Narratives of Justice

Narratives of Justice

Legislators' Beliefs about
Distributive Fairness

Grant Reeher

Ann Arbor
THE UNIVERSITY OF MICHIGAN PRESS

Copyright © by the University of Michigan 1996
All rights reserved
Published in the United States of America by
The University of Michigan Press
Manufactured in the United States of America
⊗ Printed on acid-free paper

1999   1998   1997   1996   4   3   2   1

A CIP catalog record for this book is available from the British Library.

Library of Congress Cataloging-in-Publication Data
Reeher, Grant.
    Narratives of justice : legislators' beliefs about distributive
fairness / Grant Reeher.
        p.   cm.
    Includes bibliographical references and index.
    ISBN 0-472-09620-6 (hardcover : alk. paper). — ISBN 0-472-06620-X
(pbk. : alk. paper)
    1. Connecticut.   General Assembly.   Senate.   2. Legislators—
Connecticut—Attitudes. 3. Connecticut—Politics and
government—1951–   4. Distributive justice.   I. Title.
JK3376.R44   1996
320′.01′108621—dc20   96-532
                                                              CIP

For Nicole

Contents

Acknowledgments

I have accumulated many debts in the course of this project. Obviously, I could not have embarked on or completed it without the cooperation of thirty-five Connecticut state senators, and thus I thank them first. But I owe my greatest single debt to David Mayhew, who has cheerfully nurtured and endured the project's entire life, in particular serving as midwife to its birth. For reading earlier drafts and providing helpful advice and encouragement, I am also very much indebted to Linda Fowler, Ian Shapiro, and Rogers Smith. I received helpful comments on various fragments of earlier drafts from Kristi Andersen, Joe Cammarano, Lily Ling, and Jeff Stonecash.

I also benefited from the generosity of numerous persons in and around Connecticut's state government, many of whom, unfortunately for the state, have since moved on. Among those I would particularly like to thank are The Honorable Joseph Adamo, William Dyson, Linda Emmons, Robert Jaekle, and Janet Polinsky; and Brian Allen, John Berthoud, John Brautigam, Joan Donahue, and George White.

Yale University supported the project through a University Dissertation Fellowship and a John Enders Assistance Grant. Syracuse University supported the later stages of the project through a Summer Research Grant. Through Syracuse's Undergraduate Research Program, I also benefited from the assistance of Stephen Lisauskas and David Gates.

No less essential for the successful completion of the project were the voices of encouragement and enthusiasm that were expressed at several key stages in the work. Among those I would particularly like to thank are Richard Hall, Burdett Loomis, Roger Masters, Dwayne Mefford, Gary Orren, Samuel Patterson, Robert Sickels, and the late Charles Tidmarch.

I also thank Malcolm Litchfield, Rebecca McDermott, Charles Myers, and Christina Triezenberg, my editors at the University of Michigan Press, for helpful advice and encouragement. Three anonymous readers also provided helpful advice.

Finally, I thank my parents, Elizabeth and David Reeher, for their patience, kindness, and support. My debt to my wife, Nicole Reeher, is beyond measure. Suffice it to say that she is better than I deserve. This book is dedicated to her.

CHAPTER 1

Introduction

What I want to see above all is that this country remains a country where someone can always get rich. That's the one thing we have and that must be preserved.

—Ronald Reagan

I have no problems, I've been very supportive of taking care of retarded people, mentally ill people, people who can't help themselves. I *detest* giving one dime of the taxpayer's money, of my money, to anyone who if they tried a little harder, wouldn't have to ask for it. . . . In general, people end up where they deserve to be. They may not end up where they want to be. . . . If somebody has no motivation to get off welfare, and they die on welfare, then that's what they deserved. . . . (12)

We seek not just freedom but opportunity. We seek not just legal equity but human ability, not just equality as a right and a theory but equality as a fact and equality as a result.

—Lyndon Johnson

. . . [A]dequate wages and benefits, that are adequate to maintain people at a middle class lifestyle—that's what I would call justice. A system that distributes the results of the labor of the workers and managers in such a way—there's clearly a differential needed . . . but a better distribution than we currently have, so basically we don't have people on welfare, people who are hungry, people without adequate health care, people without adequate homes to live in, simply because they can't afford these things. I sound like Huey Long. . . . (6)

The issue of distributive justice has inflamed the human mind for as long as it can remember. In the name of justice, citizens have instituted wholesale changes in their governing arrangements, revolted against their own governments, and fought wars against other nations. Over the centuries, philosophers have written volumes about the theories of distributive justice. More recently,

---

Each interview subject is given a number between 1 and 35. The numbers are kept consistent throughout the book so that the reader can follow each respondent's account. This numbering system is sometimes suspended beginning in chapter 3 to help preserve the anonymity of the respondents; these excerpts will be indicated by (*).

social scientists, journalists, and others have written even more volumes about the distributive justice of governmental, corporate, and social policies and practices, while historians, survey researchers, and interviewers have attempted to tell us what private citizens at one time thought, and presently think, about distributive justice. I attempt here to add to this knowledge, through extended semistructured interviews I conducted in 1988 with members of a middle-level political elite, the state senators of Connecticut.

Through my investigation of this set of state senators, I attempt an inquiry into the following kinds of questions: What are the sources of our basic political disagreements, and how do we go about resolving them? How do world-views and basic normative commitments shape political behavior, political argument, and perceptions of political issues? More specifically, I want to investigate whether or not there are patterns in the senators' thinking about distributive justice. If there are such patterns, what are they? What are they based on? What are the relations between the patterns? Do they share certain significant features and are they essentially based on consensus, or do they spring from different frameworks and are they essentially contestable?

The recent trend in economic distribution in the United States invites a reconsideration of American beliefs about distributive justice. It is now widely recognized that conditions have become more unequal since the late 1970s. The rich have gotten richer, the poor have gotten poorer, and minorities have fallen further behind whites.[1] The data are striking. Consider the following items regarding incomes: from 1977 to 1990, the real income of the poorest fifth of the population fell by 12 percent, while the real income of the richest fifth rose by 30 percent.[2] And from 1977 to 1989, the real income of the richest 1 percent grew by 77 percent. This richest 1 percent also received 60 percent of the total national increase in after-tax income during this period. Perhaps most revealing, a Census Bureau report found that during the 1980s, the percentage of full-time workers receiving less than $12,195 ($6.10/hour, in 1990 dollars) rose from 12 to 18 percent (this salary figure was assumed to be the amount necessary to lift a family of four out of poverty). During the 1960s this percentage had dropped, while during the 1970s it had remained constant. In the same vein, during the 1980s the gap in incomes between college and high school graduates increased by 16 percent for men and 12 percent for women (DeParle 1992b; Nasar 1992c). Data from the early 1990s show a continuation of these trends (Bradsher 1995; DeParle 1994; Kilborn 1995).

Government has not made up the difference. Between 1977 and 1989, the effective total tax rate for the richest 1 percent of families dropped from 35.5 to 26.7 percent; for the top 20 percent of families the rate dropped from 27.2 to 25.6 percent. The effective total tax rate for the bottom fifth remained constant at 9.3 percent; for the next fifth the rate increased from 15.4 to 15.7 percent. Government expenditures have also tended to favor those who are better off, or at least middle class; the vast majority of federal nonmilitary spending, for example, goes to families earning more than $20,000 (Wines 1994).

Changes in private worth generally followed the changes in income, though the relative growth among the top was not as dramatic. Nonetheless, the absolute inequalities are extraordinary. The Federal Reserve found that between 1983 and 1989 the richest 10 percent of American families increased their share of the total private wealth from 67 to 68 percent, while the share of the remaining 90 percent of families fell from 33 to 32 percent. The richest 1 percent increased their share of the total from 31 to 37 percent. Thus, in 1989 the richest 1 percent of American households was worth more than the entire bottom 90 percent (Nasar 1992b). A host of other studies have demonstrated persistent and growing inequalities in upward mobility, education, health care, and life expectancy.

Regarding racial inequality, Census Bureau figures indicate that in 1988, the median wealth of white households was ten times that of blacks (if this figure is limited to households with married couples, the ratio is still three and a half to one). A 1989 congressional study, based on federal statistics, found that children were the largest poverty group, that the poverty rates for black and Hispanic children were up to three times higher than that for white children, and that, in general, conditions for black and Hispanic families significantly worsened during the 1980s. A study by the Children's Defense Fund found that between 1973 and 1990, real incomes for white families headed by someone under thirty years old dropped 22 percent, while incomes for similar black families dropped 48 percent and incomes for Hispanic families dropped 28 percent (also note that all young family incomes had dropped during this period, even those headed by someone with a college education).[3] Other studies have pointed to similar inequalities regarding imprisonment, mortgages, health insurance, and life expectancy.[4] And again, income data from the early 1990s indicate a continuation of these levels of inequality (Holmes 1995).

These inequalities at first appear quite paradoxical in light of the fact that Americans have long fancied themselves as being distinguished by a high degree of equality. Indeed, many outside observers from Tocqueville to Myrdal have also pointed to the strength and salience of the norm of equality. This paradox has consequently generated much interest in American beliefs about economics and distributive justice, prompting questions like Werner Sombart's (1976) famous "Why is there no socialism in the United States?" or more specifically, why are there no significant, organized political movements that are critical of capitalism or that advocate a downward redistribution of wealth? The apparent truth that has emerged from the resulting studies is that while Americans insist on high levels of certain forms of equality, in particular formal political equality and social equality, they will also tolerate high levels of economic inequality.[5] This is due in large part to the intense individualism in their socioeconomic thinking. The tolerance for economic inequality is a primary component of the various accounts of a comparative "exceptionalism" regarding American thinking about economic issues; indeed, it is often cited as a principal explanation for America's economic inequality in comparison to other advanced industrialized nations.[6]

My findings call this received wisdom on American beliefs, or at least a significant portion of this wisdom, into question. As the reader will discover in chapter 3, there are a number of Connecticut state senators who do not easily fit the standard American characterization. While this group of senators retains some of the more traditionally held notions of American thinking about distributive justice, the story about fairness that they tell is startling when set against the stereotype. Their story, or narrative, contains critical treatments of economic power, race, and class; distributional norms invoking need; and an emphasis on improving human nature. For these senators, distributive justice results from the establishment of basic patterns of distribution responding to needs and the establishment of forms of social interaction emphasizing empathy, which in turn undergird, reinforce, and enhance these patterns of distribution. Thus, the range of American political thought is perhaps broader than we have assumed. I will pursue this claim in subsequent chapters.

Distributive Justice and Beliefs

Since this is a work purporting to relate and interpret beliefs about distributive justice, before doing anything else, I need to set forth briefly how I am using these two terms. A more detailed discussion of beliefs appears in the next chapter, but what follows here will lay the groundwork.

In defining the term *distributive justice,* I follow the common path in recent years of a broad construction. In addition to the just distribution of social goods, the elements constituting distributive justice also include notions about just relations in the production of goods; the proper position of the worker in an economic institution; the responsibility of the individual for her own economic status; and the responsibility of the government regarding all of these matters.[7] In important respects, these issues turn on perceptions of the economic realm itself, specifically the perceived prevalence and nature of power relations and social stratification within it and society more generally; the degree to which it is seen as zero sum, or marked by scarcity, versus abundance; the relative emphasis placed on production versus distribution; and the different conceptions of what will generate productivity.

In their work on American political beliefs, Sidney Verba and Gary Orren (1985, 52) discuss three levels of thinking about equality, which I shall borrow here and apply to distributive justice: an abstract level, including the meaning of the concept and the justification of the values involving it; a more pragmatic yet general level, including broad policy and social objectives and notions about such things as the proper extent of government involvement in the economy; and the finite level, including specific laws, regulations, and policy plans. I attempt in this study to reveal thinking at all three levels, from deep beliefs to specific policies. The basic kernel of what I am after, however, I take from the ancients, in particular Aristotle: the notion of giving each person his due. This is the fountainhead from which spring the various streams of justice.

In addition to attention to *what* the senators think, I also need to pay attention to *how* they think. Briefly, the kinds of items that will concern me here are similar to what Robert Putnam has termed the "style of political analysis" (1973, 34–35). These include the level of analysis; that is, the extent to which the senators employ broad principles and abstract concepts, or instead rely on specific examples and details. They also include the kinds of statements that are emphasized—normative, causal, descriptive, ontological, assertive, referential—and the method of ethical reasoning—consequentialist versus nonconsequentialist (rights), personified versus impersonalized, and personally responsible versus nonresponsible or structurally responsible.

Political Elites and State Senators

If one is going to study beliefs and values, there are many obvious reasons for studying those of the political elite. One does not have to subscribe to a ruling elite model of politics in order to accept the notion that political elites and their ideas are critically important and at least to some degree independent factors in the framing of our social, economic, and political world. Elite beliefs and values help shape and set the boundaries on policy debates, not to mention the role they play in the specific legislative realization of various policy directions. Thus the views of the American elite on distributive justice have a direct connection to the reality of the state of distributive justice in America (Verba and Orren 1985, 3–4, 51; Verba et al. 1987, 7). Furthermore, if the learning model of mass beliefs advanced by Herbert McClosky and John Zaller (1984) is accurate, in which values are interpreted by the members of the elite and then translated through them to the mass public, we can then conclude that changes in elite thinking reflect the social thinking to come, and that by gaining an in-depth understanding of the beliefs of certain elites, we can perhaps predict the future direction of social thinking.[8] In summary, then, the focus here on the political elite assumes that in some important ways members of the elite, to quote F. Scott Fitzgerald on the very rich, "are different from you and me," and not simply, to paraphrase Ernest Hemingway's rejoinder, in that they have more power.[9]

But why study the legislative elite? Why not study bureaucrats, interest group leaders, or members of the judiciary? Some advantages of studying legislators present themselves immediately. First, all matters of social and economic public policy must ultimately pass through their heads and hands, concerning funding if nothing else. Thus, an examination of legislators and their beliefs is in many respects an examination of public policy; an examination of "who gets what, when, how"; an examination of the stuff of politics (Lasswell 1936; Prewitt and Nowlin 1969, 298). Second, legislators reflect more of the diversity of opinion found in any given geographic area, instead of bearing the stamp of a particular executive, as is arguably the case with bureaucrats and judges. Third, being subject to periodic elections and facing an institutionalized opposition, legislators are more directly involved with the political aspects of policy questions, as well as the programmatic and philosophical aspects. By studying legislators, we can better see beliefs rubbing against and through what are perhaps more pragmatic considerations.

But why study state senators from Connecticut? For many years state legislatures were the backwater of American politics; they were outdated, backward institutions, lacking in competence and institutional capacity. This has changed drastically, however, beginning with the early 1960s. Through reapportionment, salary increases, and staff and facility growth, state legislatures have become more representative, active, and professional, and have also become less dependent on lobbyists, state party officials, and governors.[10] State legislators have thus become both more important and more interesting as subjects for interviews, and perhaps more similar to national legislators.[11] Connecticut has provided a typical example of the developments resulting in these changes. With the completion in 1988 of a $54 million office building adjacent to the capitol, the state's legislature rounded out three decades of significant institutional advancement. A recent ranking of the levels of professionalization in the fifty state legislatures, based on a variety of indicators, ranked Connecticut's legislature seventeenth (Squire 1992).

State legislatures have also been directly implicated in the distributive changes described at the beginning of this chapter. During much of the 1980s, they were forced to respond to changes in spending and taxing priorities at the national level that left them with fewer funds. This forced state legislators to confront real tests of the kinds of beliefs under study here, as they had to decide whether or not and in what ways to make up for the slack in national funds. This slack was complicated by greater demands on social support networks during this same period. In states such as Connecticut, which were undergoing dramatic economic growth during much of this period, this adjustment was not that difficult; however, as the Northeast underwent a deep recession in the late 1980s, issues of distributive justice began to receive a thorough workout. This workout came to a climax three years after I conducted my interviews, in the fracas involving independent Governor Lowell Weicker and the institution of a state income tax.[12] In 1990 a budget crisis and a new governor brought an income tax to the front of the legislature's agenda, and in the summer of 1991 an income tax was finally pushed through the legislature by Governor Weicker on the slimmest of margins, after a protracted deadlock. It is interesting to note that, as late as 1989, most influential legislators in both the senate and the house did not think an income tax was likely at any point in the near future. And at least up until the 1992 elections, a stand against an income tax had been almost a requirement for election in many districts in the state.[13] Within the state (as well as in New Hampshire, a state without an income or sales tax), this stand was referred to simply as "the pledge." Since two-thirds of the senators taking part in the passage of the 1991 state income tax were also interviewed in 1988 for this work (the tax in fact passed because of a last-minute switch by three of the senators I interviewed), the beliefs uncovered here are of particular interest for anyone concerned with that event.[14]

There are still other reasons for concentrating on state legislators from Connecticut. The first, to paraphrase Mallory, is because they are there.[15] The kind of study I wished to undertake required in-depth interviews. Since it is difficult to engage members of the political elite in such in-depth interviews, I determined that I would be more likely to meet with success at the state level than at the national level. Because of its location, the State Senate of Connecticut was particularly accessible to me, and its size (thirty-six members) provided me with the opportunity to attempt to interview the entire body, rather than taking a sample. Furthermore, I surmised that through in-depth interviews of a portion of the political elite with less experience fielding and parrying questions than elites at the national level, I had a better chance to penetrate through the party and campaign rhetoric, and the "button pushing" answers that the respondents might think they ought to give to an academic interviewer.

Granted, the conclusions that we might reasonably draw from this study are obviously limited to some extent by the attention to one legislative body within one state at one moment in time. But as I have already suggested, even with such an approach we can hope to extrapolate from the findings here to other bodies in other places at other times. And more importantly, from such a study we can gain, in the words of Alan Rosenthal, a better "feel for the broader subject under examination," in this case beliefs about distributive justice (1991, 656).[16] In addition, Connecticut's politics are not remarkably dissimilar from those of other industrialized states, and its political climate during the time in which I conducted my interviews was not remarkably different from that of other periods in its recent history (at least prior to 1990). In most respects it was a time of "politics as usual."[17] An attention to the specific contexts of the state's demographics, political climate, and recent political history is nonetheless called for, and can be found in appendix A. This appendix also includes a brief description of the senators.

Beliefs and Behavior

Any study proposing to concentrate on beliefs as a way to add to the understanding of politics must face several challenges. A senator's beliefs about such things as distributive justice may not be strongly connected to his behavior in the senate; instead, he may act out of self-interest, either material or political, or in response to forces that are largely removed from his particular beliefs, such as party or interest group pressure, or reciprocity toward another senator. In other words, his behavior may be determined independently of his beliefs. Furthermore, his beliefs themselves may be rationalizations for his own or his class's material interests, or rationalizations for emotional drives (Putnam 1976, 103).

These matters are treated in more detail in later chapters, but for now let it suffice to say that I view beliefs as filters that intersect with and affect a legislator's perceptions of other kinds of pressures on her decisions and behavior. Beliefs can filter in a number of ways. They can influence which issues and policies a legislator will try to advance within the chamber, alter perceptions of constituency and constituency interest, and affect which of her fellow senators she will seek out for advice or voting cues (Kingdon 1989, 72–106). They can influence her attitudes toward conflict, which in turn affect the process of legislative bargaining and logrolling, and whether or not and with whom she will join in a coalition.

The study, then, is informed by the commonsense position that beliefs matter—for behavior, voting, and policy. It is also informed by a position as to *how* beliefs matter—as a filter.

Methods

A rich, thorough, in-depth understanding of the senators' beliefs about distributive justice requires in-depth, qualitative interviews.[18] In *What's Fair?* Jennifer Hochschild provides an eloquent argument for the in-depth interview that merits inclusion here:

> Topics as complex and slippery as beliefs about income, property, justice, equality, and the role of government in the economy and vice versa require a research method that permits textured, idiosyncratic responses. The researcher must permit—even induce—people to speak for themselves and must be wary of channeling their thought through his or her own preconceptions about what questions to ask, how answers should be shaped, and what coding categories best subdivide the responses (1981, 21).

In-depth interviews provide the best vehicle through which the researcher can truly understand the respondents' points of view, gain genuine insight into the sociopolitical and personal contexts of their beliefs, and understand how this context fits in with and shapes their positions.[19] Survey items, regardless of the sophistication of their statistical analysis, cannot provide this information. They also introduce the problem of interpreting the meanings of answers to simple, fill-in-the-blank questions. Furthermore, they are particularly vulnerable to having the researcher force her own notions of the relevant dimensions and types of thinking upon those of the respondent.[20] Roll-call voting studies, the tool of choice for locating legislators' ideological positions, are subject to the same set of limitations. They also tend to foist preconceived notions of dimensions of thinking onto the data, and then interpret that data in terms of those dimensions. And even if they can in fact present impressive correlations, they cannot explain why the voting cleavages are the way they are, why the correlations they might find exist, and what it is about the legislators' beliefs or situations that make them vote the way they do. These roll-call studies also limit their focus to an overly narrow, albeit important, sliver of the entire compass of legislative behavior (Putnam 1973, 26–27).

The central claim behind the use of the in-depth interview is that in order to find what we are looking for we need to talk to these people and, as Robert Lane once advised me before I began the interview process, to let them talk, in order to discover the patterns and organizations of their thoughts and to let the bases of their views come forward. This charge brings us to the method of first listening carefully and then seeing what patterns we can pull out, rather than starting with a definition of the ways in which or the dimensions upon which people think and then trying to find out where the respondents fit in.

In constructing the interview, I attempted to leave it open enough to allow the senators to formulate their views as they wished, yet structured enough to allow for a systematic though at almost all times qualitative analysis.[21] Following Robert Merton, I attempted to achieve a *range* of subject matter that was wide enough to allow for the emergence of as many relevant elements and patterns as possible; a degree of *specificity* that was sufficient to compare their responses at certain points; a *depth* that allowed for the emergence of the affective and cognitive meanings of the expressions and experiences they chose to relate; and a sense of the personal *contexts* that gave their present situations and expressions meaning (Merton, Fiske, and Kendall 1956).

I managed to interview thirty-five of the thirty-six senators. In most cases an individual interview was spread over three to five meetings; the time of a complete interview ranged anywhere from fifty minutes to six hours, and typically ran about three-and-a-half to four hours. In addition to questions designed to reveal the senators' beliefs about distributive justice, the interview also contained questions about the workings of the senate body, some specific bills and policy initiatives that were considered during the 1988 legislative session, and the senators' political and personal lives. A complete transcript of the interview schedule is provided in appendix C.

In addition to the interview materials themselves, I make use of a number of other sources and techniques. These include observation of the legislators at the capitol and in their districts; observation of public hearings, committee meetings and caucuses; transcripts from public hearings and floor discussions; materials used by committees; interviews with selected house members regarding the specific bills discussed earlier; individual senator voting scores generated by several lobbying organizations; and senate voting records on selected bills. My interview methods, the interview itself, and these other sources are all discussed in greater detail in appendix B.

Of course, the success of this project depended almost entirely on the cooperation, honesty, sincerity, and seriousness of the respondents; I had to be able to talk with them for a sufficient length of time, and in talking with them I had to be able to get past the already organized and easily accessed stock campaign-style rhetoric that they might offer as answers to an academic's questions and more into the realm of their deeper inner beliefs, where definitions and organization are less clear, even to themselves.

I think I was able to accomplish these goals. Most of the senators found the questions themselves interesting, enjoyed answering them, and in one way or another found them helpful. They often thanked me before I thanked them at the conclusion of the interview and offered to provide any further assistance I might require. Although I did not code or rank their honesty as other researchers have done, in the main I sensed that their answers were honest. Several joked that they were glad that their answers would not be circulated to other senators or their districts. One senator I interviewed as the election approached sometimes caught himself giving a political answer, and would apologize and begin over. Another confessed to making the "wrong votes" on several occasions; that is, voting differently from the way he would have voted had he known more about the basics of the bills in question. But there were also a few cases where I thought that on a particular topic or question a senator was trying to be deceptive, or more often intentionally vague. The worst case of this occurred with a senator who would soon announce his candidacy for another office. But in general, my experience was similar to that of John Wahlke and his colleagues when they interviewed state legislators over thirty years ago:

> Our experience suggests that there is little justification for believing that politicians are unapproachable for interview, or that, if they can be approached and subjected to formal interview by a stranger, they will be evasive if not deceitful in responding to questions concerning themselves

and their activities. . . . A major conclusion, then, is that a specialized population like American state legislators will provide reliable data when directly and intensively interviewed (1962, 449–51).

Aims of the Study

The next chapter discusses beliefs in greater detail, lays out my methods of conceptualizing and organizing the senators' responses, and in particular develops the concept of narrative. But before moving on to these tasks, I wish to conclude this chapter by briefly summarizing the overall aims of the study.

First, I am venturing to go beyond simply taking the pulse of opinions of a set of the political elite, a group for which such in-depth study is rarely attempted. Although the political elite has been the subject of much recent study, scant progress has been made toward a complete and rich understanding of its beliefs about distributive justice. Research on the political elite has generally placed little emphasis on the subjective side of the political process, preferring a more objective, behavioral approach. This is particularly true for legislative research. This lack of emphasis should not exist. If politics is indeed about "who gets what, when, how," then it is important to study what the political elite thinks about who *should* get what. And if politics is also about "the authoritative allocation of values in society," then it is important to study the values of the people we select to carry out this allocation (Lane 1972, 80). To put the case even more simply, it is important to know how important people really go about thinking about important things.

Second, although the contours of American political ideology have been widely mapped, they remain highly contentious. I am thus also attempting to provide a detailed and nuanced ideological mapping of my own, using political elites and concentrating on the issue of distributive fairness. Included in this endeavor is an inquiry into how competing and apparently conflicting sets of beliefs might be reconciled.

Third, I want to take a specific look at what has been a contentious issue at all levels of social inquiry, the relation between deep beliefs and actual behavior.[22] Do these beliefs influence behavior? How do they influence it? Here my focus will be on the manifestation of justice beliefs in actual policy proposals, voting, and other related forms of legislative behavior. I hope to add to the understanding of both why and how such connections between beliefs and behavior occur or fail to occur at the elite level.[23] My attempt to add to the understanding of legislative behavior is itself perhaps another argument in favor of studying deep beliefs rather than attitudes about contemporary issues. As Robert Putnam points out, in order to predict and understand future behavior, we must know something about the broader—and I would add here the deeper—patterns of beliefs, since the most interesting future political problems will most likely involve issues that have yet to be faced (1976, 80).

Fourth, I hope to contribute to the study of democratic representation. Elite beliefs, and consequently the study of elite beliefs, are critical in a democracy and in democratic theory. V. O. Key makes the point most forcefully: "[T]he critical element for the health of a democratic order consists in the beliefs, standards, and competence of those who constitute the influentials, the opinion-leaders, the political activists in the order" (1961, 558). While we might sometimes like to think that in a democracy our political representatives are nothing more and nothing less than the delegates of our will, in reality we know that they enjoy a significant degree of independence. It is thus important, regarding the democratic links that can exist between representative and represented, to understand representatives' beliefs. And if elite beliefs differ from those of the public, whether or not in ways that make us think that the control over social resources and policies is better off in their hands, then it is of interest to further understand how and why they differ.

Finally, my findings should also be relevant to Werner Sombart's question, "Why is there no socialism in the United States?" The attempt to answer this question has generated a subfield of its own, so that by now we might want to conclude that the absence of socialism in the United States is overdetermined (Lipset 1988; Foner 1984; Hochschild 1981). Furthermore, the individual, ahistorical approach of my investigation may not be the preferred method for studying such an issue. Nonetheless, I will investigate a part of this question concerning the American political elite: Although the public apparently does not have patterns of thinking that support equality and redistribution in the economic realm, why do at least some members of the political elite not recognize the large inequalities of economic distribution and advance causes and proposals to counteract them? In other words, even if members of the public—including those who are poor—do not support equality and redistribution, why do others who are in responsible political positions not support such measures for them? Is it because they share the same thinking? I have already indicated that perhaps some legislators do in fact support some such measures, if not for radical redistribution, then at least for some significant alterations in the patterns of distribution and the structure of the economy (see also one of the brief interview excerpts appearing at the beginning of this chapter).

My principal contributions regarding these questions are found in the detailed renderings of the senators' beliefs about distributive justice, organized around the concept of narrative, which appear in the chapters that follow. These renderings cast doubt on much of the received wisdom about the narrowness of American beliefs regarding distributive justice, and at least suggest the potential for a stronger and more salient leftism than has generally been acknowledged. In terms of their influence on political behavior, deep beliefs appear to have their greatest impact through their filtering effect. Finally, although the respective narratives of justice are quite different in many key respects, they nonetheless appear to share some significant points of contact.

The chapter that immediately follows discusses beliefs in detail: their organization into belief systems and narratives, their manifestations in behavior, and their sources. It lays the theoretical groundwork for the study. The rendition of the narratives themselves follows in chapters 3 through 5 and constitutes the balance of the book. Chapters 6 and 7 consider the connections between the senators' beliefs and behavior and include a review of the senators' discussions of some specific bills and policy initiatives. These two chapters detail the workings of the senate based on information provided by the senators themselves in the interviews and on other sources. The book then concludes with a consideration of the relations between the narratives, some attempts to cull political lessons from the material, and some ruminations on the implications of the findings for politics and ideology.

CHAPTER 2

Beliefs, Behavior, and Narratives

Any study that concentrates on deep political beliefs such as those about distributive justice must overcome many challenges. Before anything else, we must properly understand these beliefs themselves, and approach them in a way that yields clear evidence and politically relevant conceptions, as well as theories that ultimately contribute to the pursuit of the good life.[1] As part of this understanding, we must also have a proper sense of the sources of these beliefs. Are they for the most part environmentally determined, and if so, what are the mechanisms through which people acquire their beliefs? Or are they subjectively determined, and if so, how then do these beliefs develop within individuals? Are beliefs that appear to be content-oriented in fact only the rationalizations of self-interest? Are they part of an ego defense, a means of coping with and responding to inner psychological conflicts, particularly those caused by repressed desires? Or again, are they the result of a reality-screening process required by certain psychological needs, or simply by the limits of cognitive capacity? Once these questions are answered satisfactorily, we must then understand the relevancy of the beliefs to the political process. An understanding of deep beliefs may prove quite interesting intrinsically, but to be meaningful to the understanding of politics it must carry with it a sense of how beliefs matter. Regarding legislators, this requirement means that our understanding must include a sense of how deep beliefs operate in the legislative process. Political behavior may be independent of beliefs; regarding legislators, it may be a product of electoral or even material self-interest, or it may be mostly a product of independent, external forces. These are all difficult questions. To be sure, we cannot expect to arrive at the ultimate answers, but nonetheless, we do need to realize some understanding as a base from which to proceed with the investigation and analysis.

What follows is a brief treatment of the issues that are most relevant to the concerns of this study, and a presentation of the theoretical approach that I will adopt. I begin with an examination of the study of political beliefs themselves, which includes a look at both their nature and their sources. I then move to a discussion of the connections between beliefs and behavior, which more directly involves the Connecticut State Senate.[2] I conclude with a brief presentation of the concept of narrative, which I use to organize and understand the senators' responses.

Studying Political Beliefs

The Converse Model and the In-Depth Approach. Throughout the past three decades, the study of political beliefs and ideology has been dominated by the behaviorally and cognitively oriented works of Philip Converse and the Survey Research Center, and the controversies these works engendered. *The American Voter* studies (Campbell et al. 1960) concluded that public citizens were by and large unsophisticated in their thinking about politics. What this meant was that they did not think abstractly and therefore did not think ideologically. In his work in "The Nature of Belief Systems in Mass Publics" (1964) and also in *The American Voter,* Converse concentrated on the notion of constraint, or the degree of coherency of and connection between issue positions held at any one time, and similarly concluded that the mass public by and large did not think in constrained, connected terms, and therefore did not think ideologically.[3]

In the Converse treatment, ideology was seen as a belief system, with attitudes toward things constituting the basic building blocks. These attitudes stood in certain relations to each other. A belief system was marked by constraint, which meant "the success we would have [at any given time] in predicting, given initial knowledge that an individual holds a specified attitude, that he holds certain further ideas and attitudes" (Converse 1964, 207). Adopting a social-psychological perspective, his model considered the relations between these attitudes as culturally defined and in turn learned by individuals. If the relations were learned well, they would be prominent and would remain stable over time. The relations were not hypothesized to vary with individuals, and they were defined in traditional liberal/conservative terms. To the degree that citizens had not learned these relations, that they did not think in liberal and conservative terms as defined by Converse, and that their attitude relations were not stable over time, they were considered to be unideological, unconstrained, and unsophisticated. The vast majority of the citizens fit this category between 1956 and 1960.[4] At these lower levels of constraint, attitudes were guided by considerations of group benefit, the "nature of the times," or factors completely lacking in issue content, such as which candidate they liked better personally. Elite political actors (candidates for the U.S. Congress) and elite members of the general population, on the other hand, did think in more ideologically constrained terms.[5]

In addition to providing what would become the dominant model for thinking about political beliefs, Converse and the Survey Research Center also supplied the dominant method for studying them, namely, the survey.[6] The typical survey of this kind usually consists of close-ended questions regarding issue and candidate preference, often appended with a few short-answer, open-ended questions. The data are then analyzed statistically with correlational analyses, which are in turn complemented by the content analysis of the short-answer responses, if they are available. Most studies of elite political beliefs employ similar survey instruments and analyses.

The Converse findings have generated much controversy and attracted much criticism, due largely to the pessimistic conclusions they draw regarding the attitudes of the public. In particular, the findings compromise the rosy view of a U.S. "civic culture" made up of informed, rational citizens, thus casting a dark shadow over the entire U.S. political system. The ensuing criticisms have taken many forms, which although interesting and important, are not integral to my most central concerns here. I will therefore set aside much of this debate.

Although the Converse approach has made many valuable contributions to the study of political beliefs, it has profound limitations for the deeper understanding of beliefs of which this study is in pursuit. The concern for such deeper understanding has driven other approaches that attempt to probe more deeply and more subtly into individuals' beliefs. Perhaps foremost among these are the in-depth, psychologically oriented approaches, advanced most notably by Robert E. Lane (1962, 1972, 1973). These approaches attempt to respond to the likelihood that constraint is individually psychologically driven and idiosyncratic as well as social. They begin with the notion that in order to understand beliefs and their functions, we must also understand the psychological purposes and motivations of a set of beliefs; that is, we need to understand what people are doing with their beliefs.

Ultimately, anyone studying political beliefs faces some kind of trade-off between the deeper and more subtle individual understanding afforded by the probing, in-depth approach, and the representativeness and reproducibility of the survey approach. For my purposes here, the in-depth approach is much better suited. In order to gain a better understanding of beliefs—what they are, how they are organized, and how they work—a more in-depth, individual approach is indicated, one that makes use of extended, semistructured interviews. Surveys can certainly tell us much that is of interest, but we need to go beyond them to deeper analyses. Surveys—and regarding legislators in particular, voting studies—are subject to the law of the instrument: "Give a small boy a hammer, and he will find that everything he encounters needs pounding" (Kaplan 1964, 28). Though their use is legion, they are not always the right tools for the job. What the respondents think and what they say is of obvious importance, but how they think and how they say it is also important, especially in the attempt to discover patterns and relations. A sensitive appreciation of both of these elements requires an alternative approach. These considerations call upon us to take the time to listen carefully to the respondents, to listen deeply to their inner voices, with the third ear, to extract the meanings of the narratives through careful attention and interpretation, and to record them with the left hand.[7]

A few examples will illustrate these lessons. One of the leading recent survey-based studies of elite political beliefs uses a scaled response to a single question in order to determine what kind of equality elites endorse: specifically, to determine whether they endorse an equality of opportunity or an equality of result. The respondents were asked to indicate their preferred position between two statements, located at each end of the scale: "Equality of opportunity: giving each person an equal chance for a good education and to develop his or her ability" and "Equality of result: giving each person a relatively equal income regardless of his or her education and ability" (Verba and Orren 1985, 297). In addition to missing the subtleties and nuances such a subject involves, this question appears to be loaded in favor of an equality of opportunity. Furthermore, it tells us little about the different kinds of equalities of opportunity that may be favored (my study, for example, uncovers radically different constructions of equality of opportunity among the senators). The meanings of phrases and words also may vary with both individuals and context. In my study, for example, one senator repeatedly invoked the idea of self-reliance. What began to emerge after time, however, was that her emphasis in invoking this idea was not so much the value she placed on self-reliance per se, but rather her belief that we unfortunately live in a society where people rarely help each other. Self-reliance was all that was left.[8] Similarly, another senator repeatedly invoked the idea of equality as a standard for judgment and as a goal to be striven toward. What emerged here, however, was that for him equality involved a rollback of various equalizing policies of the welfare state, in order to restore a "degree of balance" that he felt had been lost over the past two decades.

The in-depth individual approach allows for closer attention to several important items. First, it clearly allows for more subtle interpretations of the content and structures of beliefs and the patterns of reasoning and organization, which would be missed through surface-oriented surveys. Second, the in-depth individual approach better allows for the fact that people may think in different ways. Rather than positing that beliefs and their structures are simply social products, this approach better allows us to see the subjectively determined influences that are simultaneously at work. Furthermore, it also gives us a better handle by which to grasp *how* the environmental or social influences operate, something that is lacking in the mainstream approach to belief systems. In short, it offers a more contextually sensitive approach. Third, this approach better allows us to go beyond simply taking an inventory of the respondents' attitude positions or preferences on a given set of issues and move toward an understanding of the genuine nature of these positions, their subjective *meanings,* and the ways in which terms are defined and used. Fourth, and related to the third point, it allows us to get a better sense of the affect-based as well as the cognitive-based elements of political beliefs. Furthermore, it allows us to begin to understand how these two elements interrelate. For all these reasons, the individual, in-depth approach has the potential to yield better insights into certain important aspects of political thinking, particularly into the nature and influence of deep beliefs. It can produce information that in many significant respects is less ambiguous and more reliable, and it can yield a more complete portrait of the way people think about political issues. In so doing, it offers a distinctive contribution to the study of politics, and ultimately to the pursuit of justice.

The Problem of Contextual Dependence. But with such an in-depth, individualized approach, my results face the danger of having their validity limited to my particular set of respondents at a particular moment in time; that is, of being contextually overdependent. Indeed, in responding to some of his critics urging a more subtle, individual, and in-depth approach, Converse himself argues that going too far beyond the traditional liberal/conservative dimension regarding mass political beliefs, into the personal organizations of individuals, may simply yield organizations that are of interest and use only to the individuals themselves and that cannot be meaningfully registered in the political process, since they cannot be generalized or readily applied to particular policy questions (Converse 1975; Hochschild 1981, 236–37).

I offer the following responses to this concern. First, since I am studying the beliefs of a set of policy makers, the admittedly personalized information I gather is prima facie relevant and meaningful to the political process. Furthermore, I make an explicit attempt in the later portions of this book to discover the ways in which such beliefs are relevant to particular policy issues. Second, although my descriptions of the beliefs of the senators may at some ultimate level be inherently piecemeal, the respondents themselves and the circumstances under which they presented their thoughts were not remarkably different from other members of the elective political elite whose views we would also be interested in knowing. Third, the in-depth interview renders the truest and most complete portrait of beliefs and their patterns of organization. Thus, in studying this group of respondents in this fashion, I am attempting to blend a theory-driven, "top-down" approach with an individually oriented, "bottom-up" approach that allows us "to *read* a text [or set of beliefs] for its meanings, and by doing so to elucidate the art of its author" (Bruner 1986, 9–10). In short, I am attempting to draw on both the context sensitivity of literary criticism and the context independence of science (Bruner 1986, 50).

The Sources of Political Beliefs

Where do our political beliefs come from? To provide just three possibilities, beliefs and their organization may have their sources in ego defenses and psychological conflicts, such as repressed desires; they may be rooted in early experiences or socioeconomic background; or they may derive mainly from self-interest. Regarding legislators in particular, their roles in the chamber and the attitudes of their constituents (however unconstrained) could also supply sources for beliefs. Even just a partial listing of the characteristics that we would want to take account of in tracking the beliefs of legislators would include a host of disparate items: age; sex; party identification; seniority and experience in the chamber; political career; education; wealth and income; occupation outside of the legislature; district type, including rural, urban, or suburban; parental political characteristics; childhood experiences; early political involvement; and future political goals. A consideration of some of the extant research on the sources of beliefs follows.

In Lasswell's (1960) famous equation ($p > d > r = P$), political man (P) is driven by private motives (p), which he displaces onto public objects (d), and in turn rationalizes his views and activities in terms of the public interest (r).[9] Lasswell based his model on case studies of historical political figures, psychiatric patients, and local judges and politicians. For politicians, political activity and political beliefs are compensatory, a public response to the basic conflicts that afflict us all, but that have damaged them more deeply: "All men are born politicians, and some never outgrow it" (Lasswell 1948, 39). One study supporting the Lasswell model examined political activity within an Illinois mental institution, and found that paranoid individuals were more likely to be selected as leaders in democratic settings; their sensitivity to negative communications apparently led to attempts to control the situation (Rutherford 1971). In addition, James David Barber's (1965) interview and survey-based study of the freshmen members of the Connecticut House of Representatives found that while the best, most effective legislators possessed high self-esteems, the majority of legislators were engaged in one fashion or another in compensatory behavior for low self-esteems.[10]

But though the psychopathology model remains popular, most current evidence points away from it as a description of the motivations of the political elite (Putnam 1976, 74; Matthews 1985). As Robert Lane and others have pointed out, it is more likely the case that inner conflicts require so much psychological energy that there would be little left over to cope with the great psychological demands political life puts on the individual. Political withdrawal and alienation, rather than activity, are most likely to result from a damaged ego (Lane 1959).[11] Modern psychology has found that the actions and qualities required of political leaders are at odds with insecurity; therefore, higher levels of political activity should indicate fewer inner conflicts. As a final point it should be added that even if the Lasswell model were generally valid, it would still be important to study beliefs and values. Though beliefs would represent rationalizations of private needs in terms of public interests, the content and form of these rationalizations could still exert a significant and somewhat independent influence on behavior.

Another possible source of political beliefs is self-interest. From the standpoint of self-interest, political man is primarily considered as a rational, utility-maximizing creature regarding his beliefs rather than a compensating creature. As in the case of the Lasswell model, rationalization emerges as a key concept. The most powerful statement of the interest view comes undoubtedly from Marx. In this view, ideas are ultimately determined by material relations, and the ruling ideas are the ideas of the dominant economic class.[12] More subtle formulations of this relation are of course also possible, and have been put forward. Regarding the political elite, this self-interest could include not only financial self-interest, but also political power self-interest, electoral self-interest, and the ambition for higher office.

But recent research on U.S. mass beliefs suggests that something other than financial self-interest is driving the core beliefs about economic issues.[13] Donald R. Kinder and D. Roderick Kiewiet (1981), for example, have found that U.S. voters assess the economic performance of incumbent elected officials, and ultimately vote, based on "sociotropic" rather than personal "pocketbook" considerations; they base their assessments and decisions on the economic health of the nation as a whole.[14] Another study of the American electorate found that in most cases a subjective sense of class position did not structure the opinions of respondents regarding social welfare policies. It found only a weak relationship for individuals with strong senses of class ties (Jackman and Jackman 1983). Regarding the political elite, Sidney Verba and Gary Orren's study of specific attitudes toward equality found that attitudes were not derived from economic self-interest (1985, 2–4, 248–49). Electoral ambition, however, may exert an influence. A survey-based study of 372 city councilmen in the San Francisco area found that councilmen with ambitions for higher offices tended to adopt policy views that were generally associated with those higher offices (Prewitt and Nowlin 1969). But in the main, these empirical studies indicate that self-interest simply cannot substitute for the varied sources of political beliefs, even when those beliefs specifically concern issues related to distributive justice. On a more psychological plane, it should also be pointed out that beliefs about such things as distributive justice can (and probably do) structure the individual's very conception of self-interest, particularly since interests are not always self-evident. Given these findings and considerations, we should agree with Clifford Geertz, that the "main defects of the interest theory are that its psychology is too anemic and its sociology too muscular" (1964, 53). Let us then consider another source of beliefs.

While psychological compensation and self-interest undoubtedly influence the formation of beliefs at various points, perhaps a more profitable overall approach is provided by attention to the background and experiences of the legislators themselves. This is often related to self-interest, but is nonetheless both theoretically and empirically separate from it. Although Donald Matthews (1985), in a review of the research on legislatures, concludes that the available evidence does not point to a clear and consistent relationship between social background and policy attitudes, there are nonetheless strong indications that background and experiences do play a large role in the formulation of attitudes. The influence of background and experiences is by no means consistent between countries or even individual legislators, but it is there. Studies of various political elites have discovered the influence of religion, social and economic class, childhood experiences, and family background, including parental attitudes, party identification, and status.[15] These findings support the notion that beliefs are acquired and developed early in life and remain fairly consistent thereafter.

The influence of background and early experiences is of course mediated through the context of the dominant cultural beliefs. In addition, specific attitudes are subject to the later influence of institutions, which may involve certain kinds of education or training, or have a certain ethos. Richard Fenno (1973) has found, for example, that different types of congressional committees socialize their members in different ways.[16] And in a study of a dozen citizens, Craig Reinarman (1987) has carefully presented how work life, its relation to private life, and more generally "lived experience" affect adult political beliefs. Regarding the formally part-time Connecticut senate, the outside occupations held by many of the senators may also be a powerful influence on attitudes, in addition of course to their positions as state senators.

The notion of early socialization leads to the idea of political generations. As society changes, each generation coming of political age will live in a distinctive time, will be socialized in a distinctive way, and will have to some degree a distinctive set of attitudes. As each generation matures and takes its turn governing the nation, it leaves the stamp of its respective socialization upon affairs. There is thus a delay or lag time between generational events and their ultimate manifestation in elite beliefs (Putnam 1976, 102). Theories of generational effects face the challenges of defining with some meaningful specificity the beginnings and endings of generations; specifying the causal paths between individuals, events, and the eras in which they exist; and accounting for the effects of life cycle changes, natural selection, and the uniform effects of historical period. Nonetheless, the available evidence points to the existence of political generations. Regarding elites, the most persuasive evidence comes from cross-national studies (Putnam 1976, 100–102; 1973, 237–39). Within the United States, the most likely candidate for a recent generational watershed is the period of the 1960s. The effects of this period in U.S. history have only begun to be written about in a systematic fashion, but it is clear—through almost any observation of mass culture—that the period exerted and continues to exert a profound influence on the thinking of U.S. citizens who came of age during the period, and also on many of those who were already politically mature, though their perceptions during this period were conditioned by their earlier experiences.[17] Many of the senators' statements clearly reflected the influence of this period. This influence was not all positive, however. Some senators reacted negatively to the ideas of the 1960s, but in these cases the influence was no less profound.

Beliefs and Behavior: A Cognitive Filter

Now that we have some understanding of the nature of political beliefs, the way in which we might go about studying them, and the sources of these beliefs, to complete our foundation we need a sense of the consequences of these beliefs, or the connections between beliefs and behavior. The influence of beliefs about such things as distributive justice on actual legislative behavior may be strictly limited. Laundry lists of factors other than beliefs that could influence or even determine legislative behavior have been provided at several points already, and do not need to be repeated here. While later chapters will consider in greater detail the realms of behavior that deep beliefs best account for, the argument that will be made here is more general: Although other forces greatly affect behavior, beliefs about such things as distributive justice exert a significant influence on behavior through their role as cognitive filters.

The Case against Beliefs. Although it would be absurd to claim that no causal connections exist between beliefs and legislative behavior, many researchers look askance at the focus on beliefs as a preferred way to understand behavior. A broad survey of attitude research, for example, found that

> after more than seventy-five years of attitude research, there is still little, if any consistent evidence supporting the hypothesis that knowledge of an individual's attitude toward some object will allow one to predict the way he will behave with respect to the object. (Fishbein 1967, 477)

Researchers in psychology do not agree that in general, attitudes predict behavior. The assertion that deep beliefs predict behavior may be even more hazardous. Students of legislatures have not routinely made the connection between beliefs and behavior. For example, John Wahlke et al.'s classic 1962 study of state legislators came to a fairly negative conclusion regarding the impact of ideology on legislative behavior. In considering the recollections of state legislators about their interest in politics and their basic orientations toward service, they concluded (after noting the low salience of political beliefs among the public via *The American Voter*) that

> state legislators are only slightly more ideology conscious than the electorate as a whole. . . . It would seem that for the great majority of politi-

cians active at the state level . . . the "great issues" are relatively devoid of salience. (Wahlke et al. 1962, 93–94, 107)

While legislators' specific attitudes toward abortion, for example, could predict their votes on that issue, Wahlke et al.'s conclusion suggests that beliefs and belief systems may not have much influence. Other students of the national legislature have raised similar doubts about the connections between beliefs and behavior. Regarding Congress, Aage Clausen cautions that "the ideologist theory appears to have serious shortcomings as an explanation of congressional decision making" (1973, 31).[18] Similarly, in studying the U.S. Senate John Jackson concludes that his findings on Senate voting are "inconsistent with an explanation based on the notion that senators' votes are the products of individual experiences and philosophies" (1974, 81). Particularly in recent times, the technical nature and technical complexity of legislation may produce a specialist, non-belief-based thrust in legislative decision making. Studying U.S. House members, John Kingdon cites the following difficulties other researchers have found in translating beliefs into legislative voting decisions:

> [I]deology is an inadequate guide to decision, since it is difficult to connect one's general policy attitudes with specific amendments, since congressmen often do not have well-formed or intense opinions on many subjects before them, and, even if their opinions are well defined, they still need the advice of specialists in areas not immediately within their own competence. (Kingdon 1989, 9)

When one begins to observe a legislature in action, there do indeed appear to be too many amendments, bills, proposals, and issues floating around at any one time for legislators to keep track of all of them well enough to make informed decisions that by and large reflect their beliefs. The frenetic pace of the legislature and the resulting fatigue endured by the legislators add to this difficulty. Furthermore, the nature of the process itself can at times become so complicated and confusing that the salience of ideology and deep beliefs may fade behind the attempt to simply keep track of everything, and to understand what each bill actually does. When policy is discussed, it is usually in bureaucratic, technical terms, with heavy use of statistics and little use of any kind of theory. Much time is spent figuring out just what bills or proposals purport to do, how their terms are defined, and how their implementation will be carried through. Frank Smallwood, a government professor who spent a term as state senator in Vermont, makes the following kindred observation about the legislative process:

> For the individual participant, the legislative process becomes a baffling series of divergent experiences without any apparent logical sequence at

all. It often seems to be disjointed and unrelated because it is charac-
terized by a bargaining process that consists of a never-ending mix of
uncertainty, adjustments, and compromise. (Smallwood 1976, 80)

My observations of the Connecticut senate corroborated this description. Even
the way in which I was typically met upon my arrival at the various legislative
offices both reinforces and expands on Smallwood's observation. Staffers
would assume that I had come expecting to find the traditional responsible
governing model one finds in a civics textbook, and would quickly tell me that
I would not find what I expected, that things were "crazy here," and so on. They
would spend a good bit of time telling me how the reality of politics at the
capitol—its personal orientation, its fueling by egos, its behind-the-scenes
dealing—diverged from the models that I (perhaps they?) no doubt carried
with me. One senator would often chuckle about his aide trying to apply theory
to what actually went on. That evening, the same aide said to me: "The theory
of how it's supposed to work doesn't come close to the reality, and it makes
you wonder about the system, about how it works. You begin to wonder who's
representing who."

The most powerful limitation on the connection between deep beliefs and
legislative behavior, however, is suggested by the purposive, economic models
of legislative behavior. In this view, rational goal seeking defines the legislator's behavior. The most proximate of these goals is of course reelection. David
Mayhew's 1974 study of Congress, *Congress: The Electoral Connection,*
views both individual behavior and congressional politics through the lens of
this proximate goal, and produces, in the words of a recent reviewer of legislative research, "a resulting picture, presented in one of the most influential
essays in recent years, [that] depicts behavior and institutional practices which
are strikingly familiar to Congress-watchers" (Matthews 1985, 32).[19] The goal
of reelection leads to many behaviors that will produce electoral payments,
including (to use Mayhew's terms) advertising, credit claiming, and position
taking. Thinking specifically about matters within the chamber, it also leads to
political gamesmanship between the legislators, particularly between the parties. Skilled gamesmanship yields better advertisements, claimed credits, and
staked positions. I saw much of this gamesmanship during my observations of
the senate. Regarding legislation, it usually took the form of the minority
"flagging up" majority bills with amendments that were often fiscally irresponsible (even by their own admission) and that were fully intended to be voted
down by the majority. These amendments spent money on politically "sexy"
projects, such as a waiver of a parking card fee for disabled veterans or, in
another case, some additional money for an elderly nutrition program, which
would have been financed by a proposed cut in the pending salary increase for
legislators. Party-based votes against these amendments would be placed on a

roll-call vote by the minority, and then used against both the majority party and the individual legislators during elections. Sometimes press releases on the votes were generated that same day. Technical and definitional questions asked of the majority legislators in committee and on the floor are also part of this gamesmanship; they are efforts to embarrass the majority party by making it appear to be incompetent.[20] These practices were not limited to the Republicans; several Democratic senators told me that they did exactly the same sorts of things when they were in the minority between 1984 and 1986. On the majority side, this gamesmanship takes the form of automatically voting down the minority proposals and amendments to majority-sponsored bills. This shuts the minority party out from harvesting the political fruits of governance. The concern here regarding gamesmanship versus the influence of beliefs is that such gamesmanship ultimately affects the larger, prior decisions of legislators about what kinds of things to pursue and what kinds of things to attack, and that deeper beliefs about what kinds of things are right or fair will fade away in importance under the glare of more proximate concerns.

The Case for Beliefs. Two commonly made assumptions, one about legislative behavior and the other about American ideology, contribute against the focus on beliefs in legislative research. One of the reasons that so many researchers get thrown off the trail of beliefs in considering legislative behavior is that their notions of legislative behavior are overly constricted; more specifically, that they are limited to voting. Since legislative voting is easily quantified and does not require intrusive methods of study, it is understandable why it is researched so heavily, often to exclusion. Legislative behavior includes much more than voting, however. As Robert Putnam has noted, to a large degree legislatures are talking shops (1973, 27). This talking—debating, taking positions, mobilizing support, and so on is important, and it is probably more open to the influence of deep beliefs than is voting. Another problem specifically concerning the U.S. case is that since U.S. legislators (and citizens) are generally not thought of as ideological, but rather as more pluralistic and pragmatic, it may not even occur to us to look to beliefs in explaining behavior. This assumption was no doubt bolstered by the "end of ideology" thesis asserted during the early 1960s (Bell 1960). "Ideology," particularly in U.S. parlance, is often associated with intolerance and hostility, and U.S. legislators are not considered to have these qualities. They are thought of as pragmatists, pluralistic compromisers, and logrollers. The quality of being ideological, however, is not synonymous with hostility and intolerance. Putnam, for example, compares the ideological qualities of Italian and British elective elites with an index of partisan hostility, and finds no significant tendency toward hostility among ideologues. In fact, when he looks only at extremists he finds a *negative* relation between hostility and ideology (1973, 62–63).[21] Thus, extrapolating to the U.S. case, U.S. legislators may in fact be ideological and belief-motivated after all; we are just unaware of it because we have always assumed otherwise. If ideology is properly seen in broader terms, rather than in narrow, polemical terms (as a mechanism of dogmatism and distortion), then it becomes a more relevant concept in the understanding of legislative behavior. Furthermore, the fact that legislators often act pragmatically does not necessarily argue against the influence of deeper, more ideological beliefs on their behavior. These beliefs can still significantly affect the kinds of pragmatic decisions legislators make.

But there is more direct evidence that beliefs matter. To be sure, beliefs do not tell the whole behavioral story, but nonetheless they are a salient part of a large, complicated process that begins with previous collective outcomes, takes place through the behavior of the individuals these outcomes have shaped, and then ultimately ends with new collective outcomes. Let us first look at voting behavior, since it is studied so heavily in the United States and since voting is after all a key activity for legislators, one that is no doubt indicative of many other activities. Although the literature in this vein has generated controversy and remains somewhat scattered, it does indicate that the focus on beliefs is relevant to the understanding of legislative behavior and therefore to policy outcomes.[22] Support for the relevancy of beliefs is found among studies that look at voting behavior in the collective format, as well as from studies that concentrate on individual legislators' voting decisions.

On the individual level, the seminal interview-based work by John Kingdon is most instructive. Kingdon finds that the actors that are most influential in a congressman's voting decision are fellow congressmen, followed by constituents, interest groups, staff, and executive and party leadership. The attitudes of the individual congressman, however, significantly affect his choice of informants: "In selecting congressmen upon whom to rely, the first rule appears to be, as one respondent put it, 'Choose those you agree with'" (Kingdon 1989, 75). Along with expertise, this criterion emerged as the most important consideration in the selection of informants.

Kingdon goes on to develop a "consensus mode of decision" (1989, 242–61). If a bill is noncontroversial, then a congressman votes with the consensus. If a bill is controversial, then a congressman looks to his personal "field of forces," which includes his own policy attitudes and the views of relevant actors, such as constituents, trusted associates, and important interest groups. Again, if there is no conflict between these elements, he votes with the consensus. If there is a conflict within his field of forces, a congressman considers his goals. Kingdon assumes that congressmen have three, Fenno-like goals: the satisfaction of constituents, intra-Washington influence, and good public policy. If there are conflicts between these goals, the tendency is to go with the goal of public policy, which is in turn largely determined by the congressman's own attitudes. Although, as I have stated several times already, attitudes or beliefs are not the whole story, Kingdon concludes that "it would be tempting to adopt an ideological model as one's sole explanation for legislative voting behavior" (1989, 273). He sticks with the consensus model because it can accommodate the other influences that result from the complexity and volume of legislative voting decisions, and because the other influences often provide links between attitudes and particular decisions.

Similar findings exist on the state level. In an interview-based study of the Oklahoma and Kansas state legislatures, Donald Songer et al. (1986) found attitudes and values to be consistently important in the choice of voting cues for all the issues they studied, with the exception of redistricting. Values and attitudes were found to be either a determinative or a major factor in 63 percent of the specific voting decisions they studied. Eric Uslaner and Ronald Weber's comprehensive fifty-state survey-based study of legislative decision making also found that beliefs had an important impact on behavior: "Our analyses have thus suggested that to a certain extent, the subjective orientations of members of state legislatures do play a major role in the behavior of the legislators and also in shaping policy alternatives" (1977, 184). In an earlier work, the two researchers had discovered that legislators' orientations toward "social welfare concern" had affected the level of redistribution policies in the states (Uslaner and Weber 1975).[23]

Moving further beyond studies of voting, Steven Kelman's study of U.S. policy making takes direct aim at economic purposive models of legislative behavior, and adduces many pieces of evidence from other researchers, in addition to his own, in arguing for the significance of "public spirit" and ideas over self-interest as the wellspring of public behavior (1987, 60–67, 213–47).[24] Sidney Verba and Gary Orren's comprehensive survey-based study of U.S. elite attitudes toward equality found, in opposition to utility maximization and self-interest theories, that values were both autonomous and influential in their effects on both political thought and action (1985, 2–4, 248–49). In an extensive interview-based study of Congress, Steven Schier (1992) concentrates on members' economic beliefs to explain budgetary policy during the 1980s. And in a comparison of bureaucrats and elected politicians from several Western democracies, including the United States, Joel Aberbach et al. found that both role (bureaucrat versus politician) and ideology (defined broadly as "a coherent system of beliefs and values") have independent impacts on the approach to policy (1981, 115).[25]

With care not to fall into the fallacy of claiming that the rationalizations people offer for their actions are in fact the motivations behind those actions, I offer several additional points in support of the significance of normative beliefs.[26] First, legislators must give reasons for whatever courses of action they take, and when they do they must invoke norms other than naked self-interest. Once invoked, these norms can develop a life of their own and affect decisions independently. Second, the fact that there is a need to at least rationalize decisions in this way is important; it tells us something about our fundamental premises, and may itself influence what self-interested options can be successfully pursued (Williams, Jr. 1979). Third, it may not be possible to separate interests and ideology or deep beliefs, because the beliefs themselves define the conception and content of the interests, in terms of what is desirable. As I have pointed out earlier, interests are often unclear. And even if ideology or beliefs have their source in interests, this may only be the case because of other prior beliefs that assert and justify the connections between them. Indeed, E. E. Schattschneider claims that "it is futile to try to determine whether men are stimulated politically by interests or by ideas, for people have ideas about interests" (1942, 37). Finally, it may be the case that the very nature of beliefs is to serve the holder's interests (Reinarman 1987, 164). Thus, to say that beliefs are epiphenomenal because they are self-serving is to misstate the case; rather, the question is how these interests are constructed, and how legitimate they in fact are. Beliefs are important subjects for study in the attempt to answer both parts of this question.

Beliefs as Filters. Many of the above studies supporting the focus on beliefs, in particular the individually oriented studies, also imply a mechanism through which beliefs influence behavior. They suggest that in addition to directly influencing legislative decisions, beliefs also act as filters that influence the legislators' perceptions of the many other forces acting on them. Taking John Kingdon's treatment again, for example, we find that the influence of attitudes and beliefs is reinforced through lobbyist activity and the congressman's selection of staff. Staff members are selected in accordance with the congressman's views, and staff often select a congressman in the same way.[27] Lobbyists are found to be most successful when they aim their persuasive efforts at values the congressman already holds (Kingdon 1989, 165, 272). Kingdon also finds that through their policy attitudes, congressional members to a large degree subjectively control and edit the larger field of forces to which their decisions are subject. Their attitudes are important factors in both the selection and perception of the environment and events to which they will pay attention in their decision making. In other words, they act as filters. Furthermore, Kingdon's very model of consensus decision making, with its emphasis on attitudes in the selection of fellow members as voting cues, adds to this filter notion of beliefs.

Operationally, we might compare the filter effect of beliefs to that of the tint on a pair of glasses. As beliefs become more intense (due to the certainty with which they are held, their importance to the holder, and the ego involvement they entail), the tint becomes darker, and in turn either filters out entirely or leaves its imprint on an increasing number of objects. A recent piece of research on a state legislature supports this operationalization. In an interview-based study of committee work in the Minnesota lower house, Jon Hurwitz (1986) found that on issues of high salience and controversy, individual legislators' own attitudes proved critically influential in their perceptions of the issues and the political characteristics surrounding them. This effect greatly intensified as ego involvement in an issue increased.

The notion of beliefs as filters is consistent with the commonsense view that both internal-subjective and external-environmental forces influence an individual legislator's behavior. Beliefs and environment are not separate items; they are complementary and linked (Greenstein 1971, 12–13). They are intertwined in a "push-pull relationship"; as one gets stronger, it exerts more influence vis-à-vis the other (Greenstein 1969, 29; Putnam 1973, 2–3). Some environmental situations will even enhance the effect of beliefs, just as the effect of our glasses will vary depending on what we are looking at. By the same token, beliefs can enhance the effect of situational forces, just as our glasses can at times allow us to apprehend some things more clearly (Greenstein 1971, 15).

The notion of beliefs as filters also leads to two final conclusions about the approach toward political beliefs. First, it further bolsters the need for and the place of the in-depth interview in the study of political beliefs. If beliefs act as filters, then we need to gain a subtle understanding of their tints through in-depth interviews. It is also through in-depth interviews that we can best understand the nature of the filtration process. Second, we should bear in mind the fuzziness of such a concept as filtration and the difficulty in assessing the effects of different shades of gray, and adjust the standards of proof and evidence that we demand from our investigations accordingly. This fuzziness holds true as well for the beliefs themselves. Thus, the standards of validity that fit such a project are those of plausibility—of perspectives that "we can imagine or 'feel' as right"—rather than scientific proof, and the evidence that is most persuasive is that of thick description rather than correlation and covariance; the subject does not allow for any more specificity than that (Bruner 1986, 52).[28]

With this in mind, let us now listen to the narratives of justice.

The Narratives of Justice

In my earlier arguments for the use of in-depth interviews, I emphasized the method's greater sensitivity to the subtle idiosyncrasies and personal contexts of each senator's beliefs. But I must also of course be able to tease out meaningful conclusions and themes from the interviews in order for the study to be of any use. In this analysis I must be able to discover (but not impose) structure in the material yielded by my open-ended and largely semistructured approach in the interviews, to submit the material "to the discipline of a 'more detached and abstract understanding'" (Hochschild 1981, 22).[29] I must attempt to pull out the meanings of what the senators tell me, and locate the enduring underlying themes (Bruner 1986, 7).

Are there patterns of response? Yes, there are. I found that when I asked the senators my questions concerning distributive justice, their answers did have patterns, which took the form of shared stories, or narratives. The concepts of script, story, and narrative have been widely used recently to understand how people both think about and relate information concerning a variety of subjects. There is no reason to expect that narrative would not work equally well in understanding normative thinking about politics and justice, where the mind confronts a complicated world, from which it must generate both meaning and prescription. As Alasdair MacIntyre claims, humans are essentially storytelling animals (1984, 216).[30]

Narrative fits well with the research in cognitive psychology that considers the individual more as a cognitive miser in the processing of information, a seeker of efficiency and satisfaction, than as a seeker of consistency and mastery (Lau and Sears 1986; Mandler 1984; Kluegel and Smith 1986). Limits on cognitive powers force one to process, retain, and organize information selectively. In the same vein, the construction of a narrative provides a way of "compacting vast ranges of experiences," and, I might add, the meanings of those experiences, "in economical symbols" (Bruner 1979, 6–7). This compaction is a necessary process, given the limits on our capacity for processing information. Narrative supplies cognitive shortcuts, provides an organization for the other, more specific organizations of attitudes, and places them in a familiar context. It tells us what items of information are to be treated as evidence and what items are irrelevant (MacIntyre 1977, 454–55). It also invests the information with both meaning and purpose.

In addition, narrative, and the cognitive research with which it can be linked, also complements the notion of beliefs acting as filters. The filtering process sorts information and enhances one's ability to make sense of the world and to take appropriate action. Indeed, John Kingdon's work on the way beliefs affect behavior, from which in part I derived my notion of filters, has many points of contact with narrative and cognitive research. They share a similar set of assumptions and starting points, which highlight the importance of time limits and cognitive miserliness among individuals.

More specifically, the narratives that I discovered are similar to those described by Jerome Bruner. They are "instantiation[s] of models we carry in our own minds" (1986, 7).[31] The teller of a narrative is engaged in a certain kind of enterprise, one that is distinct from the construction of a logical argument. Narrative is more concerned with deriving meaning from experience than with explaining it; it is concerned with the "vicissitudes of human intentions" (1986, 11–12, 16). As a speech act, narrative intends "to initiate and guide a search for meanings among a spectrum of possible meanings" (1986, 25). Bruner identifies a common structure in the theme of narrative: Narrative "contains a *plight* into which *characters* have fallen as a result of intentions that have gone awry either because of circumstances, of the 'character of characters,' or most likely of the interaction between the two" (1986, 21; emphasis in original). Alasdair MacIntyre makes a similar point in stating that "narrative requires an evaluative framework in which good or bad character helps to produce unfortunate or happy outcomes" (1977, 456).

The narratives found here include accounts of history (often rooted or woven into the senators' own life tales) that in turn lead to explanations of present conditions and views about the future. Though they differ in the meanings they extract from the information and experiences on which they are based, to a large degree they share Bruner's organizational structure. In terms primarily of content, there are three basic kinds of narratives, in the naming of which I have concentrated on the attitude toward the existing economic order: the critic's narrative, the supporter's narrative, and the ambivalent's narrative. I did not place each senator's responses into one of the three narrative types based on some prior set of criteria; rather, the responses sorted themselves empirically. What held each narrative type together and distinguished it from the other two narratives were the salient properties of the narrative itself; that is, the way the narrative constructed the characters and the circumstances, the locus of responsibility for the plights the characters find themselves in, and the nature of the interactions between characters and circumstances. Different sets of heroes and villains populate the critic's and supporter's narrative, for example, while the characters in the ambivalent's narrative become more uncertain. To a large degree, the senators telling these narratives are also arranged by party; only Democrats tell the critic's narrative and only Republicans tell the supporter's narrative.

Were there close calls in the sorting? Of course there were; the most problematic were two cases of ambivalents-cum-critics. Not every senator told a paradigmatic version of a narrative type. And in addition to the few senators who mixed some parts of two different narratives (none mixed all three), there were a few who I spoke to for relatively short periods of time, and with whom I would have needed to spend more time to really nail down. But there were surprisingly few close calls; for most of the senators, the basic three-part distinction was strikingly apparent.

Each narrative ranges over several topics and contains several core episodes or chapters. The chapters within the narratives both illustrate and organize the senators' views on the issues involved in distributive justice. The critic's narrative, for example, consists of four chapters, which I have named "The Big Fish Eat the Little Fish"; "To Each According to His (or Her) Needs"; "Love Thy Neighbor as Thyself"; and "Government as Hero."

The most interesting and unusual findings are undoubtedly contained in the critic's narrative. Senators telling the critic's narrative are much more critical of the American economic system than the existing research on political beliefs would lead us to expect. Although at various points throughout their stories there are indications of the more traditionally held notions of American thinking about distributive justice (support for differentiation versus equality, emphasis on opportunity versus result, emphasis on education, and so on), in the main the narrative is somewhat startling. It contains critical treatments of economic power, race, and class; distributional norms invoking need; and an emphasis on improving human nature. Distributive justice results from the establishment of basic patterns of distribution responding to needs and the establishment of forms of social interaction emphasizing empathy, which in turn undergird, reinforce, and enhance these patterns of distribution. There is also, however, a backing off on the depth of the critique that occurs between the diagnosis of the distributive problem and its treatment, which again indicates the presence of traditional American thinking. While the problems perceived are quite deep and structural in nature, the solutions offered are softer and more individually oriented.

The discovery of this narrative is particularly interesting, owing to the fact that the people telling it are established politicians. That this narrative was found among a group of established politicians within a state not known for extremely progressive or radical tendencies, but rather as "the land of steady habits," is quite remarkable.[32] This narrative thus suggests the question, for what kind of political theory might this narrative form the normative base? Therefore, in describing the narrative in the next chapter, I will consider the links between the critic's narrative and various American, as well as European, political theories.

Given the political successes of the New Right (in its various forms) during the 1980s, the reader may be less surprised by the elements found in the supporter's narrative, but nonetheless some items will not fail to startle, appearing to better fit into the thinking of an earlier era. Supporters tend to reject notions of economic class, locate the problems of the have-nots in elements of their own characters, and endorse distributions based on narrowly constructed notions of merit. They also tend to take human nature as they find it. Distributive justice consists mainly in following certain procedures, which are believed to respond to merit.[33]

The ambivalent's narrative tells its own distinct story; it does not simply mark out a middle area between the critic's and supporter's narratives. Ambivalents support both the market system and its resulting patterns of influence, but they are left queasy due to the numbers who either fail to participate or fail to thrive in the system. They recognize, as George Orwell once noted, that the problem with free competition is that someone always loses. Explanations of poverty and underachievement take a historical approach; forces such as past legacies of racism and poverty and rapid changes in the economic structure that either displace people or leave them at a competitive disadvantage are held accountable for much of the problem. More simply, the failures of the system, or of those within it, are seen mainly as the result of certain characteristics about those people, but characteristics that are not their own fault. Thus, ambivalents favor more strongly redistributive policies than do the supporters, but do not begin with considerations of need, as do the critics. Distributive justice is largely achieved by controlling the externalities of a system that is essentially fair. In addition, the ambivalent's narrative contains a motif that is not found in the other two narratives: a technical approach to justice issues. The technical approach is distinguished by an emotional coolness, a tendency to reach for facts, a hesitancy to place blame, and a proclivity toward specific incremental policy proposals.

There were also several large and overlapping subthemes or subplots that permeated these narratives. Again, some of these were more oriented toward content, while others were more oriented toward form and approach. First, regarding content, there was substantial evidence in the interview materials for Thomas Sowell's (1987) two-part division of constrained and unconstrained world visions.[34] Relying on such thinkers as Adam Smith, Edmund Burke, and Alexander Hamilton, Sowell describes the constrained vision as rooted in a static conception of human nature limited to self-interest and thus requiring incentives and trade-offs to motivate behavior. Relying on such thinkers as William Godwin, Thomas Paine, and Jean-Jacques Rousseau, he describes the unconstrained vision as rooted in a dynamic conception of human nature filled with the potential for good intentions and impartial acts—man as perfectible. These notions resonate through the different respective positions each vision has regarding knowledge, social processes, liberty, equality, power, and of course justice. I found a similar resonance in the senators' narratives; the unconstrained vision was most sonorous in the critic's narrative, while the constrained vision was most sonorous in the supporter's narrative. Second, a finding from Robert Reich's analysis of American political thinking is also present in the narratives: attitudes regarding inclusion and exclusion, or the treatment of "the other," are of central importance (Reich 1987, 16–19).[35] Variations in these attitudes are critical in understanding the differences between the narratives uncovered in this study. Third, as many other observers of American beliefs have discovered, I also found that in the senators' treatment of economic and social mobility there was an enormous emphasis placed on equality of opportunity, and on education as the key to realizing that opportunity. Within this shared emphasis, however, there is much room to differ. Differing definitions of equality of opportunity and beliefs about education entitlements figured greatly in the differing views of distributive justice.

Regarding the basic form and approach of the responses, several other subthemes emerged. Most notable was the presence of personal experience, particularly early experience, in the formation and perpetuation of beliefs. Particularly salient within the theme of experience is the decade of the 1960s. The personal experiences of the senators during this period, in addition to the period's political ideas and political leaders, exerted a profound influence on the thinking of many of the younger and even some of the older senators. Also prevalent was the relative tendency toward the personal and individual plane rather than the abstract and structural plane as the preferred level of analysis and prescription. This was particularly true in the case of prescribed solutions. Though problems of injustice were often accounted for in individual, personal terms, even when they were outlined in more abstract and structural terms the solutions and prescriptions offered tended toward the personal, individual level, rather than the level of the economic system as a whole.

Two other subthemes that combine both content and form also emerged. First, consistent with the concept of narrative as a way to describe the senators' responses, views about distributive justice and in particular about equal opportunity can be seen largely as statements or views about history. Implicit in the statements about the existence and provision of equal opportunity for socioeconomic advancement were different accounts of what had happened to individuals and groups in the past. These accounts structured both accounts of current circumstances and future prescriptions.[36] Second, as many other students of American beliefs have found, there was often some degree of inconsistency and ambiguity within a given set of responses, as well as a substantial degree of ambivalence regarding the attitudes of many of the respondents toward their own views.[37] This was most present in those senators telling the ambivalent's narrative, but was not limited to them alone.

Finally, I found a gender factor at work, which for any individual senator could overlap with the three narratives just presented. In the course of the interviews I found that the female senators, as a group, more strongly resisted answering the questions in terms of abstract, objective, rules-based types of answers than did the male senators.[38] Relative to the male senators, their responses were also marked by a more personal and individual approach, a heightened sensitivity to needs, a deeper concern for the well-being of others, and a stronger desire for harmony.[39] A more elaborate examination of the effects of gender on beliefs about justice in a legislative context certainly would be useful and called for, but it is well beyond the scope of my inquiry here; indeed, it would require a separate book. I will thus refer only marginally to these effects as I present the narratives.

CHAPTER 3

The Critic's Narrative

Life is unfair. (7)

Those who are rich control everything. (9)

You could be rich . . . [and] basically you do what you want to do, and you can get away with anything you want to do. (8)

There are injustices that occur in anyone's lifetime, in any generation, that aren't corrected. . . . It just seems that no matter what we recognize is necessary to correct them, it doesn't seem to happen. . . . That's just sad. (6)

Sometimes you get so frustrated with not seeing the results about something, you get these flashes where you say, "Gee, I wonder if we'd be better off burning this fucking place down." (6)

Nine of the senators, a quarter of those interviewed, fit the mold of the critic. Their narrative may startle. What makes the account presented here particularly surprising and interesting is the fact that it is the product of a group of established, elected politicians. Although the stories these nine senators tell vary in significant ways, the critic's narrative is held together by a strong sense that American society is not just; that equal opportunity, the metaphor for upward mobility that Americans of all ideological shades endorse, means much more than the requirement that openings in employment and education be filled in a formally nondiscriminatory fashion; that this stronger form of equal opportunity does not exist in fact; that society is highly stratified—into classes—and that it is stratified unfairly; and that the poor and racial minorities are kept down socially and economically, and in some cases exploited.

What is the solution to these problems? In abstract terms, most critics share the view that the ultimate solution to the problems of poverty and inequality lies not so much in the traditional welfare state efforts to sustain and eventually change those at the bottom end of the socioeconomic distribution, but rather in the transformation of the socioeconomic structure itself and the larger environment within which individuals operate. But when they come down to the more specific, concrete prescriptions of measures to achieve these goals, the critics' views become softer, gentler, and more subjectively oriented than what their original diagnosis, taken alone, would appear to warrant. They concentrate not so much on structural reorganization, but rather on meeting individual needs and engendering compassion and understanding among individuals. Thus, though the critic's narrative presents a challenge to the commonly held notions about American patterns of economic thinking, the apparent contradiction between diagnosis and treatment points to two distinctively American traits: the endurance of the norm of differentiation concerning the economic realm, and the individualistic framework and approach toward social problems (Hochschild 1981; Lamb 1982). The critics appear to be different, perhaps unique, but are nonetheless American.

Nevertheless, the critic's narrative remains in many important respects remarkably different from the generally accepted notions of American beliefs about distribution, at both the elite and mass levels. To better set the stage for the critic's narrative, as well as the other narratives that follow, I shall begin by briefly expanding on the account of these accepted notions I offered in chapter 1. In painting this backdrop I use the broadest of strokes, but I believe the portrait is in the main accurate. My portrait also will be limited to a contemporary representation of American beliefs; I will not discuss the historical and philosophical origins of these beliefs in such elements as the early absence of a feudal order or the Anglo-Scottish versus the French Enlightenment.

When looking across the landscape of American economic thinking, most observers are struck by the premium placed on economic individualism, which in turn tempers support for public assistance, government regulation, and any significant moves toward economic equality. At the same time, this premium bolsters support for the norm of differentiation in the economic realm. This premium is in part reinforced by (and also reinforces) a sense that there is at least an acceptable supply of available opportunity for economic advancement.

The notion of equal opportunity is key in this belief system. Varying conceptions of equal opportunity are of course possible. Stronger conceptions imply a greater degree of government intervention in the economy. The brand of equal opportunity found to be most supported, however, is a comparatively weaker, more formal and negative variant; protections against overt discrimination, for instance. Within the notion of equal opportunity, the framework is again an individualistic one; there is comparatively little emphasis placed on the social and economic realities that may undergird and often determine—and thwart—individual achievement.

On the other hand, public intervention in economic matters is favored to the degree that the practices of industrial corporate capitalism are perceived to obstruct economic individualism, individual development, and opportunity. But though big business is often mistrusted, the commitment to capitalism remains strong, particularly in what Herbert McClosky and John Zaller identify as the held values of "individualism, competition, achievement, private property, the profit system, differential incomes, and the unlimited acquisition of wealth" (1984, 159).[1] Freedom is the most dearly held of all values, and in the American mind it is thought to be both wrapped up in and dependent on the free enterprise system. As Irving Kristol has observed, the American way of life is infused by capitalism; the United States is in fact the paradigmatic capitalist nation (1983, chaps. 12, 15).

It is not surprising, then, that economic inequality is highly tolerated. Even the poor, who would have the most to gain from greater equality, apparently seek only what Jennifer Hochschild has called "fair differences" (1981, 111). And in his study of working class men in "Eastport," Robert Lane found a support for income inequality that led him to remark: "Surely, beyond the grave, there is a specter haunting *Marx*" (1962, 70). American arguments about economic equality become arguments over marginal adjustments in the size of the gaps; the gaps themselves are taken for granted.[2]

Due not only to assumptions of economic individualism, but also to a shared sense of social equality, American perceptions of economic class are very weak, if not entirely absent (Seligman 1987, 164–66).[3] The political and economic realms are largely considered separately, so that while economic inequality is tolerated, a norm of political equality exists alongside it. There is some concern that inequalities in the economic realm may sometimes spill over into and influence the political realm in ways that threaten the dominant political norm of equality, but these realms are not considered sufficiently linked to warrant a challenge to the norm of differentiation and inequality in the economic realm.

There are variations on this overall theme, to be sure, particularly concerning the proper degree of state involvement in the economy (Reinarman 1987). But nonetheless there is thought to be a broad consensus around this theme, which acts to constrain the range of legitimate politicoeconomic dispute. Generally, critical analysis is absent. There is a felt sense of justice concerning economic and public affairs. Citizens do not challenge the fundamental beliefs, and ambivalence rather than challenge results from any incongruities between support for the system and an awareness of its shortcomings in practice.

Observers of the views of the political elite on these issues have found them to be roughly similar to those of the mass public. The elite does tend to have more extreme views—to both the left and the right—than does the public, but its views are still within the boundaries of the dominant ideology or consensus described above.[4] In general, the political elite also tends to be more tolerant of government intervention (for obvious reasons), and simply more tolerant; that is, it is more strongly supportive of civil liberties (except for the economically conservative elite vis-à-vis the economically conservative nonelite) (McClosky and Brill 1983; McClosky 1964).[5]

The contrast between this portrait of American beliefs and the critic's narrative immediately suggests some questions. First, how and why does the apparent gap between the critic's narrative and the dominant pattern of American thinking about distributive issues exist? Second, have the critics staked out a position that is fundamentally irreconcilable with the other positions found in the senate? Third, looking at the actual legislative products of the Connecticut senate, one finds little evidence of the strong views that the critic's narrative contains. How and why, then, do the critics' views become lost or hidden in the legislative process? How do they become lost in the translation of thought into action? Granted, the critics constitute only a minority of the senators, but in a situation where they constitute a quarter of the entire membership, and more importantly, over a third of the majority party, we would expect to see some evidence of their views in the legislative output. I will investigate these questions in later chapters concerning the relations between the different narratives and the role of justice beliefs in the legislative process. For the moment, however, let us listen to the critic's narrative itself.

An Overview of the Narrative

In the critic's narrative, persons who find themselves at the bottom, in destitute living conditions and facing thoroughly bleak economic futures, are seen as victims of a social and economic system that at some significant level of responsibility put them there. The posited levels of responsibility vary with the degree of purposiveness posited in the logic of the system's dynamics; the criticisms are located at different levels of the corporate order. Some critics, for example, locate the problems in the deeper, more structural levels of the capitalist order. In the most critical version of the narrative, identifiable groups are seen to hold a monopoly of power, through which they direct the system's operations and profit from its maltreatment of others. The abusive nature of this system, particularly in the most critical tellings, is ultimately driven by greed.

Unlike Jennifer Hochschild's (1981) citizen respondents, the critics do not appear to divide their world into separate economic, political, and social realms that are in turn subject to separate standards. At least they do not do so to the same extent. More specifically, critics believe that economic resources invariably seep into the political process and influence political outcomes in profound ways. Concentrations of wealth translate into disproportionate amounts of political power, which in turn serve to reinforce this wealth. This view leads to less acceptance of concentrations of wealth, as these concentrations exert undue influence in a domain where there is already in place a strong (and culturally reinforced) norm of equality.

Race figures prominently in the critics' consideration of socioeconomic relations; the hatred built around racial distinctions is held to contribute significantly to the gulf of wealth, income, and opportunity that separates certain racial groups. As several critics put it, entirely too much of one's future depends on nothing else but race. When minority status is combined with poverty, the resulting mixture fastens a socioeconomic yoke around one's neck that is almost impossible to throw off.

Concerns about socioeconomic class as a division that engenders hatred and results in unjust treatment exist alongside and in some cases are woven through and around the concerns about race. In some tellings of the narrative, expressions of hatred and prejudice extend beyond race specifically to economic status or class more generally. In these tellings, class can encompass race, with the discussions of minorities by and large absorbed within the discussions of the lower classes.[6] The critics perceive an overall prejudice against the poor and working classes, which acts to keep them from rising into and being accepted by the middle and upper classes. Concomitantly, critics see the existence of a significant underclass and, more generally, assert the very existence of economic and social classes. Critics define classes by wealth and income as well as by type of occupation, and see their populations distributed in the form of either a pyramid or a distended bell curve, depending on the dimensional level employed. They also perceive a tension between these classes, or at least between their economic interests, which is for the most part dichotomous between those with greater and fewer resources. Though not overt and openly engaged, the conflicts between these groups and their interests are nonetheless won by those with the greatest resources.

The general theme of the story regarding these racial and economic groups is one of abuse: Persons at the bottom of the socioeconomic distribution have been and will continue to be used by those persons in the top half of the distribution. The little people are the protagonists of the critic's narrative, but there is no necessary, predestined, ultimate vindication of justice for their hardship; the little people do not rise up and displace their taskmasters. Government, however, is capable of acting for them. It can be the hero in the narrative by satisfying people's needs, by exhibiting care, understanding, and compassion, and by engendering these qualities within others. Under these circumstances, the narrative becomes epic saga. But as things actually stand, government does *not* act as the hero and the injustices for the most part go unavenged. Government's potential remains for the most part unrealized. And in all likelihood the situation will not change. In the critic's narrative the future remains problematic, both for the future prospects of those in need and for the larger health of the entire economic system.

Though all tellers of the critic's narrative are Democrats (and all supporters Republicans), their stories do not appear to originate from their partisan attachments. The narratives may be largely sorted by party, but they do not appear to be driven by it. The critic's narrative instead resonates with experiences in the senators' own lives, in their own stories of how they grew up and how they became politically aware. Sometimes these experiences are challenges or hardships lived through personally by the senators or by members of their families. Sometimes they are the challenges and hardships of others who were near enough to them to be seen firsthand. Not all the tellers of the critic's narrative have experienced or personally witnessed difficult lives, however. Although they are not the senators from the wealthiest families or those with the most wealth presently, many of the critics grew up in financially comfortable situations and presently lead financially comfortable lives. For a few senators, the guilt over this fact in the face of the knowledge of other people's situations seems to have played a part in the formation of their beliefs about justice. What appear to be more important, however, are the formative experiences in their childhood and early adulthood. These formative experiences seem to have substantially shaped both the organization of and meaning derived from the experiences and information gathered later in life.

Four Core Chapters

Four dominant themes, or core chapters, emerge from the critic's narrative. These chapters present the dynamics of the economic system and the sources of its distributive injustices, the endorsed norms of distribution, and the means of solving the problems of injustice. They organize the critics' specific views on the great variety of issues involved in distributive justice: wealth and income distribution; taxes; entitlements; education; social and economic conflict; bias in the marketplace; and the place and meaning of work in one's life, to name but a few. I have called the four chapters "The Big Fish Eat the Little Fish," "To Each According to His (or Her) Needs," "Love Thy Neighbor as Thyself," and "Government as Hero." "The Big Fish Eat the Little Fish" describes the workings of the market economy, how distributional patterns came to be the way they are, the difficulties of socioeconomic mobility, and the way businesses are run and people are treated. "To Each According to His (or Her) Needs" delineates what distinguishes a successful economy and a fair system of distribution. "Love Thy Neighbor as Thyself" discusses solutions to the problems laid out in the first chapter. It also locates the sources of injustice and puts forward possible cures for it. "Government as Hero" concerns the potential role of government versus injustice. Although these chapters each deal with distinguishable themes, they inevitably flow into one another, and thus in my presentations of each chapter the reader will no doubt notice elements of the others.

Taken as a whole, the chapters may appear to be somewhat contradictory. The optimism and lack of reformist teeth in "Love Thy Neighbor as Thyself," for example, do not seem to fit well with either the gravity and depth of the problems laid out in "The Big Fish Eat the Little Fish" or the benefits of public intervention found in "Government as Hero." Furthermore, when we look at specific, quantifiable responses such as the perceived and preferred yearly incomes of selected occupations, the resulting numbers are not what we might expect, given the qualitative responses contained in "To Each According to His (or Her) Needs" and "The Big Fish Eat the Little Fish." These contradictions point to larger ambivalences that haunt the critic's narrative, ambivalences that appear to result from the clinging persistence of the traditional liberal assumptions dominant in American political culture. Critics identify problems that cut deep into the core of the individualistic assumptions underlying the notion of the market-oriented corporate economy, but when offering desired distributions and outcomes, they remain largely guided by those assumptions and by the actual outcomes of the corporate system. In the critics' view, incomes, for example, are skewed in the way they are mostly because of greed and injustice and the lack of a genuine sense of shared community and mutual understanding, but directly changing this skewness means endangering a necessary incentive system, which is seen to motivate individuals effectively. In a perverse rendition of "American exceptionalism," these ambivalences may be due in part to the situation in which the critics find themselves in an American legislative body. Since they believe it is virtually impossible to persuade a majority of the legislature's members to allocate the means through which to genuinely address the problems that they identify (a perception I will return to in chaps. 7 and 8), the critics rely on more psychological, individual solutions. In this sense, their apparent ambivalences may in fact be cognitive strategies through which to cope with the problematic nature of their own beliefs.

I should also point out that the latter two chapters of the critic's narrative have many points of contact with the style of the women senators' responses, which I described briefly in chapter 2. This is seen in particular in the personal and individual approach, the heightened sensitivity to needs, and the emphasis on understanding and empathy. But note that the women do not constitute a majority of the critics, nor do the first two chapters of the critic's narrative ("The Big Fish Eat the Little Fish" and "To Each According to His [or Her] Needs") necessarily match the style of the women senators' responses.

A more detailed rendering of the four chapters constituting the critic's narrative follows. These chapters are succeeded by a brief discussion of several additional, disparate items of interest in the critics' responses, a presentation of their views about specific incomes, and a further discussion of the limitations on their critique of the economic system. This discussion is followed by the critics' stories of their own personal and political lives and a consideration of how these experiences might have influenced their narrative of justice. I then conclude with a consideration of the question of what political theory this narrative might be a part.

Before proceeding to the details of the critic's narrative, however, I wish to make a preliminary point concerning the place of justice itself. Since this work concerns beliefs about distributive justice, a significant and in some respects prior aspect of the senators' beliefs about justice is the relative emphasis the senators place on the concept of justice itself. Out of the three basic narratives, the critic's narrative places the highest priority on justice; that is, a concern that the rules of distribution are fair, in that they give each person or group its due, and that these rules are in fact followed (Lane 1962, 469). Indeed, this priority constituted one of the most striking aspects of my conversations with the critic senators; to a much greater extent than any other group of senators, the critics spontaneously reached for justice in discussing economic and social issues. This phenomenon is perhaps due to the fact that their narrative is after all a critical one; it asserts that things are not as they should be. One has a greater need for normative standards when expressing criticism than when expressing approval or ambivalence. Nonetheless, the reader should not overlook the fact that in the critic's narrative the notion of justice occupies a greater prominence and a higher profile as a criterion for assessing economic conditions than it does in the other narratives.

The Big Fish Eat the Little Fish

This is a story of the imbalance of power and the use of power that largely accounts for the perceived imbalance of income and wealth distribution, the very existence of the poor, the difficulty in social and economic mobility, and the apparent political acquiescence and cooperation in this system of many of the disadvantaged. It also describes how businesses are run, how people are paid, and who profit most from the general success of the economic system. Versions of this chapter vary in the degree to which they are framed by race, and the degree to which they are infused with a moral critique, but they are always stories of injustice. The chapter does not trace this injustice back to its historical origins, like Rousseau's "first person," who "fenced off a plot of ground, took it into his head to say *this is mine* and found people simple enough to believe him" (1964, 141), but nonetheless the notion of greed, and as another narrative chapter will demonstrate, a lack of understanding and empathy, emerge as the fuel for the engine of injustice.[7] In contrast to the ambivalent's narrative and especially the supporter's narrative, this chapter does not hang responsibility for the plight of the have-nots—in particular its minority members—upon the have-nots themselves.[8]

The critics' suspicion of those at the top of the corporate order is not surprising. Bureaucratic corporate capitalism has always had a difficult time fitting into the classical capitalist notion of individual entrepreneurship (Kristol 1983, chaps. 12, 15; Miller 1976, 308–17). Large corporations are the objects of much negative sentiment among the American public, and are only slightly more popular than big government. But "The Big Fish Eat the Little Fish" is more a story of specific kinds of socioeconomic relations. In "The Big Fish Eat the Little Fish," corruption has a particular face, which looks in a particular, class-oriented direction. The notion of corruption is part of a larger economic problem; it has a critical ideology.

I have already stated at several points that the critics' views are more extreme than what one might expect to find among almost any group of U.S. politicians. One facet of the critic's narrative that reveals this unusual quality is the extent to which actual conditions are seen to fall short of posited norms; that is, the perceived degree of injustice present. Even though many of the norms and ideals of the critics are cut from the traditional American fabric— equal opportunity, liberty, freedom—the way they are construed and the per- ceived size of the gap between what is and what ought to be contributes to the radical and anomalous appearance of the critics' views. But the critics also go beyond these traditional values. A lens through which this can perhaps best be seen is the notion, highly contentious within the field of political philosophy, of negative and positive liberty (Berlin 1969; Macpherson 1973).[9] Negative liberty—an individualistic notion, a "freedom from"—is the conception of liberty that has anchored mainstream American political thinking. But in the critic's narrative, and particularly in "The Big Fish Eat the Little Fish," a notion of positive liberty emerges—liberty in a more progressive, developmental sense, a "freedom to," a notion of empowerment. In the critics' view, the promise of liberty is not so much realized through the establishment and preservation of the largest possible private sphere within which the individual is left unencumbered and uncoerced (though this concept is not cast aside entirely), as it is through the promotion of conditions under which individuals, in a community, can develop themselves as individuals and can gain access to the means of producing a materially adequate and emotionally fulfilling life. A good example of this distinction is found in a critic's comment about bus service to better public schools. The senator criticized the state supreme court, on the grounds of freedom, for a decision requiring students to pay to go to a better public school than the one they were already enrolled in.

> I'm appalled at the state supreme court justice's decision on this busing thing. He has denied certain poor kids the right to equal education and to access to education, by saying they have to pay 97 dollars for busing for each of their kids, times three. That 97 dollars may be what they use to outfit those kids with proper clothes so that they're not laughed at when they go to school. That 97 dollars may be the money they send with that kid to eat their school lunches. And for the supreme court . . . to deny access and opportunity—that decision I find very, very hard to swallow. I couldn't believe that decision. . . . If you're going to have freedom from fear, freedom of religion, freedom from want, freedom of equal oppor- tunity, you've got to have—some of these things in life are necessary to

achieve that. The right to assemble, free speech—all of those things are important, but through some of our other avenues we deny people. (3)

There are three ways in which the big fish eat the little fish. The critics are almost evenly divided between giving more weight to the first two ways, or variants, together, versus the third variant. In the first, most critical variant, the wealthiest minority controls the economic system for its own profit in both the short and long term by structuring the system so that those in the bottom echelons rarely move up and at the same time receive unfair incomes. In this view, American capitalism represents for the most part a power relationship and an opportunity inhibitor. It is based on a politics and economics of exclusion. The theoretical framework of the system itself may offer the potential for inclusive opportunity, but that opportunity is denied in fact.

Ultimately, the rich get their money off the poor. Wages and consequently distributions of wealth are determined by these power relations. The market economy is not directed by a hidden hand, but by specific, locatable power. The problems presently threatening the overall health of the total economic system, such as declining productivity and the loss of a competitive edge against overseas corporations, are the fault of those at the top of the corporate structure due to their own greed and their creation of a system that cannot plan ahead, and that keeps the majority underfoot and thus destroys cooperation. There are direct links between wealth and political power. Political democracy exists only for those with resources; democracy is distressingly incomplete.

In the second variant, exploitation is not as locatable in a specific group that actively controls the system's dynamics. The problem is more in the system's organization. In many respects, this account is as critical as the first variant; in some ways perhaps more so because the problems are systemic and are embedded in the very nature of the economic enterprise, and not specific to a particular group wielding a disproportionate amount of economic and political power. But the two accounts ultimately merge, for a specific group is able to retain an inordinate amount of power and resources largely due to the structure of the system, and the structure of the system becomes skewed and accumulates biases largely due to specific actions, repeated over time. The following excerpts add flesh to the skeletal descriptions of these two variants of the first narrative chapter.

> Knowledge is power, and the more people understand the more powerful they get, because then they start understanding what's going on. The less you know the more controllable you are. And you have too many people who are at the bottom, that don't know. . . . They don't understand how the system's actually telling them . . . "You're excluded out of this, this is not your territory." . . . If you're uneducated, I think the system likes it

better, because you're more controllable, and the people at the top have a better handle on you and they can also more or less dictate your lifestyle. . . .

They [the wealthy] throw it [consumer goods] out there and the poor buy. They know that poor people have money and poor people don't save money, they spend money. . . . And that keeps them right at that level, because once you start understanding the system, you're going to say, "Wait a minute . . ." The wealthy benefit off you on the retail side or they benefit off the poor or the poor working people on the economic side, because of the pay. They pay you less money; you work harder but you get less pay. And they justify it, they say "This is all the job is worth." . . . You might be doing more work than his exec, but that's the way they keep people at a certain level. . . .

Basically, [the rich] got their money off the poor, and I think they have a moral obligation to actually put money back in, to . . . help the poor. . . .

The poor—that's one group or segment of people that politicians really don't deal with. . . . What we have is more or less segments of a demo-cratic system. If we had a true democracy, we wouldn't be in the positions that we're in now as far as oppression of people, also hunger, problems that an industrial country that we have shouldn't be having. And a country that's as advanced as this country is, and we're still having problems that third-world countries have. And also as far as people being educated to the political system, and to the process of democracy—there's too many of them that is left out of it. . . . For some, they live a true democracy, and for others, they're left out of it. . . . With this big stress on capitalism that we have in this country, we go beyond being a democratic type of govern-ment; we become a country that's involved basically in monetary, and also in ownership of property, rather than [being involved] into peo-ple. . . . If you don't have money . . . you can be left out of that pro-cess. . . . You could be rich . . . basically you do what you want to do, and you can get away with anything you want to do. (8)

In some cases, I feel there's that conspiracy out there; how many young-sters do you really want to be educated. . . . The way the system's been in the past, in which they would always say we need a few at the top, and everyone down here works, the working people. . . . They keep raising the [education] standards. . . . (8)

GR: I'm wondering about the conspiracy. Who is the "they" there?

I would say probably the white Anglo-Saxon Protestant group, the power makers, the ones who actually say "We're going to make the economy do

this, we're going to make the economy do that." And they can do it. . . .
There's a network of "good ole' boys" that is nepotistic. (8)

I think . . . [classes] are very important. I think they pretty much control
how the system works, how our government works. Those who are rich
control everything. . . . Through the control of government. Through the
legislative process. . . . They occupy positions in government, they occupy positions in the private sector of our society, and they are the controlling factors of every facet of our lives. And they control that—those
facets. . . .
    I just don't think that [incomes and wealth being more equal] will ever
happen. Not in this country, because I think that one of the key or principal factors is that there has to be a poor class of people for the rich and the
middle class to survive. Just think if there were no poor. All the middle
class people would be out of jobs. The people who service the poor, they'd
all be out of jobs. . . . The system makes it happen. I don't think people
who work there are working to augment the poor, but they're working
within the system that's geared to it, keep people poor. . . . It'll never
change. (9)

There's clearly an upper class. . . . They're the people who use their
money to influence and buy influence, exert power. . . . In terms of political influence they constitute, in national and even statewide circles—I
believe in an elite theory. I don't believe in a ruling class theory of power,
because I don't think everybody in the upper class participates, but I think
certain individuals do so more than others. And I think being a member of
the elite is in a large part—not totally—related to your economic wealth.
    . . . Some people get to places they want to be—you have to bring in
the factor of moral scruples—some of them, they have no moral scruples.
The end justifies the means—that explains why they're successful. They
don't give a shit about who they hurt, whose lives they affect. They don't
care about . . . the personal, social, other kind of fallout from their
activities.
    . . . In any business, there's a natural tendency towards an exploitative
relationship with your workers in the sense that no matter how good you
treat them you still want to get the most out of them. . . . I guess that's
what Marx referred to as an exploitive relationship. What I think constitutes bad business profits is when your profit and your success is predicated on an exploitive relationship that views the employee in more of a
negative way; in other words, you don't see them in human terms, you see
them in a dehumanized way, and they're simply objects for your manipulation and your exploitation. . . . Simply thinking, these are objects of

mine for exploitation, for manipulation. I'm a good businessman because I can devise clever ways of getting more work out of them without doing much for them. That to me is what I call the short-term, fast-buck approach, which does happen in a lot of industries. . . . The owner don't give a shit as long as . . . there's a new wave of cheap labor coming along. . . . I think a business could be just as successful where it sees people in a more human way.

. . . You know all this talk about declining standard of living and increased trade deficit and so forth, and how this impacts U.S. competitiveness and U.S. standard of living. And solutions like devaluing the dollar, they're not total solutions. You've got some real problems with the values in American management, starting with what's an acceptable level of greed. . . . Basically leaving these solutions for the most part to what the ownership of companies choose to do and what government makes available. . . . It's really kind of wishy-washy intervention by government. . . . I don't know that I would jump to the conclusion that we need public ownership . . . but we certainly need some more intervention in terms of planning and regulation. . . . (6)

The third variant is less critical. There is a stronger belief in the justice of a free market and a stronger support for the place of large corporations within that market. At the same time, however, there is also a belief that in practice the market is not free and that corporate business is often run unfairly. Over time, people accumulate economic power and skew the workings of the market. The system is not just. This imbalance also finds its way into the political realm, but in this telling the connection between economics and politics is not as direct and complete as in the first two variants. Again, let us listen to some of the voices.

How the first person became poor . . . I really don't know. I would assume—sort of in crude terms—I would assume that someone got pushed around by somebody else, number one, or someone was not as ambitious as someone else, and relative gaps opened up and they've been maintained since. And the social structures that then proceeded to develop through social evolution tended to make those gaps part of the system and make them impermeable. . . . I can't speak historically, because I don't know. . . . I guess all I'm saying is that however that happened, the social system tends to maintain that. . . .

Within sort of the parameters that I've gone at—certain minimums [of income] and in effect, certain maximums, although not quite—my bottom line is that the market should decide that. That takes us back to a previous discussion about the idea that there are no free markets. So, what we're doing is, we live in one regulated market, or one structured market, and all I'm proposing is we change to a slightly differently structured market. . . . I'm not saying the free market should set wages, . . . I'm saying that public policy should set the parameters and then within those parameters, the market should set the wages. . . .

[The market] is open to abuse. It's not just a manipulation of power; it's open to abuse . . . by people rigging the market economically. . . . So people get corners on various things, including power, and then can use their corners on power or wealth, or whatever, to further tilt things in their direction, so . . . that's why I say there has to be a social structuring of the marketplace and then let the market occur. . . .

People who have a lot of economic power would probably argue that my goal is too far out of sync with theirs. And I could say, "Okay, that's just a difference of opinion," . . . or I might say, "Well, there's an element of greed to it." (5)

The eight-hour day or the ten-hour day that anybody is putting in yields them a bounty or product of wealth that is roughly equal. I don't expect it to be perfectly equal—I don't think it should be equal. But I think that it can be too exaggerated. I think that when one person is barely able or unable to put a roof over their head and another person can live in the most lavish or extraordinary lifestyle, and each is putting in an eight-hour day, this isn't fair. The gap is too wide. . . .

[Our society is] not as just as I'd like to see it. It's not bad, but it's not good either. I get the feeling that we're not moving in the right direction. . . . And I do think that the gap is too great, and some salaries are entirely too high. The ability to corner huge amounts of wealth seems to be too weighted in favor of certain groups and individuals. . . . When an Ivan Boesky can pay off a hundred million dollar fine or a two hundred million dollar fine with a check, and he was able to accumulate that wealth in a relatively short period of time . . . then I think there's something wrong with the system. And another man, relatively bright and perfectly willing to take risks and so on, trudges away, barely able to keep a roof over his family's head and educate his children, there's something wrong with that system.

. . . I think the vast majority of people—virtually all people—want to do productive work and want to please other people, and want to do something for other people, and be rewarded for good work. I think it's human emotion. I don't buy the notion that large segments of any population are lazy or incorrigible. I think—I'm much more willing to believe that problems of that sort flow from bad management, injustice, unfairness, poor organization. . . . (4)

Returning to the critic's narrative as a whole, power relations are asserted to be behind the operation of the economic realm. They are at work in the determination of what people will earn, in the ultimate formation and maintenance of distributions of wealth, and more generally in the operating procedures of business. These relations are joined by the forces of supply and demand, the larger sociohistorical forces in society, and the educational requirements necessary for certain kinds of occupations. The critics think that wages should be determined by considerations of what constitutes a living wage and what value the work in question brings to society, in addition to the skill, education, and experience it requires. Implicit and sometimes explicit in the concern for the value of the work is the notion that labor occupations have been historically undervalued and underrewarded in comparison to professional and managerial positions. The critics' concern for a living wage presages a larger concern for supplying human needs, a concern that will be discussed in greater detail below.

I think the most important thing to employers—private sector employers . . . in determining a wage level is how critical a function somebody performs is to their making a profit.

. . . I think there's an overemphasis on the value of work performed by people who are managers, marketers. . . . There would be no incentive for these people to do their work if there was no differential. But I think there's too great a differential, to the point that the value of the labor of the person on the production line in America, historically, is undervalued. . . . I think there's too many people in the workplace, in terms of a minimum wage and a minimum pay base, are really not paid adequately. . . . The biggest dispute concerns what constitutes an adequate minimum. . . . Maybe a range, say, that nobody gets less than $30,000 [per year], nobody gets more than $80,000; maybe that's fair. I'm not sure. (6)

Not surprisingly then, the critics' view of work itself, as an activity, is fairly bleak. For most people work is something that is endured, something that one does to secure the material means of existence, rather than a means through which one creates a meaningful existence.

For a lot of people, work isn't a fulfillment, for a variety of reasons. . . . More poor people are dissatisfied with their jobs for a number of reasons, not totally dissatisfied. It could be pain level or it could be interest in the job. And a lot of people who get paid well are not too excited about what they do; they think they do boring work. They're not stimulated. (6)

The notion of socioeconomic class is central to this chapter of the narrative. Many of the critics brought up the term on their own, and the others affirmed the existence of classes much more readily and definitively than the senators telling the other narratives. The critics' conception of class is based primarily on wealth and income, rather than social status or background, although in a few tellings the nature of the occupation played a role in determining class. To a significant degree economic and political power is also a component of class, but power differences based on class are perceived to have their origins in differences of wealth and income. The perceived divisions of class are generally three-part rather than two-part. One critic, however, conceptualized classes in terms of relations to the distribution of economic power and divided them into just two groups, depending on that relation.

Critics see the existence of classes in ways that the other senators tend not to; that is, they see classes more as sets of ascriptive traits than as simply handy (and necessarily nonstatic) statistical categorizations of wealth and income. Though economic classes are not viewed as social and economic castes that completely determine one's destiny, the prospect of upward mobility is seen to be quite bleak for most of those in the lowest class. In the critics' view, upward mobility certainly poses a deeper challenge than that suggested by what many critics referred to as the "American myth" of upward mobility. Class defines many of the terms of one's future prospects. This is particularly true if one is a member of a minority.

Critics describe the general distribution of classes and wealth either in two-dimensional terms, as a bell-shaped curve, distended, with its mass weighted more toward the poorer end, or in three-dimensional terms, as a pyramid. These descriptions are in marked contrast to the more popular notions of an evenly proportioned bell or a diamond, with the great majority of people occupying the middle-class center portion (the evenly proportioned bell is more common among the other two main narratives). Among the different critics, the delineations of each particular class vary, but in the main the critics identify a small class of very rich, followed by a wide band of middle class, within which the highest and lowest strata have more in distinction than in common. This is followed by a large block of working poor, employed in both service and manufacturing, which is followed finally by the destitute or non-working poor, often referred to as the underclass.

Both the objective and subjective interests of these classes are thought to conflict over the distribution of wealth and power. The battle line of this conflict is found between those of lower and higher socioeconomic status.

There's a natural friction between employer and employee, whether it's a union shop or not, in that the employee is obviously looking for more money or benefits and the employer is doing what he or she can to keep that mythical number [profits] at whatever level it should be at. But I think that the employer probably has more responsibilities as an employer than most of them either admit to or take on. (2)

White people who work very hard to maintain a middle class lifestyle somehow think that issues like affirmative action, racial equality, economic justice issues, are the kinds of driving forces that could put a crimp in their style. . . . That becomes a form of conflict between middle and lower class groups. The upper class groups . . . who own businesses, have investments at stake, I think they see the demands of both middle and lower class groups for an improved standard of living as something that comes out of their pocket. . . . (6)

I think there's a real fear. Otherwise, I can't see any reason for wanting to keep whole blocks of people down and out. There has to be some benefits for those who have, to want to keep people out. And the only thing that I can conceive of is fear that it will reduce what they have. (1)

Obviously, the poor does not like being poor. They don't have the opportunity to share in the wealth in this country. Those people who are in the middle class resent the poor people . . . their hard-earned tax dollars have to go to in many cases to support the people, so they are resentful of the poor. And they are resentful of the rich because they feel sometimes the rich people who have the money have ways of avoiding paying money out of their pockets—tax money. . . . (9)

We have a class system set up where if you're born into wealth, basically you're going to stay into wealth. . . . In most cases you'll find that people who are born poor are going to end up, basically, being poor. . . . You have that 1 percent or 2 percent that just refuse to be poor . . . and they break out of that cycle. In this country we'll always have a class system because you have to have a work force. . . . The system basically lives off the poor. . . . Everybody benefits off of that poor group of people—the poor, the middle class poor, the upper poor—because they're basically locked in. They're the ones that need the most services. . . . [Classes] are important because they keep the economy going. . . . (8)

The people who are structurally unemployed or are third generation welfare families—their interests don't have too much in common with the guests on Robin Leach's television show. I'm not sure either one does much good for the other. But [even] cutting the extremes off—yes, I think the same analysis applies. . . . We do not have anywhere near the permeability in the class structure that one would like to, you know, by myth, assume. . . . So, the myth would have it that, well, it's all a meritocracy; you start out anywhere you want and end up where you deserve. And the myth just isn't true. (5)

But if the critics are correct about classes, why do we not see more political movements to increase equality and change the organization of the economy? The political paths for such activity are formally open to those with the least amounts of economic resources, so why do we not see more people at least making the attempt? Why are there not stronger forms of labor politics? Why is there no socialism? To explain such absences critics reach for larger, social forces, in addition to characteristics of the have-nots themselves—but characteristics that are not their "fault." It is not simply that they are uninterested in politics and prefer instead to concentrate their efforts on their own private lives. It is more that they are left exhausted from the demands of their labor, and are left without the leisure time conducive to political activism. The economic system in which they find themselves instills within them a frustration and resentment that produces more political alienation than motivation. Furthermore, in some accounts the dynamics of the economic system, acting over several generations, have profoundly influenced poor people's own subjective perceptions of their political opportunities and economic interests in such a way as to hold back or subvert potential political movements on their part.[10] Additionally, many persons in the lower economic brackets are deeply suspicious and distrustful of the efficacy of political activity, due to their own experiences in dealing with government. This emphasis that the critics' account places on subjective factors presages another chapter in the critic's narrative, "Love Thy Neighbor as Thyself," which will appear below.

I think that what happens is that people who are in a situation where they are in the underclass—if that's what terminology we're going to use— may not have the energy and may not have the desire to get out as a block or as individuals to rally around an individual who says that "I'm going to help the poor," and use their power as individuals. I think that's the result of many things. One, the energy level. Presumably, many of the working poor are working at jobs that are clearly more physical than those of us that sit around on our duffs all day and answer phones and push papers, and [they] also may have to work longer hours to attempt to get food on the table and move further ahead. . . . But I think maybe more to the point is the fact that they may have tried at one point or they may have observed at one point, and not feel or believe that either their voice individually or their voice as a unit has any effect. (2)

[The poor] don't believe in the system. I remember going to public hearings in my freshman year [in the legislature], and this is when they used to have all the big welfare debates, because the government never put any welfare increases in . . . and I'd go out in the audience and take people aside, and we'd have the welfare mothers bused up to the capitol. . . . I'd talk to these people . . . I was very amazed at their lack of belief in the system. "'The Man' is not there to . . . is not going to let us get out of this system." . . . I think that comes from being beaten down by the system. Also, if your concern is getting food on the table, clothing someone—all these other things that we take for granted—you're not going to have too much energy left to change the system. I think it's also having access to the system. I don't think the people have been empowered to access the system. And that takes ongoing involvement. It does not just entail one-time demonstrations, but an ongoing process. (7)

The social value system of this country does not positively sanction poverty, not only from a standpoint that it's not good to be poor, but there's something wrong with somebody if they're poor. The social value system in this country looks at poverty as a dysfunctional—it says something about a person's psychological makeup, something about their personal worth and value because they're poor. Rather than it being looked at in a more objective, socioeconomic—this is a state of affairs for some people, but it's something beyond their control. So I think a lot of people who are poor or near-poor . . . will lie about it . . . will not say they're poor, because it will bring some form of social objection. It's not acceptable. (6)

In what I have presented thus far, the issue of race has been for the most part underplayed, emerging only in the margins of the excerpted passages. But this lack of appearance has been more my doing than the senators'. I have deliberately held aside explicit discussions of race in order to present them alone. During the interviews, racial discussions were for the most part oriented toward blacks. This was apparently due to the questions in the interview as well as the assumptions of the senators.

In the critics' views about race and justice, there is a split between less critical accounts of racial disparities in distributions and more critical accounts that posit the existence of explicit racial discrimination. In the less critical variant, minorities experience particular difficulties because they occupy places in the economic system, largely due to historical discrimination, that make them particularly ill-equipped to adjust to and benefit from new directions in the economy, such as the trend toward high-technology and service industries. In the more critical variant, minorities are still actively being held back because of their race. In both accounts, however, critics share a keen sense of the depth of difficulty, despair, and hopelessness gripping those who are both poor and in a racial minority.

> The last ten years have been tremendous years of economic prosperity for the people who were positioned to do that. And the black community was not as positioned as the white community to take advantage of the last ten years of economic growth. . . . I think the relative gap will close. That's my personal view . . . based on the fact that I think the positioning has changed. (5)

> At this moment in time, while the racial attitudes are the root cause, they're not the direct proximate cause today. . . . [Blacks] are not as well prepared to overcome these hurdles . . . that have to be cleared to achieve an economic objective, a social objective. (4)

> Although we as a society claim to be less racist and less prejudiced than we were twenty years ago . . . I think that there is still a feeling of, there are still underlying racist and prejudiced feelings among members of society, and I think this is one of things that . . . that because of this, even though, again, ABC corporation—not the television network—but "ABC" corporation is required by law to hire x amount of minorities, et cetera, that's where they draw the line. They come to their quota and that's it, and I think that . . . I certainly go to enough social functions as a senator and overhear things directly, to know that in general society still feels that, still has prejudicial feelings. People come up to me frequently and make racist remarks, that you would least expect, from people that you'd probably least expect it. . . . On the surface we at least seem to be doing the right thing, but the underlying attitude is still there. (2)

> A lot of these people [minorities] started out in companies, but they can never make it, so they have to come out and start their own businesses, instead of these corporations saying "Okay, well I don't care what color you are, we're going to promote you, because you're doing the right things that we want you to do." They're just excluded. And that's where you have economic injustice. . . .
> A lot of them give up on the system because the system has been beating up on them. They just quit. . . .
> Color plays such a large part in determining people's lives. We need people to be blind for about a year to get over it. (8)

> Nothing has changed. It goes back to my earlier point that the leader of the country sets the pace, sets the agenda, or sets the attitude. And I think the

attitude of the last eight years has been antiblack. . . . There was a period of time when blacks were making progress. . . . We find now that things are no different now than they were twenty years ago. . . . Color still plays a major part in the quality of life in our society. (9)

It should also be noted here that some of the critics offer similar kinds of views about gender discrimination, though they perceived gender discrimination to be in the process of breaking apart, at least in the workplace.

Among those critics offering the more critical view of racial discrimination, one also finds what is at first glance a curious emphasis on self-reliance. This emphasis, however, is defiant and accusatory in tone; a poor member of a minority must be self-reliant because that is all there is. No one else is there to help. And so the only way out of the ghetto (at least for the present) is to rely on oneself and break out on one's own.[11] Occasionally included in the exhortations to self-reliance are criticisms of those members of the black community who have managed to climb out of the ranks of the poor, but do not help those remaining below them.

Related to this discussion, but going beyond specifically racial terms, is a critique of the workings of the welfare system over the past twenty years. Critics see the welfare system not as a potential liberator from poverty, but rather as a perpetuator of poverty.[12] It is set up and administered in such a way as to keep the poor continually poor, and in the more critical tellings it is purposely designed in this way, since the system needs the poor in order to function as it does. Many people benefit economically from the variety of occupations generated by a system that continually supplies submaintenance levels. The welfare system is also seen as a way to control the poor, both economically and politically. But some of the recent attempts to change the welfare system—workfare and related proposals—are castigated as means of further punishing the poor and as consignments to dead-end occupations.

To take a person who is—we're talking about people who are on general welfare, general assistance, and most of them have real problems; they're either drug addicts, or alcoholics, or a lot of them are sick and unable to work—and to take them and say that they have to work for the money that the city is going to give them is unjust, I think, because their needs—we have to consider their needs. . . . I'm saying it's all right to tell them that they have to go to work. But number one, don't put them out sweeping streets, cleaning leaves, and doing unrealistic work that's not going to fit them for the marketplace, not going to give them any skills to go any further. They're going to be locked into minimum wages, probably never move from there, and . . . still live below what I would consider a normal standard of living. So you haven't done anything.

. . . I think that [welfare] is the government's way of controlling people's lives. . . . I think it's a plan by the government to control people, because as long as they pay their wages—give them money to live on, they can determine how far they're going to go. . . . They can control a group of people. (1)

People who are on welfare . . . I would say the overwhelming majority, are willing to work. We then provide disincentives to prevent them from working. We tell them that we're going to give them 100 percent marginal tax brackets and that every dollar they earn we're going to take off their welfare checks. That's the highest tax bracket in the country . . . that's really good thinking, they really thought that one out. And then we tell them that in addition, we're also going to have them go into the marketplace in the least, low paying jobs where there's the least health insurance, for example. And when they do that, because they're trying to save the public money by getting off welfare, we're going to reward them with that effort by cutting off their health insurance. So, of course people don't move out of that system. . . . You just wouldn't do that and that's common sense. (5)

A lot of our social programs, like the antipoverty programs, people were put in charge of running poverty programs, which included a number of different types of programs. . . . In many communities, and I witnessed this in my community, people were put in charge of these programs who came from the ranks of poverty who probably got . . . hired because they had been somewhat politically active, involved with radical politics, that they were basically a pain-in-the-ass, a nuisance, to the establishment.

So in many respects the poverty program was a failure because it didn't take as serious the objective of trying to end poverty or reduce it. It really looked more at how do you manage to stop it from being a nuisance, to the haves, to the political establishment. And you do that by using it to buy off the more vocal problems, the more vocal objections. . . . Money has been spent just to cushion political fallout, cushion social fallout. . . . I don't really think there was that kind of commitment . . . necessary at the upper echelons of government to see these things work. (6)

The way the system was set up . . . designed to help people that basically didn't have an income. . . . A lot of these programs started off as basically good programs to help a certain class of people to move up. Once these programs get into place, it goes beyond that; something happens. . . . These programs eventually end up being part of the system that's actually keeping people at a certain level. . . . People benefited from it, right down from the social workers, to the policemen, to the fire department, to the judges, to the lawyers. Everyone is benefiting off these poor people. . . . In order to really deal with the problems in this country . . . with poverty, which is getting worse . . . homelessness . . . infant mortality . . . you have to declare war on the problem and put your forces into that problem, a lot of forces into that problem. (8)

To Each According to His (or Her) Needs

This chapter concerns distributional norms more specifically. The principal distributional norm that emerges from the critic's narrative is one of providing for human needs, over the concerns to reward merit, induce incentive, and abide by the results of market transactions. Merit, equity, and market incentives are also concerns of the critical senator, but the provision of human needs, at least at a minimum level of entitlement (which in most cases extends well beyond the present "safety net" provided by the welfare state), is the paramount concern.[13] This concern is based on a deep compassion and sense of empathy for all humans, but particularly for those who are less fortunate (I will return to this sense of empathy in the presentation of the next narrative chapter). In the critic's narrative, individuals' needs should be met simply because of their status as human beings. There is a strong sense that each individual has an equal moral worth, which in turn carries with it distributive implications.[14] The provision of needs should be tailored to each individual's situation; persons in dire economic straits have greater needs, and should receive more assistance and attention than those who have been able to stake a claim in the economic system. Furthermore, as was seen in the first chapter of the critic's narrative, poor persons are in dire straits largely because of an unjust system that has taken advantage of them.

I should note here, however, that the concern for needs does not necessarily translate into support for complete economic equality, or even an equality of need fulfillment, although some critics were supportive of substantial moves toward equality. Alongside the concern for needs, support remains for some amount of incentive, and the economic differentials perceived to be necessary in order to provide and maintain this incentive.

The concern for the provision of needs appears in the narrative through two primary channels: in the discussion of a successful economy and along with that in the approach toward large-scale politicoeconomic policy decisions; and as an explicit principle in the discussions of income, jobs, and entitlements. It is to these two channels that I now turn.

In broad discussions of the criteria for evaluating the overall success and justice of the economic system, the critics reach for the normative principle of needs. These needs are constructed broadly and include not just economic resources, but also the psychological health of the individual and the social health of the community.[15] The provision of economic resources contributes to the fulfillment of these noneconomic needs, but it alone does not satisfy them. The critics' impulse for reform and change is not driven solely by a concern over empty stomachs; stomachs are not the only empty things needing to be filled. In the critics' view, profound changes in the values of society are necessary both for moves toward satisfying these noneconomic needs and for the provision of the economic needs themselves. For the critics, the satisfaction of needs is not just a deep concern, but also a standard of evaluation against which the American economic system is perceived to be sorely lacking.

> My own view of human life and humanity is that there are certain principles that should govern human existence, that . . . argue against the tenets of a survival of the fittest viewpoint. I believe in certain inalienable rights for every human being, which I think I outlined before. So I look at society as being obligated. I believe the strong have an obligation to provide for the weak, just by virtue of their humanity. Just because somebody lacks the capacity or ability to be as strong as someone else doesn't entitle them to less, in terms of a certain standard. . . . There is a certain standard to which everyone should be entitled to live. . . . Everybody's not where they deserve to be. (6)

> I'd want people not to be taken advantage of within the system, in the sense that a person's productivity should be measured by an ability to make a living and some sort of a decent quality of life. (7)

> If everybody has the same opportunity for education, employment . . . access to things that they need—I think that would be a just society. (1)

> I think the first thing I would look for [in an economic system] is the basics; I'd look to see that people are well housed, well fed, well clothed, well educated, and then beyond that I would look at things like . . . is that a short-term thing or is there long-term security in that. . . . On the one hand, [justice] . . . means that the system provides those fundamentals, and on the other hand, it is a system which allows people to retain the fruits of their own labors. (5)

> The level of acceptable greed. What is the value system of the owners of business. What is an acceptable level of profit. Does the government regulate that. How do the owners of business view their social commitment to the workers, in terms of not just something basic, say medical

care, but what about the flexibility with respect to present situations . . . sensitivity to the needs of the individual. . . . How well does government support a human services system that is vital to providing and addressing needs of families who have to work. . . . Given the wealth, there is a rather unacceptable level of poverty in a country like this. People fall through the cracks and there's no safety net . . . to catch them. . . . [Justice] would mean fair profits for businesses. It would mean full employment. . . .

[A]dequate wages and benefits, that are adequate to maintain people at a middle class lifestyle—that's what I would call justice. A system that distributes the results of the labor of the workers and managers in such a way—there's clearly a differential needed . . . but a better distribution than we currently have, so basically we don't have people on welfare, people who are hungry, people without adequate homes to live in, simply because they can't afford these things. . . .

You first of all need a legal and judicial system that is predicated on the principles of fairness, equity, that assumes people are entitled to live at a certain standard and quality of life.

. . . There's definitely people I would call lower class economically, people who are just on the fringes of subsistence. They just make enough money to stay off the streets, not starve, wear enough clothing. How it affects them personally varies. . . . There are people who are always struggling, and therefore their life has more stress and anxiety in it. There is other people whose state of poverty is more easy to depict just from a visual perspective; you can see where they live, you can see what they eat, you can see what clothes they wear. These other people, I'm trying to say, I don't think they realize they're poor. They don't realize what they go through, what they put themselves through, their families through, their personal lives through. They're basically the kind of people Marx— they're basically proletariats in a true Marxist sense but they don't see it that way.

I know a person who is a secretary for some corporate executive. And she thinks of herself just because of her occupational station in life, the status that goes with that, I'm sure she says "I'm a middle class person." Yet, I wonder how happy some of those people are, based on their ability to pay for the kinds of things, the lifestyle they're trying to lead. . . . If they're not divorced, they're probably living in a relationship that is fraught with a lot of problems because they put so much stress on themselves just to maintain a certain lifestyle, a certain visual perception— they want people to see them as successful. . . .

To me a successful life is not something measured strictly in terms of acquisitions, wealth. . . . When a person that's able to show they own this home, they own this car, they're able to dress a certain way, they can afford a certain vacation, but they got kids that are fucked up, they got a lousy relationship with their spouse, . . . a variety of neuroses. . . . Those things are a result of the total environment in which they live and work, and play—something's wrong. . . .

What are you allowing your socioeconomic status to do to you? How does that interrelate with the way you think about yourself, your general level of contentment? (6)

Needs resurface in the discussions of incomes, minimum entitlements, and levels of social support. Consistent with this concern for needs, one finds the critics taking a dim view toward incomes that are thought to be very high, such that they surpass all reasonable needs.

You can still work forty hours a week at a very productive job . . . but we don't treat their productivity, compensate their productivity enough, to justify moving them out of poverty. . . . For instance, you compare someone [in] maintenance compared to someone who does something else, and [although the maintenance person] is very very valuable and productive, . . . that's not going to be compensated, of course, and we still might have very productive people who still might not be able to make a liveable wage. And I don't know if they're ever going to change that—probably not. . . .

It would be great if we give everyone a salary where they could have a middle class, American, "Pledge of Allegiance" type of lifestyle. . . . It would be nice to determine, is if you could take an individual's circumstances and try to have that play into what you pay them; however, that is not the way it is and it is not the way it will ever be. (7)

Some of the salaries that are paid to people on the top are horrendous. . . . It's a sin for people to be making that much money—and playing with it. . . . Enough is enough—having money to just squander. When there's so much hunger in this world, and homelessness. It's sinful. (1)

I think that all the jobs . . . at the low end of the scale are probably underpaid. I think the problem is I would like to think that people should be able to make a living, enough money, so that they can live comfortably—not luxuriously, but comfortably. And I think in this society, for an individual with a family, a man or a woman, whoever happens to support a family, to live comfortably means a house which they own, adequate clothing, transportation which obviously means a car, some recreational funds, cultural funds. . . . I suspect at the very top, I suspect that the top by definition are abuses, just like the bottom, by definition, are abuses. (5)

Need also dominates the discussion of minimum entitlements and social support. Success in the economic system depends in large part on one's education, and thus education, usually through the college level, is an element that is often included in discussions of minimum levels of entitlement. Need concerns are also reflected in the consideration of actual and preferred levels of welfare spending. The critics' estimated levels of public welfare spending tend to be lower (and more accurate) than those provided by the other senators, and in turn critics support both increasing these levels and directing the money more toward those most in need of it.

> Everyone is entitled to a job, housing, education. . . . I believe college education should be free. (9)

> The paradox of the whole damn thing [present welfare system] is that when you look at the levels, in effect they do not ensure the pursuit of happiness. . . . It would be a standard that permits an individual or a family to live in adequate housing; provide adequate food; . . . the basic necessities to operate a household, money so they could pay their utilities, including a phone; . . . income so every household could own an automobile; . . . and education for the children beyond public high school education—I don't think that's something people should have to scratch for. We have public institutions, but there are some people who can't go to them, still. Those are minimum needs and essential opportunities. (6)

> I think there is a basic level that we have to achieve. . . . I think that government has a role to play in assuring that these standards are met, and it's not just by giving out things. It's by regulations and support; it's by philosophy; it's by direction that's set. Just because you believe that people have a right to live . . . that we have a right in a democratic society to live in a decent home, to have a chance at a decent education, to have equal opportunity and equal access to a decent job. I don't consider that as being a government handout. I think if anything it's very positive for the community at large . . . in terms of society. Ignorance doesn't produce progress. Discontent doesn't produce unity. All those factors tend to negate those kinds of values that we think about: honesty, integrity, caring for one another, utilizing our resources in cooperation, instead of a "give me" attitude. . . . We have to ensure people—whether you're disabled physically [or] emotionally, whatever your color, wherever you come from . . . that there is in this country a standard of life that we are willing

to protect and to foster. . . . It's there, and it's a standard that we are going to abide by. (3)

Love Thy Neighbor as Thyself

If they [the rich] have so much . . . then it's sinful, it's sinful, not to give something to the poor. It's inhumane. . . . Just the thought of someone being hungry, of children being hungry, it really hurts. . . . People consider me liberal. I think I'm just a human being that cares. (1)

In the critics' eyes, distributive injustice is rooted in greed, fear, and hate, and the economic structures that institutionalize them. But the solution to these problems lies not in dramatically changing the structure of the economic system, but rather in instilling the values of empathy, understanding, and compassion among the individuals within that structure and among the individuals controlling it. The value of education emerges as a motif within this theme of understanding and compassion. Like the other senators interviewed and like other political elites and private citizens, critics emphasize the importance of education as a means of leverage in the economic system and as the vehicle through which opportunity can be realized. But education takes on a much broader meaning and significance in the critic's narrative. It is not only the means through which those in the lower half can make it into the upper half; it is, more importantly, also the means through which everyone can learn about and understand one another, so that each will no longer fear and hate other individuals and groups, particularly minorities, and so that the majority will no longer desire to keep these minorities in a subjugated status. In short, education runs in two directions. Even concerning members of the bottom economic groups, critics place less emphasis in comparison to the other senators on education as a means through which they can enter a system that is waiting to receive them (if they are qualified), and more emphasis on education as a means of changing the structure of attitudes and expectations that limit their sense of possibilities. Education extends to the personal experiencing of other persons, and requires integrative encounters. This holds true for members of different classes, but holds particularly true for members of different races. Integration, then, thus becomes not only a necessary component of equal opportunity, but also a means to the understanding and compassion required for a truly just society.

Injustice comes from a lack of leadership, a lack of knowledge, a lack of commitment, a lack of interpersonal relationships. Easy enough to say "I hate the Jews, and I hate the blacks," if you never have any contact with them. It's all of those things, it's experience. And it's not just for the adults. You will never have true justice unless you begin to understand that the formation of justice occurs . . . with our youth, and I mean at an early age. They must be taught justice, and they are taught how to be a just person. And that comes from experiences and from relationships with people. . . . Why don't we stop and think once in a while, "Suppose I was the minority?"

. . . There's a fear. There's a fear that you, your security is threatened. Then, coupled with that fear of security is the fear of the unknown. We live by a buzzword, . . . by what we see on television and what we read in the newspapers. And look at the headlines as they deal with these minorities when it comes to crime, for example; when it comes to welfare fraud; when it comes to all those negative things we as individuals do not want to see in our society. They tend to be mostly minority groups that are involved in this. And so we perpetuate a perception that black is bad in the cities, that being an Asian is, you've got to be careful—look at what the Japanese did to us in World War II, now they're infiltrating here. If you look there's beginning to be a turn against Orientals. . . . And then the fact that we really don't know about those people. We just don't have a thorough knowledge of minority groups. (3)

[The rich] just don't give a damn. I don't think they give the poor—that's the problem—the poor any thoughts at all. (9)

I think—and not necessarily in black-white prejudicial terms, race terms—but I think in overall terms, in this country people have an underlying prejudice—anybody that's middle class, or lower middle class, or above in terms of class, in terms of earning income and where you live, et cetera—have an underlying prejudice of people who are poor, whether they're black or white. Maybe there's even more of a prejudice in a general sense against minorities that happen to be poor. But I think that that's one of the real moral crises that we face as a nation today, and that is the prejudice that people have against the poor. (2)

I don't think there's a lot of understanding between the employer and the employee—probably not enough time spent together . . . where each [employee] can express, openly, how they feel about their job, how they think they should be compensated, and that employer, in return, stating what it means, what benefits he gains by the quality of their work. . . .

If everybody understood the benefit that they had to somebody else, it would be easier. (1)

I think one thing that would promote injustice is . . . people really not knowing each other. . . . If you don't understand people's culture . . . then once you go into the work force, you're going to be more or less discriminating against that group of people. . . . Once you understand people, it's very difficult for you to be biased toward them or attack them. . . . If people really started looking at people as being human beings, and if people would say that, "Yeah, I like you. You're all right. . . . If I'm feeling good I should want Mary, John, and Sue to feel good. I want them to enjoy some of the things that I enjoy." (8)

I think basically the system functions because of people. Despite what you write in your laws and espouse in other forms of doctrine . . . people have got to run it. And as long as people don't have attitudes that are compatible with the principles and attitudes that I've talked about, you basically get dysfunctions in the administration of justice and you're definitely going to fall short of achieving what I have defined as the just society. Humans are imperfect. . . .

I think the real cause of all injustice. . . . What is injustice? What do we mean when we say someone is unjust to somebody? Well, they hate them for some reason. . . . Underlying all this activity is usually a great sense of fear that an individual or group has towards another individual or group. That is the unresolved problem. . . . (6)

I would go a step further [than integrating schools]. The degree to which we can equally start to integrate places in which to live will have the same effect, in fact it would go a step further, and I think decrease the level and degree of racism, and fear and hatred among people who are different. . . .

My parents brought me up to discriminate. . . . I was not given positive reinforcement to play with the [minority] kids. . . . We moved into a . . . neighborhood that was clearly mixed. Only over a process of years I freed myself of prejudices, simply because I was forced to live around and associate with [minority] people. . . . I can relate to that process on a personal level. . . .

How do you desegregate housing? Well I think that's very much a process of government. . . . The lack of a policy that would in fact desegregate neighborhoods, desegregate schools, is tantamount to endorsing injustice—silently, quietly. . . . (*)[16]

I think people need . . . education, because you need to try to understand that we're all human beings, we all have the same needs, really. Everybody has the same needs, generally. If you have an education, you can understand the historical reasons for the conditions of people, of all people—how everybody got where they are. (1)

In addition to building empathy and understanding, there is a concern to give people a stake in the system, and thereby build a community in which all feel they have a part. This concern for inclusion extends to the function and administration of government as well, presaging the next chapter concerning the role of government as an activist hero.

> I think if you have a society that generally believes that all members of the society who are willing to participate—and that would be 99 percent— should have a stake, should be given a stake in society, and should have an opportunity to succeed, and that their labor should get them somewhere off the treadmill, I think if society believes that, then they would go about setting in place the mechanics to do it. . . . I have the sense from Japan that they do manage to convey to the whole society that they care for each other as a community, and that no one is going to be left far behind. . . . I don't think that we have managed to convey that sense in this country to large, large segments of the population. (4)

> I think sometimes we have to get into the worlds [of poverty], these various worlds that we know about, and bring the opportunities to people rather than asking them to go to them [the opportunities]. My vision of working in a city would be to bring everybody into a large neighborhood area, bring in people who were willing to train people, day care centers. . . . Do it right on the spot. You see you just don't have to move people out of environments all the time, to make them better. You can make the environment better. And that will make people better. If government is responsible for their environment we better get off our duffs and do something about the environment, and I think we can do something about it. Instead of saying, "People, come here and we'll train you," my theory is "Stay there, right where you are and we'll come to you." That does two things: Besides bringing a service to you, what it says to you as a person is, "Hey, someone out there is worried about me, is thinking about me." . . . We go out; that's government's function, that's the responsibility of government—to take government to the people.
>   . . . That's what I see as my vision: that the government has got to open up to more people, and listen to their concerns. (3)

The emphasis on empathy and compassion evokes a theme of the American morality tales identified by Robert Reich: exclusion versus inclusion, we versus they, or the attitude toward "the other" (1987, 16–19).[17] As Americans, we define ourselves to a great degree through contrasts with those whom we are not. Common "others" include the poor and the nonwhite. Reich deftly presents the dangers of such divisions and our standard responses:

> As we attribute to "them" . . . the problems that bedevil us, we simultaneously limit our repertoire of responses to two broad categories: First, we can discipline them. By being tough and assertive, we can compel them to repent, lay down the law on acceptable behavior, and punish them when they transgress. Alternatively, we can conciliate them. Through generosity, understanding, and toleration we can socialize them, bring out the best in them, and seduce them into changing their ways, into becoming more like us. (1987, 18)

Thus, public discourse and policy options are constrained within a one-dimensional scale ranging from toughness to appeasement. In addition, one of the most important elements of public debates concerns the boundary between us and the other; that is, who is entitled to the considerations and benefits reserved for us.

The critics, however, reach for a third alternative. Their emphasis on empathy and understanding is a call to transcend "the other" in our social thinking, to love our neighbors—the "others"—as ourselves. Indeed, in their responses critics often became the other, adopting the perspective of the poor, the disadvantaged, and the minority. Their ability to empathize appeared to come from their own experiences of hardship, their own experiences as the objects of racial or ethnic prejudice, or their integrative encounters with members of other groups. These experiences, and their place in the narrative, will be discussed in further detail below in the section on the sources of the critics' beliefs. But one might argue that the critics are in fact drawing a dividing line of their own between the self and the other, particularly in "The Big Fish Eat the Little Fish."[18] Such a view may not be entirely fair, however, for although the critics certainly assess blame upward for the injustices they see, at the same time they include this top economic group in their desired community of understanding and empathy. They do not consider them as an "other" that is outside their realm.

This narrative chapter on empathy and compassion appears to be the softer, more lenient side of the critic's narrative, perhaps as well the Neo-Kantian side. It relies on a notion of human personality similar to the dynamic conception of human nature that undergirds Thomas Sowell's (1987) unconstrained world vision. People can change; they have the potential for good. They can be born again.

But the narrative chapter on empathy and compassion may also represent one of the limits of the critique of the economic system. The individualistic solution of loving thy neighbor as thyself appears somewhat paradoxical when set against the depth of the problems that the critics identify, and in some tellings the problems' apparent structural nature. The solution, however, is both individualistic and communitarian; the values to be instilled are those supporting a genuine community of individuals, but the method of instilling and engendering these values is not large-scale social and economic change, but rather enlightenment at the individual level, through experience and education. This paradox may become less perplexing when we consider that at the core of the matter, much of the structurally generated injustice identified by the critics is engendered and sustained by each individual's lack of understanding and empathy.[19]

Government as Hero

The onslaught against government popular in conservative and neoconservative circles is given little truck in the critic's narrative.[20] Government is instead the hero of the critic's story, coming to the rescue in order to correct wrongs, attend to needs, nurture individuals, and establish by example and by more direct means the values of community, fraternity, and equality. The narrative becomes epic. Instead of being part of the problem (as Ronald Reagan once prominently claimed), government is a force for justice. Critics believe that through its leadership, government can set a tone of compassion, empathy, tolerance, and mutual respect that will have a real effect on society.[21] Concerning distributive justice more directly, government is often seen as a beneficent equalizer. This equalization is primarily achieved through a progressive taxation policy.

> I think the whole role of government, probably, is to make society and the economy more just. (7)

> In that you're dealing with a value system, the system won't change on its own. So I would consider that an enlightened form of government would impose that value on them, and say, through some form of planning and control, "You can exist privately, but you know. . . ." That kind of intervention. . . . (6)

> [Government] can act—and I think on the federal level at times it's been negligent in acting—to show people that there is reason not to be prejudiced against people who happen to be poor. . . . And to me that's frustrating.
>   . . . I think it [government] affects our lives both positively and negatively in different aspects. . . . Environment protection, for example. I

think government has been doing many positive things to protect our environment, but on the other hand, they're really laxing [*sic*] in other areas or they have commitments to do things but don't do them. That's a specific area where government can go both ways. . . . There are some negatives that are just inherent in government. . . . Military spending, excess military spending. (2)

Dissatisfaction, ill health, . . . the homeless, lack of proper education for the children—at some point in our society it's going to affect us all. So you're putting your head in the sand if you think that you're getting away with something and you're going to cut back on some of these programs that basically form the foundation for our democracy. But it's a tremendous political thing to do. You see, people talk about getting government off our back, but government should be walking beside people. Government is a force that can bring into our society the positive things that are necessary to keep the society healthy, safe, content. . . . Where there has been discontent, there has been rebellion. Look at South America. The problem in South America is the gap between the rich and the poor. It's an economic factor; it's a social factor. . . . The basic line is that government does have a role. And you can't negate that role on the local, state, or federal level, because if you do your foundation becomes weak, and so we all have a role to play. (3)

Government needs to put a floor under the market, and then mechanisms to prevent the riggings of its workings, which is the abuse. People are in positions where they can tinker with the market to skew things in their direction. . . . The types of control? Tax policy is one kind—the graduated income tax is one way to limit this control. . . .
    The first thing I would do is I wouldn't tax people who made less than what I considered to be sort of the minimum required income. And then I would tax the balance progressively. (5)

In the critic's narrative, government should and can be the hero, but this does not imply that it does in fact act heroically. A case in point is the welfare system, which the critics attacked on the grounds that it tends to perpetuate a class of poor rather than enabling poor individuals to break out of their poverty. In its actual manifestations in the United States, the government is in fact heavily criticized, but it is usually criticized for being inactive and ineffective rather than constrictive and intrusive.

A legislative branch and executive branch of government that is crisis-management oriented as opposed to proactive, meaning it looks at and analyzes problems and proposes solutions. I think that's more the case than not—I mean that on the federal, state, and local level—government generally tends to be crisis-oriented. It's passive until a major calamity or crisis occurs. And the existence of that type of government, I think, encourages injustice. (6)

Sometimes I get so frustrated. People are always saying to me, "But that's the system." At a public meeting I once screamed "But we *are* the system!" You have to look at individual humans. . . . I think government is people, and that if you don't understand that, you've lost the concept of government. (3)

I think the kinds of things that promote injustice are, first of all, a great deal of it simply is inertia. There are injustices that exist and yet there is a great deal of difficulty in getting them addressed because . . . to address them costs money and someone's ox is going to get gored in that process and all of that. So I think . . . a tremendous amount of it has to do with just inertia. (5)

This vision of the role of government is also present in the critics' discussions of their own roles as individual senators within the senate body. They see themselves as activists, working to raise the collective consciousness, and acting in the interests of the persons, groups, and geographic areas most in need.

I look at myself as trying to be a social conscience, someone that tries to inform people about certain things. (8)

Number one, [I see myself] as a social reformer. The reason we get elected is to change things; otherwise, we could stay at home and check "ditto." (5)

Certainly I see myself in the role of a senator, but I also see myself as someone who very much likes to side with the underdog. (4)

I guess I see myself as some degree of a reformer, an advocate for people who need government to help them. A reformer in the sense that I see myself as having a responsibility to try to correct things that are wrong. . . . I think of myself more in terms of a popular representative than as someone who represents any particular segment of my constituency. . . . I think populist is probably a better term. (6)

Three Other Items of Interest

There are three particular items in the interviews that are not constituent components of any of the four basic chapters, but which nonetheless are of interest and should be included in the description of the critic's narrative. They are the critics' views of the economic future of the nation; internationally comparative assessments of the success of the American economic system; and the manner in which the terms *capitalism, socialism, liberal, conservative,* and *radical* are defined. Though these three items do not fit easily into one of the four chapters, they are consistent with and add further substantiation to the overall narrative.

An optimistic attitude toward the future has long distinguished American thinking.[22] An assumption of limitless possibilities seems to be part of the standard set of American values; it is certainly required baggage for successful presidential aspirants. But in general, the critics' vision of the future is much more pessimistic than that of the other senators; at best it is contingent and problematic. For the critics, a brighter economic future depends on more long-term planning, a real attack on collective goods problems such as the environment, substantial progress toward a state of fairness in the treatment of the ever-growing minority groups, and better technical education for the members of the increasingly displaced working and poor classes. In its strongest and perhaps most pessimistic variant, the critics' view of the future contains the possibility of some form of revolution, or serious backlash, if the nation continues on its present track.

> I think it's definitely a fact that the minority population in this country, both black and Hispanics, particularly Hispanics, is growing. They are the labor force of the future. And you look at today, the dropout rates between blacks and Hispanics is quite high; the prison population of blacks and Hispanics is quite high. You ask who's going to do the work in the next twenty years, it's going to be blacks and Hispanics. How can they do that when they're not educated, not trained? That's a serious problem I see the country facing in the next twenty years. (9)

> The other thing that we better watch out for is the fact that the minority of today is going to be the majority of tomorrow. You can step on them all you want today, but don't forget that they're the majority tomorrow, and if you don't build a coordinating effort, if you don't build the solidarity that we need between all peoples, you're going to have a discontent that you can't contend with. It's not going to go away. What makes anybody think it will? (3)

In the next forty years, there might be a rebellion, in which the poor people say, "I've had enough of this, and it's time for a change, it's time to equalize some of this wealth." And I think we might have some type of revolution. I hope it's not a violent type of revolution, . . . [but something] where people are going to stand up and say, "We're not wealthy, but we do work and we deserve some of these benefits that the wealthy have." (8)

The international comparisons drawn in the course of discussing the elements of a successful economy make for another set of interesting features. While supporter senators were adamant in their view that the U.S. system offered the richest and fairest set of arrangements in the world and most ambivalent senators held out the hope that the U.S. system at least offered the best of the actual, albeit imperfect worlds, many critics asserted that the United States could in fact learn from other nations about the organization of a fairer (if not richer) system.

Take a country such as Sweden, in which they have more of a socialized government, a socialist government, and in which they have low unemployment, low crime. Basically, their system is a democratic type of government. I don't think they emphasize capitalism like we emphasize capitalism. . . . (8)

I think there's probably something we could learn from the Japanese and the Germans in terms of treating people more fairly within the system. (4)

One of the things that particularly some of our Oriental competitors have over us is they have a different value system. Basically, their capitalists are not as greedy as we are. They look at success and profit in the long term, not the short term. (6)

Finally, in the course of the interviews, I asked the senators to provide their own definitions of five terms: liberal, conservative, socialism, capitalism, and radical. Although the specific contents of these definitions varied, patterns emerged in their general content and style that contrasted with those offered by the other senators, particularly supporters. In some crude sense, the styles of definition reflect the degree of ideology informing the responses, a constituent element of what Robert Putnam has termed the "style of political analysis" (1973, 34–35). The most extreme critics provided value-laden definitions of liberal and conservative, while the remainder offered more neutral or emotionally cool definitions that distinguished the two terms by the relative degree of government involvement and spending, and/or openness toward change. Critics tended to offer neutral and even positive definitions of socialism, and either neutral or polemical definitions of capitalism. In the neutral definitions, the two terms were distinguished by the relative degree of public involvement in the economy. Notions of capitalism were not folded into or conflated with democracy or freedom. One critic was quite clear in differentiating capitalism from democracy. A few critics made efforts to separate socialism from the negative connotations with which it is usually associated in the American mind, such as the notion that socialism is undemocratic, and also took issue more generally with the common American negative stance toward it. By the same token, the term *radical* did not evoke negative reactions from critics, as it did from many of the other senators, but rather more neutral and in some cases even positive renderings.

When asked whether they thought of themselves as liberal or conservative, they all sided with liberal, sometimes with reservations that took the form of fiscal caution and responsibility, or with reservations about being labeled. When asked whether they had ever considered themselves to be radicals, many replied that they had at one time or still did consider themselves in this way.

Some of us are called liberals when we try to get more money into programs that help people: welfare programs, or skill training, those kinds of programs. . . . The other way I think about it is caring, truly caring for people and their needs—liberals. On the other side of the coin, conservatives never seem to understand the real needs of poor people, and sort of have a sense of pull themselves up by their own bootstraps type of concept. And if you don't have any boots, it's tough. So there's a coldness on the other side. . . .

Capitalism has to do with huge sums of money, and socialism deals with people's needs. (1)

A lot of times people look at capitalism as democracy. I think they mix up the two. I tell people they're totally different. I say "Capitalism—that's money. . . . They're going to tell you that you can get ahead, but there's criteria . . . or certain stipulations you're going have to make in order to move up." It's that special group of people that's controlling everything. . . . You're looking at the white Anglo-Saxon Protestants, the old line. . . . Those are the ones that are still in control of the real money in this country. . . .

Capitalism has scared the death out of people because people are saying, "When you mention socialism you're talking about communism," and people are getting those two confused. What [Sweden] is doing is saying "We are responsible for our people, and we're going to give you these services." Capitalism is saying "We're not responsible for you, you can make it on your own." . . . We have socialism in this country, but it's limited. . . . They don't call it that but that's what it is. . . . "Socialism" in this country is more or less a taboo to use. (8)

Socialism means a move away from that [competition and private ownership], into government ownership. I think in this country we actually have a mix of both socialism and capitalism, and I think that people don't understand that because they think of socialism in terms of foreign governments rather than in terms of what this government is doing. And when you talk about, for example, the project in Tennessee for electricity, which was a government program—they sold electricity to the people, it was less expensive than letting private industry do it at the time. So I think those terms [capitalism and socialism] are easy enough for people to understand. I think that what they do, though, is that they equate them with other forms of government. They don't see them as a form of democracy. (3)

GR: So socialism might be compatible with democracy?

It certainly could be, certainly could be. The nationalization of major means of transportation, for example. That would be just one example. Socialized medicine; you know, we've come a long way in that field alone. . . . We condemn, I think, labels, because we place labels on certain things. So, "socialism" is very European; it's not American. (3)

Socialism simply means to me that there's certain activities of the economy that should either be planned, regulated, or owned by the government sector, but not planned, regulated, or owned in a totalitarian sense—that is what I would term communism, the totalitarian control of economic activity. (6)

Radical to me is not a bad word. I think radical—sometimes inherent in the word is creativity. I think one of the greatest radicals or revolutionaries in our time is Thomas Jefferson. . . . Radical means a departure from what is considered to be the norm at that point in time. The freeing of slaves was a radical movement. . . .

GR: Was there ever a time when you considered yourself to be a radical?

Yes, I think my political career was the point where I was treading on some ground where it wasn't really the norm for women to be involved; my whole political career has been a first. (*)

Limitations of the Critique: Equal Opportunity and
Other Sources of Economic Differentiation

Although the critics do indeed relate a narrative that is in many important respects harshly critical of the American socioeconomic system, there remain significant limits on the degree to which these critiques are carried through and brought home. We have already seen some of these limits in the focus on compassion and interpersonal understanding as ways to solve deep, sometimes structural problems, and in other parts of the narrative as well. The limits presented here add to these, and attest to the enduring vitality of the norm of differentiation in American thinking about the economic realm, in spite of the overall themes of the narrative. Beginning at the systemic level of the economy, side by side with the critique of the corporate market system, one finds a support, at least in principle, for the system of profit and the private ownership of productive means. These institutions are defended in terms of providing economic differentials necessary for incentives, which in turn make the economic system function and grow, and are also defended in terms of a fairness similar to equity, in that one should get back from something what one has put into it.[23] The critics retain reservations, however, concerning these two institutions.

> I think competition is good, and competition is best served by private ownership, and permitting the making of a profit. I just think that appeals to a side of human nature—I mean that is a side that for good or bad motivates people towards effort. (6)

> I'm sort of saying that there are two valuable goals and there's obviously a tension between those goals. You can't allow the private acquisition goal or private satisfaction goal to overwhelm the tension because then you lose the community justice goal; you can't allow the community justice goal to overwhelm the system where you lose the private justice goal. So there are tensions that are inherent. (5)

But even more profound than the support for profit is the emphasis placed on equal opportunity. As I have pointed out, many other researchers have found in their studies of American beliefs that equal opportunity is the key metaphor in discussions of equality. Similarly, although the critics often cited what they called the "myth" of equal opportunity in the United States, as a concept the notion of equal opportunity, properly realized, nonetheless dominated their discussions of equality. When asked specifically about equality—about how people are and should be equal, critics almost always reached for equal opportunity. Equal opportunity as it is usually constructed is itself a somewhat paradoxical notion, because it uses an equality of one kind—certain basic rights and opportunities—in order to justify an inequality of another kind—results. As Jennifer Hochschild has phrased it, equal opportunity thus bridges "the gap between the promise of political and social equality and the fact of economic inequality" (1988, 168–200).

The critics' particular conception of equal opportunity, however, is stronger than the popular metaphors of a level playing field at the start of an athletic contest or a footrace with an equal start. This stronger view has already been intimated in the different chapters of the critic's narrative, particularly the two concerning the role of government and the attention to needs. According to the critics the genuine realization of equal opportunity requires an equipping and empowerment of the disadvantaged that goes far beyond the establishment of a level playing field and a fairly played game. As a couple of the senators phrased it, equal opportunity requires that government act not just as an umpire, but also as trainer and coach, again with an eye toward needs. When asked specifically about affirmative action and racial quota policies, the critics expressed strong support for affirmative action, and most supported quotas. Those that resisted quota policies did so on the grounds that they were overly race-oriented, and that they hurt everyone involved, including those they were designed to help, since they did not really train and equip those persons and since they engendered resentment along racial lines.[24]

> Equal opportunity really means that there's an understanding that where people need assistance—at any stage of the game—where they can use help, they get it. That's in a perfect world. And that would conceivably continue throughout anyone's life.
>
> . . . [A quota] is too drastic, too easy, and too cheap an approach to solving a problem, and it has a very big downside: It's racist. . . . I have no problem with making a judgment on the basis of need as opposed to merit, but I have a difficulty with making that judgment on the basis of race rather than need. (4)

> I think that the use of quotas in job hiring was a necessity to begin to develop this whole business of equal opportunity. It's unfortunate, but sometimes we have to mandate in order to reach objectives. . . . My only concern was that we don't insult the people that are part of those quotas by letting the public think that they're getting in there because they're black or because they're a woman. I want them to understand that yes, they're part of a quota—and it's the same thing with the veterans of the United States—they still have to pass a certain criteria. We give extra points to the veteran when they take an examination. That's not to negate the worth of that person as an individual, it's just to give him a little bit extra because

of the years he spent away from this country while another person may be getting opportunity experiences. So you have to be very careful of that. (3)

If [equal opportunity] is in terms of a footrace and it's a black person and a white, they start off at the same starting line. However, the white runner has track shoes on and a track uniform; the black may not have. Some days he runs in his bare feet; some days he runs in his sneakers. He doesn't have a track uniform. Hasn't had the proper coaching nor the proper facilities to train in. . . . The government's role is to remove a lot of the obstacles that the black runner, or the minority runner may have. . . . I believe that it's a tremendous role that government has to play, it must invest in human capital. . . . You must understand that there are a lot of minorities who come to the starting line with, again, a lot of problems. . . . They're not able to get a good night's sleep because they have to sleep in a room with five or six others. They may not have had a nutritional breakfast before the race because of their economic condition. . . . (9)

We should all get the same start in life. And if we all get the same start in life, then I think you can look at, it would be easier to determine if a group is slow—if they're slow learners—what the problem is. Until we all get the same start in life, with all things equal, you're never really going to know whether those kids that are not getting a good education, not able to live in a decent house. . . . You're never going to know whether that's the kid that could find a cure for AIDS. (1)

The beginning of the race is never fair. (8)

One also encounters the endurance of economic differentiation in the critics' discussion of specific incomes. I have already presented the critics' general views of the ways in which wages are in fact and should be determined. But in the interviews the senators were also asked to estimate the average annual salaries of several specific occupations, and then to suggest what they thought the occupations ought to make. An exercise similar in many respects to this one was performed by Sidney Verba and Gary Orren (1985) in a survey-based study of the beliefs about equality held by various leadership groups.[25] I will thus compare my findings with theirs. My income data are presented in table 1.

In the main, the critics' estimates of the incomes are accurate. The ratio of the highest estimated income to the lowest estimated income is much lower than it is in actuality, due mostly to the underestimation of the executive's income; otherwise, the estimates of real incomes are fairly accurate.[26] The

TABLE 1. Incomes (Annual, in K) Estimated and Preferred by Critics, with Percentage Change, Actual Incomes, and Ratios of Top to Bottom Incomes

Occupation	Estimated	Preferred	Percentage Change	Actual[a]
Bank teller	14	19	+36%	12
Janitor	16	21	+31%	13
Production worker	17	24	+41%	18
Police officer	24	29	+21%	22
High school teacher	26	35	+35%	26
Press operator	22	23	+5%	35
Engineer	52	53	+2%	43
Physician	140	134	−4%	106
Executive	500	298	−40%	1,167
Ratio of top to bottom income	36	16		97

Note: N = 9. The actual interview question reads: "I am going to read to you some occupations. For each one, tell me what you think it makes for a yearly income, on average, across the nation: a police patrol officer; the top executive at a top financial services corporation; a doctor; a middle-level engineer, without supervisory responsibility; a janitor; a high school teacher; a bank teller; an industrial production worker in private industry; and a printing press operator in a large city." After the respondent completes this part of the question, the second part reads: "Now for each one, tell me what you think it should be paid, if it is any different from what it is paid."

[a]The actual income figures for the occupations are taken from the following sources. All occupations except the executive: Bureau of Labor Statistics, U.S. Department of Commerce, *Occupational Outlook Handbook 1988–1989* (Washington, D.C.: 1988), 51–53, 121, 129, 229, 349, 376. The executive: financial services section of "Executive Compensation Scorecard," *Business Week,* May 2, 1988, 57–58. Incomes taken from the Handbook are for the years 1985, 1986, or 1987, depending on the occupation.

critics' averaged responses corresponded correctly with the relative order of lowest to highest incomes, with the exception of the printing press operator.[27]

The preferred income figures are somewhat surprising in light of the critics' more critical views about wage and income determination in the abstract. The critics' specific income preferences are significantly more egalitarian than those of either the ambivalents or the supporters, particularly the supporters; yet they are still less egalitarian than we might expect. Notice that although the critics cut the executive's income almost in half and more than halve the ratio of the highest to lowest income, in the preferred case the ratio of these two incomes remains sixteen to one. The relative order of the incomes is also left intact, with the exception of the printing press operator; in the preferred case, the production worker slightly edges out the press operator.

When considering Verba and Orren's data on leadership groups, it would seem most relevant to compare the critics' responses with those of the black, feminist, labor, and Democratic groups. In these comparisons, the critics' responses do not appear to be significantly more egalitarian. These results are surprising since the critics' views are in many other respects more egalitarian and more harshly critical of the economic order than those of the Verba and

Orren respondents. The total results of the comparisons, however, are mixed. The ratio of the critics' highest to lowest preferred income (sixteen) is higher (less equal) than that of any of the Verba and Orren leadership groups except for business and Republicans, although the critics do start with a greater degree of spread between the occupations' estimated incomes before expressing their preferred incomes (the ratio of the critics' highest to lowest estimated income [thirty-six] is higher [less equal] than that of any of Verba and Orren's leadership groups, and the executive's actual income is much higher in my set of occupations) (Verba and Orren 1985, 160–64).[28] Thus, looking at the relative difference between the ratio of the highest to lowest estimated income and the ratio of the highest to lowest preferred income (in other words the relative difference between estimated highest/estimated lowest and preferred highest/preferred lowest, or the relative change toward equality), the critics' responses appear to be comparable to those of labor and academics, and more egalitarian than all the other groups, except for feminists and youth. Looking at the ratios of the preferred incomes to the estimated incomes for particular occupations, the results are different still. The ratio of the critics' preferred to estimated income for the executive (0.596) is comparable to those derived from the responses of blacks, Democrats, and the media, but is higher (less equalizing) than the ratios of feminists, academics, college youth, and labor. On the other hand, the ratio of the critics' preferred to estimated income for the lowest paid occupation, the bank teller (1.36), was higher (more equalizing) than the ratio of any of the Verba and Orren groups, including feminists (1985, 160–64).[29]

The Personal

You know, I left college . . . because the aid levels I got were not sufficient to live on. I had to go to work. That was . . . when they thought there was so much aid. And fortunately I landed a job through politics. I got involved in politics when I left. . . . That was one of the things that motivated me to go into politics. I admit that I wasn't just in politics for altruistic reasons; I saw politics as a way of bettering myself. And it worked. . . . I still had my ideals. . . . And after I was in politics and got a good job working for the [local government], I went back [to college]. . . . I paid for it out of my pocket. I was so angry at the system I wouldn't even apply for any goddamn loans or anything. I was so sick of it, when I think of what I went through to get that pittance. . . . (*)

You see I was [in] a minority once. I know what it's like to be hit with rotten apples and pears and called [an epithet]. I know what it's like to go to a high school and be told I didn't have the proper background, the proper family background, to become a [professional]. It hurts, and the younger you are the more it hurts, and the deeper the scar. . . . If it wasn't for my mother and father the scars would have probably been much deeper. But the compassion of my mother and the strength of my father did a great deal to teach me about justice and what happens when you have intolerance and bigotry, and all those awful things that really aren't "justice for all."

. . . I've been interested in government's role for a long, long time, and part of it did come from my background. I'm [from an ethnic] background. If you look at the area where I was born and raised, I was born on "the wrong side of the tracks." We had two high schools, a vocational-technical high school and a college-preparatory high school. The [one ethnic group] and the [other ethnic group] were shoved into the vocational-technical school. I was able to get into the preparatory school as a minority. I faced many minority kinds of things. Because of the position and the place where I lived, I was almost denied the right to apply for [professional training]. . . . I had a strong, strong family support.

. . . I lived in an area where right across the street were the [minority ethnic group], in downtrodden tenements run by [a] Judge . . . , a big political figure in the town . . . , who kept them in bondage. (*)

In relating their views about justice, many of the critics explicitly referred to the importance of their own personal experiences in the formulation of their thinking. Even for the remaining senators who did not draw such explicit links as those indicated by the above excerpts, their personal stories nonetheless reverberate throughout their narratives of justice. These stories include personal experiences of hardship and struggle and experiences of unjust treatment, or the witnessing of hardship, struggle, and injustice experienced by others. One of the critics, for example, had lived for a time in the public housing development where a supporter had once been a bill collector. Not surprisingly, the views of the critics' parents were also significant factors in the development of the critics' thinking. But though the critics' basic party identifications are generally consistent with those of their parents, they did not simply inherit their views from them. Their beliefs appear instead to be the products of dynamic interplays between personal experiences, parental input, and their own learning.

When I was a kid we used to have chuck roast, which my mother would say, "We're having steak." So we'd get that steak and my mother would beat it to death, and put tenderizer on it, and it's still tough. And I couldn't figure out why you hear people saying, "There's nothing like a good steak." . . . Until I got to be nineteen. . . . (*)

When I was in high school, that's when I started learning about America, the real America. It wasn't in the civics books. It was in other books I started reading—listening to Malcolm X, Martin Luther King—reading about black history, which we didn't read in school. By the time I got into the military, I said "Something's definitely wrong with this country." So when I came back, that's when I became involved more with the political side. (*)

I witnessed discrimination on a firsthand basis and that to some degree influenced my thinking about social relationships, you know, relationships between groups. (*)

I was always for the underdog. . . . As a child, I could remember, the family used to come to our house, congregate there. And they would talk politics, and I was just fascinated. (*)

Many of the critics, like many of the activists in the movements of the 1960s and 1970s, either grew up in liberal, progressive, or left-of-center families and social environments, or had formative experiences in late adolescence or early adulthood that engendered in them progressive or left-of-center views.[30] Moreover, the larger cultural era and educational environment in which most of these critics grew up and politically came of age—the 1960s and early 1970s—helped to foster progressive modes of thought among those persons who were potentially receptive. Most of the critics were in their early forties at the time of the interviews, which put them in their late teens and early twenties during the heart of this period.[31] During this period social activists, as well as many academics, were successful in raising concerns among significant blocks of the American public about the conditions of poverty, racism, and inequality; the desire to meet needs and establish fairness; nonviolence and pacifism; integrity versus corruption; and participatory democracy versus hierarchy, authority, and elitism. Many of the critics took active parts in this culture, and even if they were not involved in it they were at least, in some significant respects, products of it.

I was very upset with the civil rights issues that were going on in the sixties. . . . I can remember always being somewhat controversial within my family. . . .
I remember when I first got back to Connecticut after graduating from college, . . . I was almost tarred and feathered and run out of town, because I was antiwar. That wasn't radical, but it was radical for [my city/town]. (*)

I remember my father and I probably being two of very few white faces picketing Woolworth's when I was a kid, because they wouldn't allow blacks. . . . (*)

The accounts of how the critics became actively involved in politics to the point of running for office reflect these experiences as well. Perhaps most notable in these accounts is the fact that most of the critics were not recruited "party agents." They were not "coopted" or drafted for public office from the local party organizations or the community at large by the party operatives.[32] Instead, they tended to pursue political office more through their own initiatives, responding politically to the social and economic concerns born and developed in their political comings of age.[33] Similarly, a few initially became involved in politics through local community movements.

The personal stories also point to the influence of later experiences and environments on beliefs. Though one's predispositions certainly affect how one experiences and interprets subsequent events, the ongoing context of life experiences cannot help but influence beliefs. Foremost among these are the relations found in the family, society, economy, and workplace. And wrapped up in these experiences is the influence of the region and neighborhood wherein one lives and works. For reasons of anonymity I cannot go into detail on these issues concerning the critics, but nonetheless it should be pointed out that not surprisingly, many (though by no means all) of them live in urban surroundings. The connection between these surroundings and the critics' beliefs seems clear: urban surroundings provide more immediate and pervasive exposure to those persons for whom the market has failed (though supporters might say that those persons have failed the market), and more intellectual and social support for the critics' views. This relation is no doubt a mutually reinforcing one; because of their views critics are likely to fare better politically in urban environments.

Other demographic data reveal patterns that are also of interest. As we might expect, critics earn substantially less money and possess fewer assets than the other senators. They are also somewhat less educated; this statistic mostly reflects the comparatively lower incidence of lawyers among critics.[34]

The popular wisdom about political beliefs asserts the tendency of one's beliefs to become more conservative with age, particularly with the transition from early adulthood to middle age.[35] This assertion has been particularly popular concerning the generation that came of age in the 1960s and early 1970s. Reasons for this tendency include the assumption of family responsibilities, embarking on a career, improvement in economic status, and change in peer group. Some of the critics cited similar conservatizing effects regarding their own views. These effects did not influence their values of justice so much as their views about the possibility of realizing these values within the present politicoeconomic system.

> I sort of found the radical approach to things an appealing way of participating in government. When I got active in government—I did not run for politics or get into politics waving a radical banner, interestingly enough—and soon after I was in government I became convinced it wasn't really the way to get things done. This system repulses radicalism. It's just not acceptable. Those who choose radical approaches, their careers and time in the business is short-lived. You've got to have the long-term view of things, what you want to accomplish. And you're going to have to do it by playing by certain rules, it's as simple as that, or get out of it, because I don't see any other way working. (6)

> I've noticed to some extent over the past couple of years . . . that I may be a little less liberal than I have been . . . in terms of fiscal conservatism. I'm tending to be a little bit more conservative in terms of certain fiscal issues. (2)

The Political Theory of the Critic's Narrative

Taken as a whole, the critic's narrative of justice prompts questions about the political theory, or theories, within which it might fit, or for which it might constitute a normative base. Since from an American perspective the critic's narrative appears to be somewhat unusual, it is instructive to begin an investigation into these questions with a consideration of some present and past forms of Left-oriented American political thinking and movements. I will then consider the relations between the narrative and two contemporary European political theories, social democracy and Christian democracy, as they are reflected through their respective political parties.

Much literature has appeared recently concerning a resurgence of Populism, on both the Left and Right.[36] Connecticut is not a state in which we would expect to find the traditional versions of Populism; it is not an agrarian, or southern, or western state. But the "New Populism," although linked historically and philosophically to the Populism of the late nineteenth century, is a more generalized movement (though still decentralized and local). According to Harry Boyte:

> It emerges from the conviction that an elite has dishonored an historically, culturally, or geographically constituted people, its memories, origins, common territory, ways of life. Thus there is a certain class feeling in populism—the belief that common people are mistreated by the power-

ful. . . . Most simply, populism calls for the return of power to ordinary people. (Boyte and Riessman 1986, 8)

There is certainly a link between the critic's perspective and Populist attitudes toward the corporate powers. There is a moralism in the Populist view about value and labor that is also present in the critic's narrative, in particular the critics' views about class; class-oriented thinking takes the form of a dichotomy between "producers and parasites, workers and predators, the robbers and the robbed" (Tindall 1976, xii). Furthermore, Populism's notion of the connectedness of individuals, a communal aspect found in both the early and present versions of Populism, echoes in the critic's narrative, particularly in the narrative chapters on need and love. Populism encourages even those who have been exploited to balance the pursuit of their own self-interest with a concern for the interests of all people.

But the differences between Populism and the critic's narrative are almost as profound as the similarities. These extend beyond the obvious discrepancies, such as Populism's lingering nostalgia for preindustrial agrarianism and its enduring regional orientation, to broader points concerning Populism's economic and social vision. To the degree that Populism has an economic point of view, it is more about power and the experience of powerlessness than it is about distribution and fairness (though the two are obviously linked).[37] Although Populism opposes the large institutions that it perceives as the sources of economic injustice, it focuses not so much on taming, resisting, or changing these institutions as on circumventing them through local activities and self-help. Populism is even less clear than the critic's narrative about how we must approach and solve the economic problem itself. As a current Populist acknowledges, "[t]he central question a serious progressive populism must answer is how it will deal with the overall problem of economic management and structure. Else it will end up as just one more effort to change the subject without facing the main question" (Alperovitz 1986, 167). Concerning organizational issues more specifically, the critics are not as suspicious of large organizations and bigness per se—especially big government—as were (and are) the Populists (or the Progressives of the early twentieth century) (Hofstadter 1955, 215–22). The critics concentrate their wrath more specifically on the management of these economic organizations and the members of Populism's "plutocracy."

Standing next to Populism's emphasis on decentralization and localism is its "darker side" of racism, nativism, and xenophobia, of which one can still see a faded image in the current Populism (Hofstadter 1955, 77–93; Miller 1986, 132–40). The critics clearly do not share these views. The sense of connection with others contained within Populism remains a profoundly local, parochial experience, while the critics stress the importance of developing a much broader consciousness.

This Populist parochialism, however, is also part of a concern with genuinely involving people in the activities and decisions that affect their lives, that is, with realizing the promise of democracy in meaningful ways. In this sense, past and present Populisms are linked to the New Left movements of the 1960s and 1970s. Indeed, many students of the New Left have observed that it has a healthy heritage in older American lefts, including Populism, abolitionism, war resistance, nuclear weapons protests, the Wobbly movement, and various nonorthodox, or libertarian, Marxisms.[38] I have already noted the influence of the period of the New Left on many of the critics. "Participatory democracy" was the term that the activists of this period used to describe their democratic project, and in its full meaning it shares several points of contact with the critics' concerns about engendering and sustaining empathy and caring for others in the face of a competitive, exploitative socioeconomic system. As Nigel Young points out:

[Participatory democracy] offered itself not merely as a practical principle, but as ideology or political philosophy. At its heart lay an idea of mutual aid, as against individual competitiveness; cooperation rather than opposition; it could simply be extended to a socialist critique of the individual status-striving of capitalist society. (1977, 132)[39]

But of course it rarely was. And the critics share this failure as well.

Participatory democracy also includes a notion of individual duty, a responsibility to become an active part of an authentic community where the personal is connected to the systemic (a popular feminist phrase of the period was "the personal is political," and in *The Port Huron Statement,* Tom Hayden called for "a reassertion of the personal"). There is a moralism in this political imperative that resonates in the critic's narrative. This moralism depends on a view toward others that is based on a faith in common values, common ground, and a common love of man. Indeed, the critic's narrative seems heavily influenced by what Samuel Beer (1978) identifies as the "romantic revolt" of the 1960s. Such a view of political life leads to the idea of changing and reforming individuals through democratic experiences, which provide people with opportunities to develop empathy and understanding. This notion of reform has an American heritage in the Progressive period, which drew on the Yankee Protestant ethic of personal responsibility, the potential for redemption through involvement in the lives of others who are less well off, and the possibility of changing individuals through moral appeals.[40] These ideas correspond to a facet of the critic's narrative I have referred to earlier as its "softer side," which emphasizes changes in tone and attitude over changes in structure. In particular, they evoke the critics' views about the double-edged value and purpose of education, as both a means of achievement and as a means of understanding others and developing empathy.

Progressivism, however, also featured the Protestant-based norm of allocating economic rewards based on individual qualities and merit exercised within a competitive system, at the time called "the race of life" (also a phrase of Lincoln's) (Hofstadter 1955, 219–27).[41] This norm is somewhat at odds with the critics' primary emphasis on needs, although the Progressives also advocated a maximum participation in this competitive system (Hofstadter 1955, 224). To continue chronologically from the Progressive period, I should also note that New Deal thinking does not seem to correspond well to the critic's narrative. The critics' views are not in direct conflict with the ideas of the New Deal, but the narrative does emphasize certain priorities and concerns that were not at the center of New Deal thought (Hofstadter 1955, 313–25).

In a 1986 essay, J. David Greenstone offers a view of American political culture that encompasses many important elements of the political movements that I have referred to, as well as perhaps the critic's narrative itself. He identifies two strains of liberalism that have been present throughout American history: a secular Lockean strain and a Protestant, non-Lockean strain. The non-Lockean strain, which ran particularly deep in Yankee areas and drew much of its strength from Yankee intellectuals, figured prominently in both the Populist and Progressive movements and in the protest movements of the 1960s and 1970s. It emphasizes "the commands of duty and the overriding role of conscience, rather than Locke's more sober concern with an enlightened self-interest," although it retains a "liberal commitment to republicanism, capitalism, and individualism" (Greenstone 1986, 22). It offers a broader conception of liberty than the Lockean strain: liberty involves more than the absence of restraint (the negative concept); it also involves "the development of those human faculties that make freedom truly meaningful" (the positive concept) (1986, 20). It also offers a different notion of what the national union is about. Instead of concentrating on the territorial and economic importance of the union, that is, the union "as a particular political regime that provided human happiness or utility," the non-Lockean strain locates the significance and value of the union in moral terms: the union is based on a "commitment to equality of rights, to the love of justice, and to the extension of positive liberty for all" (1986, 20, 43). These differences turn in large part on the two strains' respective notions of human personality. The non-Lockean strain assumes a more dynamic notion of human personality, similar in fact to the notion assumed by the "unconstrained world vision" described by Thomas Sowell (and which I have discussed at several earlier points). The Lockean conception is more static, evoking Sowell's "constrained vision." Greenstone thus summarizes his point: "[A]lthough the central tenets of American liberalism are widely shared, they are interpreted in different ways. And these differences of interpretation may be of fundamental rather than secondary importance" (1986, 28).

The critics share the non-Lockean strain's views about duty, liberty, the union, and human personality. But the non-Lockean strain of liberalism does not seem to go far enough into the critics' views about economic and social justice to genuinely characterize the narrative. Something more is at work here.

The narrative's unusual qualities (from an American standpoint), along with its general leftism, also invite brief comparisons with political theories and ideologies from other countries. European social democracy seems a good place to start, because it too goes further into economic and social justice than non-Lockean liberalism, while at the same time remaining within a reformist rather than a revolutionary approach. Indeed, sympathetic American observers of European social democracy have pointed out its correspondence to elements of the American Left.[42] Social democracy's commitment to equality and its views of the aims of equality are similar to those of the critics; social democracy desires to move beyond equal opportunity, narrowly defined, but stops short of complete equality. As C. A. R. Crosland has observed, the social democrat "seeks a distribution of rewards, status, and privileges egalitarian enough to minimise social resentment, to secure justice between individuals, and to equalise opportunities; and he seeks to weaken the existing deep-seated class stratification, with its concomitant feelings of envy and inferiority, and its barriers to uninhibited mingling between classes" (1956, 113). Appropriate welfare levels and redistribution are to be achieved through progressive taxation rather than expropriation.

At the same time, social democracy remains committed to instituting these changes through the procedures of parliamentary democracy and national legislation, rather than through the creation of alternative institutions that stand in opposition to the state (Esping-Andersen 1985, 6–10). And in this endeavor, social democrats do not pursue a majoritarian, class-conflict style of political action; they instead emphasize inclusiveness, harmony, cooperation, and solidarity between classes and peoples. Social democracy's orientation on these issues matches up well with the chapters of the critic's narrative on the love of fellow humans and the role of government. The critics may represent a genuinely radical point of view, but they are not revolutionaries. Changes from within the system—most notably through the state—can be genuinely beneficial, with long-term positive effects. Unjust individuals can learn the errors of their ways through new experiences, and can change. Thus from an economically critical perspective, both social democracy and the critic's narrative are open to the same criticism—that they ultimately rely on a utopian brand of politics since they fail to identify and develop "the agency of socialist transformation" (Birchall 1986, 17).

But social democracy should not be overly equated with the critic's narrative. First, social democracy may be more egalitarian than the critic's narrative, though such judgments are problematic. Note, for example, that based on the income exercise presented earlier in table 1, the critics favored more income inequality than did all the groups of Swedish political elites in Verba et al.'s sample (1987, 263). Second, social democracy remains primarily an institutionally oriented program, heavily concerned with management, production, and employment (Paterson and Thomas 1986).[43] Its assumption of economic growth makes possible theoretically the institution of progressive policies without great socioeconomic conflict. Third, social democracy gives comparatively less attention to much of the moralism in the critic's narrative, particularly the emphasis on inequities and need satisfaction and the concern with building empathy through participatory experiences. We may thus wish to consider another European political program with a more explicitly moral overtone, but also with a less explicitly egalitarian focus: Christian democracy.

Christian democracy is an unlikely candidate for correspondence to the critic's narrative. It is generally considered to occupy the center to center-right position in the spectrum of European political programs. Christian democracy, however, is more complex than this, and merits at least a cursory examination here (Irving 1979, xvii–xxii, 29–57). Christian Democrats support state interventions in the economy and are concerned with socioeconomic democracy and sociopolitical integration and inclusiveness. These concerns follow from their attempts "to reconcile liberal democracy and industrial society with traditional Christian teaching" (Irving 1979, 30). Christian Democrats attempt to chart a middle path between capitalism and socialism, to create, to turn a phrase, "capitalism with a human face" (Irving 1979, 57). The chapters of the critic's narrative on need satisfaction and love of others appear to be similarly informed by Christian-based ideas. But Christian democracy is also marked by conservatism in its attitudes toward individual rights and property rights, as well as in its sense of the proper limits of economic intervention. In addition, its emphasis on inclusiveness and compromise is at least in part based on the fierce pragmatism that guides its political programs and strategies. Like the other theories, then, it offers a mixed bag of comparisons.

Overall, the best analogy in political theory and praxis for the critic's narrative appears to be some form of populism, with a social democratic tinge.

CHAPTER 4

The Supporter's Narrative

Any American, no matter what their background, can rise to whatever level he
or she is capable of. . . . I think it's very fluid. People who were born in
poverty can become multimillionaires. I know people like that, and there are
plenty of examples. And I think America is almost unique in that sense. We
have more opportunity in that sense. (10)

In comparison to the critic's narrative, the supporter's narrative occupies more
familiar American terrain. Although the stories that the supporters tell vary in
significant ways, they are held together by views about economic justice that
we would associate with a conservative position. This narrative's story line is
markedly different from that of the critics: the heroes become villains, the
villains become heroes, and the alleged victims become culpable. As with the
critic's narrative, the supporter's narrative also contains four core episodes or
chapters that organize the supporters' views. In many respects, the supporters
sketch negative images of the portraits drafted by the critics in the chapters of
their narrative. I have called the four supporter chapters "Every Man a Trump";
"Render Therefore unto Me"; "More Like Us"; and "Government as Villain."[1]
These chapters cover roughly the same topics as those in the critic's narrative.
"Every Man a Trump" describes the workings of the market economy, the
history of distributional patterns, socioeconomic mobility, and the operations
of business. "Render Therefore unto Me" concerns the makings of a successful
economy and the norms of distribution. "More Like Us" advances remedies for
the problems the supporters recognized in the course of putting forward the
first two chapters. "Government as Villain" describes the impact and role of
government. As in the critic's narrative, the material in these chapters inevitably bleeds together, and in each chapter the reader will undoubtedly discover
elements from the others. Taken as a whole, the supporters' chapters are more
consistent than those of the critic's narrative, but they nonetheless contain
ambivalences of their own, which I will flesh out in the following discussion.

An Overview of the Narrative

Supporters believe that, by and large, society is just. Their sense of justice is
based not on the egalitarian impulse to provide for human needs, but rather on
the notion of equity, of being able to keep what you make. Supporters believe

that the allocations yielded by market exchanges preserve and promote equity. They locate the immediate threat to justice not in the accumulation of wealth, privilege, and power by those of traditionally higher status (which critics might say distorts the workings of the market), but rather in governmental redistributions of wealth and restrictions on the market, and the political power of the have-nots. These forces lead to unjust allocations of resources through unfair confiscations of fairly earned rewards; supporters view these allocations as forms of special, illegitimate privilege. These allocations and confiscations are in turn the sources of market disruptions; they ultimately result in inefficiency, in addition to being unjust.

Like the critics, supporters reach for conditions of opportunity and equal opportunity as the indicators of justice, but they differ from the critics in the way in which they construct these terms and in the degree to which they see them to exist in reality. A negative conception of liberty and freedom is prominent in their thinking. Equal opportunity is also constructed more negatively; it is thought to be more concerned with direct exclusion from economic pursuits than with assistance and empowerment in order to take part in these pursuits. Implicit in such a notion of equal opportunity is the assumption that an adequate supply of opportunity exists. And supporters do claim that economic opportunity does in fact exist, and that it is available to all persons. They believe that in most important respects, America still operates under its traditional ideals. Supporters thus share the premium on economic individualism held by most Americans and express criticisms of public assistance, government regulation, and policies to increase economic equality.

Supporters resist any strong notions of socioeconomic classes and deny the existence of an underclass.[2] They instead posit a naturally occurring cooperative relationship between employers and employees, which unfortunately is often disturbed by employees. Their description of the distribution of wealth is a normal distribution, with a center of mass located slightly toward the poorer end. They recognize that there are great distances between different income and wealth levels, but in their view the boundaries between them, to the degree that they are clearly identifiable, are not impenetrable barriers to upward mobility.

The notions of distribution that follow from the supporters' principles of equity and market exchange are generally laissez-faire. In responses to questions about specific occupational incomes, the incomes are mostly left alone, and no occupation's income is lowered (see table 2, p. 105). The people at the top deserve to be there; they have earned their positions. Success should be rewarded, not punished. In general, wages are not determined by power relations but instead by a market that responds to qualifications, education, training, and ability; in short, a market that reflects merit. This is both how it is and how it should be. Supporters thus give market allocations an explicitly *moral* quality that is lacking in some of the philosophic and economic defenses of the market system.[3] Another pillar in the supporters' endorsement of the allocations of the market is the notion that market transactions reflect uncoerced agreements between buyers and sellers. Markets promote freedom because they do not presume to determine anyone's preferences; the public good is determined by private, free choice.[4] Note that this construction of freedom through the market is somewhat at tension with the above defense of market transactions in terms of merit.

Supporters maintain an uneasy approval for a minimum standard of living that should embrace all people; however, they believe that this standard is either met or exceeded by the present levels of welfare spending. But the idea of providing assistance to people who provide nothing in exchange for it seems at odds with their idea of equity. Indeed, the supporters' approval of such measures remains problematic, even within their own minds. They find the concept of workfare, for example, to be quite appealing for this reason. But in their acceptance of even limited measures of public support for the poor, they recognize that some persons' economic circumstances remain beyond their own control.

Yet the difficulties here regarding the supporters' views about poverty and economic failure run even deeper. In fact, it is not just a few people who are falling through the cracks. Even with the existence of genuine economic opportunity, a widespread, intense poverty still exists. People who are born poor tend to stay poor. Supporters must acknowledge and explain these facts, and they account for them with a politics of blame. Since by their account opportunity does exist, the persistent lack of upward mobility on the part of some people indicates more about them than about the structure of the economic system. Poor people, rather than being the innocent victims found in the critic's narrative, constitute a morally suspect group that ultimately ends up leeching off productive society. Thus supporters' solutions to the problem of poverty mostly consist of efforts to change those at the bottom, to make them more willing as well as more able to participate in the economic system.

For the most part, supporters see our own government—especially national government—as the evil empire. It intrudes upon personal and economic freedom (although it is also the vehicle through which the poor can mend their ways). Lacking a profit motive, it is inherently inefficient and wasteful. Its reactions to the problem of poverty are wrongheaded; through its welfare policies and other efforts it removes incentives to work and produce. It undercuts responsibility and discipline. It destroys individual initiative and corrupts the very people it is supposedly trying to help, and thus compounds the problem of poverty.[5] The primary instrument through which government effects these evils is the confiscatory tax scheme. Supporters prefer flat tax schemes over progressive ones.

In spite of both government's evils and powers, the supporters' view of the future remains for the most part optimistic; America is the best country on earth and will continue to be so. Supporters may be critical of the state, but they remain intensely supportive of the nation.

Several additional paradoxes in the narrative merit separate attention. In the critic's narrative one finds a deeply critical, collectively oriented, even structural diagnosis of the problem of injustice, yet at the same time one also finds a relatively gentle, individually oriented prescription. In the supporter's narrative one finds an intensely individualistic approach toward distribution and economic activity more generally—making it on one's own is valued above almost all else—but at the same time one also finds support for the traditional, organized, collective sources of authority over individuals.[6] This authority may be vested in the management of a large corporation (versus nonmanagement employees); in social mores (versus individuals' preferences); in the collection of producers (versus consumers); or even in the government (versus individuals or group protests). As one example, supporters posit a natural cooperative relationship between management and nonmanagement employees, which is ultimately manifested in the nonmanagement employees doing what management tells them to do; that is, in following its authority. Disruptions in this cooperative arrangement are due to the nonmanagement employees, often acting through unions. As another example, in the questions about specific occupational incomes, supporters raised the income of police patrol officers by a greater proportion than for any other occupation.

In this endorsement of authority and social order, the supporter's narrative comes closer to the older, traditional European version of political conservatism than at perhaps any other point. The motivation for this endorsement, however, may lie more in a simple concern for law and order, or in a strain of patriotism, than in the epistemologically conservative notion that these traditional sources of authority are the repository of collected wisdoms and trusts that have been handed down from one generation to the next. It could also be the product of a generational effect—supporters tended to be older than the other senators—or the distant echo of an American version of civic republicanism, with its obsessions over decline and moral corruption. Finally, this paradox may reflect an inherent paradox within both the argument for and the reality of economic individualism: in practice, economic individualism can ultimately lead to collective patterns of organization in the economy and in society that compromise individual economic autonomy and achievement.[7] Thus, individual autonomy, or at least its harmful effects, must be constrained in some ways.

There is another related paradox—perhaps tension is a better word—that also merits attention here. The supporter's narrative exhibits a duality in its notions of human nature and motivation: On the one hand, there is an emphasis on self-interest and incentive; persons are fundamentally motivated by their own self-interest, and to be effective, institutions and policies must be constructed around this fact. This fact about human nature is not challenged; it is taken as an unproblematic given. One finds this view of human nature more prevalent, for example, in discussions of wages and incomes. Yet on the other hand, there is also a more traditional concern for moral character and for the engendering and maintenance of this character through institutions and policies. Supporters place a heavy emphasis on the qualities of self-reliance, diligence, and discipline. Policies need to go beyond an attention to incentive and self-interest. They must instill character. One finds these concerns more prevalent, for example, in discussions of why the poor do not take advantage of the many opportunities to make themselves better off.

These two views of human nature are not mutually exclusive. One could argue that both views are elements of Thomas Sowell's "constrained" world vision, which was discussed herein in chapters 2 and 3 (Sowell 1987). It is not inconsistent to state both that people are motivated by self-interest and that people differ in their abilities to realize their interests due to differences in character. Nonetheless, the two emphases tend to lead in different directions in thinking about the issues that concern distribution, political institutions, and policies. They may represent competing reflections of the older and newer conservatisms, both of which are present in the supporter's narrative. The supporters' concern for moral character, as well as their politics of blame more generally, may also indicate a link with the religious wing of the new conservatism. None of the supporters, however, emphasized religion in their responses or framed their comments in religious or spiritual terms.

Just as all the critics are Democrats, all the supporters are Republicans. But again, their stories do not seem to be driven by their party identifications. Like their critical counterparts, their narrative appears to be largely the product of early experiences. In this respect the political views of their families while they were growing up emerge as important sources of their beliefs. What also seem important, however, are later work experiences outside the senate, as supporters took on business and management roles. These experiences do not mark supporters as unique within the senate, and exactly why and how they drew the lessons that they did from them remains to some extent a mystery. One fact, however, is clear: Most supporters tended to lack early firsthand experiences with poverty; the few that did have such firsthand experiences were children of the Depression. Thus their experiences with poverty were arguably strikingly different from those in modern urban poverty. Poverty was considered to be less deviant during this time, and this perception may have become even more prevalent in retrospect.

The format of what follows is similar to that of the critic's narrative. A more detailed rendering of the four core chapters immediately succeeds this overview and is followed by brief discussions of several other disparate items of interest in the supporters' responses, and the limits of their support of the economic system. I then consider the supporters' statements about their own political and personal lives, and examine the effects of the personal element on the supporter's narrative. I conclude the chapter with a review of the relations between the supporter's narrative and various political theories.

Every Man a Trump

In *Tales of a New America,* Robert Reich identifies a mythical morality tale essential to the American self-image, which he calls the "triumphant individual."

> [The triumphant individual] is the story of the little guy who works hard, takes risks, believes in himself, and eventually earns wealth, fame, and honor. It's the parable of the self-made man (or more recently, woman) who bucks the odds, spurns the naysayers, and shows what can be done with enough drive and guts. He's a loner and a maverick, true to himself, plain speaking, self-reliant, uncompromising in his ideals. He gets the job done. (1987, 9)

Though the triumphant individual is a loner, and a bit different perhaps from the average person, he is nonetheless just plain folk; everyone can identify with him, and moreover, everyone can be him. In "Every Man a Trump," supporters think that the path of the triumphant individual is open to anyone if he will only try hard. And the ascent has no practical limits; one can climb all the way to the peak. It matters little who one is and from where one starts. Environments and circumstances can be overcome. The "log cabin myth" of yesterday becomes, in the hands of the supporters, the "ghetto myth" of today.

> If [a couple] lives in a public housing project . . . and has a son. And there's another couple that has a son born the same the day, that lives down here . . . in a two million dollar mansion. Assuming that the [mansion] kid doesn't have a business dumped in his lap, I think if the [public housing] parents are determined to see their son get a good education, they give him good values, I think he has an equal chance to succeed with the [mansion] kid. (12)

The notion of economic justice embedded here involves opportunity and equity. Supporters explicitly reject notions of equality of distribution, and instead think of a fair economic system as a game in which all players have the opportunity to play and win. Accumulations made during the game do not necessarily threaten the fairness of the future of the game. Rewards for work performed, products produced, or services rendered are distributed through the market. Justice means having the opportunity to engage in market transactions and to prosper from them. Equal justice means equal opportunity. People must make their own way in the market; a large part of the justice of the market is found in the relation between one's own contributions and the rewards one earns, and in the judgments that we make of others' work through the market. The justice of the market is that its distributions match some roughly objective assessment of one's contribution; that is, of one's merit. But at the same time, the very process of exchange yields a fair result. Thus to a large extent, the supporter provides a self-reflexive justification of the market.

How well does reality conform to this ideal? The supporters share a strong sense that the economic system itself, if left alone, is fair. People do have opportunities to enter it, and they are rewarded for their efforts. What occurs *prior* to market exchanges—socioeconomic circumstances; personal disadvantages; in short, one's life chances—are viewed as starting points that we all have and that we all must deal with.[8] Some people will struggle; that is the way of the world. It is not, however, a significant issue of fairness. There is also a sense that the struggles that do occur are good for the character and perhaps even for the soul. Life should not be easy. There is a drama of work and redemption in the supporter's narrative, which takes place on a secular plane, in the market. I will return to this concern with character in the narrative chapter named "More Like Us."

Such a view about the market and justice would seem to depend on, or at least to imply, a belief that conditions of upward mobility do in fact exist. This is indeed the case in the minds of the supporters. What the critics referred to as the "American myth" of upward mobility and opportunity is seen by the supporters as a treasured reality. Upward mobility exists because opportunities exist, and people can take advantage of them. And by and large, the opportunities are available equally. Making the upward move depends on the individual, and how much she is willing to work and persevere. If she is so willing, then she will be rewarded.

> I don't think there's any problem at all [in moving up]. It depends on the individual, and if they have the incentive, if they have the chutzpah— whatever you want to call it—to improve themselves. I don't think there's great restrictions on it. If we were in Europe, I'd say: a hell of a lot of restrictions. (14)

> I believe, and I hope—and they better—employers take a look at the applicants, as individuals, as human beings, and hire them on that basis.

And once an MBA is hired as somebody's executive assistant, then it's up to him; all he has to do is achieve. Where the hell he was born and what his father was putting in his pocket every month—he doesn't even have to have a father; the mother can be brought up on welfare, but if she instills the proper values and the proper motivation. . . .

. . . Opportunity, but they have to walk through the door on their own. . . . Everybody in this country has the same opportunity to achieve that someone else does. No goal can be out of the reach of anyone. (12)

I think we give [people] the opportunity [for jobs]. We give them the opportunity of whether you want to go to college, or whether you want to go to voc-tech college. . . . The opportunities are there; the door is open if you want to walk through it. It might be a little bit difficult, but that's good character building. . . . The opportunities are there for the people to educate themselves in whatever manner they want. There's something for all of us . . . . It depends on what you want to do and what goals you set. . . .

In every strata there is—I don't want to say good and bad, but—there are those that make it and those that don't. . . .

This is a place of opportunity. Just look at some of the people we have. Jesse Jackson . . . Martin Luther King; I'm sure they set their goals and got where they wanted to be. . . . Andrew Young, Julian Bond. . . . There are an awful lot of the others that have come a far way, simply because they've decided, "This is the way I want to go." And when the opportunities have presented themselves they've taken advantage of them.

. . . What is fair in the economic world? It's all fair, simply because anyone has the opportunity to go as high as he wants to go, and his capabilities allow him to go. I think it's up to the individual. If the individual sets the goal, that they can achieve whatever they want. . . . We have it [equal opportunity], but I don't think too many people take advantage of it. (11)[9]

I don't see any kind of holding down, if the person has the capability of doing something. . . . I don't see any barrier for a person that applies themselves from going right up that ladder. I don't see any barrier that says because you are here you can never move to here. I don't see that. We have people that can't read or write that have broken through that and have become owners of industry, owners of enterprise. They have the innate ability but just not the formal training. (13)

People have control over their own lives, . . . ultimately control their own destiny. . . . They all have a shot at doing whatever it is they so desire. You can see some very rich, wealthy people, very good families, who have done nothing and gone down the tubes. And you can look at those who started out with nothing and built it into something. (15)

Education also figures prominently in making the upward move, but again, a decent education is seen to be open to those who want it, though some of the supporters grant that more could be done by government to insure that at the early stages at least people can receive a good education. It is interesting to note here that the supporters' conception of education is as an enabling device, as a credential of learning and training, and even in itself as a reflection of the work ethic and a proper upbringing. It is not, however, a broader vehicle for promoting interpersonal understanding and empathic compassion, a function to which the critics drew much attention.

> As a general rule all of the kids have the opportunity to go to school, to get an education. And if they do that that opens the door into all the—a great number of them don't take advantage of it. Look at Jesse Jackson. . . . Here is a guy that came from dirt poor—the way he describes it—to being nominated for the president of the United States. That is the story of Lincoln—from the log cabin to the presidency. (13)

> In the poorer classes, I don't think education is important to them, and I think that's a conflict, because we feel it's important, and it should be important to them. . . . Obviously, to me, education is a road for everybody, and I find it very difficult that we don't have a way of conveying the message to those who don't take advantage of it. (15)

The particular vision of opportunity, and more specifically equal opportunity, that emerges here is a fairly narrow one. As the concept is defined by the supporters, equal opportunity is both endorsed and thought to actually exist. Equal opportunity means the right of anyone to *try,* the right to compete. It means a chance to do what one is capable of doing, an opportunity to achieve. It means not being actively excluded. The emphasis here is on qualifications and capacity. Stronger forms of equal opportunity, such as affirmative action and quotas, are rejected on the grounds that they yield inefficient results (the people given these opportunities cannot do the work), and that they are reversely discriminatory and therefore unfair to others who deserve the rewards for their labor. Government's role concerning opportunity is as an umpire with limited jurisdiction; certainly not as a trainer. Later, in the narrative chapter "More Like Us," we will see that government may also be a drill instructor.

> I believe blacks, Hispanics, browns, yellows, should be given a job, providing they can produce and perform the same as—I'd like to say one of us—but you know what I mean. Affirmative action to me is a joke. I

believe they should be working, but when you say, hey, John Jones, because he's black or Hispanic, gets a 40 point edge or 20 point edge when they take a test, I'm against that. . . . Just to put them in a slot because they need a black man in there or a Hispanic in there is a big joke. Who ends up paying for it? The consumer. Because they infiltrate their work force with minorities who are not capable of doing that [work]. (16)

[Equal opportunity] means government stepping in to prevent overt discrimination. . . . Not government creating the job so that a particular person or group can fill the job, and certainly not mandating those who create the capital to do certain things that, just frankly, may not be in their economic interest, which is what makes them thrive as capitalists. . . . If you're physically and intellectually capable, and government can assist you in getting a college loan, that's terrific. But government shouldn't say, "Well, generally speaking, you're not qualified to go to the University of Connecticut, but because you're from a disadvantaged group we're going to let you go anyway." I'm not sure that's doing that student any good, or the rest of the students, for that matter. Maybe that means that they have to go to community college, for instance. The government shouldn't break the rules—sort of artificially lift people—because if they're not capable and qualified . . . I don't think they're doing them any favors. . . . (10)

The supporters' construction of liberty follows from this vision of opportunity. The conception of liberty contained within the supporter's narrative is a clearly negative one, as opposed to the positive conception of the critics. Liberty is not related to or dependent on empowerment; rather, it means a field of unencumbered activity, a space within which the individual is not coerced. At the same time, the perceived forms of coercion that might invade such spaces of freedom are limited by the supporters to overt, easily identifiable kinds of intrusions, rather than more subtle forms of power and coercion. According to the critics, these more subtle forms of power can inhabit both political life and market transactions. Since the supporters limit themselves to a relatively narrow notion of coercion, they are less likely to perceive threats to liberty in the everyday business of the economic system.

The supporters' fluid conception of upward mobility, along with their notion that there is a large supply of economic opportunity, leads one to wonder about their beliefs about socioeconomic class. The very conception of class implies salient barriers, distances, and discrete placements. The supporters' sense of economic mobility would seem to obviate these distinctions. Another related issue is whether they advocate the interests of a particular class in their responses, regardless of their own class analyses, or lack of them. Regarding the second issue, the supporters' general statements about upward mobility and opportunity, as well as about the poor and the levels of welfare spending, are certainly in the interests of those in the upper income brackets. And it would seem that, relative to the current state of affairs, the haves would profit from the more specific policy positions of the supporters.

Regarding the supporters' own analysis of class, the statements are marked most by an absence. Supporters either completely reject the existence of socioeconomic classes or confirm their existence in only a weak sense. They do perceive differences in the socioeconomic statuses of people, but these differences are conceived of as a continuous distribution, or ladder, without significant social meaning, rather than as discrete, meaningful groupings. They perceive this ladder to be weighted more heavily, that is, to be wider, in either the middle or the bottom half of the ladder, but this feature is not considered to present a problem. The differences between the spots on the ladder and the fact that its width narrows as one nears the top are useful incentives for achievement.

That supporters do not see the clear class distinctions that critics see consequently means that they also do not perceive a conflict of interests between the various economic groups. Rather than cleavage and conflict, a better model of the supporters' view of economic relations is that of an escalator, or a mountain. All can compete to get to the top; the fact that only some make it does not put them at odds with those who only get a short way up the peak. The distance up the peak that each person travels does not depend on the distances achieved by the others. And as more people work their way up, the peak becomes open to ascent by even greater numbers.

Supporters not only reject the notion of significant conflicts between economic strata in society, they also reject the notion of significant conflict between employers and employees, and managers and workers. They identify a natural partnership in the production of a good or service, with each element in that production playing its role. In the supporters' view, strife does of course exist, but when it occurs it is due mostly to the unnecessary disruptions of labor and nonmanagement employees, and not to the way management treats its employees or the possibility that the nonmanagement employees do not have an adequate voice in the actions of the institution. A more specific critique of labor unions accompanies the general assessment of blame for labor strife. Labor unions by and large have a negative impact on both the productive process and the interests of their own membership. They disrupt the process and introduce discord into a naturally harmonious project. They demand more than their membership deserves. They weaken the health and the vitality of the productive system as a whole, and therefore compromise the long-term interests of their own members.[10]

It is not surprising, then, that the supporters' conception of work itself, as it is experienced by the average worker, is a more positive one than that of the critics. For the average employee, work is more a source of fulfillment and meaning in life than it is in the view of the critics, who conceived of work more as a chore, necessary in order to secure the material means of existence and to enjoy other more private pleasures. For supporters, both the necessity of work and the place of work in the larger system of equitable market exchanges and productive effort lead to a widespread appreciation of everyday work, even as it is presently experienced.

The supporters' weak notion of class, as well as their views about upward mobility and work, also imply the notion that over time the distributions of wealth and income have steadily become more even. This is indeed the case in the minds of the supporters. In their view, classes used to be more clearly defined and more meaningful than they are now. There has been a gradual, naturally occurring middling, which is good.[11] If there is a degree of class consciousness that does exist in the supporters' views, it is their middle-class orientation. The middle class is the great unsung hero of their narrative. The plain folk of the middle class do their work without complaint, dream American dreams, realize some of them, and pay for those who are not as good as they are. They carry the country on their backs.

> Four or six percent of the people in our society are filthy rich, and would be totally incapable of handling that 20 percent who are in the poor category. If you stripped them out dry and took every cent away from them, you still couldn't support that 20 percent. Then you have that group that's in between, 75 percent or so. They're the moderate, that is, moderate-low to moderate-high income type people, who can manage on their own, that seem to get the burden, ultimately, for whatever reason, be it that there's a better lobby for the uppers and the lowers. And the guy caught in the middle has to pick up the tab for 99 percent of it. (14)

Render Therefore unto Me

As I have already made clear, the principal distributional norm that emerges from the supporter's narrative is an individually oriented market mechanism. The market mechanism is supported both because it contributes to the health of the entire economic system by making efficient allocations of resources and because it is properly attentive to merit and desert. As with the critics' endorsement of need satisfaction, the supporters' endorsement of the market appears through two primary channels: in the discussions of a successful economy and as an explicit principle in the discussion of specific occupational incomes.

In discussing the overall success of the entire economic system, the supporters look more to the health of the system as a whole, in terms of its total wealth-generating powers, than to the welfare of any specific group of citizens, or to a minimum level of provision that all enjoy. The size of the economic pie is their main concern, rather than how it is divided up. Some supporters take the condition of the middle class as an indicator of the state of this health, but all supporters concentrate their attention on the entire economic system. They accept the notion of a trade-off between efficiency and equality, and come down squarely on the side of efficiency.

Regarding incomes and wages, supporters endorse a market system because its allocations reflect such items as qualifications, skill, training, seniority, and education—the investments that people make in themselves by way of their own labor or payment. The wide differences in incomes generated by the market system provide the necessary incentives to produce and achieve. The market keeps the system productive. Supporters pay little attention to the satisfaction of human needs, outside of the need to be rewarded for merit. The needs of the economy come before the needs of the individual. Supporters think both that the wage market ought to function in the way that I have outlined, and also that it does in fact function this way.

> I'm not saying, for instance, that some aren't overpaid or underpaid, but I think the market has to dictate that. I may not agree with it, [but I wouldn't change it] . . . because ultimately you're hurting many of the people that you want to help. If you artificially mandate salaries, then you're ultimately going to put people out of work, because the market dictates price, and the market dictates one's value to a company. . . . [Changing incomes] is not for me to say. (10)

> I would not go for that [a redistribution of income]. I think it depends on what you have succeeded in doing. . . . If you have reached the stage where people are paying you a good salary, it's because you deserved it. And if you didn't deserve it they'd kick you out, I would hope. (11)

In the discussion of specific occupational incomes, supporters were quite reluctant to alter with their preferred incomes what they perceived to be the actual situation (table 2). They made the distribution of incomes only marginally more equal than they found them. This comes as no surprise, nor does the fact that the changes that they did make were far less equalizing than those made by the critics. Critics were perfectly egalitarian in the direction of their changes—the lowest incomes were raised the most, comparatively, and the highest incomes were decreased the most. The supporters did not show such a pattern. They raised the middle incomes the most, raised the bottom incomes somewhat, and left the top incomes alone (the income of the police officer was raised most of all). No supporter cut any occupation's income.

It is also interesting to note how the accuracy of their estimates compares with that of the critics and with reality. The supporters' estimates of the lower incomes are high in comparison with reality and with the critics' estimates. This fact may reflect the supporters' notion that conditions at or near the bottom of the income distribution are adequate, and that upward mobility and economic opportunity are available. It also may reflect the supporters' sense of the power of labor organizations. But given this pattern of comparison with the critics' data, it is notable that the supporters' preferred incomes for the lowest occupations are equivalent to those of the critics, and higher even for the production worker. This fact, however, appears to result from the supporters' comparatively higher original estimates. Regarding the relative order of the occupational incomes, the supporters duplicate the critics' pattern, by leaving the relative order unchanged, except for the press operator, which is downgraded.

In discussing the critics' income data in chapter 3, I made several comparisons with similar data on elites collected by Sidney Verba and Gary Orren (1985, chap. 8). How do the supporters' estimated and preferred incomes compare with those of the leadership groups they surveyed that were predominantly conservative, particularly the business leaders and the Republican leaders? The overall results of the comparisons are somewhat mixed. The supporters are at least as equally laissez-faire about income distribution as was any group that Verba and Orren surveyed. The ratio of the supporters' highest to lowest preferred incomes (29) is higher (less equal) than that of any of the Verba and Orren groups of respondents (business leaders were the least equalizing, with a ratio of 26.9), though I should point out that in the supporters' case the executive income represents a higher high end, and the spread of the estimated incomes is substantially higher for the supporters. Looking at the relative difference between the ratio of the lowest to the highest estimated incomes and the ratio of the lowest to the highest preferred incomes (in other words the relative difference between estimated lowest/estimated highest and preferred lowest/preferred highest, or the relative change toward equality), the supporters are less egalitarian than any of the Verba and Orren groups, with the exception of the business leaders (1985, 164). The ratio of the supporters' preferred to estimated incomes for the highest paid occupation, the executive (1.0, or no change), is higher (less equalizing) than that of any of the Verba and Orren groups (the ratio for business leaders was 0.94; for Republican leaders 0.81). The ratio of the supporters' preferred to estimated incomes for the lowest paid occupation, the bank teller (1.12), is lower (less equalizing) than that of any of the Verba and Orren groups, with the exception of business and farm leaders. The supporters' ratio for this occupation is about the same as the Republican leaders' ratio.

The supporters' views of the welfare and entitlement system will be

TABLE 2. Incomes (Annual, in K) Estimated and Preferred by Supporters, with Percentage Change, Actual Incomes, and Ratios of Top to Bottom Incomes

Occupation	Estimated	Preferred	Percentage Change	Actual
Bank teller	17	19	+12%	12
Janitor	21	22	+5%	13
Production worker	30	31	+3%	18
Police officer	25	37	+48%	22
High school teacher	29	37	+28%	26
Press operator	28	28	—	35
Engineer	46	48	+4%	43
Physician	123	123	—	106
Executive	550	550	—	1,167
Ratio of top to bottom income	32	29		97

Note: N = 5. Data are missing for two supporters, due in one case to an incomplete interview, and in the other to a failure to engage the second half of the question, concerning preferred incomes. See table 1 for the complete text of the interview question and the sources of the actual income figures.

treated in greater detail in the next narrative chapter, but it should be pointed out here that regarding minimum levels, or the standards of living to which everyone is entitled, the supporters seemed genuinely ambivalent, sometimes indifferent. A sense that there is a certain standard of living to which everyone is entitled is also accompanied by a sense that that standard is either met or exceeded by the present levels of government welfare spending.

More Like Us

It is a fact that not everyone participates in the American ethos of advancement and upward mobility. The difficulties involved in jumping onto the escalator are particularly acute for certain minorities. These problems are apparent to the supporters, though they did tend to downplay their significance. But how do they explain them? What do they claim is happening here? Supporters claim that the failure on the part of some segments of the population to tap into this ethos of advancement must say more about them than about the system itself.[12] They lack the motivation, desire, character, and self-reliance necessary in order to move up. Thus in the supporter's narrative, explanations of the large pockets of poverty and economic failure largely take the form of a politics of blame, although the narrative also contains reservations about whether the characteristics of these people that cause them to remain stagnant are their own "fault." The poor are blamed not only for failing to make it in the system, but also for ruining it for the rest of us. They take our money, drain our economic system, disfigure our cities, and threaten us with crime.

I have no problems, I've been very supportive of taking care of retarded people, mentally ill people, people who can't help themselves. I *detest* giving one dime of the taxpayer's money, of my money, to anyone who if they tried a little harder, wouldn't have to ask for it. . . . In general, people end up where they deserve to be. They may not end up where they want to be. . . . If somebody has no motivation to get off welfare, and they die on welfare, then that's what they deserved. . . .

Poor people lack the motivation not to be [poor]. And I think often the government encourages them. . . .

Poverty will never be wiped out, and we're kidding ourselves if we ever think it will. If you were to put two men on a deserted island, each with $1,000, eventually one man would wind up with $2,000 and the other nothing, and that's just the nature of the beast. We can be given equal opportunity, but we are not going to be created equal. . . .

There are people who are going to be poor people no matter what. Those who want to be poor—that's their choice. Don't come around to me complaining about it. There are some people, without realizing it, if they move into an area that's not a slum, it will soon become a slum, because of their attitude toward life. They're tearing down [a public housing project] in [a city]. [It's] maybe 40, 50 years old. It's made with brick, concrete, and steel. And it's falling apart. And yet there are people living in wood houses that are over 200 years old that are not in disrepair at all. That has to be people. If anything I think our system encourages people to not make the effort. I think everybody has different needs, and if somebody will give me enough money to satisfy my needs, then I'm not going to work to achieve any more. (12)

I feel that a person who can work and won't work should get nothing. But a person who can't work and wants to work should get something. (16)

Reading a story the other day: the only black tactical fighter pilot in the United States Navy, and he was challenging a group of high school kids, and it was in Washington, D.C., and it was obvious that they were all black. The reason there was only one of them [pilots] is because they didn't do their job, they didn't work, they didn't study. The opportunity is there, if they applied themselves. And that was his whole premise; is that it's your fault that there's only one of us at the top of the ladder.

. . . You have a bottom rung, which would be those individuals . . . that have dropped out of the work force. They are dependent on government to supply their necessary needs, and are willing to accept that level. . . . The bottom group is a drain, and I think that is where a lot of our resources are going but not being effective. Can we ever eliminate that bottom rung? I doubt it. But it's a goal. (13)

What are the sources of this blame? There is almost certainly a cognitive aspect to it. Recall that the critics were probably subject to a cognitive pressure moving them toward the softer, more individualized solutions contained in their narrative chapter "Love Thy Neighbor as Thyself," a pressure emanating from the facts of limited public resources and a policy environment that virtually precluded any profound changes in the politicoeconomic system (not to mention the inherent limitations of state-level initiatives in a national economy; see chap. 7 herein). By the same token, the supporters are subject to a pressure to blame the poor, in that the plausibility of the existence of a system with an unencumbered market that rewards merit is at least prima facie threatened by the concomitant presence of large blocs who are not prospering and who are in fact becoming worse off. Such facts require an explanation of some kind, and if the explanation does not locate the source of the problem within these blocs, then the system takes on a harsher, more sinister quality than that advanced by the supporters.

A form of racism may supply another source of blame. As it is clear to the supporters that large segments do not participate in the ethos of socioeconomic advancement, it is also clear that racial minorities are overrepresented in these segments. This also must be explained. It does appear that a streak of racism is present in the supporters' account of poverty. When race and poverty are discussed together, explanations of poverty that locate problems in the poor tend to flow into explanations that locate problems in certain posited features of minorities. This emerged most clearly when the supporters were confronted with the notion that the conditions of certain minorities—most notably blacks—in many respects have not improved significantly in recent years. Supporters also echoed a complaint made by some of the critics, that black leaders and successful black individuals had not demonstrated sufficient loyalty to other less fortunate members of their community, and had instead abandoned them on their way up.

> When I drive through [a city] on the [city] road, into the black section, I see a hundred cars double-parked in the road, littering all over the streets, some of them bottle in hand, consuming alcoholic beverages I'm sure, and some of them perhaps high because they just sniffed some coke or had a couple of marijuana cigarettes. . . . I drove through there one day. I was going up the hill, and there was a car parked in the road right in front of me, and cars parked on the side. And I tooted my horn, and a big black came over and says, "Where are you going, why are you bothering me? You wait here and take your time." I'm sure he was prompted by intoxication, and maybe he hated whites. I like blacks. I don't want you to feel I don't. When I was a kid I played in a neighborhood up the street where there were several black families, and they were great black families. . . . Many of them [blacks] want to better themselves, and do. (16)

In the case of blacks, I think a lot of good was done under Roosevelt, and ultimately during the civil rights era, to bring black Americans up to a more level playing field. But I also believe that there are many black leaders in this country who refuse to recognize why many others who were poor over the years *did* manage to get ahead. And I blame many black leaders for being out of touch, and for patronizing the very people they purport to represent by suggesting that they can't get by without a government handout, which in many instances destroys the incentive to get off welfare, to try to get ahead. And I think that's a tragedy.

. . . If everything is given to someone, some people don't have any respect for it, and that has also led to the decline of the housing stock in the public sector. . . . Some people have no respect for property. (10)

Genetically, there are things that you are capable of because of the genetic strain . . . . I'm not trying to talk like an Aryan dictator, but I know damn right well that there are things that are inborn. . . . (14)

[The recent loss in black incomes, relative to white incomes] is because of their attitudes. I don't think it's because of lack of opportunity. I think that we're certainly giving them the opportunities. . . . The minorities are in positions now where, say, 25 or 30 years ago you would never consider it [possible]. . . . Either they're not taking advantage of it [opportunity]— either by education or by applying themselves—I don't know. But I think there are more and more of them, and . . . that's why I think the gap is widening. . . . Those that want the opportunity take it and run with it. . . .

I don't think there's anything as an underclass. If there is, it's because the individual wants it. But I don't like that word because I feel that this is a free country; we have all the privileges and the rights. If they want sympathy and to be martyrs, and consider themselves an underclass, but I don't. . . . The word is offensive to me. . . . Because it means that these people feel as though they're being stepped on. (11)

I think there's an attitude within the black community that they are being discriminated against to a far greater extent than I think they are. Every time you read the paper and a black is having a problem with somebody, that black is crying discrimination. . . . I think if black people will begin to look upon themselves as equals to a much greater extent than they do, they will be accepted as equals to a much greater extent. The one thing I hate to hear is that I owe them. Even if my ancestors were all southerners and owned slaves, that's not me, and I don't owe them. (12)

What are the solutions to these problems of poverty? The supporters' discussion of the solutions brings us back to attitudes toward the "other."

Traditional efforts to help the "others" in poverty by simply giving them things, such as money, food, or housing, will not accomplish anything because they will either fail to take advantage of them to better themselves or, worse, they will ruin what they have been given. Supporters endorse one side of the dichotomy of reactions to the other that is identified by Robert Reich, a dichotomy that the critics would have us move completely beyond. The supporters wish to make the poor "more like us," but the way to do so is by being more assertive and punitive than accommodating. There must be incentives and punishments, opportunity and coercion. But ultimately, there is little that government can do.

> Those people that need [welfare] should get it. But I would suspect that a lot of people are getting it third and fourth generation, that should be forced into some kind of training program to break the cycle. . . . Once they get on the cycle we almost force them to stay. (13)

> I have not seen [a public housing project] in years, but they tell me it's a disaster. And yet when that was put together it looked like a very nice place. There is some woman, a black woman, from St. Louis—but I'm not certain—who is going around to these different housing projects and instilling this in people. . . . And she was making each one—she had a captain in each unit, and so on, and said "All right, we're going to do this." And it was perfectly marvelous, it was working. And that's what you need. You come with your leadership, and your attitude towards life. . . . If one woman can do it, then there are ten other people who can go around to different locations and do it. (11)

One issue that arises out of the supporters' views on poverty and race, similar to an issue that arose out of their views about class, is whether the supporters are genuinely committed to a notion of rewarding merit, or whether they are instead offering a rationalization for a position that serves the social and economic interests of those who are already better off. One way to investigate the issue is to observe how they treat situations of downward mobility that are analogous to those of the poor and the nonwhite, but that are also clearly due to factors beyond the control of those who are not successful. Another way is to observe how supporters treat situations in which the economic groups that they always appear to support are on the losing side of the market system. Two questions from the interview allow us to make both of these observations.

First, how would supporters divide their time and attention if they were teachers in a class half-filled with slow children and half-filled with smart children? Since it is presumably not the slow children's fault that they are slow, if the supporters side with the smarter children, then perhaps they are indeed prejudiced against the less fortunate for reasons other than those rooted in considerations of merit. In general, the supporters did in fact direct their attention to the slower children (as did the critics), though a few expressed a concern about the middle. One supporter did not address the question, insisting that the two groups should never be put together.

Another question concerned government assistance to large corporations in financial trouble. If supporters argue that individual economic failures are mostly the fault of individuals, and therefore deserved, then how do they react to the failure of large corporate enterprises? Should the corporation be left to twist in the wind? Again, the supporters were true to their principles. They universally rejected the *concept* of such government assistance, though two supporters reluctantly accepted its *practice,* if the enterprise was large enough and if certain conditions were attached to the aid.

The supporters' responses to these two questions also lead one to ask whether the narrative that they are telling is not a survival-of-the-fittest story, a reincarnation of the Social Darwinism popular in America in the late nineteenth century.[13] The response to the question about allocation of teaching time would argue against such a view, but the response to corporate bailouts seems to support it. And the moral element that supporters attach to their emphasis on self-reliance evokes the notion of a social duty involved in taking care of oneself, a notion that echoes earlier Social Darwinist theories (Sumner 1982, 98). But there are two important respects in which the supporter's narrative differs from a survival-of-the-fittest story. First, although there is a keen desire to preserve incentive in order that the economic system will remain healthy, there is no inkling in the supporter's narrative that there must be failure in order to have progress and evolution, or that opportunity is inherently limited and without the failure of the weakest the system itself will become weaker. It is theoretically possible for all to succeed, and for all to merit a comfortable life. The goals of society do not depend on inequality, though inequality is almost wholly accepted. Thus, supporters do not follow the nineteenth century apologists of the robber barons in confusing social and economic progress with species evolution (Hofstadter 1948, 167–68). Second, there is no sense of a social identity that is found in the collective struggle to conquer scarcity, an identity that each individual experiences through his own efforts to take care of himself and his family. The goal of society is the preservation of the triumphant individual himself, not what triumphant individuals, together, accomplish. I should also note that supporters themselves do not appear to be corrupt like the politicians of the Gilded Age of Social Darwinism. They do not convert their economic ideas over into the political realm in order to take what they can. Instead, drawing on that period, supporters are more of the model of Grover Cleveland, with *principled* beliefs in laissez-faire, which lead to policies that may be cold and uncaring in the eyes of many others, certainly the critics (Hofstadter 1948, 169–85).

Government as Villain

Government, particularly big, national government, is the source of much evil in the supporter's narrative. It is as big a culprit in explaining economic and social problems as the underachievers to which it is seen to cater. Its shortcomings take two forms: (1) its failure to do its tasks well and (2) the harms inflicted by much of what it does accomplish. Supporters conceive of government largely as an agent of income transfers (through welfare payments and taxation) and a regulator of business, rather than as a provider of generalized (non–means tested) services and a superintendent for the infrastructure of the economy.

Putting aside for the moment what supporters see as the problematic nature of much of what government attempts to do, government suffers from a basic ineptitude in performing its tasks. Its large-scale, impersonal bureaucratic organization and accompanying lack of incentive mechanisms constitute the sources of this ineptitude. Government feels no real pressure to produce. The problems of big government are particularly acute in the area of welfare; its inefficiency keeps much of the money from ever reaching those it is supposed to help.

> Government is a poor manager. There's no incentive. The guy managing the department that's responsible for maintaining the [public] housing doesn't have the same pressures to produce that someone in the private sector has. And I really think that sums it up. . . . There's no profit motive. . . . I don't want to paint everybody with the same broad brush, but many of the people who are in administrative positions are political appointees, and are given consideration for those jobs through political connections, which isn't nearly as pervasive as in the private sector. (10)

> I have a feeling a lot of [government] money is spent and not necessarily getting directly to where it's supposed to be going. . . . That it's lost in the bureaucracy somewhere. . . . I'm just watching what's happening here— look at what we did: we opened up this wonderful building [a new legislative office building], and look at the increase in staff. It's just taking us further away from the people that we should be meeting with all the time, making us more reliant—if we allow it to happen—upon staff. (15)

But more importantly, to the extent that government is effective in what it does, it corrupts. First, through its intrusions as a regulator, it corrupts the workings of the market, constrains freedom, and invades privacy. Second, by intruding on freedoms and by attempting to do too much for people, it corrupts self-reliance. Furthermore, its system of welfare provides an incentive structure in which people choose not to be productive.

I think government has gotten more intrusive into people's lives, and people aren't even paying attention until maybe it becomes an issue somewhere down the line for them personally—be it with taxes, be it with certain statutes that are sitting on the books that prevent or allow you to do things.

. . . Maybe the expansion of the welfare program placed people into a prison that never should have existed. If they were not in that prison, maybe they would have gone through the school system, gotten jobs, and been motivated to do something. Maybe we've locked the door without realizing it. (15)

The more government gets into something the more people are going to expect. . . . You're going to get the people who are living there [housing projects] to say "Wait a minute. Why should I bother if the government's going to come in and paint the apartment?" Or if the sink plugs up, or the dishwasher doesn't work. So, the less government we have the better off we are. (11)

Capitalism is beaten down to death by legislators because they all like to pick on the corporations. Little do they know that the number of people they employ—without some of these corporations we could not exist. (16)

I believe that our welfare system is in the condition that it is in because of the individuals that work for the welfare system—they perpetuate the welfare system, because it's their livelihood. And anytime that we see any reform legislation being offered, it's always fought by those individuals that are not served by the welfare, but that work for the welfare. . . . I'll give you a prime example. I hired a young woman, a single parent—one child, as my secretary. And she was having difficulty on the salary that the state paid her as my secretary, surviving. And so we made arrangements for her apartment, arrangements for furniture. But the welfare worker came along, and said to her, "We can pay you more if you stay home and take care of your child." So she quit the job. I see the woman a year and a half later. She now has *two* children. And so this was a perpetuation as I saw it, by the social worker in the welfare department. (13)

We make our giveaways too easy to get. (12)

One way to limit the evils perpetrated by government is to limit its available resources and to alter the ways in which it collects its resources. What kind of tax system do the supporters endorse? They prefer flat tax rates, without, or at least with drastically reduced, deductions. These taxes are fairer and are less punitive toward those who produce the most wealth.

> If I were doing a change in the federal income tax structure right now I would say everybody pays the same percentage, whatever that may be. . . . And set a bottom group that would not be involved in paying an income tax. A flat rate with no deductions. . . . I think it's more equitable . . . I don't feel that we should unequally penalize somebody who's earning more, either. (15)

> I have my own theory on taxes. I would much prefer a flat tax, with no deductions. . . . We have so many loopholes. . . . If I had my way we would have a flat tax . . . and that would treat everyone equal. (13)

> I am not one who supports repressive tax rates. If I pay 15 percent of what I have and you pay 10 percent of what you have, and the reason I'm paying 15 of what I have is because I have a little more than you, you're not paying your fair share. (12)

What then is the supporters' view of the proper role and function of government? Their vision appears very close to the traditional liberal notion of a night watchman, or umpire. There are connections between libertarian positions and the supporters' minimalist vision of the state. The supporters' vision differs from a pure libertarian vision in the coercive role advocated for government (government as drill sergeant), which was described in the previous narrative chapter. Government is the potential vehicle through which the have-nots, rather than being cared for and pampered, are induced to become productive, responsible members of society. In addition, government is supported against various challenging groups, such as open government advocates and peace activists.

> Government is there—it's their responsibility to make sure that all competition remains fair, and nobody abuses whatever power and influence they may obtain to take immorally from someone else. (12)

What is the supporters' view of their own roles as legislators within government? The supporters' vision of their own roles is most distinguished by their eschewal of what they see as special-interest groups and limited constituencies. Though they did not describe themselves as crusaders within the assembly for less government, their notion of their own role is defined largely in negative terms, in that they are not for any group in particular.

Two Other Items of Interest

Two additional items that were discussed in the previous chapter on the critic's narrative are also of interest here in the supporter's narrative. They are the supporters' views of the future of the nation and their definitions of the terms *capitalism, socialism, liberal, conservative,* and *radical.*[14] As one would no doubt expect, supporters share much more of the traditional American optimism about the nation's future than do critics. But the supporters retain serious reservations of their own, which include concerns for the moral fiber of the citizens and for fiscal restraint on the part of government.

> I believe that the country will continue to prosper. I see no indication that we will go through the throes of the Depression of the 30s. . . . I see a real change. The 60s, that group of people that are now in their 40s and 50s that came out of the 60s, they were a "gimme" generation. I see that changing drastically. The generation of the 80s, and I base this on my experience of six years of interviewing juniors and seniors [in high school] for [a legislative program]. The students that came to us six years ago: "When's lunch? How much am I going to get paid? Do I have to work on Saturday? When's the next party?" The students that I interviewed this year: "How can I get this into my résumé? What can I do that will help me in the future? Are there some things that I can do that will give me some insight into how government works?" Almost a 180-degree turn. This generation is going to be looking for the things that they can do to better themselves and the society that they're in. That's the difference I see between the 60s and the 80s. (*)

> [The future] depends on who's running the country at the time. If we have a liberal up there, he could run it into the ground, with big giveaway programs. I think if we have a fiscal conservative then the country's going to do just great. (11)

The overall style of the supporters' definitions of terms reflects a high degree of ideology, or a value-laden quality (Putnam 1973, 34–35). Liberal and conservative were defined in respectively negative and positive terms. A liberal was described as a profligate spender and an advocate of overactive, top-down government, while a conservative was championed as attempting to hold the mark on public spending. They tended to ally themselves with the conservative mantle, particularly with respect to the economic facet of their definitions, though some of them also thought of themselves as moderates. Capitalism was defined in positive terms, and sometimes equated with freedom and democracy. Concerning socialism, supporters committed what the critics identified as a dangerous fallacy, by conflating socialism with communism and totalitarianism. While the critics viewed radicalism as an extreme of any opinion and located its essence in the attitude toward existing organizations and structures, most supporters considered radicalism solely in terms of the extreme Left.

> Liberals . . . have the answers for everything. They invariably cost you money. They require the involvement of government in developing a program, and invariably it shows people what they should be doing and how it ought to be done, from a governmental viewpoint. . . . Government wants to go in and solve the problems more from the top down, rather than having it develop from the inside out . . . . (14)

> With liberals, their first attempt at a solution is to spend money. . . . Often it aggravates the problem. A liberal will attack the results of the problem. I think the best example is all the urban programs we've had—there is no question that there are serious problems in our cities . . . I think our cities are much worse today than they were when we started attacking the problems of the cities, despite the fact that we have spent across this country billions and billions of dollars. . . .
> Liberals seem to feel that you reach a point where you have too much [money], and you shouldn't have that much. And that somebody should have more regardless of whether or not they've put forth the effort to gain that. (12)

> Liberals are people who are willing to give the store away. They almost border on the radical. I can't understand their reasoning or their thinking. I think they go after a cause, and it's almost like tunnel vision. (11)

> Socialism, Nazism, communism, they're all the same; the only difference is with socialism, you can vote it out of office if it doesn't work—which it won't work. . . . The government runs the economy . . . decides everything. In capitalism, everyone is free; every man for himself. The incentives are great. (12)

> Some of the socialist countries later develop into communistic states. They start off with helping people, helping do this, do that. The first thing you know a cancer has erupted, and you either destroy it immediately or let it lie terminally, and then it's too late. (16)

> Radical . . . destructive activists who want to do it by force. I can remember during the 60s . . . during a public hearing, the college kids all coming

in with their long hair and beards, . . . the American flag sewed on the seat of their pants. It just made me want to vomit. (16)

Ambivalences in the Narrative

In spite of the supporters' high level of approval for the economic system, they recognize a number of circumstances in which the system fails to realize its ideal, and in which problems or failures are not due to the characteristics of the individuals who have failed. These recognitions are rooted in the supporters' own experiences or firsthand observations of problems. They are the problems that affect the middle and upper end of the income distribution, as well as the poor. Most notable among these problems are the difficulties encountered in securing affordable housing and the difficulties small businesses face in gaining access to capital. The cost of housing in Connecticut is among the highest in the nation, and supporters have either experienced struggles of their own in affording a home or have seen their own children, or others like them, face similar struggles. People who are known to be decent, hard working, and moral are having troubles; the market is not functioning as it ought to function. Consequently, supporters assert that the government can do more in the area of making housing available, and identify housing as an issue on which they are more "liberal" than they are on most other issues.

> My two boys can't live in my town, and that's wrong. Because they simply, as starting out, they can't afford to buy land or a house in the town that they grew up in. That has to be corrected in some way; I don't know how. (*)

Supporters have also either experienced or witnessed difficulties on the part of small businesses and entrepreneurs in getting access to needed capital. They have observed that large corporations are sometimes able to drive smaller enterprises out of business through underselling and collusion. This occurs regardless of the diligence and effort of the small enterprises. There is thus a desire in these cases for some measure of countervailing power or balance, but it is unclear exactly where such power should come from.

The supporters who are women exhibit ambivalences of a more general kind. There is among them a relatively deeper concern for those who are on the bottom, a less materialistic perspective, as well as a more compassionate tone throughout their narrative. But the compassion is limited to the individual, interpersonal level (as it tended to be in the critic's narrative); it is not carried through to social programs or policy proposals. In addition, the impulse toward compassion and understanding is most prevalent on the more noneconomic social issues, such as gay rights, for example, rather than on purely economic and distributional issues.

We have to go back to very basic things, such as home, family, values, what a family instills in its children and carries on with it. And then into the larger world, how they treat others, and how they look at others, and how they view others—whether they try to help or not help. . . . I think . . . if you go back to the elements of what this nation was founded on, which was initiative, risk, but everybody worked together and tried to forge ahead and make the best of the situation. I guess that justice was built into that. . . . I guess I tend to look at it more in a social—how people treat one another, how people care for one another, or do not care for one another, because we are people, and I guess that's important to me. . . . We have the rules, but it's the rules that people inherit, the unwritten rules, that bother me, because a lot of people don't follow those. (*)

I don't know whether they [the poor] are happy or unhappy. They may be very satisfied with their lives. And their values are obviously very different, and maybe we shouldn't thrust our values on them. It does become a query for me . . . because I really want to know what their feelings are. . . . I don't know how the poor children feel in terms of being poor. And the contacts have just been lost. (*)

What bothers me is that there's such an awful emphasis on materialism right now. . . . I do see a tremendous amount of it in a lot of the families in my area, and I don't understand it. (*)

I think people have to have a feeling of self-worth, and it's incumbent upon us to help them gain that feeling of self-worth, which is not always through financial reward. (*)

The Personal

I think there's enough choice now that people tend to be happy, or content [with their jobs]. I hope I'm not in a dream. . . . When I worked at [a factory]—I was just a high school kid—there were other young kids that were working there that wasn't a summer job [for them]. And I can remember thinking, are they going to be doing this for the rest of their lives? And yet they seemed to be very happy doing what they were doing. They were learning a skill, and it was a skill that they were proud of learning. . . . I could barely take the summer [in a nonmanufacturing position in the company]. . . . It was just too mundane. (*)

When you're brought up in the suburbs in [a rich] county, everything is run by who belonged to what club, you know, what family, stuff like that.

Which I've got to tell you, I enjoyed, because I didn't know anything else. . . . I had a very nice upbringing and a very happy one, and I can't fault it—that was the league my mother and dad were in and both my [siblings] and I enjoyed it to the fullest extent. But as you grow older, you begin to see, you know, another part. (*)

I guess I grew up a little rich kid, went to private schools. (*)

I was in the army. It was a slow evening, and I was in a drugstore, and I bought the book, *Conscience of a Conservative,* by Barry Goldwater. And I spent the evening reading that. A few days later I went back to the same drugstore—it was a slow evening—and I bought another book, *The Liberal Answer to the Conservative Challenge,* by Eugene McCarthy. And I read that. And that's when I decided that Barry Goldwater made a hell of a lot more sense than Gene McCarthy. It was at that point that I decided that he wasn't such an ogre. (*)

I was born and raised on a farm. . . . So I don't see that barrier. Take a little farm boy . . . and become a senator in Connecticut. So I can't say that there have been barriers placed in front of me. (*)

I'm a product of the East side of [a city]. We would be considered from a moderate to a low-moderate income group in those days—I'm talking going back to my childhood. And yet I can tell you almost every one of those people . . . moved out of that neighborhood. . . . Some of them are real success stories. I think there was a hell of a challenge. (*)

We still haven't recovered from the 60s, in my opinion. . . . I think that . . . a large percentage of the teachers and professors that we have in colleges today came out of that 60s culture. And just today reading an article in *The Hartford Courant* about a fellow here in Connecticut that graduated in 1968 . . . from East Hartford or West Hartford High School, and they followed those [graduates]; where are they, what they're doing. And he marched in the parades against the Vietnam War, and all of those activities that grew out of that culture at that particular time. He now is an attorney for the federal government. I would expect that some of the decisions he makes are still tempered by what he saw and what he participated in in the 60s. I'm sure that some of the approaches that were used in education came out of that culture. We're seeing the effects of this in our education system today . . . when the largest city in the state has less than 50 percent of its student body able to pass the minimum test. . . . It will take another generation or two for the attitudes that were developed in the

60s at our colleges not to be a part of the underlying philosophy of the professors. . . .

When I was growing up as a youngster—it was in the late 30s and early 40s—it was a time when everybody was motivated to be in the right mode. (*)

As with the critics, personal experience appears to play an essential role in the construction of the supporter's narrative. In contrast with the critic's narrative, there is not a generalized theme or type of experience. In addition, later experiences exert a comparatively greater influence on the supporters' beliefs. This is particularly the case for those supporters who are (or were) involved in business or administration. Nonetheless, the supporters' experiences do coalesce in their effect on the narrative. One supporter's experience of growing up in, and ultimately out of, a poor neighborhood contributed to his belief that anyone can be upwardly mobile, if they will only persevere. Another supporter's views were heavily influenced by experiences in business. If there is a theme, it is that many of the supporters lacked firsthand experiences of poverty or economic hardship, and most had little knowledge of the lives led by the poor. Those that did have such experiences, such as the supporter just described, grew up during the Depression.

Supporters grew up in either Republican or conservative Democratic families, which for the most part were politically inactive beyond voting. As with the critics, supporters did not simply inherit their views from their parents (though they are substantially in agreement with them), but rather developed their views through a dynamic interplay of family, personal, social, business, and political experience.

Some other information about the supporters is also of interest in considering their beliefs. For many of them their first formal political experiences, as well as their first real grapplings with political issues, came relatively late in life. They are older and whiter than the rest of the senate, but not more male. Supporters possess more assets and earn slightly more income than the other senators, yet they are also less educated.[15] While critics tended to come from urban districts, supporters came from upper or upper-middle class suburban districts. As in the case of the critics, it would appear that such a relation is a mutually reinforcing one; supporters are likely to fare better in suburban environments. In contrast to the critics, there is no overall pattern of recruitment; some supporters were recruited to pursue public office by others, while others were ambitious self-starters.[16]

I was sitting in rotary [club] one day, complaining about something. . . . [My friends] said to me, "If you're so damn mad about it, why don't you do something about it?" And we laughed and went on our way. Two or three weeks later the subject came up again. So I said, "You guys are out of your gourd to think that I would run for state senate." (*)

I always had my eye on the state senate seat. That was the only elective office that I had my eye on, that I thought about. (*)

The Political Theory of the Supporter's Narrative

Of what kind of political theory might this narrative be a part? For what political theory might this narrative form the normative base? In presenting the supporter's narrative, I have commented along the way on the connections, as well as the breaks, between the narrative and different political theories, mostly conservative. Before leaving the supporter's narrative for the ambivalent's narrative, let me now briefly summarize what the connections and breaks appear to add up to.

Though this narrative is in many respects consistent with the New Right, that is, the deregulatory, anti–welfare state, free market economic conservatism of the 1980s, there are several points of tension between the supporter's narrative and this brand of conservatism.[17] First, the supporters demonstrate a concern, at least at the level of the individual, over shortcomings of character and restraint. This concern is combined with a reassertion of traditional forms of authority that extend beyond the reassertions of traditional religious and social authority identified within the New Right itself. Reminiscent of older conservatisms, there is a paternalistic concern for the moral life of the individual, which does not easily fit with the individually acquisitive attitude of much of the new conservatism. Second, there is a positive role for the state in the supporter's narrative as a keeper and promoter of character and moral values, through punishments if necessary. Though selfish and/or lazy, human nature is not taken completely as a given by the supporters; however, to be effective policies must also employ incentives. There is a reform impulse of sorts embedded in the supporter's narrative, although it is not a particularly compassionate one. Last, there is lacking in the supporter's narrative the neopopulism that many students of the New Right have identified. Supporters are not against bigness per se, only big government that is economically intrusive and overly redistributive. Corporate management is endorsed.[18] Regarding all these points, however, note that many observers of the New Right have also identified similar tensions and contradictions within it.

This apparently problematic set of concerns within the supporter's narrative is also reminiscent of Samuel Huntington's (1957) situational definition of conservatism, where conservatism is marked by its affirmation of existing institutions and conventions.[19] The supporters are indeed supportive of the authority of most of the contemporary political and social institutions, with the exception of the state's authority in economic and socioeconomic matters. Supporters may also display what is termed radicalism by Huntington's criteria in their critique of the institutions of the welfare state, but this critique appears to be based in part on the supporters' view that this institution violates other, more important conventions and institutions. Thinking of the supporter's narrative as an underpinning of contemporary conservatism in these situational terms, however, does little to illuminate it based on its actual content versus its relative ideological positioning.

Finally, while the supporter's narrative is clearly not a facet of the more traditional, European brand of conservatism, there are several points of contact between them. Although a reverence for the state qua state is completely absent in the narrative, there is support for the state on law and order grounds and as a taskmaster for the poor. Although there is little sense of the state as the repository and the promoter of moral values, there is a notion of the state acting to reform the poor. At the same time, although there is no reverence for an upper class, nor is there a support for hierarchy and inequality per se, success is certainly admired and the incentives offered by inequality are considered positively. Although there is no necessary reverence for the past, nor for tradition, nor is there a sense of a pact between generations, or of a set of collected wisdoms handed down from generation to generation, supporters do worry that moral character and virtue are in decline.[20] Finally, and perhaps most importantly, although there is little suspicion of capitalism or distrust of the impulse toward self-interest, there is a concern for individual moral character.

Like the critic's narrative, the supporter's narrative is profoundly reformist rather than revolutionary. To be sure, the object of reform has been turned upside down. But the supporter's narrative is not based on class conflict, or Social Darwinism; all persons can come along and work and be well rewarded. Though the supporters may exhibit a relatively harsh attitude toward the poor, the poor can change, and they can be changed. But in changing, the poor do not undergo the kind of transformation of consciousness that the critics hope for on the part of those persons who practice injustice. Rather, they are simply exercising diligence and self-control. The enterprise of reform remains within the confines of a more static notion of human personality, within the confines of the constrained world vision of the supporter's narrative.

CHAPTER 5

The Ambivalent's Narrative

Remember, I'm an egalitarian, not a liberal. (17)

[L]ife is both fair and unfair. (20)

It would be tempting to assume that what I have called the "ambivalent's narrative" consists simply of an amalgamation of disparate parts of the critic's and supporter's narratives, that it is only a residual category of responses lacking an evident narrative structure (albeit a large residual category). This is not the case. Though the ambivalent's narrative does indeed share significant characteristics with each of the other two narratives, it remains its own distinct account.

Ambivalents struggle with many of the same concerns about social and distributional justice that engage the critic's narrative, but they do so against the backdrop of a keen sense of the limits of government effectiveness, as well as a concern for a healthy, growing economy, which they perceive to be at tension with the equalizing demands of justice. Thus the ambivalents' views are informed by a perception of the classic trade-off between equality and efficiency. They are, of course, not alone in this regard, for the negotiation of the apparent trade-off between equality and efficiency constitutes the field over which much of the battle between contemporary liberalism and conservatism has been waged. As Arthur Okun (1975) has observed, we might think of this trade-off as a bucket that carries resources from the rich to the poor. Unfortunately the bucket leaks; in making the transfer we inevitably lose some resources. The relevant questions are thus: How much leakage do we tolerate before we disapprove such transfers, and what kinds of transfers are worth given rates of leakage?

The outcome of the ambivalents' struggle with this question yields many points of contact between their narrative and a set of views that has become known as neoliberalism (Rothenberg 1984). Both ambivalents and neoliberals, for example, tend to describe themselves as social liberals and fiscal conservatives. In fact, in ideological terms ambivalents can be thought of as neoliberals without great distortion. I will summarize these points of contact in the final section of this chapter.

In the ambivalent narrative's story line, heroes and villains are less starkly drawn than they are in the other two narratives, and their characters are in general seen in more problematic terms. To invoke once again Jerome Bruner's conception of narrative form, narratives contain "plights into which characters have fallen as a result of intentions that have gone awry either because of circumstances, of the 'character' of 'characters,' or most likely of the interaction between the two" (1986, 21). In the ambivalent's case, these plights are more the result of circumstances than of character. And the ambivalent's narrative offers a less emotive, cooler account of circumstances. Although it does locate socioeconomic victims, they are neither perceived to be the products of a particularly blameworthy system on the one hand, nor are they themselves the objects of blame on the other.

As in the other two narratives, I have isolated four core episodes or chapters in the ambivalent's narrative that largely organize the senators' views. I have called the four chapters "A Crimeless Victim," "Cleaning up the Margins," "Educate! Educate!" and "Government as Empowered Umpire." "A Crimeless Victim" describes the actual conditions of the market economy and its distributional outcomes, and socioeconomic upward mobility. "Cleaning up the Margins" relates the ambivalents' notions of distributional fairness and their suggested approaches to correct the perceived problems of distribution and upward mobility. "Educate! Educate!" describes the approach toward the deeper socioeconomic problems that are perceived to lie behind the distributional problems. And "Government as Empowered Umpire" sets forward the significant though decisively limited role of government. Here, the ambivalents' sense of the limitations of government effectiveness in promoting economic fairness, along with their concern with securing strong systemic economic performance and efficiency, appears to lead the narrative toward an emphasis on educational programs and governmental enforcement of civil rights instead of economic rights. As in the other two narratives, the material within these four chapters overlaps, but here each chapter is infused by a profound ambivalence and internal tension that is the trademark of the narrative as a whole.

An Overview of the Narrative

Ambivalents generally support the market system and its method of distribution. In their view distribution should be based most heavily on merit, considered as a combination of one's effort—primarily labor—and the quality of one's performance—primarily output. The market is seen to respond to these values pretty well in most cases.[1] Fairness resides in following these rules of distinguishing merit *within* market transactions, and in maintaining genuinely open access *to* the market itself. Thus, like both the supporters and critics, ambivalents look for conditions of upward mobility and equal opportunity as indicators of economic fairness; equal opportunity is once again a powerful concept. And ambivalents believe that, for the most part, conditions of equal opportunity exist and the mechanisms of upward mobility are firmly in place.

But although they do not wish to change the basic structure of the distributional system as they find it, they are nonetheless left queasy about this system, due to their recognition of the large number of those who either fail to thrive in it or do not participate in it at all. They perceive that many people, especially members of racial minorities, encounter serious difficulties in their efforts to advance themselves solely by dint of their own labor and diligence; avenues of opportunity are not always open to them. Granted, the very concept of a market implies failures as well as successes (it may in fact depend on failure, though note that the supporters take a different view). The ambivalents are aware of this, but they also seem to sense that the failures may undercut the viability and the value of the system itself. They remain particularly concerned about the social and racial patterns of market outcomes.

Explanations of the patterns of poverty and lack of economic achievement take a historical approach in the narrative; forces such as the delayed and enduring effects of past racism or rapid changes in the economic system that displace certain people or leave them at a competitive disadvantage are seen to account for much of the perceived problem. The main reason why certain people have a more difficult time participating in the American ethos of upward mobility is their lack of sufficient education and the skills required in the newer economic enterprises. Thus, though many individual cases of socioeconomic failure are perceived to be the most proximate result of aspects of those individuals who have failed, the existence of these aspects is not seen as the fault of those individuals.

Though the ambivalents locate serious violations of distributional fairness resulting from these aspects and historical circumstances, they believe that there are enduring limits to what government can do to change them. Government is inherently inefficient due to both its large size, and as a collective, public organization, its severance from profit-oriented incentives. Even worse, through overactivism government can be counterproductive; that is, it can pervert those very characteristics that allow individuals to compete and succeed in the market system. The ambivalents do retain many of the ultimate goals of welfare liberalism's social activism, but at the same time they perceive deep-seated problems in the attempt to achieve them through government activity.

There is, then, a strong conviction in the ambivalent's narrative of a trade-off between equality and efficiency, which in part takes the form here of a trade-off between being fair and helping those who really do not deserve to have less, and damaging incentive and initiative—the two essential components of a private market economic system that is perceived to work pretty well, at least in general. But for the ambivalents this trade-off is not just a contest between basic fairness and the provision of needs and the maintenance of an incentive system necessary to a growing economy; it is also a contest between the values of cooperation and competition in the promotion of that growth.

> I think any system that's going to be successful has to be incentive-oriented. Whether that incentive be the common welfare, or the ability of individuals to thrive, the incentive has to be there. (17)

> What happens when Calvinism meets Buddha? Or Mohammed? . . . Calvinism gave birth to the industrial revolution; Buddha controls technology. . . . We're seeing a lot of this coming out now with short-term profits. Remember Calvin taught us that God loves those whose fields were fertile, covenants are fair, children were blessed. But Reaganomics, situational ethics, some of the most honored people are thieves; I swear. . . . The business of America is to make money, I guess. . . . (33)

Granted, in both the critic's and the supporter's narratives, one can also find perceived trade-offs between equality and efficiency. In the critic's narrative, however, efficiency is a less central concern; other concerns such as the provision of needs and the engendering of mutual understanding enjoy a preferred status. In the supporter's narrative, the trade-off is easily accepted, and is itself used as a reason to endorse policies of efficiency over equality. For ambivalents, this trade-off remains decidedly problematic. In grappling with it, ambivalent senators emphasize careful government spending, targeted on areas where they believe it can be the most effective, such as child development and early education. And where it is targeted, they emphasize acting positively to permanently change outcomes, rather than creating self-perpetuating systems of public spending.

Though ambivalents believe that the economic system works pretty well, that is, that it extends the genuine possibility for individual advancement and a rough equality of opportunity, they also recognize, as I have already noted, that there remain for many individuals significant challenges to upward mobility and socioeconomic success. This recognition, combined with their belief in an equality-efficiency trade-off, leads them into a delicate balancing act when it comes to addressing distributional problems. This act requires the reckoning of the interests of disadvantaged and powerless individuals against the interests of the haves and the established business and professional community. Such a reckoning is in turn designed to ensure a balance in the workings of the market; the ambivalents think that though it works reasonably well, if left completely alone the market has the potential to fall out of balance, and more specifically, to become skewed in favor of the haves.

The ambivalents' attempts to remedy wrongs thus take the form of controlling externalities, or, as I have called them, attempts to clean up the margins. "Cleaning up the Margins" indicates, in fact, the ambivalents' larger approach toward the entire question of justice. The search for justice becomes an eternal quest to first discover and then establish the appropriate balance between normatively legitimate but competing interests. In contrast, the supporter's narrative has a more uniform conception of interests—rendered in a way that favors the upper strata, while the critic's narrative rejects the normative legitimacy of many of the interests of those in the upper strata.

Education is the most prominently featured component of the ambivalents' social policy; it is the principal means through which the state can provide individuals with the equipment to enter into and succeed within the market. The ambivalents place particular importance on early education and programs of early development. Not only do these programs complement the ambivalents' predisposition against interfering with the market, they are also thought to have the highest probability of success. In addition to education and programs of early educational support, the most distinctive role for government advocated by the ambivalents is that of a vigorous protector and expander of rights. This role of government appears to follow in large part from the perceived tension between social justice and economic growth. The limits on what government can and/or should do in strictly economic terms lead to other methods of addressing socioeconomic problems, which do not entail direct government activity in matters of economic production and resource distribution. The expansion of rights, most notably civil rights, is one such method, although this does entail a high degree of government regulation of some hiring practices. Like education, civil rights offer a less explicitly redistributive cut at these problems, by opening up avenues of access.[2] One could argue, in fact, that although it too has incurred its share of attacks, the field of civil rights has constituted the sole growth sector of the industry of American liberalism during the past twenty years.[3]

The norms and ideals of the ambivalent's narrative are cut from the heart of the traditional American moral landscape: opportunity, achievement, liberty, freedom. One of the ways in which I distinguished some of the values of the critic's narrative from this tradition (although the critics shared many of these traditional values as well) was through the concepts of negative and positive liberty. The critic's narrative emphasizes a more positive notion of liberty, a liberty that involves development and positive empowerment, as well as protection from intrusion. In contrast, the ambivalent's narrative works within a more negative liberty perspective; ambivalents believe that a condition of freedom exists when there are private spheres within which individuals can act without constraint. Thus, regarding the theoretical conception of liberty, the ambivalent's narrative is comparatively closer to the supporter's narrative, but ambivalents separate themselves from the supporters by their perception of how deeply and widely this conception is realized in everyday life. Ambivalents perceive that a significant number of people do not in fact enjoy wide spheres of unencumbered activity; their liberties are constrained by the activities of others in the marketplace or by the conditions that they have inherited. Ambivalents thus believe that the public authority must act positively to balance these private activities and to aid people in overcoming their inherited conditions so that all may enjoy a substantial measure of freedom.

Certain other features of the ambivalent's narrative also merit prefatory comments. In chapter 2, I mentioned that the ambivalent's narrative is marked by a motif that is not as prevalent in the other two narratives. This is the technical approach toward socioeconomic problems. I have already described an element of this technical approach, in the ambivalents' hesitancy to impose blame. This hesitancy to impose blame is part of a more general aspect of the style of the ambivalent's narrative, which tends toward a coolness of approach in contrast to the more highly emotive, blame-imposing styles of the supporters and critics. The technical approach is also distinguished by a general pragmatism, a proclivity to reach for facts and specific, incremental policy proposals, and an emphasis on prioritizing and targeting programs to specific social problems.

In sketching the critic's and supporter's narratives, I argued that in their own ways, both narratives are reformist in nature. In contrast, the ambivalent's narrative is far less reformist. There is little emphasis in the narrative on changing the source of the perceived problems of injustice; indeed, the sources themselves remain somewhat murky in the ambivalent's account. I also noted that certain elements of the other two narratives sometimes take on an evangelical cast. There is far less of an evangelical cast to the ambivalent's narrative; although ambivalents wish to help persons to achieve, they leave people's characters pretty much as they find them. Part of the source of this attitude may lie in the fact that the distributional problems that the narrative identifies are not perceived to run as deeply as those identified by the supporters and critics. Ambivalents apparently think that these problems may in fact be overcome through the careful, reasoned application of practical measures, rather than through the transformation of basic human attributes (as they are respectively perceived by the other two narratives).

The view of human nature itself that emerges in this narrative is thus an ambivalent one as well. It does not fit as neatly into either of Thomas Sowell's constrained or unconstrained visions as do the notions held respectively by the supporters and critics. Human nature appears more static than dynamic in the ambivalent's narrative (closer to the supporter's constrained vision than the critic's unconstrained vision), but at the same time, in being static it does not pose intractable problems for social progress (closer to the critic's notion than the supporter's). Human nature is thus left comparatively undefined.

In contrast to the other two narratives, tellers of the ambivalent's narrative include senators from both parties. The influence of party on beliefs thus becomes much more conceptually complicated when ambivalent senators are considered as a group. One way to get a handle on this influence is to investigate whether the ambivalent senators in each party tend to have different views on certain issues or stress different things. Such an investigation indicates that party membership appears to have only a limited effect on the ambivalents' beliefs. Party membership overlays the ambivalent's narrative but does not change its essential character, much in the same way that the effects of gender overlay the supporter's narrative. But party does, however, seem to have a significant effect on the assumptions made about others' beliefs. Republican and Democrat ambivalents are saying roughly the same things, but they appear to be carrying on arguments with different sets of people in their responses. Republicans seem to be arguing with both the Democrats, whom they consider to be more liberal than they are, and with a subset of Republicans whom they consider to be more conservative; while Democrats seem to be arguing solely with the Republicans, whom they consider to be more conservative. This indicates that Republican ambivalents have a sense of themselves as being unusual within their own party, a perception that is verified when we tally up the numbers of each narrative type (15 of 24 Democrats are ambivalents, compared with 4 of 11 Republicans).

In describing the critic's and supporter's narratives, I also commented on the effects of gender. It plays a comparable role in the ambivalent's narrative. In particular, for those ambivalents who are women, the motif of the technician is mitigated and there is a comparatively greater emphasis placed on understanding and empathy.

The ambivalent's narrative is not the only narrative where one finds ambivalence in beliefs. Recall that the critic's and supporter's narratives are also marked by certain discrete paradoxes and ambivalences. The ambivalent's narrative, however, appears to constitute a more generally paradoxical position. Ambivalents think that the system is fair, but that it is not fair; that it works well, but that it does not work. Internal contradictions run high in the ambivalent's narrative. These contradictions threaten to rend apart the narrative, and spawn an ever-present struggle to keep the account coherent. During the interviews themselves, this struggle was palpable; as they moved through their accounts, the senators seemed to wrestle with the lines of their own story in an effort to keep them concordant.

There is thus a deep tension that pervades the entire narrative. The narrative is a distinctively modern story, punctuated by its wrestling with morality within perceived constraints, and its attempt to somehow move beyond these constraints; with its uneasiness with the world, and its pragmatic assertion that it is of this world. It does not accuse, but neither does it accept.

A Crimeless Victim

"A Crimeless Victim" is a somewhat tangled, self-contradictory story that contends that society is relatively fair—largely defined as openness of access, but that also attempts to explain why so many people fail to sufficiently participate in the socioeconomic system. Individual tellings of this chapter vary to some extent in the degree to which they are framed by this ambivalence, but they all share it. They also share a characteristic that separates them from both the harsh critique of the socioeconomic system found in "The Big Fish Eat the Little Fish" of the critic's narrative and the support of that system found in "Every Man a Trump" of the supporter's narrative: a lack of a moralistic tone.

In spite of the ambivalents' perception that there are large numbers of those who do not thrive in the socioeconomic system, they stand by the assertion that the system is by and large fair. It may have shortcomings regarding the meeting of each individual's needs and it may at times allow a few individuals with ability and greed to pervert its workings, but overall it rests on a basic framework of fairness, which is visible in its day to day operations. The problems are not embedded in the system itself; they are correctable at the level of the individual. And in any case, the system is much more just than other extant economic systems.

> I think [our society] is the most just that has ever existed. And I think overall it's pretty reasonably just, considering the obstacles that there are. . . . I think this country has come a long way in the last 30, 40 years in ending discrimination. It's made enormous achievements, and I think it continues to do so. . . . Just this last session in the legislature there was a measure that prohibits discrimination against people who have handicaps or who are mentally retarded—discrimination in housing. There are whole new frontiers where this country is way ahead of the rest of the world in that area. (20)

> Overall, I'd say that our society has the best structure for justice of any society. But our justice is administered by human beings, so it's always subject to inequities, interpretation. (17)

> I think by comparison to most other [societies] in the world, and in an overall sense, yes [we are just]. I think there are still significant pockets

of our population who have not yet had the opportunity to compete on a level . . . playing field. There are still long-term discriminatory problems. . . . In the overall sense, yes; but we still have a ways to go with it. (30)

Our society is very unjust, and then I would say as a rejoinder, but more just than all the rest. . . . I'm trying to equalize everybody so that everybody has the same shot at the system. . . . This is all the ideal; I'm pragmatic enough that I've got to function day to day here. . . .

I think that's one of the greatnesses about America, that one can really amass a fortune in the course of a generation. That's pretty unique. (24)

If, as I have already suggested, the ambivalents view justice primarily as consisting of access to the economic system and responsiveness to merit, then it follows that they will look for conditions of upward mobility and economic opportunity as indices of justice. Once again, in the ambivalents' view there are obvious shortcomings in the state of upward mobility and opportunity, but in the main a mechanism of mobility is firmly in place; the challenge is in bringing more people into this mechanism so that they can take advantage of it. It is acknowledged by the ambivalents that those at the lower end of the socioeconomic spectrum have a more difficult time availing themselves of this mechanism, but they maintain that even for these people, the prospect is realizable. And although the ambivalents, like the critics, believe that some of the problems in upward mobility among the worst off are quite deeply ingrained in the system, they do not perceive these problems to be the result of any one person's or group's *agency*—in particular the agency of the group at the top of the corporate order (as do many of the critics). And once again, the conditions of opportunity and mobility in America compare favorably with those of other nations. The best summary of this ambivalence is found in one senator's assertion of the existence of upward mobility, an assertion that sounded at the time as if it were being made more to the senator himself than to the interviewer.

People have a lot more control over their destiny than I think they realize. I think work is rewarded. People *can* move up, damnit. (24)

Other ambivalent senators had similar comments.

I think in this country you can do it [move up]. I don't think it's that hard, because of economics. . . . Economics is such an overriding concern in this society, more so than in any other society, that there is upward mobility. . . . There are obviously exceptions. I think the minorities do have a tougher time, no question about that. (18)

I think it's hard to move up the ladder, no matter what income group you come from; harder if you start with nothing. But easier than it is in any other country in the world. (20)

I think we have opportunity in America. The degree to which it is equal will require eternal vigilance, because we also have a system that is incentive-oriented, but really highlights the individual, and focuses on individual performances. Unchecked, there's a tendency for greed to be the dominant factor. When greed is the dominant factor, that would mean that you have a situation of the haves and the have-nots. (17)

I think for all its drawbacks and all its limitations [our society] still provides people with that opportunity, who would make the effort. They have to be extremely motivated, but I think they can still succeed. But there are people who need more than that; they don't have that ability, that impetus. . . . I don't feel hopeless. I feel that we have a wonderful opportunity. People are taking it; those who don't are fettered by circumstances that we have a responsibility to remove, to better. (26)

I think in this country you can move from any class to another class with more ease than anywhere else. But the likelihood is that someone born into a family in the very poor is probably going to stay in that group the rest of their life, though there are opportunities to get out. It's just much harder. . . . The vast majority of people in this country, maybe 90 percent, fall in between, and I think people just sort of slide up and down, and their children shift this way and that way, and there really is no strong class structure. . . . I think people have in this country a greater opportunity to live a life based on their own effort, and not feel that they tried for X but the system forced them to settle for only half, or 40 percent or 30 percent of that X. . . .
    But I don't think anyone deserves to be poor. . . . I mean, I can sit there and say, "look, [some] people have not made any effort to go beyond, in fact they won't even avail themselves of the opportunities that are sitting there . . . to help them move up." . . . Therefore maybe I won't lose sleep over them, but to say that they deserve to be where they are tends to lead to some sort of punitive sense towards the issue. (32)

For those of us in the middle, I think it's possible to make it up, and many do. That to me is the enduring greatness of America: You can do that. If you're in the bottom, I think it's near impossible to climb that mountain past the middle and get to the peak; near impossible, but not totally impossible. The things that are most likely to stop you are education, child care—lack of it, and opportunity. (22)

How then does the narrative account for the existence and persistence of poverty, which it recognizes as a fairly widespread and salient feature of the economic landscape? The previous excerpts on the presence of upward mobility preview the answer to this question. In the most immediate terms, poverty is seen to result from a lack of the qualities necessary for upward mobility; foremost among these are a sufficient education and a self-perception and self-expectation for success. Ambivalents agree that one's early life experiences largely condition the likelihood that these qualities will take hold. Thus, patterns of poverty are thought to result from patterns of early development, and poverty in general is explained from this perspective. The environment of poverty hinders the development of an outlook that values education and initiative.[4] When someone is born poor, everything surrounding her reinforces her continued existence in a poor state: a lack of resources, a general environment and ethos of stagnation, and an overpowering sense of hopelessness.

This view obviously rubs against the ambivalents' notion that economic opportunities do in fact exist—and the ambivalents seem to be aware of this tension, but they attempt to resolve it by arguing that if public and private efforts were effectively directed at the early stages of development, then those who are presently poor could and would enter into the system of upward mobility that is currently in place. Thus ambivalents do not hold those in poverty accountable for perpetuating the lack of early development, as do the supporters. In the ambivalents' view, poor persons have more immediate concerns, such as survival. It is not their fault that they are poor. Nonetheless, ambivalents do reach for aspects about poor persons themselves in order to explain why poverty exists in the first place. At the same time that ambivalents do not blame the poor for being poor, they do not blame either the system, or a supposed elite that controls that system, for perpetuating poverty. Their views are not infused by the moral outrage over the conditions of poverty that permeates the critic's narrative.

> I think the problem probably is that for a lot of people there is the perception . . . that you can't make that choice . . . you get to a point—if you've been on an assembly line all your life, and you're forty-five years old, the options of moving ahead and changing suddenly aren't very real for you. On the other hand, I think there's evidence, particularly for women in this society, some degree for minorities, and I think also with increasing higher education, I think for everyone in general, that children of families who have been at the lower and middle . . . can move up, and have. . . . (30)

> A lot of it goes to the makeup of the individual: what the parents have done with the child, how they've educated him. . . . These [poor] people

that are [moving up] are exceptional; they've been nurtured, they've had an aunt or uncle, or mom or dad who has taken a particular interest in them, sweat hard, do two jobs, wash floors, and so forth, to get their kids an education. . . . I'd say that's the exception rather than the rule. Hard-core poor people—people who are unemployed, because they want to be, or because they can't get a job, or because they have problems, or because they live in a poor environment, so forth. . . . Why are they there? . . . They're born there, primarily. Their mother and father that left, that type of thing; they became welfare recipients; mainly attitude of parents, or parent. . . . I'm not so sure that there's enough commitment on the part of haves to help the have-nots. (27)

[Moving up depends] on education, as a base. And then much of the rest of that is based on personal initiative, clearly to get from the great mass in the middle up to [the top]. . . . Personal initiative, luck, the ability to have some access to capital. . . . People in the very poor, it's not just education; I think government support programs can help. . . .

I think the vast majority of [poor] people are born into the very poor. And in the cities in the United States, there may be an increasing connection between them and certain types of immigration. . . . Most of the people who are born into it can never make the climb out. (32)

Certainly if someone's born of a low income family, it's more difficult [to move up] because again, the generalization is that they're coming from an area of low income people, . . . the public schools are the less desirable schools for public education. It's not because of the caliber of teacher; it's because of the more difficult nature of motivating the kids because if they're from a low income area . . . one presumes that there's going to be social problems that may not exist in other homes. And so they're less motivated, and . . . so they're getting less of an education. And the lesser their education, the lesser their ability to move up that economic ladder. . . . (23)

Equal economic opportunity is very difficult to achieve because if you're born into poverty, born into an area where there are drugs and prostitution, and heavy crime, and high despair—no hope, chances are you're going to be locked into that cycle. You're going to become a parent at the ripe old age of fifteen. And the welfare cycle or the economic cycle will continue. (21)

Just as their moral outrage over poverty is restrained in comparison with the critics, so is their concern and outrage over racism. They are concerned about racial patterns of achievement, and in explaining these patterns they assert that to some degree racism still exists, in both overt and more subtle forms. Much of the class conflict that the ambivalents do perceive is based on racial differences, so in this regard race becomes quite important. But once again, their explanation of the present situation takes a cooler, more technical approach, drawing on history, demographics, and the changing structure of the economy. Ambivalents thus come to terms with racial patterns of achievement and racism in a way that satisfies both their basic commitment to the notion of upward mobility and opportunity and their particular construction of that notion. In fact, many ambivalents appeared to become palpably relieved as they explained racial patterns of achievement in these terms. Ambivalent women senators were more aware of and concerned about racism, perhaps from their own experiences; many had themselves been seen as "others" or deviants simply because of their careers in politics.

As is the case concerning poverty, ambivalents also draw on aspects of the members of minorities themselves in order to explain patterns of achievement. These aspects include attitudes about the self and one's environment, the value placed on education, and the lack of proper role models. Again, experiences in the earliest stages of one's life are the most important determinants of these aspects. Ambivalents alluded to these aspects somewhat reluctantly, however, and with some trepidation. They were also careful not to assess responsibility for these characteristics to the minority members.

> Access to capital, access to property. . . . Although we've used a lot of different methods—banking laws, lending policies, civil rights acts, so on—we've broken down a lot of those barriers. But the fact remains that to accumulate property and capital for nonwhites is going to take at least a generation, under the circumstances that we have now. And certainly we've seen the emergence of a black middle class, for instance. And we've seen the rapid advancement of Amerasians. It is clear that barriers still exist. But I don't think that those barriers have as much to do with public policy as they do with the values/attitudes side of the equation. . . . Have we done a lot? We've done better than most of the rest. Is there discrimination? Yeah.
>
> . . . Perhaps [the growing difference between blacks and whites economically] is because the very poor stayed very poor. Certainly the data on single parents, single poor, that's increased. Perhaps that cycle of teenage pregnancy is perhaps one of the root causes of poor. Then you're dealing with a rise in that. Who are the poor? . . . I'd like to see the data between twenty years ago and today, that isolates black males versus white males. (24)

There are certainly circumstances, I believe, in hiring and promotion and opportunity, where choices are made, however guardedly, nonetheless invidiously, about rewarding and promoting people who are more like the mainstream or less like the mainstream. Even where that doesn't happen, you have a legacy, and the legacy is grandparents didn't have opportunity to offer an opportunity to son and daughter who didn't have opportunities to offer opportunities to son and daughter. And that is a slow process of unraveling. . . . Affirmative action . . . is intended to deal with the discriminatory consequences over time. . . . Black children simply have not had the exposure to educational opportunities that white children have had in this country. You also still I think see the consequences for many black families, though less and less so but it is still there, of the shift from rural . . . to children growing up in an urban background. . . .

It's not just the legacy of discrimination; it's coming late to the work force. Jobs in the service sector generally pay less than in the manufacturing sector. . . . To the extent that the manufacturing sector is disappearing, and is largely taken up by people who have been in it a goodly while and therefore are probably not black and Hispanic, the service sector is what then becomes available to blacks and Hispanics. . . . And if you're talking about high-tech, which is the other option, that assumes a fairly good level of education and technical preparation, which again has not been available. (30)

I think blacks who are making it today are those who are the best educated blacks. . . . Education and I guess the wrong role models [are the problem]. . . . When you're about six, seven, eight years old, it's like walking down a path. And you come to that fork in that path. And because it's so easy to go off on this one, which is the same path your mother chose before. And at some point in the past, it was because of discrimination; it may even be the most recent [point]. . . . I think [black poverty] is due to education, due to past discrimination which has encouraged that treadmill. . . . I think too many minority children are having children. . . . When that kid starts off, it's two strikes against him, and Righetti's about to throw the third one by him. . . . How do you come out of that? . . . I think not enough examples are made to young, black children that education is the answer—early on in that path. . . . They don't need a handout, they need a hand up, to use Jesse's [Jackson] phrase. (*)[5]

Lack of education—that's a major factor. Certain groups of people prioritize education. . . . I think the reason that blacks [earn less] is probably the fact that in many instances the mother is being called upon to provide most of the economic and moral leadership. . . . The lack of a strong parental example is missing, and I think that's important. And that's not primarily a black issue; that's white and Hispanic also. . . . A lot of it boils down to inner fiber, desire, to really want your kids to do well, to work at them, to spend time, be patient, and so forth. And sometimes the mother has too many chores, so that she can't handle everything. (27)

As a group, their [nonwhites] education, job preparation, contacts within the community, and all the rest, and location of jobs, tends to restrict them to a larger degree to lower paying job opportunities to begin with. There probably isn't much overt discrimination anymore. It's just that a young, black kid, . . . whereas the comparable national average white kid might have a 3 percent chance of being a doctor, 6 percent chance of being a lawyer, the comparable shift is that the young black kid has a 1 percent chance of being a doctor, 2 percent chance of being a lawyer. . . .

You do get the feeling, as someone . . . who remembers the late '60s and the riots, and Martin Luther King, and that stuff, very vividly, the passage of civil rights acts; you get a sense of a great deal of progress being made. It may be consoling to think that perhaps what is going on is a tremendous economic growth for white people versus better opportunities for black people, but that it just hasn't managed to keep pace. But that's not much consolation. (32)

In discussing differences in economic achievement, ambivalents largely accept and use the notion of class divisions, but they are also uncomfortable with it. Class is not a prominent feature of their narrative more generally, nor is it generally perceived as a pernicious source of boundaries between people, as it is in the critic's narrative. Different persons' interests, particularly those of employer and employee, are generally seen to complement each other. Ambivalents do perceive the existence of some relatively muted class conflict, which occurs primarily in the lower echelons. The fact that they locate conflict in this sector of the wealth distribution is not surprising, since they perceive that the system of mobility functions well in most instances. The ambivalents' sense of class is perhaps best expressed in their view of how a successfully performing economy affects the individuals within it. While critics claim that growth aids those in the higher echelons of the economic structure to a much greater extent than it aids others, particularly the poor, the ambivalents believe that growth aids everyone; to the extent that ambivalents do divide up the benefits of growth, they tend to do so by industrial sectors of the economy rather than by class.

In support of these views ambivalents believe that the distribution of wealth has not changed significantly since World War II, and do not expect it to change dramatically in the future. Like the supporters, they perceive the distribution of wealth and income to be shaped like a bell curve, with a slight bulge in the bottom part of the middle half. In contrast, the critics perceive more inequality in both income and wealth.

But the ambivalents' views are also distinct from those of the supporters. The very nature of their conception of the proper role of public intervention, that of striking the right balance between helping people and maintaining incentive, implies a kind of economic dualism that attempts to reward both halves. This balancing effort is largely missing in the supporter's narrative. The general statements and policy positions of the supporters profited the haves at the expense of the have-nots. Regardless of the supporters' own lack of class analysis, there appears to be a class-based effect to their prescriptions. This effect is less clear in the ambivalents' prescriptions. In addition, ambivalents accept and use the notion of an underclass as a group that does not take part in the ethos of upward mobility, a concept largely rejected by the supporters. But ambivalents usually give it a curious definition; they consider the underclass mostly in terms of deviant behaviors or conditions, such as drug addiction, teenage homelessness, and adult homelessness. We thus see once again their ambivalence toward the economic system, this time through their conception of a term that has become politically charged and symbolic. Ambivalents accept this term but define it in a way that does not imply that the economic system routinely expels a segment of its population into a bottom caste.

> Class connotes two things, among others: number one, a consciousness of being within a certain group; and number two, a static quality to one's being part of an income group, a social group. And that just doesn't exist in this country; people are not class conscious. People do not regard themselves as part of the lower class, as they do in England, or did in England. . . . Nor are there legal barriers to moving from one class to another. There may be social barriers, economic barriers, but those are surmountable also. (20)

> I'm treading very lightly here. . . . I just have such a fuzzy view of [classes]. . . . There are poor people in this system and there are rich people in this system—I don't deny that that exists. I just don't want to perpetuate a class distinction, because I want poor people to be better off. . . . I want to see everybody earn their own way. (24)

> A decent employer—as his success grows, certainly many levels of success for the employee will grow. It doesn't have to be a one-to-one relationship. But then again, if the employer gets too greedy, then he's got discontented employees. . . . As the success of the employer grows, the level of security of the employee will grow. Hopefully, the amount of pay

to that individual will also grow. . . . Any reasonable employer will real-ize that if they've got a motivated group of employees, the productivity from those employees improves, and if the productivity improves then the bottom dollar [improves]. . . . Again, if a employer's looking for too much money, too great a return, trying to get every ounce of blood out of every employee, without the employee seeing any benefit, whether it be psychological or financial—that's not a good employer. . . .

I would say your ultrawealthy are very very small, less than 1 percent of the population. Your poor . . . based on my definition, would probably be 20 percent of the population, maybe a little bit more. And so that middle income group is the group . . . but I've also made that rather broad. A lot of people would think someone, a household, making $125,000 a year is wealthy; I don't think that's wealthy in today's day and age. Not when that family's going to spend $300,000 to buy a house in [a small town]. . . .

I don't think [their interests] would conflict at all. . . . Their interests are all to improve their level in that . . . [distribution] curve. The poor person dreams of being richer—richer's the wrong word, more secure. And even the wealthy people strive for greater wealth. So they all have the same interests. Depending on the level in that curve, there are levels of hostility. . . . Instead of using the word hostility, we ought to use the word envy. . . . When the curve is almost [double] humped, wealthy and very poor, then the hostility is very great, because there's very little hope of moving from this hump to that hump. But when the majority are in the middle, I think you're less likely to have any upheaval in society, because there's a natural progression. . . . There's the hope that you can move forward in the economic scale in the United States. Can someone go from the poverty level in a lifetime to the ultrarich? Probably not. (23)

Class has kind of a caste, a rigidity, that I'm not sure I can really apply in this country. That may be because we have such a mythology of oppor-tunity that it's just tough to fit the two together. I do know statistically that there is not as much upward mobility as we would like to think there is. . . . People do not make rapid shifts from the bottom of the society to the top in great numbers. . . . If one were to find some sort of caste system, I think it would be a racial caste system. . . . But I don't think in general, when people go home [from work], and drive home—most of them—in their own cars, sit down in their own living room—most of them, and watch their own TV—most of them, go to their own ballgame or movie—most of them; I don't think [class] is something that is really constantly there. It's not like going to the theater, and sitting on the benches, because somebody else is sitting in the loges, because some-body else is sitting in the balcony. Society is not like that. In moments of crisis . . . people may have more of a sense of being better off than others, or some people who always seem better off, others who always seem less well off. But I don't think it's something people wake up with every morning. . . . (30)

I don't think [class divisions] are very important. Although I think we have to become more concerned about almost an institutionalization of an underclass in the country. You know, South Bronx, that kind of stuff. . . . The existence of the very wealthy is in some ways almost irrelevant, . . . except for the fact that that be an open, crackable class. (32)

It is also interesting to note that the ambivalents who are women tend to have a stronger conception of class and class conflict, and perceive more people in need, than do their male counterparts. This finding is consistent with the apparent effects of gender more generally, as it reflects the difference in the relative sense of and concern over social disharmony.

From what we have seen thus far, it appears that the ambivalents reject the notion that power relations and the coercion that accompanies them are lurking behind the operations of the economic realm and ultimately dictating the outcomes. Though many of those at the bottom of the economic distribution suffer from a set of beliefs and attitudes that undermines their potential success in the system, ambivalents do not assert that a set of power relations is behind such beliefs, as do the critics. In the ambivalents' view, market outcomes can exhibit patterns of bias; if left completely unregulated, they are subject to prior influences that have more to do with positions of advantage than merit. But for the most part market outcomes are subject only to surface manipulations, which are in turn correctable through adjustment and regulation; their correction does not require the massive shift in our perspective toward economic life implied by the critic's narrative.

One of the best lenses through which to view the ambivalents' distinctive position on market outcomes is their explanation of the determination of incomes. While critics point to power relations as the ultimate determiner of income structures, ambivalents emphasize the way in which the market responds to such appropriate considerations as skill, education, responsibility, and amount of competition for a given position, though they do recognize pay inequities based on gender and race. According to the ambivalents, the appropriate considerations can be subverted under the right circumstances, but both employers and employees have the power to throw the system out of its proper balance, although employers have comparatively more power in the lower status occupations. And while critics pointed to members of the business elite as examples of people who were extremely overpaid, ambivalents tended to identify the most popular and highly paid entertainers and sports figures.

If you didn't have an adequate supply of engineers, the salary would go up. . . . I believe the supply and demand cycle, specifically in salaries, will work. We're not as in the Soviet Union, where they dictate, you will be paid such and such. It's generally voluntary here. If it takes less education and training to become a janitor, and the salary for a janitor is such and such, then I can't argue with that. . . . I think when you have an occupation that's underpaid, then the supply and demand cycle will work on it, because people will generally stay away from that occupation . . . . The cycle will come around eventually. . . . Are schoolteachers underpaid? Are nurses underpaid? Yes, but society has its own evolutionary ability to adjust to that. (23)

Cleaning up the Margins

According to the ambivalents, economic fairness is marked by accessibility and impartiality. The system must be open to all, and its structures must not explicitly favor any one person or group over another. Individuals are entitled to fairness because they are of equal moral worth. In the ambivalents' case, however, this belief in equal moral worth does not carry with it the same distributive implications that it does for the critics, in part due to the ambivalents' beliefs about the existence of upward mobility and opportunity. These implications are further muted by concerns for the efficiency of the entire economy.

> This gets into an area where my personal beliefs are a little split. . . . There's a sense of economic justice, where—I don't mean to say that an economic system, it's necessarily a negative that some people are left out of the economic rewards, because I think any economic system will, and that's where government comes in to assist people—but there is a sense of economic justice, which goes back to the rewards to individual initiative, where if the system is closed by allocation of power, resources, through inheritance, rather than equal access. Or it's a closed, oligopolistic type of structure. That's an economic justice issue which is to me different from the question of taking care of the needy. . . .
> We're all born with the same innate worth. . . . Everyone should have equal opportunity to achieve what they work for. . . . If for some reason they face a personal problem, tragedy, disability, whatever, society has an obligation to respect that innate worth that each person has, and not to allow them to become driftwood on the public byways. (32)

[Justice is] opportunity; not equity, but opportunity. I think an economically just society is one in which all people have the resources and the opportunity to choose to be what they want to be. The choice, thereafter, is theirs. A just society is not a leveled society. (30)

[Justice is] equal access to goods and services, that includes education, includes many fundamental goods and services. (24)

Justice to me connotes equilibrium, balance, equality of opportunity, fairness of opportunity. That we don't have excesses of one kind or another. . . . Not . . . somebody owning the entire pie, and hoarding it. I think it's good that some people can rise and earn more and produce more, but I think at the same time there are others who don't have those same opportunities and advantages, and that basically, there has to be some sort of sharing, some sort of sensitivity to those who are incapable, disadvantaged. . . . (33)

The ambivalent senators who are women placed comparatively more emphasis than did the men on compassion, understanding, the provision of human needs, and shared responsibility as constituent elements of economic fairness.

Are people doing well in the system? Does the system allow for the weakest members of that society—the weakest being the handicapped, the sick, disabled, those who are poor for reasons beyond their own control—is there room for trying to help those people? . . . Or is it every person for himself or herself? . . . We should pay a little more attention, make adjustments, make an effort to help, and I think the system should do that—within its financial means. I'm a pay-as-you-go fiscal person, I guess. (*)

Because [our society] is so make-it-on-your-own, take-care-of-yourself, kind of attitude—although we give you the opportunities—we don't look at others through their eyes, and try to put ourselves in their positions. And therefore we don't understand the different backgrounds of people, and why there are problems in certain urban poor areas. I think that's one of the problems we have between middle class whites and blacks, and upper income versus poor; I don't think we understand each other. . . . So therefore I think their opportunities are reduced, and that's where you've got a problem with fairness and justice. (*)

If there was adequate housing, if there was adequate services, if the medical needs of people were being met, then I think the economy would be working well. If also a newcomer could find work, a newcomer could

start a business, if there's access to the system, I think it's a good system. . . . That's what was so exciting about this country, and still is, even
though it's very hard. . . . (*)

The ambivalents' concept of fairness also appears to correspond to equity:
conditions of openness and equal treatment in the economic game will certainly promote equitable outcomes.[6] But like the critics the ambivalents go
beyond the value of equity. One can see this most clearly in their discussion of
how wages ought to be determined. In discussing the basis of rewards in a fair
wage system, ambivalents endorse equity-related criteria such as the amount of
ability, education, and skill required for the position and the value a given
activity adds to the final product. Such criteria are the constituent elements of
the norm that rewards should be proportionate to the amount of input (considered in various ways), rewards that are in turn meted out through the market.
But the ambivalents extend these criteria to include rewards for the amount and
importance of decision making required, and the unpleasantness and danger
involved in the activity. The market works well not just because it yields
efficiency and secures a relative equality of treatment, but also because it
responds to these other values, which the ambivalents also hold important.

> I'm a believer in pay equity, for example. I believe that people who are
> doing reasonable jobs with reasonable merit should receive similar kinds
> of pay. By the same token, I believe one's limit to achieve should be
> boundless. (17)

> In business situations what you add to the process [should determine
> income]. Also some determination in the market, demand and supply,
> balance; you're talking about the ability to attract sufficient people to a
> business. And all positions should reflect some kind of premium for
> decision makers. There should be a premium for people who have to
> endure some special kind of risk, . . . people whose jobs require enormous
> emotional drain. (32)

> I think the difficulty of the task and the skills necessary to carry out the
> task; that involves particularly education. But I also feel . . . if it's a
> particularly objectionable area of employment or hazardous area of em-
> ployment, then those are considerations that should be figured into com-
> pensation. Certainly the general marketplace in terms of supply and de-
> mand plays a key factor . . . with a particular need or shortage, you're
> going to see that in compensation. (29)

> Ability to do the job [ought to determine incomes]. And I think demand is
> a fair way to determine that also. If there's a highly skilled position of one

type or another, that just naturally reduces potentially the number of people working in that area. I think those are fair ways to determine actual salaries or pay. . . . I think that if we were able to make that leap [to more income equality], in some ways it would be more difficult to attract people into the professions that are rather demanding. The medical profession offers an example. . . . You'd tend to find some areas that there are not many people in, because of the physical or mental difficulty, if the pay is not commensurate with the effort. (28)

What do the ambivalents' responses to questions about specific occupational incomes reveal (table 3)? In general, the ambivalents' perceptions of actual incomes are fairly similar to those of the supporters; their perceptions are lower (and more accurate) than those of the supporters concerning the lower paid occupations, but they are not as low (or as accurate) as those of the critics. They are more redistributive than the supporters in their preferred incomes, and less redistributive than the critics. In addition, in comparison with the critics they are less egalitarian in the direction and relative magnitude of their changes from estimated to preferred incomes. Ambivalents are, however, more egalitarian than supporters.

These findings fit the general contours of the ambivalent's narrative, when placed against the other two narratives. While the ambivalent's narrative certainly perceives more actual and potential problems in the economic system than does the supporter's narrative, at the same time it does not see the extent of problems and injustice that the critic's narrative sees. These differences are supported by the fact that ambivalents perceive a lesser amount of income differentiation than do the supporters and a greater amount than do the critics, and also by the fact that in advancing preferred incomes for specific occupations, ambivalents recommend incomes that yield more overall equality than those recommended by the supporters and less equality than those recommended by the critics.[7]

Like both the critics and supporters, ambivalents embrace a condition of equal opportunity as a cornerstone of economic fairness. Their emphasis on opportunity is perhaps even stronger than that of the supporters and the critics; they have a faith that by itself opportunity can solve the fairness problem. But how exactly do the ambivalents conceive the condition of equal opportunity? Do they endorse the stronger form of opportunity of the critics or the weaker form of the supporters, something in between, or something quite entirely different? As we might have expected by this point, the concept of equal opportunity that the ambivalents endorse appears to blend elements of both the critics and supporters, and in so doing it creates its own distinct version. Ambivalents perceive that many persons experience problems in gaining access to the economic system, and this perception leads them to the stronger

TABLE 3.   Incomes (Annual, in K) Estimated and Preferred by Ambivalents, with Percentage Change, Actual Incomes, and Ratios of Top to Bottom Incomes

Occupation	Estimated	Preferred	Percentage Change	Actual
Bank teller	16	19	+19%	12
Janitor	17	22	+29%	13
Production worker	25	27	+8%	18
Police officer	25	29	+16%	22
High school teacher	29	36	+24%	26
Press operator	27	28	+4%	35
Engineer	52	57	+10%	43
Physician	202	194	−4%	106
Executive	538	413	−23%	1,167
Ratio of top to bottom income	34	22		97

Note: N = 15. Data are missing for four ambivalents. See table 1 for the complete text of the interview question and the sources of the actual income figures.

conception. At the same time, they are deeply concerned with protecting a system of incentive, which they believe is threatened by overassisting disadvantaged persons, regardless of their history of past hardships. Helping some persons too much means hurting others who deserve to be rewarded, and therefore compromising the prior values of merit to which the market responds, at least in most cases. As we have seen, access to education is especially important to the ambivalents, and regarding that particular realm of opportunity, they endorse a comparatively stronger position. But overall, they once again attempt to strike a balance between helping those truly in need and preserving a system that grows and is competitive. It is also in the ambivalents' conception of equal opportunity that their conception of liberty in largely negative terms becomes most apparent.

> There's got to be a balance. Although people really need the opportunity and freedom to go out and take that chance, and work hard and make it, they also have to be stopped if their drive to make it steps on people, and really holds them back. That's when we've got to stop and say, hey, we've gone too far. . . .
>
> I sense that to make it more fair you've got to go out of your way to push somebody forward [in order] to make it even, on the one hand. On the other hand, what you're doing is making it unfair for the guy that hasn't been held back yet—he hasn't had the impediments, but he also . . . now somebody has the extra help. My sense is that if we at least remove all the impediments, yes, certain people or groups are going to have an advantage for a bit. But in the competitive spirit of capitalism and

democracy, we will eventually be equal in terms of opportunity. A lot of people, to have gotten the advantage, had to work like heck to get there, and they got there. And I think our system is based on that, so I don't think we ought to artificially help people move ahead of others. Then you've got a different situation, where others are being discriminated against. Hopefully if you just remove everything, eventually we will come out even. (25)

What constitutes equal opportunity, you'd have to look at it holistically. . . . Often times, if you've been neglected for a long time, it's "out of sight, out of mind." And so if government is going to have an equitable policy, they almost have to guarantee that a certain segment of society that has been left out of the mainstream [is able] to perform, to prove their worth, to prove their ability, and to demonstrate that they can do the job. (17)

Equal opportunity should mean that somebody who is of the minority or group that we're trying to promote should have the same chance as someone who is in the mainstream of the country. . . . [Do we have this opportunity?] No. I do think it's changing. I think our attitudes are better than they used to be. . . .

   Again, we've got to balance the haves and have-nots. I think we do that pretty much in government. I also feel if we do too much, then we . . . I don't think you can legislate it [equal opportunity] either. You can offer incentives. In the long run, it's got to be something where society comes around. But if things get bad enough you've [government] got to do it. . . . (18)

We all know . . . in terms of the nature of man, that some people are going to be chiefs and some people are going to be indians, and some people are going to amass power and wealth because of different personal traits. So, are we supposed to equalize for that? Hell no. We should start with the same basic opportunities, and then we all accede to do whatever we want to do. . . . To get the same educational background, to be able to grow up, be healthy, be educated, and be prepared to function in a productive capacity as an adult. . . . Opportunity to access. . . .

   Government's trying, within their means, we're trying around the theme of education. Certainly, that's a costly formula. . . . In terms of health care, the government definitely has a role. (24)

In the ambivalents' view, economic growth solves much of the problem of distributive justice. It allows us to direct the necessary funds into changing the circumstances and characteristics of those who do not fully participate in the system (which will itself contribute to growth in the long term), while still attending to the immediate health of the entire economy. When discussing the trademarks of a successful economy, ambivalents thus reach for macroeconomic indicators of efficiency and production, rather than focusing on the criteria of need fulfillment, particularly for those at the bottom strata, as the critics do. But they are not entirely like the supporters, since their reasons for ensuring an ever-increasing economic pie include an active concern to provide opportunities and at least minimum levels of support for those less well off.

> A successful economic system has close to full employment, close to full production of goods and services at a competitive price, and it has little or no inflation. These things reflect the health of other things. (19)

> You'd have to look at [the economy] on an overall basis: . . . the number of people that are employed, whether or not your employment rate is high or low. . . . You'd have to measure it to a large degree by what the middle class can do; whether or not they're buying automobiles, buying refrigerators, whether or not they're able to educate their kids. . . . I think the true measure . . . is what the middle class is able to do. . . . There's always going to be poor and there's always going to be wealthy, and their status is not going to change to a large degree, although we try and balance it out and try and develop more middle classes. (27)

> We should have a system like ours; that encourages personal initiative, that puts controls on the public good, but only when they're needed— whether that be environmental, or labor laws, for the protection of people. But I really think you've got to have that incentive, for individuals to make it. And if it works wrong, then taxing to help those who can't make it, rather than controlling businesses to the point where they're not working well or are discouraged from trying to make them work. Then everybody loses. . . . It's a balancing act. (25)

> Is the system producing, to a large extent, those goods and services that the people need to lead a fulfilling life, to exist? Is it a system that provides for upward mobility, allows for talent to come through? (33)

These statements, however, beg an important question: During the time in which the lower strata are waiting for economic growth to bring them opportunity, and before they have profited from the early development and education programs that are recommended by the ambivalents, what are the minimum levels of support to which they are entitled? Recall that critics posit a relatively generous set of entitlements, while supporters endorse a much more modest level of assistance. Ambivalents willingly assert a minimum standard of living to which everyone is entitled, but the level that they support appears to be lower than that of the critics and more closely linked to what is presently supplied by the public support system already in place. Society as a whole has a shared responsibility to supply these minimums, but those at the very top carry a greater share of this responsibility. This greater responsibility, however, is seen as more of a personal ethic, which does not involve the profound transformation of personality that the critics envision; furthermore, ambivalents are reluctant to mandate that those at the top carry a separate, special responsibility to help those at the bottom.

Educate! Educate!: Government as Empowered Umpire

Ambivalents believe that although the economic system, if left to itself, tends to fall out of balance, there is an inherent cost to government involvement that must always be considered. Government should watch over the game and see where the inequities lie, but should still let the game be played. It should not become a player itself, as it does in the critic's narrative. Programs must be carefully targeted, money carefully spent. There are limitations on what government can and should do because funds are limited—public-sector spending ultimately takes money away from the private economy; because government overinvolvement threatens incentive; and because human nature is such that the potential for profit is necessary for people to undertake the variety of activities that society requires of them.

The ambivalents' view of human nature is a key component in their views about the role of government. People are basically self-interested, and there is little emphasis in the ambivalent's narrative on changing this orientation. Thus any real redistribution of wealth or other similar kind of government intervention inherently carries with it great costs, which in the minds of the ambivalents outweigh the benefits.

> I think a lot of people would like to have one class of people. But I don't think the net result is going to be what they think it is. I don't think you're going to pull a lot of people up; I think you're going to pull a hell of a lot of people down. In the balance your poor may become slightly less poor, but overall, you're going to have a hell of a lot more people who are [with] a substantially reduced standard of living if we adopt that system, with no incentives. . . . To some degree, we need stratification [in economic status] to have incentive, to provide incentive and initiative. The economy depends on it; otherwise we'd have a society of slugs. The base level in society is lazy. You need incentive to drive it. (19)

The whole Yuppie thing, I don't think that's anything new. . . . If it [equality] were government imposed, then it would be very negative, it would take the incentive away from those creative people. . . . Unless there's some way for the person to excel, and unless there's some way for the person to be rewarded for that excelling, then I think it's very negative for that profession. (23)

I get worried about social activism that tries to legislate the distribution of wealth. I wrestle with this personally. Morally, you could say that we have to take from the rich and give to the poor, which is a philosophy. But you cannot homogenize society; man is an aggressive animal, there is competition. You cannot say everyone is going to be equal; we're not here for that. This is a terminal existence. . . . I think promulgating equal opportunity, and keeping the doors at least ajar, is the healthy way to go. . . . You can't legislate values; you can't legislate effort. You can't legislate it in a negative sense; you can't punish those people who work their ass off. . . . I wrestle with this—I think I'm a social liberal and a fiscal moderate—I wonder if sometimes we handicap minority groups by extending so much help that we destroy initiative. And I see some of that. . . . (33)

The most effective means through which government can have a positive influence on the game is through directing its spending at disadvantaged people at a very early stage in their lives. If opportunity is available, yet segments of the population do not avail themselves of it because they lack the requisite skills and mental outlook, then steps must be taken early in their lives both to equip them and to put them in an achievement-oriented frame of mind. The focus on early intervention is driven in part by the ambivalents' concern for cost-effectiveness. They believe that once patterns of underachievement establish themselves, it becomes extremely costly—perhaps too costly—to break them.

The key component of this early involvement is education. The function of education in the ambivalent's narrative is something between that found in the critic's and supporter's narratives. Education is for the most part an enabling device, a vehicle for upward mobility, rather than a source of personal transformation; it does not have the socializing and empathic functions that it has in the critic's narrative (though the ambivalent senators who are women conceive a comparatively broader role for education, which includes education as a promoter of justice, mutual understanding, and compassion). But at the same time education also enables persons to overcome a wide range of environmental and historical challenges, which the supporters tend not to see in the first place.

In the other two narratives, we saw that the approach toward what Robert Reich (1987, 16–19) has described as "the other" supplies a particularly telling aspect of the senators' views. By now, the ambivalents' approach toward the other should be apparent. Through educational efforts, especially early education and early development-oriented programs, ambivalents are trying to change these others at an early age, to change what are perceived to be basic aspects about them: their values, their level of initiative, their very level of intelligence. Ambivalents focus their efforts on making these changes, rather than on attempting to change the basic framework of a system that has hurt their parents and that has brought them into this condition. But in trying to change the others, they take the second of the two standard approaches identified by Reich, whereas the supporters tend more toward the first. Ambivalents try to change the others through assistance and understanding. They try to provide them with inclusion into the perceived ethos of achievement—more of the carrot approach—while supporters emphasize a more assertive, disciplinary approach—more of the stick. Recall that critics attempt to move beyond the concept of the other entirely.

> The major ongoing commitment to reach those [poor] people has to be through public education. I mean schools, and schools that try to reach these people at an even younger age, and reach them in a greater way throughout their childhood life. . . . Take a far more active involvement in helping them mature and develop and get skills and education, and all the rest. . . . Take a close look at public assistance programs that make an addiction out of dependence. . . . (32)

> I'm not so sure that they're doing enough in starting with [poor] people at a very early age, at an age when they should be going to day care centers. But to take someone who is twenty-four or twenty-five, and essentially hit the welfare rolls, and has drug-related problems or alcohol problems, and spend a lot of time trying to turn it around and have them become productive members of society—it might be a little too late in most instances. . . . But I think if you start at an earlier level you'll get a better return, by providing better education, better support for the families, economically and otherwise. (27)

> Education is the key. . . . I think education is key to a lot, I really do. And mixing with people, which we can do through our education system too. . . . I think day care is such an important thing, for the development of kids, helping to get them to the point where the schools can help them, and give them some additional intellectual stimulus. Hopefully, that will give them the ticket out. (25)

[We need] a recognition that we have to make the future better for our children. And the best way, the most effective and efficient way, is to renew this country's historic commitment to public education. . . . (22)

So much in terms of potential is determined very early in people's lives. . . . One of the things we can do is do a better job of targeting what investments we are able to make in people. We tend to put our money in at the wrong points in time as a government. We tend to invest a great deal of money at a point that's much too late. We tend to spend a lot of money maintaining people rather than challenging them. . . . We put a great deal more money into high school education—more resources, more attention, support—than we do into elementary, and certainly, pre, early childhood. The money you're spending in high school, particularly on remedial education and dropout prevention, and dropout return, is money that need not have been spent, largely, if you had done more at preschool, early childhood. . . . I think government really has to rethink where and how, and what it is we're investing in. We do a super job of keeping people where they are, and that's not what the system is supposed to be about. It's supposed to be about helping people to progress, to do for themselves. . . . (30)

I've always been an advocate in terms of certain social programs that put aside money . . . that come from a cost-benefit analysis. Something like nutrition programs for pregnant women. . . . Kids born in this country who do not get proper nutrition in the womb enter life without the capabilities that they would have as human beings, because they did not get proper nutrition in the womb. That's like from day one. . . .
    Certainly that's a key aspect of it—the educational aspect, because that provides the opportunity to break out from the poverty situation. (29)

The ambivalents' posited role of government as a source of balance between competing interests, as well as their resistance to direct economic redistribution, leads to the characterization of government as an umpire. One of government's principal roles is to ensure fairness, but it is limited in the ways it can effectively do this. Explicit redistribution threatens incentive and threatens to upset a market system of allocation that is generally efficient and fair. Furthermore, government is not a good manager. Ambivalents are thus critical of welfare programs as they are presently set up because they do not effectively promote economic achievement (and therefore do not serve the interests of the disadvantaged), and because they constitute a glaring example of the limits of government's abilities as a manager. At the same time, ambivalents do not have the same concern over welfare fraud that the supporters displayed, and neither do they support the "workfare" programs as they have been set forward in the present policy debates. These programs are seen as forms of punishment of the poor.

Although ambivalents do significantly limit the appropriate sphere of government activity, in many important respects their view of government's proper function goes beyond the image that the label "umpire" evokes. In addition to simply watching over the economic game, government does act, in order to educate, to develop, and to expand rights. Thus government is an empowered umpire, empowered to actually change the game, at least at the margins. The assistance programs ambivalents support are informed by their basic pragmatism and are targeted where the probability of success is highest.

> Trust everybody, but cut the cards. And in this instance it's government, in the free enterprise system, that cuts the cards, to make sure everybody gets a fair deal, or a square deal. . . . Opportunity is all you can provide, an equal opportunity. . . . It's government's role to serve as a catalyst. . . . We're a collective enterprise with the business, or private sector, the academic, or intellectual sector, and the volunteer sector. All too often the government has tried to do things on its own, or the volunteer sector has tried to do things on its own, or the business community has gone off on its own. . . . Rarely has there been an opportunity in the national community to come together. . . . In our society, it seems to operate out of synch with one another. . . . Government's role in the future will be to serve as a catalyst, making sure that social, political, and economic justice are meted out; but also to serve as a catalyst for the further growth and stimulation of business, but on a fair and reasonable manner. . . . I envision a team approach for government. . . . (17)

> The drive to make it, without government watching over the shoulders of those at the top of the drive—I think people would be walked all over. (25)

> One of the responsibilities of government is to . . . allow people to enter the system. If it's through educational opportunities, through removing some of these tremendous obstacles, like drugs. . . . I think that's our responsibility. . . . Opportunities need to be equal, and this is, again, a goal that government can play. For instance if a person is handicapped, we certainly can't remove the handicap, but we can create an atmosphere where that person can be assisted to achieve their goals by placing them near a job opportunity, or giving them the chance to compete on a more equal basis. (26)

Medical care, shelter, housing, all those things; there should be an equal opportunity for everyone. But I don't necessarily think that the state should automatically provide those services. . . . The government should only be stepping in when there's a gap there that needs to be filled. And minimum wage is one way. There are other carrot approaches in terms of tax incentives, for example, to encourage day care facilities, to enable single-parent families to have affordable child care, so they are able to work and provide an income for their families. . . . Government's role is to make the opportunity available for people, and without being the great equalizer on a taxation basis, at least have somewhat of a fair tax structure. (29)

Where government can be a catalyst toward an efficient marketplace, government's a player. I just think that those have to be fairly measured interventions. (24)

I'm a moderate, I think. There are times when I think government intervention is absolutely necessary. I think the difference between moderates, conservatives, and liberals is that moderates see an end to government intervention; in other words, government assistance early on, with the hopes that we would be able—take the welfare recipients for example—to take them eventually off the rolls. . . .

The state has a responsibility to build a program to break that cycle [of hard-core poverty], and that we look at it as an investment in people as opposed to buildings. I think in the future that's the way we're going to have to look at it. It really is not a good thing for society to have this continue. It's not good for blue-collar workers. It's not good for lower income and upper income people to basically have this drag, and that's what it is: It's a drag on the economy. . . .

That's one of the measures that we're missing in this state, is there doesn't seem to be a concerted effort to do a cost-benefit. Even if the cost-benefit doesn't have a break-even point for fifteen years—I'm not looking for a short-time resolution to this. At some point in time you have to sit down and say, what is job training all about; what do we have to do with day care; what do we have to do with birth control, you know, family planning, and the whole series of things that basically tie into the problems. What do we have to do about housing opportunities. (19)

One of the things we have to do—first of all, a preference for anything that is targeted towards helping children born into families dependent on welfare to get out of that. And that is to key very heavily into their relationship with their education, the earlier the better. My other preference would be highly targeted programs. . . . If you start off designing a program to combat poverty, that part of its goal is to make enormous strides in a short period of time, you're dealing with a disaster. We are unfortunately better off picking the closest [people] to success, and just pouring it at them, and moving them and their children up and out of the trap, rather than spreading out money all over the place, and none of it accomplishes much of anything. (32)

How should these government programs be paid for? Ambivalents believe that taxes should be progressive, but they do not support the redistribution of wealth and income as a policy goal in itself; rather, progressive taxes are advocated as a fair means by which to supply needed public services. The limits that ambivalents set on the top marginal tax rates ranged between one-third and one-half of the corresponding marginal incomes.

Additional Items of Interest

Other items of interest in the narratives that do not fit cleanly into the basic chapters include the ambivalents' view of the future and the motif of the technical approach. In describing this motif I shall also discuss the ambivalents' style in defining certain political and economic terms, and their conception of their own roles as senators. Although these items are not constitutive elements of the narrative, they further support its broad themes.

One element of traditional liberalism that the ambivalents have retained is optimism. They seem confident that in terms of their concerns about economic fairness and economic performance, the future will be brighter than the present. Their optimism about the future serves the narrative well, for if they were more pessimistic, it would be even more difficult to reassure themselves that their strategies for addressing the problems that they themselves identify will ultimately succeed. I do not mean to claim that their optimism is either false or predetermined by their policy stands, or vice versa. But their optimism does help to contain any dissonance between their perceptions of reality and the appropriateness of their proposals to improve that reality.

Ambivalents are united in their belief that in the long term, the national economy will prosper, and the economic prospects of persons in every stratum will improve in real terms. Some have concerns about the short-term effects of dislocations of certain sectors or industries, which in turn could further increase economic inequality and lessen the supply of opportunity and upward mobility, and some believe that although the economy will ultimately thrive, it may not have the same international standing that it once did. But in the main, their vision is a distinctly positive one.

The intensity of this optimism is tempered somewhat by the technician's motif. A cool, pragmatic, nonaccusatory approach informs each constitutive chapter of the ambivalent's narrative. In discussing the various topics contained in their narrative, ambivalents constantly reach for facts and historical context as a mode of explanation in a way that neither the supporters nor the critics do. We have also seen that ambivalents offer proposals of a comparatively incremental nature. Furthermore they are not interested in reforming mankind, but rather accept it pretty much as they find it. It is perhaps not surprising that the technician's motif is a trait of the ambivalent's narrative, rather than the critic's or supporter's narrative, because these other narratives are more extremely located, ideologically. Technical approaches better fit the framework of those who tend toward the middle.[8]

Integral parts of the technician's motif are the ambivalents' way of defining certain key terms and their descriptions of their roles as senators. In contrast to the other two narratives, the ambivalents' definitions of socialism, capitalism, liberalism, and conservatism contain almost no emotion or moral judgment. These terms are usually defined based on the relative degree of governmental involvement in the economy, the amount of public ownership, attitudes toward public spending, and certain issue stands. But not surprisingly, ambivalents do tend to offer disapproving definitions of the term *radical*. To ambivalents, radicals are too extreme (in either direction), impractical, and close-minded; they are not effective political players. Ambivalents generally do not think of themselves as radicals.

In describing their visions of their own roles as senators, ambivalents consciously shy away from descriptions based on specific points of view or based on certain subsets of their constituents. When they do describe themselves in these terms, they ascribe to themselves a moderate label, or claim that they represent the broad middle class or "working middle" class. Concerning their roles within the senate body itself, they emphasize those of compromiser, balancer, mediator, expert, and legislative craftsman.

> Capitalism to me means the creation of capital, which is wealth owned by private individuals. Socialism means to me state ownership of the means of production. Those are definitions that whether accurate or inaccurate in terms of political philosophy, really have been diluted in terms of their practical application. And as we've seen, socialist countries like China and the Soviet Union have begun to try to develop free enterprise—even more so the satellite countries. And in this country we have a fairly high degree of state regulation and in some cases outright ownership. (20)

> Capitalism is a belief . . . that the private production of wealth ultimately benefits all, and is the engine of social democracy. Socialism—I would

take it from a more collective point of view—and simply say that [it means that] the collective sharing of wealth and labor is more beneficial. . . . Capitalism in this country obviously has a much more positive image than socialism does. Not many people would identify themselves as socialists. (30)

Conservatism would be maintenance of the status quo, and moving more towards a capitalistic society, where equal opportunity might be an ideal. . . . Liberalism would be an emphasis on equal opportunity and moving towards a goal of socialism, where people might not actually be receiving the same, but there would be caps on wealth and on poverty. . . . I think the American society swings back and forth between the two extremes, in a middle, narrower limitation; the Great Society being the liberal maximum and the Reagan Revolution being the conservative maximum. . . . I'm torn between the two [labels]. I see strengths in both. . . .
    Capitalism means that if you have economic power you can enhance it, you can strengthen it. If you have no economic power you can strive for economic rewards and power, but if you happen to be in a different group you may not be able to get into the economic mainstream to really have an equal chance. . . . Socialism is where no one is extremely poor, no one is extremely wealthy—which has its negative impact. You lose the individual's competitiveness and dedication to strive for economic gains, because government provides equal benefits to all, and you lose the incentives to work hard and to take risk and improve oneself's status. On the positive side, it's where no one is locked into a cycle of poverty. . . . The conservative element would mean less government restrictions, and the socialistic element would mean more government intervention; government would be the redistributor of wealth and opportunities, and institutional support, whether it's education, or welfare. . . . I believe in essentially socialistic capitalism. (21)

A radical . . . is somebody who works through confrontation, and does not think that we can change the system quickly enough to suit them, through the system. . . . I may have had hair down to my shoulders, but I was not a radical. (*)

[A radical is] someone devoid of and divorced from that sort of pragmatic approach to change and progress that I would be an advocate of. Someone who is extreme in their advocacy, extreme in their solution, far out of the mainstream. Not necessarily a bad thing, unless there's too much of it. . . . There is need always for a certain expression of radical thought in society. . . . I don't think [I've ever been a radical]. And that's for someone whose first political experience was in the antiwar movement and the civil rights movement. (*)

Of course I consider myself a moderate. . . . I'm interested in helping people. I'm also interested in trying to pay as you go, whereas I think a liberal is just the opposite. A conservative probably would not have enabling legislation except in the very last extreme. . . . Of course there's strength in both sides, but somewhere down the middle, I find that's the best approach. . . . (18)

The only way you can survive, and the only way this country can survive, is that of the moderate. You can't be too far to the right; you can't be too far to the left, and to remain the kind of economy that we have, the kind of political system that we have. You can't benefit just the workers, because then you lose the incentive of being the employer. We have an economy that requires the interaction of both groups. So you don't really find radical, deviation far from that middle, and people whose minds can't be changed, running for office. Because they can't win. They can win in little pockets . . . for one term, two terms. It doesn't work. (23)

[I am] a representative, a communicator. . . . I think also a pragmatist, I think I bring that here. And a craftsman. There are some of us who tend to be simply show horses, and others who tend to be work horses and enjoy the craftsmanship of legislating . . . really managing the process. (30)

I don't really have an agenda. I'm not a crusader. I'm more of a technician, in terms of making the system work. I guess I like to be somewhat of a conscience, not from a "this is right, this is wrong" position, but I try to stop things that are being done for the wrong reasons. And more, really, just being a voice for [my] region, which I think it has lacked. (*)

[I have] a concern for trying to protect the benefits of the middle class, and to try and make the economic ladder possible for the lower economic strata, through education, equal opportunity for jobs, through a healthy economy. . . . Trying not to gouge business so as not to alienate the state and local businesses—helping labor at the extreme expense—I try not to be extreme in my supporting of issues on the labor side. . . . Where there is no natural constituency that the business issues have been for—when business is for something and there's no group out there with a great concern against it, . . . I have been probusiness. Some people will be antibusiness, no matter what, and some people will be antilabor, no matter what. I try to weigh the benefits and costs. (21)

If anything, during the time that I've been in a leadership role is that the actual proposals that we put forth tend to be more moderate as a caucus than they otherwise would have been. . . . You won't see a lot of extremes coming out of this caucus, and I think that's more a manifestation of my own beliefs than anything else that I do here. . . .

I see my role, particularly in a leadership position, as one who tries to present a moderate stance on all issues. Not exactly middle of the road, but someone who reflects on the issues, looks at them very carefully . . . I bring a certain expertise into the process, which is [my field of employment], a very technical background. . . . (*)[9]

The Personal

I can remember at the age of eight, Kennedy came right up this street. . . . I was on my bicycle—my father was a [local officeholder] then. And my mother was nine months pregnant with my little brother. . . . I'll never forget looking at Kennedy . . . I'll never forget how thrilled I was when he looked over and saw my mother and me, and he went like that to my mother [patting his stomach] and he went like that to me [a thumbs-up gesture], and then I drove my bicycle up alongside him. And the Secret Service were looking at me. And he yelled out, "keep going!" And that was John Kennedy. I didn't know I was going to be state senator some day, but I knew I liked politics, because I liked John Kennedy. (*)

In 1969, I believed in a revolution to bring all good things to the world . . . [then] I woke up. I realized there wasn't going to be a revolution, and if there was, it wasn't going to provide a utopia. . . . Certainly, no utopia could be provided. (21)

Although the ambivalents grew up and came of age politically in roughly the same period as did the critics, their beliefs obviously developed in a significantly different direction. What are some of the factors that might have contributed to this alternative development? First are demographic factors such as age, education, wealth, and occupation. Although they are similar to the critics, ambivalents are the youngest and least senior group of senators, and as a group they have a self-awareness of constituting a new political generation.[10] This consciousness may contribute to the quality of middlingness in their beliefs, as they attempt to distinguish themselves from each of the two poles in the standard political continuum, at least as they perceive it. Randall Rothenberg and others have observed a similarly based tendency among newer generation politicians at the national level (Rothenberg 1984). Ambivalents are also the highest paid and own the most real estate of the three groups.[11] They are also the most educated; this fact largely reflects the relative preponderance of lawyers in the group.[12] Their own socioeconomic success and their investment in their own education may contribute to their basic endorsement of the market and their emphasis on education as the vehicle for achievement (though by the same token the critics are by no means underachievers).

Second, certain elements about the ambivalents' interest in politics and their careers may be important sources of their beliefs. As a group their interest in politics developed earlier than it did among the senators in the other two groups, and they were much more likely to have been "born" into politics by being raised in families that were either active or deeply interested in politics. Furthermore, their families were not notably progressive or left of center, though a few were fairly conservative. In addition, ambivalents do not appear to have had the kinds of early experiences regarding poverty and discrimination that produced the powerful empathic reactions that are found among the critics. Thus, from the combined effects of all these factors, ambivalents might have learned the art of middlingness early on.

Ambivalents in the Democratic Party tended to have been recruited for political office by party regulars, and those who were instead self-starters at least sought the office with the party's backing.[13] These ambivalents sought their offices from the inside of the system rather than the outside. Again, this insider quality might enhance their tendency toward middlingness. Ambivalents are also clearly the most ambitious of the senators; many of them openly admitted during the interviews that the senate office was a temporary stop on the way to a higher office. Concerning the other ambivalents who offered no such comments, I sensed from both the interviews and my participant observation that many were hungry for higher office. Such ambition may also reinforce middlingness, in that the ambitious senator adjusts his beliefs in anticipation of the (usually) broader constituency of the office to which he aspires.[14]

I was groomed along by the local party leaders as a young guy whom they were interested in taking care of. (*)

I was approached [to run for state senate] by others, but it was something I had considered too—I had always considered the possibility of something like this. . . . [I was approached by] people in organized politics and outside of organized politics, and for different reasons. . . . The ones who were in organized politics, including town committees and the state central committee, and the like, were looking for a good candidate for that particular slot. (*)

If there was a president of something, I wanted to be president of it. I don't know why—a lot of it was ego. I ran for [political] office in the first instance a lot more because of ego and sense of self-destiny, however pompous that is, than because of any selfless, broad political motives. . . . [I ran for state senate] by positioning myself, by methodically planning for a potential vacancy, and by deliberately seeking "the powers"—in quotes, the influence, by sheer weight of effort, and being acceded to by the decision makers. I know that sounds very calculating, but that's sort of the way I've operated. . . . I've been thinking about running for Congress since I've been in high school. And that's the only motive I've ever had in everything I've ever done. . . . I've been running for Congress since I was first elected. I'm sorry to be so acquisitive, in a pejorative sense. (*)

Finally, I should note that there is no noticeable geographical pattern in the ambivalent senators' districts; they come from rural, suburban, and urban areas.

The Political Theory of the Ambivalent's Narrative

We're not part of the grand coalitions of the New Deal . . . the New Frontier and the Great Society. . . . The new focus is on egalitarianism, it's on balance. It's on being fiscally conservative and socially liberal, and then justifying what that means philosophically. . . . I can't think of an age that's lived through more different movements and more different ages. We've been through the jet age, the space age, the microchip age, in a relatively short period of time. And look at the different social movements of the time. . . . (*)

Being a John Kennedy Democrat is, I discovered, much different from being a Ted Kennedy Democrat. If "1" were the most conservative position and "100" were the most liberal position, I would say President Kennedy was a 55; Ted Kennedy is pushing 90. But where I came out—it took a while—was when I was [an adult], and Gary Hart was running for president in '84. . . . The issue wasn't so much liberal versus conservative anymore as whether the Democratic Party was going to shake itself from the Great Society of the early and mid-60s, and develop a new set of ideas, and a new way of looking at things. Talk about fiscal management, pay-as-you-go, social programs. . . . That sort of crystallized things that had been going through my own mind; that is, you can't just throw money at things, you have to really be fiscally sound and careful. You have to look at programs not in terms of how much money is involved, but in terms of their effectiveness. . . . If I were a 90 on that scale back in college, I'm a 55 or 60 now. (*)

At the beginning of this chapter I compared the ambivalent's narrative to a recent variant of liberalism, neoliberalism. Indeed, there are numerous points of contact between the two, so many points in fact that it is tempting to consider the ambivalent's narrative as the normative foundation for neoliberalism, or at least its normative analog. Just a selection of the similarities in views should illustrate the comparison. Both ambivalents and neoliberals consider and vaunt themselves as a new political generation. Both describe themselves as social liberals and fiscal conservatives. Both tend toward a middling position.[15] Both retain many of the social equality goals of traditional liberals, but have become critical of the traditional Democratic, that is, Great Society, public support-oriented means that have been employed to achieve them. Both stress growth as the means through which to attack the problems of social injustice. Both have roughly the same sense of the limits of governmental involvement; both are against big government and bureaucracy out of concerns for efficiency and innovation. Both emphasize investment and education over redistribution. And both are notably optimistic in their outlooks and in their visions of the future. Their personal characteristics and backgrounds are also similar; although they do not necessarily come from wealthy families, both neoliberals and ambivalents are well off and well educated. In addition, both appear to be products of the 1960s, though neither were inspired by this period to take a more radical or challenging approach toward politics; the period instead seems to have fostered a drive for high achievement. The two groups are also similar in their style and orientation. They are both marked by pragmatism and a quality of coolness; the technician's motif fits particularly well with neoliberalism.

But ambivalents and neoliberals are quite different regarding party membership; the ambivalent's narrative is told by Republicans as well as Democrats, while neoliberalism is considered to be a wholly Democratically based phenomenon. This presumption suggests the question of whether there is room in neoliberalism for Republicans. If we are to consider the ambivalent's narrative as the philosophical underpinning of neoliberalism, or its normative analog, then the narrative suggests that we may need to expand our notion of neoliberalism itself, or at least rediscover the notion of a politically moderate Republican (the effects of the elections of 1994 may assist us in this endeavor).

In many respects the ambivalent's narrative (as well as neoliberalism) also matches the thinking of the original New Deal period. The New Deal resonates in the ambivalents' embrace of experimentation with new governmental approaches; its relatively friendly attitude toward business; and its emphasis on economic performance and growth, and on reinforcing the foundation of the economy. Though neither the New Deal nor the ambivalent's narrative are bereft of inspiration and indignation, they are both marked more by pragmatism than by passion (Hofstadter 1955, 325).

CHAPTER 6

How the Narratives Play Out: Three Bills

We have now heard the respective narratives of justice. In this and the following chapter I wish to examine the effects of the senators' beliefs on their actual behavior during the 1988 legislative session, the session in which the interviews took place. For many political scientists and political observers, the uncovering of these connections is the real payoff of a study such as this one; the understanding of beliefs themselves is secondary to the understanding of how they affect important political outcomes in relatively immediate ways. Unfortunately, political scientists presently know comparatively little about how beliefs—particularly the deeper beliefs found in the narratives—influence legislators' processing and evaluation of incoming information, and ultimately how such beliefs influence decision making. There have been relatively few attempts, even in single state studies, to independently determine beliefs and then examine how these beliefs affect behavior (Barrett and Cook 1991). Granted, there is a vast statistically based literature that attempts to find correlations between certain measured legislator or chamber characteristics and certain behavioral outcomes, such as voting decisions or policies (these characteristics may include many items in addition to beliefs). Indeed, I will draw liberally on this literature in making my own arguments. But this literature remains only suggestive since the correlations are only tabulated, while the actual mechanisms of linkage are left for the most part unstudied. In most cases, these works are left to speculate about these mechanisms in their final conclusions. Alas, given the narrow perspective of my own work here—my main focus is beliefs rather than behavior—my findings will be only suggestive as well.

If it is true, as I have argued in chapter 2, that beliefs have their impact on behavior primarily as filters, then we would expect to find narrative-based patterns in the way the senators discuss and ultimately act on legislative issues. These patterns begin to emerge in this chapter. I will also look for any narrative-based patterns in the relations between beliefs and behavior, as well as any narrative-based patterns in the senators' *perceptions* of the relations between beliefs and behavior. These patterns are considered in the following chapter.

The interviews upon which the narratives are based also contained questions about the connections between the senators' beliefs and their behavior, the workings of the senate, and several specific bills considered during the 1988 session. This chapter and the following one are based on those sections of the interviews, my observations prior to the interviews, other primary sources such as interviews and conversations with staff members and house members, and documentary sources such as floor transcripts, records of public hearings, and newspaper articles. I will draw on my interview and observation material throughout my examination, often without quoting or even specifically acknowledging it, so the reader should remember that this material undergirds my arguments.

This chapter examines three bills that were considered during the 1988 legislative session, and the senators' discussion of them in the interviews, in an attempt to see how the deep beliefs reflected in the narratives manifest themselves in more specific, immediate attitudes about policy issues. The bills I will examine here concern education financing, property tax, and plant closings. The following chapter considers the connections between beliefs and behavior in the senate from a more general perspective, and draws on all the sources just mentioned, in addition to the research of other scholars.

Of course, in an effort to better understand the connections between the senators' beliefs and their behavior, it would be extremely helpful to trace out in detail what individual senators within each narrative type actually did regarding the three bills. Unfortunately any such presentation would also run the risk of exposing the respondents' identities, which I have been trying to protect. Thus, I have decided to refrain from that effort. Nonetheless, the senators' discussions of the bills are at least suggestive of the effects of general normative beliefs on more specific policy attitudes, and in turn on voting decisions and other forms of legislative behavior. And beliefs do appear to matter. At the same time, the senators' discussions also preview many of the limitations on the effects of beliefs, which will be considered in the following chapter.

Education Finance

In 1977, the state supreme court upheld a lower court decision in the case of *Horton v. Meskill* (172 Conn. 615), which held that the state's reliance on local property taxes to finance public education violated the state constitution. The court ruled that the system of finance violated both the equal rights and protections provisions and the education provision of the constitution, and thus mandated the legislature to enact a more equitable education financing formula.[1] In response the legislature formed a School Finance Advisory Panel to recommend a new educational formula. In 1979, after a protracted period of study and an ensuing legislative struggle, the legislature passed a plan that would double the state's contribution to public education in five years and would allocate its aid based on a town's relative wealth. Since the money going to the towns under the new finance plan was not explicitly earmarked for local educational spending, this plan served in part as general property tax relief for the cities and towns, as well as education finance reform. By 1985, state funding accounted for 41 percent of the entire state expenditure for public education, while the proportion provided by local funding had dropped to 55 percent, from 73 percent in 1974 (Hodgkinson 1988). Riding the booming state economy during the mid-1980s, the legislature increased the state education budget by 80 percent between 1982 and 1987 (Frahm 1988).

The 1979 education finance system was based on a Guaranteed Tax Base (GTB) formula. This formula combined four factors: the number of students in a town, its relative wealth, its need, and the effort it made toward its education. A town's wealth was determined by property and income wealth per capita (not per student). A town's need was determined by the number of students on welfare; each student from a family receiving assistance from Aid to Families with Dependent Children (AFDC) would add an additional half person to the student enrollment for the purposes of calculating support levels. And a town's effort was determined by changes in its rates of school funding, holding the other factors of wealth and need constant. But regardless of its wealth and effort to fund its own education, each town was entitled to receive a minimum grant, which in 1988 was $250 per student.

The next major legislative initiative in state education spending came in 1986 with the passage of the Educational Enhancement Act (EEA; enacted by a Republican-controlled state legislature), which established a three-year trust fund to raise teacher salaries and to allow towns with high student-to-teacher ratios to hire additional teachers. The funds were distributed through incentive grants, which in turn were allocated based on changes in salaries and number of teachers employed. EEA was apparently effective; in 1982, the state's teacher salaries ranked twentieth in the nation, but by 1988 they ranked fourth (Libov 1988). But the fund was created with state budget surpluses, and there was no provision for funding beyond 1989. The fund's imminent exhaustion provided a significant impetus for the consideration of a new education finance system during the 1988 legislative session.

When the GTB system was originally implemented, the legislature also established the Education Equity Study Committee to monitor the overall system and to advise the legislature on any proposed changes in educational funding. Based on its ten-year experience with the GTB, and in light of the expiration of funds for the EEA, in 1987 the committee began to develop a proposal to replace the two systems (the committee was then headed by a former Democratic state representative, and also contained several acting senators, including the Education Committee cochair).[2] This proposal became known as the Equalized Cost Sharing Formula (ECS). Under the old GTB system the gap in educational spending between wealthy and poor towns had not widened, but it had not significantly narrowed either. The new ECS formula was designed to narrow this gap, at least to some extent, through providing additional state aid to poorer towns. In 1988, the State Department of Education recommended the Equity Committee's proposal to the legislature. The new plan would be funded entirely through the state's General Fund Budget. It would begin in 1989, and would be phased in progressively over a four-year period, reaching the "target year" in 1992. Since it would begin in 1989, the program would not become part of the budget—and would not have to be funded—until the following legislative session, after the 1988 elections.

The principal change from the GTB to the ECS formula was in the way a town's wealth and relative need were defined. Under ECS, wealth would be determined per student versus per capita. And instead of determining relative need based solely on AFDC students, ECS would also include state mastery test scores; each student on AFDC would add a quarter person to the calculated enrollment, and each student scoring below the remedial standard on the state-wide mastery test, which had been implemented a few years before, would add an additional quarter person.[3] Finally, the program would use a three-year average in determining wealth, rather than the single-year figure used in the GTB formula. This measure was intended to provide greater predictability and stability for local school board planning.

The program would also eliminate the additional rewards and punishments in state funding that were meted out in response to the changes in a town's educational effort. But perhaps more importantly, it would change the Minimum Expenditure Requirement (MER) for town education funding in order for it to receive the state funding assistance. This level would be raised to $4,800 per student—including the need adjustments—by 1992, and would be determined thereafter by a comparison with spending in the other towns. Thus, the new program would help towns to spend a required minimum amount on their education. This MER would also serve as the "Foundation" level for calculating a town's aid; towns would not receive state aid for education spending above this level. In addition, no town would receive, due to its relative wealth, less than it would have received under the old GTB and EEA programs. Thus, towns like Avon, Canaan, and Old Saybrook, which might otherwise receive less under ECS, would be "held harmless"; they would receive a 1 percent increase over their old support levels during each year of the phase-in period. And they would receive this increase regardless of the changes in their student enrollment.

Though it did not set any upper limits on what a town could spend on its education, the ultimate policy goal of the ECS program, as articulated by the Equity Committee and the Department of Education, was to enable any town in the state to spend on its own education an amount equal to 90 percent of the amount spent by the wealthiest town, with the state contributing up to 90 percent of that amount, if necessary (dubbed the "90-90 goal"). This goal, however, required a higher amount of state funding than the ECS program ultimately called for.

The plan received criticism on several fronts, from both within and without the legislature. Its use of mastery test scores in determining relative need was criticized for rewarding failure and punishing success. Representatives of the state's largest cities, especially Hartford, also objected to the inclusion of mastery test scores rather than the sole reliance on AFDC students, since this move would decrease the funds they might have received otherwise. The plan was criticized for being unaffordable and for not specifying its means of finance in the future, beyond the provision that it would be funded out of the General Fund Budget. In particular, its overall increase in educational aid was criticized, as fears grew over declining state revenues and potential budget deficits (fears that were subsequently realized). The plan was also criticized for being considered too hastily by the legislature; the Education Committee, for example, was not fully briefed on the plan until February, in a legislative session that was mandated to expire that May. But at the same time, the committee and the legislature were under pressure from town boards of education to complete and pass the program during that session, so that they could negotiate contracts and prepare budgets with firm expectations of state aid levels.

In putting forward the ECS program, the Education Committee made several adjustments, partly in response to, or in anticipation of, some of the above criticisms. The Education Equity Study Committee had originally considered a level of state aid of almost $2 billion by 1992, but in its final "majority report" it called for approximately $1.1 billion in state aid (a minority report kept the more ambitious funding levels). The Education Committee worked with the lower funding level; the bill it sent to the full legislature supplied between $1.1 and $1.2 billion of state aid in the "target year." In response to the objections over rewarding failure, it added a provision to reward towns that raised their mastery test scores over time. Finally, it added an additional measure to the provision to hold all towns "harmless," which would provide 5 percent yearly increases over the original GTB and EEA amount for any town that was not considered a minimum-grant town under the old GTB formula. This measure primarily assisted large-city suburbs and small cities such as West Hartford, Danbury, and Norwalk. An amendment was also added on the senate floor to provide 5 percent yearly increases to towns in the 1 percent "held harmless" category if 20 percent of their students met the poverty or educational need measure. This amendment increased state aid to just one city, Stamford.

The education bill passed the senate on a 32–4 vote (only Republicans voted against the bill), was subsequently passed in the same form by the house, and was immediately signed into law by the governor. Four Republican amendments were defeated on the senate floor, including measures to require school districts to increase education spending to match the increases in state aid; to eliminate the additional aid based on low mastery test scores and to create a separate grant category to aid in the improvement of the scores; and to limit state aid to 75 percent of the total local educational expenditure. Another amendment proposed an adjustment to the Grand List of property value (used in calculating a town's relative wealth) to account for the funds in lieu of taxes that the state was already providing to some towns to offset tax-exempt property located within their borders. That amendment would have correspondingly increased the aid going to many other towns, including many towns in Democratic districts (the 75 percent limit also increased the aid levels in many Democratic towns). In accord with the standard party competition strategy, these Democratic towns were read aloud on the senate floor. The chair of the Education Committee recognized the logical merit of the Grand List adjustment, but nonetheless recommended its rejection in favor of further consideration and review by the Equity Study Committee. The four amendments were defeated on party votes; there were a few defections from the Republican ranks on the amendment concerning tax-exempt property, apparently due to the fact that some of their districts would not gain from the adjustment, and on the amendment concerning the 75 percent limit, apparently due to the fact that it substantially violated the original intent of the education bill itself.[4]

The ECS-based education finance bill clearly involves issues that are central to the narratives of justice. In particular, it involves the question of how to provide, distribute, and redistribute resources that are perceived to be integral to the provision of economic opportunity. It also involves questions over the appropriate levels and forms of government spending. But other factors were obviously involved in the education bill's passage. First, as it was embodied in the bill, the redistributional issue had a certain twist: the resources were ultimately being allocated by town rather than by individual. Redistribution was thus more explicitly and visibly in the form of some senate districts receiving more aid than others; the trade-offs were between districts rather than between individuals. This fact heightened the concern to give every district something and no district less than what it had before; hence the bill's original "hold harmless" provision. It also promoted the intrusion of local interests into general interests; hence the subsequent additions to the bill that favored certain kinds of suburbs and cities. Second, although the bill was relatively bipartisan in its final passage, party strategies still clearly played a role. Witness, for example, the "record building" amendments offered by the Republicans and their summary defeat by the Democrats (see chap. 7 herein). Third, the bill's initial form, its path, and its ultimate resolution were mostly the products of the actions of a few designated experts, in particular the senate chair of the Education Committee, who also served on the Equity Study Committee. The following comment made in the full chamber by one of the senators who had also served on the Equity Committee illustrates the influence of these factors:

> I too would like to commend [the] senator [the Education Committee chair]. . . . I served on the Equity Committee with him last year trying to prepare this formula. I have to tell you that I don't totally understand it to the degree that many people do and [he] has a really good handle on it. And I think that he had especially a lot of pressure because of the district that he came from and the people that he represents. . . . I think that he really looked at the state as a whole and where the needs were and I think those needs are addressed in this bill.[5]

But at the same time, as the above comment on the floor also indicates, these factors did not completely obliterate some real struggles over deeper normative questions. And the debate on the floor appeared to reflect the genuine beliefs of the senators about these questions. But such struggles may have been an unusual occurrence, at least on the senate floor. For example, the senate chair of the Education Committee, who shepherded the bill through committee and the full senate, commented on the floor that the debate was "one of the most high minded that we have had in my first two years here." Comments from the bill's consideration before the full senate follow.

> Today we take a very important next step in the continuing commitment in educational equity and excellence in Connecticut. . . . [D]isparities, and very wide disparities, exist in the State of Connecticut. Maybe three factors will be interesting. Per pupil tax resources in the State of Connecticut: the disparity from highest to lowest town, 35 to 1. School tax rates in the State of Connecticut: the highest to lowest town, 9 to 1. Per pupil expenditures: a disparity from highest to lowest of 2 to 1. . . . The result, despite progress . . . has been that we are nonetheless facing a situation where too many school districts with too few resources cannot possibly provide equal opportunity, the equal opportunity for education which our constitution mandates. . . . So the question really before us is whether a promise made will be a promise kept.

> The bill before us today makes fair changes, needed changes, and appropriate changes in the state's commitment to public education. And I think it is something that over the next few years will serve us well, and [will] advance that commitment to free, local, public education, which is the

greatest mixing factor, the greatest contributor to a democracy in the United States over the last 200 years. . . .

I am hearing a great deal about the cost of education. . . . [I]f we do not educate our young and educate them properly, you will be spending more money, and it may be in areas that you do not wish to spend it. . . . [T]his bill . . . is a program of action . . . before the crisis comes upon us. . . .

I think this bill directs funds to those towns that need it, to our urban centers and to the poor, smaller towns throughout Connecticut. And education, in my opinion, is the key to those people to help themselves, to better themselves so that we can have better communities and less poverty around the state, . . . in this the wealthiest state.

I do believe the local community is the first place of responsibility for providing education, and it is their responsibility to determine what that education will be and how that education will be funded. . . . Where does this formula take us? . . . I believe that there are those out there who will feel that the passage of this bill and the amount of money that we are dedicating down the road without being able to guarantee that the money exists somewhere in this state is very irresponsible on our part. And I cannot, for one, accept that irresponsibility.

If it were up to me as an individual I would like to see us spend some more money on education, because there is probably nothing more important than the education of our young. And as I sat here, I listed a few items as to areas that at the top of my head came to mind as areas where I would like to see substantial increase[s] [in] spending. . . . And why don't we just go and increase the funding for these [other] programs? . . . [B]ecause we understand we have a limit to what we can do. We have to control our hearts and control our minds because we also understand that we can't just raise taxes totally out of sight. To do that would be negative to the economy of the state.

The senators' discussions of the education bill during the interviews largely reflected these same concerns. In particular, they wrestled with concerns to respond to relative need versus concerns over government spending and the desire to preserve local control over items such as education. They also discussed the more pragmatic concerns of supplying tangible benefits to their districts and cooperatively engaging in the legislative trading process. Among all the senators, as the relative involvement in or attention paid to the bill went down, the relative emphasis placed on the amount of money going to their own towns and on the norm of "going along with the others" went up. In addition, the specific content of the issues involved appeared to have an independent effect on the senators' engagement in the bill; to the degree that the content struck a chord in their own more particular legislative agendas, they seemed to have been more engaged and interested in the bill and its broader theoretical implications. There were some recognizable subpatterns within these general patterns, however, which corresponded to the different narratives. These sub-patterns held for both the content of the senators' views on the bill and their approaches in assessing both the bill itself and its path through the legislature.

In expressing their support of the bill, critics tended to emphasize its redistributional elements. They generalized redistribution from the individual level up to the town and district levels, and endorsed need—in this case the need of an entire town—as a fair standard by which to distribute a given amount of state funding. They conceptualized relative need in terms of a town's available resources and the prevalence of its socioeconomic ills. Regarding concerns over whether or not the state could reasonably afford this program, critics subsumed (and perhaps avoided) this question within a relatively expansive view of what constituted appropriate state expenditure. But this emphasis on redistribution and a broadly conceived state role may not have been a hard choice for the critics, since they represented a relative concentration of the poorer districts in the state. In this case, an apparently ideological stand coincided nicely with district-oriented concerns.

But though the critics supported the bill, they had some reservations about it, which again reflect the views contained in their narrative and also perhaps their interest in maximizing the funds going to towns in their districts. They objected to the "political elements" that intruded into the process concerning the treatment of the towns "held harmless." They believed that these well-off towns should not have received as much assistance as they did. They also expressed concerns that education funding, by itself, would not solve the problems that the bill was touted as addressing, and that the education bill might actually help to mask the need for more direct engagement of these problems.

> Some [wealthier] towns, they're not going to get less. So if you want to talk about political decisions, there were some influential people in the Democratic caucus whose communities were going to be affected. . . . I've been all for [education financing measures]. I still think we've got a long way to go; we're certainly not going to solve the problems of education through the education finance system. . . .[6]

> The issue involved in that [bill] was how the money was going to be distributed, the formula; what towns and cities were going to get

what. Here again, my basic concern was that . . . the poorer towns in the state should [receive] more of the money than the rich towns. . . . I think that . . . the big cities are called upon to carry a disproportionate burden of society's problems, such as taking care of the poor and the elderly . . . and it's a known fact that urban kids go to school with a disproportionate amount of social and economic problems than kids in the suburban areas go through. And we are calling more and more for our school systems to take care of those problems. I feel that a school system in [a rich town], to get proportionately the same amount as the kids from [a poor city], is unfair.

One of the big issues in that bill was bringing some equity into the educational process by equalizing . . . the whole gamut, so that the large city schools . . . could do all the things necessary to bring their schools up to par. Equity, really, so that all children should get an equal education, equal opportunity for education. And the best that they can have. . . . I think the state can't afford not to have it enacted; it's something you have to do, and you have to pay for it.

Not all supporters voted against the education bill; in fact it received only four nay votes from the entire senate. But those supporters who ultimately did support the bill viewed it as a somewhat unpalatable compromise that nonetheless represented a key funding item for their districts, and that deserved support due to the importance of education for both individual upward mobility and the attractiveness of the state's business climate. Nonetheless, the supporters still shared deep concerns over the bill, which for some were strong enough to overcome its positive elements and force a nay vote. Again, these concerns reflected parts of their narrative. First, the supporters were suspicious of the education funding as constituting simply an extra source of money flowing from the state to the towns and especially the cities, without any accountability attached to it. They were also concerned over installing another negative reward system through the supposed need-based funding mechanism. The funding mechanism did not make use of appropriate incentive systems, which were obvious and readily available. On perhaps a more fundamental level, they objected to the way the bill determined relative need; why should a greater number of people on welfare result in more state money going to the town for education? The bill also went beyond what the state could afford, and would probably result in an income tax. Finally, in the obverse of the critics' concerns over the efficacy of education programs by themselves, supporters doubted the ability of additional government spending to alleviate cultural problems that in fact resided deeper within the home, the family, and the individual.

I asked the Office of Fiscal Analysis to run off a comparison if we continued the GTB and Enhancement Act formulas over four years and compare that to the new formula. . . . My towns would be better off keeping the two existing formulas. . . . So I voted against it based on that; I don't think the people in my town send me to Hartford to vote for legislation that is going to take money away from them. . . .

To a certain extent, calling that an education bill is a misnomer, because the money goes down to the municipalities and goes into the General Fund. And some cities and towns spend it on education; some spend parts of it on other things. . . .

I don't have problems supporting additional funding for education. . . . We can't compete with other states when it comes to energy costs here in Connecticut. Foolishly, we have one of the highest state corporate taxes in the country. . . . The one thing that I think we can offer corporations in trying to make Connecticut attractive is a well-educated populace, skilled employees.

I think the issues were the changing of the formula, and the equity, making it equitable based on the tax structure. I'm not so sure that guarantees equitable education and a quality education. . . . I don't think that the testing helped the bill at all, the way they were using the test scores. I don't think because you have AFDC families in a school system that you get more money, for that particular reason. The fact that the money isn't necessarily earmarked to go into education bothers me, because it may never do what it was intended to do. It was also a tremendous amount of money, and a commitment into the future, and I don't know if the state can sustain it. . . . Everybody knew the state can't sustain it, and now we're going to have to look for other sources to finance it. . . .

I don't understand why we're giving money into education because a family is on welfare. It doesn't make any sense to me. . . . Does that mean because you're on AFDC you're not going to do well, and it costs more to educate you? I don't think anyone's proven that. . . . Why not just say outright, this city is not spending enough money educating its children, therefore we have to supplement all their children, not just this one particular group of children. We pick up on that in other ways with the hot lunch program, the breakfast program, and other things that are provided for the children of welfare-dependent families.

Ambivalents were more politically pragmatic in their discussions of the education bill. They endorsed the value of responding to relative need, but tempered this with an emphasis on what they considered a "realistic" answer to the state's mandated commitment to education funding. They saw the bill in large part as a measure of tax relief for certain towns and cities. They also emphasized the fact that the bill provided something for everyone, including their own districts, and that it did not overly disadvantage the wealthy towns. The bill fit into the ambivalents' desire not to pit different income groups against each other in the political system. Like the senators telling the other two narratives, the ambivalents rightfully viewed the bill as a compromise; it ultimately provided a way for everyone to be for the program, and it offered widespread, short-term electoral benefits. But as a compromise, the bill thus represented a good outcome; as a compromise it represented a successful piece of legislation.

The ambivalents also had their concerns about the bill, although their concerns did not run as deeply as those of the senators telling the other two narratives. Some wrestled with conflicts between the fairness of relative need and concerns with bringing more funding into their own districts (a dilemma spared for many of the critics). There was also concern that in the end the towns "held harmless" received too much. Like the supporters, the ambivalents had concerns with the accountability of the spending and the expense and tax implications of the program. They also doubted to some extent the effectiveness of increased government spending, even though it was in their favored area, education.

> One of the major issues there is how do we deal with the fact that we know that there are a significant number of communities, or let's say students, who live in communities that need more help and financial assistance, and aren't getting it under the current program; while at the same time there is a substantial number of communities which have enough local wealth that perhaps you could make a decent argument that they should get no or little state assistance. But politically, there seems to be a need to keep everyone in the system, and keep everyone being a winner; not only in terms of saying OK, the [wealthy towns] not only have to get something, but that something should go up every year. So, how do you balance it out? . . . There was a political necessity not to behead any towns, even though my natural instincts would be to do so. . . . The bill was written as a balancing act. . . .
>
> My attitude is if the rest of the legislature will go along with giving the towns I think need to have the help, if you're also going to help other towns, that's fine with me. . . . The marginal increase in productivity is not worth the political blood and acrimony, and probably the resulting lack of support for public education.
>
> I've been a believer and supporter of increased state aid for education for a number of reasons. . . . We've got this constitutional provision . . . that

we've never fully lived up to. This new formula gets us very close. It also does a tremendous amount to ease the local property tax burden, because that's your major local expense. . . . Also, the towns in my district did pretty well on it.

I think the end result in the final bill . . . is a compromise. . . . You have the . . . communities and . . . school districts . . . competing for that dollar. . . . If there was an effort to take dollars away . . . you're going to start losing votes left and right. No legislator in his or her right mind is going to go back home and say, "hey, I brought you home less money than you received last year." . . . I think the idea that every district will get more money than it did last year was a wise decision.

Property Tax Relief

Relative to other states, Connecticut relies heavily on property taxes for local government funding.[7] The property tax includes taxes on residential, business, and other property—mostly motor vehicles. In 1985, property taxes accounted for 26 percent of the total state and local government revenues; the average across the nation was 17 percent (Price Waterhouse 1988). Per capita, this percentage placed the state fifth nationally, while as a percentage of personal income the state's reliance on property taxes ranked fourteenth. Property taxes accounted for 58 percent of the state's local government revenues, while the average across the nation was 28 percent. These data reflect the fact that the state's towns are among the most fiscally self-sufficient in the nation (Johnson 1989a).

Within the state, the relative burdens and tax structures vary widely from town to town, but statewide, the effective tax rate on property was approximately 1.4 percent. Since the funds are generated and spent by each town or city, the general patterns across the state are what we would expect: higher income towns raise relatively more money per capita, have relatively lower effective property tax rates, and have lower property taxes as a percentage of income, while lower income towns raise less money, have higher effective property tax rates, and have higher property taxes as a percentage of income (Price Waterhouse 1988, 78–79). And urban tax rates are higher than those in suburban and rural areas. On a town-by-town basis across the state, then, there is a regressive quality to the property tax system. These patterns, of course, contributed to the debate over educational opportunity. Within a given town or city, the property tax burden is relatively flat, perhaps even regressive. Thus, most states have instituted some system of local property tax relief, usually in the form of a "circuit-breaker" program that gives tax breaks to families and individuals with lower incomes (Nice 1987). These relief systems can serve to some degree as redistributional mechanisms at an individual or town level, as well as direct aids to local governments. The specific mechanism of relief is usually the provision of funds by the state to the town or local jurisdiction to make up for the funds lost through the individual assistance program.

Certain factors about Connecticut's property tax system and its economy during the 1980s combined to make property tax relief a particularly salient issue during the time of the interviews. First, the state's towns revalue residential property—both personal and business—only once every ten years. This revaluation cycle is among the longest in the nation. Other forms of property, such as motor vehicles and nonresidential and non–real estate business property, are revalued every year. Thus, relative changes between the values of different kinds of property are stored up over a long period of time and then instituted all at once, resulting in shifts in the tax burden by type of property. The revaluation does not mean that overall property taxes must increase, since the mil rates can be adjusted appropriately, but since the taxable values of properties will shift relative to each other, shifts in the relative burdens do occur. When this dynamic was combined with the fact that in the 1980s personal property values in the state increased dramatically—exceeding an average annual rate of increase of 20 percent from 1983 to 1985, for example—revaluations occurring during the late 1980s could result in equally dramatic shifts in the tax burden, shifts that fell most heavily on owners of personal residential property (who often had not experienced income gains to match the gains in their property value). If revaluation had occurred across the entire state in 1985, for example, the residential share of total property taxes would have grown by 10 percent. More than 100 cities and towns in the state, including Hartford and New Haven, were scheduled to revalue between 1988 and 1991. All of these factors might have demonstrated the attractiveness of a state income tax system, but instead the recognition of these problems, along with a deep resistance to an income tax, fueled the gyrations and convolutions on property tax relief that were to come.

Indeed, property tax relief had been considered well before the 1988 session. The state already had in place a circuit-breaker program for elderly citizens, through which they could receive deductions from their property taxes or rent subsidies based on their income. But most of the legislative action up to 1988 had added up to a series of special, narrow provisions, reflecting a variety of interests. The acts from the 1987 session, for example, included measures to broaden the eligibility for and increase the benefits under the elderly circuit-breaker program; to allow permanently disabled homeowners to participate in the circuit-breaker program; to allow larger temporary deferrals of taxes for qualifying elderly citizens; to allow manufacturing facilities additional time to file claims for tax exemptions under the preexisting program for "distressed municipalities"; and to allow exemptions from the tax for all livestock except horses and ponies not used in farming. More significant was an act to create the Local Property Tax Relief Fund, which was designed to provide $42 million per year for ten years for future property tax relief (this legislation passed the senate on a mostly party-line vote).

But most importantly for the 1988 session, the governor called a special summer session of the General Assembly at the completion of the 1987 regular session in order to pass additional legislation concerning property tax relief, among other issues. That special session subsequently passed a bill that established a legislative task force (chaired by the cochairs of the Finance, Revenue, and Bonding Committee) that was directed to recommend specific plans for the relief of shifting burdens due to revaluation; established a Residential Property Tax Revaluation Relief Fund of $30 million in the next year in order to fund the programs recommended by the task force; and allowed towns that had undergone or were undergoing revaluations between 1987 and 1989 to ease in the assessment increases over a five-year period. This bill, subsequently signed into law, received only five negative votes in the senate, all from Republicans. This final act of the 1987 assembly thus set the stage for the reconsideration of more general and broad-based property tax relief in 1988.

The task force commissioned a study by Price Waterhouse, which did not recommend a specific course of relief policy, but instead gathered and presented data on the property tax burden and its shifts and suggested several options for relief (which in turn would frame the ensuing debate). Foremost among these were the expansion of the elderly circuit-breaker program to include all lower income residences; the creation of a flat deduction in the assessment of personal residences, subsequently known as the "homestead exemption"; the creation of separate rates of tax assessment for residential and business properties, which could be instituted at the discretion of each town or city, subsequently known as "classification"; and simple direct tax credits to homeowners (it is also certainly possible to combine these proposals in various ways; to limit, for example, homestead exemptions to those with lower incomes). Each of these options could also be gradually phased out over a given period of time, thus serving to ease the initial blow of revaluation to a targeted type of property owner. These options were by no means new; they had been pushed in various incarnations in previous legislative sessions by various individual members, but had never been passed. Immediately prior to the 1988 session, the growing concern over the state's economic health and falling predictions of future state government revenue appeared to make a system of phased-out classification or homestead exemption more attractive, since they do not necessarily involve increased aid from state to local government. In the case of classification, the revenues lost from residential property can be made up by higher rates assessed on commercial property; in the case of a homestead exemption, they can be made up through a higher overall mil rate. After receiving the Price Waterhouse relief options, the task force could not reach a consensus on the appropriate course of action, and thus made no specific recommendations. The various proposals were therefore left circulating as the session began.

In the early days of the session, the recognized leaders within the assembly on the property tax relief issue—the same two cochairs of the Finance, Revenue, and Bonding Committee who also had served as cochairs of the task force—began to make known their desire to include some form of classification scheme in the tax relief program. In turn, most of the Democratic members of the senate showed support for some version of such a program, while support in the house for classification was comparatively weaker. The governor, who had long been opposed to any system of differential classification, countered this movement with the announcement that he would soon offer a different plan of his own. The Connecticut Business and Industry Association (CBIA), the principal lobbying group for the business community, also opposed classification. The governor's specific objection to the classification scheme was that it would drive businesses away from the towns and cities in which it occurred, and that it would be a source of divisiveness among the cities and towns (Fink 1988a). The plan the governor subsequently introduced (before the two assembly cochairs presented their plan) would have provided $200 tax credits to all homeowners living in towns undergoing at least a 20 percent shift to residential property in tax burden because of revaluation. Twenty-three towns were projected to undergo such tax burden shifts, and this part of the plan was estimated to cost approximately $11 million in the following year. The plan also called for direct state aid to towns and cities to help hold down property taxes, and a requirement that residential revaluations be conducted every five years instead of every ten years. The tax burden shift element of the plan was criticized by the Finance Committee cochairs as well as the Republican leadership as an unfair way to distribute the state aid, in that there was no distinction of individual need within a given town; the entire town itself either did or did not qualify for relief.

Also at this time, a split was forming between the house and senate over the possible expansion of the circuit-breaker program. Support was growing in the house for expanding the current program to all homeowners, regardless of age, while the senate was moving toward raising the income limits on the program but leaving the age restrictions intact. Additional differences between the house and senate would mark the progress of relief through the legislature, with the house generally taking positions closer to those of the governor. There was an ideological irony here, in that the house was more progressive than the senate in preferring a general expansion of the circuit-breaker program, but arguably less progressive in following the desires of the governor regarding the homestead exemption and classification (though the progressivity of the homestead exemption was somewhat unclear; see the following).

The possible expansion of the circuit-breaker program to the nonelderly also revealed a further limitation on the redistributional impact of the other property tax relief measures being considered, which for the most part went overlooked in the public consideration of the issue. All the other measures assisted only homeowners, but those who are poor are most likely to be renters. A possible response to such a critique is that many renters would also benefit from the tax relief since their rents would not go up as much due to revaluation, but savings at the wholesale level do not always get passed along at the retail level. In fact, many renters could expect their rents to increase as a result of a homestead tax exemption policy, since larger (and more valuable) apartment units would likely receive the same standard exemption, but the correspondingly raised mil rates would cause these more valuable units to incur a raise in taxes that would outweigh the savings from the exemption. Two bills that were more explicitly redistributive were in fact introduced in the assembly. Both bills, one originating in the house and the other in the senate, expanded the circuit-breaker program to all the state's residents (the senate's version even placed the qualifying income levels 25 percent higher than those then in use for the elderly). But after a public hearing, neither bill was subsequently reported out of the Finance, Revenue, and Bonding Committee.[8]

In the month following the announcement of the governor's plan, the senate cochair of the Finance, Revenue, and Bonding Committee initiated a relief bill in the senate, despite efforts by the governor, CBIA, and other lobbyists to kill the bill in the Finance Committee. The bill combined giving towns and cities the option of granting exemptions of $25,000 from the taxable value of residential properties with the governor's plan of direct tax credits for homeowners in towns undergoing large shifts in tax burdens. Largely at the behest of local tax assessors, the bill did not include the governor's proposal to require revaluation every five years instead of every ten years. The local funds lost through the exemptions could be recouped through higher mil rates on all forms of property—personal, residential, and commercial. Though this homestead exemption portion of the bill would not cost the state anything, the dollar amount of reshifted burdens would far exceed that contained in the governor's plan; one estimate placed the total figure in excess of $100 million ("Beware" 1988). The proponents of the bill argued that it was more progressive than the governor's plan, since a combination of a flat reduction in the assessed value of a home and higher mil rates would result in a greater relative reduction in taxes for those with less valuable homes. The governor still objected to this plan, on the grounds that it was, in effect, simply another version of classification. In reaction to the governor's response, the senate leaders proposed extending the exemption to commercial property as well, but the governor and CBIA still remained opposed to any exemption plan. At this time, the governor made explicit his intentions to veto any bill containing a homestead exemption. The senate leaders responded that they would nonetheless pass a bill containing some form of homestead exemption. The governor in turn threatened to call a summer session if the tax relief issue was not resolved before the May adjournment date.

But at the same time another, and from a larger perspective perhaps a more decisive factor entered the process. Concerns about a potential state budget deficit and about future budgetary problems (which were subsequently realized) caused the addition of two house amendments to the 1988 budget. The first amendment reduced the approximately $70 million designated for property tax relief in 1988 to $18 million—just enough to cover the governor's plan—and directed the difference in the funds to the state's General Fund in order to balance the budget, while the second amendment eliminated the funding for tax relief in subsequent years. These amendments did not rule out the homestead exemption plans, since from the standpoint of the state they could be revenue neutral, but they nonetheless did place a severe set of constraints on any additional plans for relief that involved state funds.

As the 1988 session progressed, the property tax debate in the assembly and the press centered around the addition of a homestead exemption to the governor's plan for limited direct relief. The debate also began to assume the form of a Hartford versus the rest of the state contest, in addition to a governor versus the senate contest, in part because the exemption provision would considerably help homeowners in Hartford since the city was facing a revaluation, and in part because the senate leaders pushing the exemption represented districts in the Hartford area.

As the session neared its close, the bill containing the homestead exemption worked its way through the senate. In terms of direct state aid for tax relief, the bill would provide $200 tax credits to homeowners in towns and cities where revaluations between 1982 and 1986 pushed the effective tax rate to 2 percent or above, and $25 to $125 tax credits in towns and cities where revaluations in 1987 and thereafter pushed the effective tax rate to 1.5 percent or above. The credits would be phased out over a period of five years. Along the way an amendment was added to expand the elderly circuit-breaker program by raising the qualifying income limits. This was consistent with the senate's original desire to expand the program, but the timing of the amendment suggested that it might have been added to make the entire bill more attractive to both the senate and the house. The expansion of the circuit-breaker program would cost $2 million, and was funded by a corresponding reduction in the direct tax relief program. Towns and cities would not be permitted to offer more than one form of subsidy to any homeowner.

The senate bill passed the senate on a 23–13 vote, which was mostly along party lines; there were four defections from the Democrats and two from the Republicans. Two Republican amendments were rejected; the first would have replaced the homestead exemption with a phased-in reduction in the rate of taxation for all personal (as opposed to residential) property, including business and individual property, with a corresponding phased-in increase of taxes on residential property. The second amendment would have replaced the direct tax relief with an extension of the elderly circuit-breaker program to all homeowners within a qualifying town (forty towns were estimated to qualify). A third Republican amendment, similar to one that the Democrats had planned to offer, was passed unanimously. It was in response to a recent ruling by the state supreme court that allowed individual revaluations of residences that were sold in the interims between general revaluations, based solely on the sale price of the residence. The amendment made such revaluations illegal.[9]

In response to the bill's passage, the governor and CBIA reasserted their intentions to fight the exemption, from the position that it hurt business. The critique that the program was not sufficiently progressive also continued to dog the bill, in that it rewarded wealthy homeowners and commercial enterprises that happened to be located in qualifying towns, and that, except for the elderly, only homeowners as opposed to renters were helped. Furthermore, the bill only allowed tax exemptions for apartment units with three or fewer dwellings. Thus, the resulting higher mil rates on larger units were likely to result in higher rents for those living in these units. Finally, two days after the senate passed the bill, the General Assembly's Office of Fiscal Analysis determined that under the trigger mechanism for the direct state aid, only one of the eleven towns that revalued their properties in 1987 would qualify for relief, and consequently in its present form the bill would spend only $9 million of the $16 million in allocated state funds. The office had previously estimated that about twelve towns would qualify, but in the interim most of those towns set their tax rates such that they failed to reach the trigger, while a few others postponed the new tax assessments entirely.

On a 103–47 vote, the house removed the homestead exemption provision, and sent the bill back to the senate on a 142–7 vote. In order to include more towns and cities, the house also lowered the effective tax rate trigger level for revaluations in 1987 and thereafter to 1.3 percent and raised the grant amounts to between $50 and $250. Consequently, ten towns and cities would be eligible for direct relief in the following year, and the plan would once again spend approximately $16 million, excluding the elderly circuit-breaker expansion.

On the day following the bill's passage in the house, the senate, in the face of the strong negative vote in the house, in effect capitulated to the governor in passing on a 32–4 vote the house version of the bill, which the governor then signed into law. Once again, two Republican senate amendments were rejected.[10] The first would have expanded (by lowering the effective tax rate trigger) the number of towns covered under the direct relief formula, and financed the expansion by excluding from relief all properties assessed between 1982 and 1986 at over $200,000 and properties assessed in 1987 at over $300,000. The second amendment, which garnered only two votes, reinstated the governor's proposal (which originated in the Price Waterhouse report) to mandate revaluations every five years instead of every ten years. In their postsession interviews with the media, the senate Democratic leadership attempted to find victory in the $2 million in new aid to expand the elderly circuit-breaker program and in the fact that a relief package had passed in any form.

The law that was ultimately passed, then, was relatively meager. Only a handful of towns were covered in the first year of its application, and the amount of relief for any given individual was small. In terms of redistribution, the law's impact was minuscule. Thus, the larger concerns about the property tax and revaluation that initially informed the creation of the task force and the early consideration of legislative options were left mostly unaddressed in the law's final disposition. As one of the senate Republican leaders said on the floor, "We have had this pregnant elephant out there. She has been moaning and groaning all session. And she gave birth to a mouse." But some of the factors that constrained the course of the bill's development would also contribute to an expansion of the tax issue arena in later sessions. Indeed, the bill became law amidst a growing unease about its funding in future years and a growing awareness that a more substantial reworking of the property tax system could soon be thrust upon the legislature by economic events.

Like the education bill, the property tax relief bill involves issues that are central to the narratives of justice. Foremost among these are redistribution, progressivity in taxes, attitudes toward urban centers and their attendant problems, and concerns about the limitations on what the state government can afford. And also like the education bill, the redistributional issue assumed a particular form in the property tax bill, which complicated the matter: Relief funds were being distributed by town rather than by individual (except for the circuit-breaker extension).

Concerns about questions of distributive justice and the limits of public spending were certainly evident in many of the comments offered on the senate floor during the bill's consideration. Running underneath them, however, were more immediate electoral and interpersonal chamber concerns, which were revealed both in the interviews and in some of the additional comments on the floor. Thus, ideological, regional, district, and interpersonal concerns all overlapped and intertwined, sometimes reinforcing each other and at other times working at cross-purposes. Comments from the bill's first consideration by the full senate, before the house amended it by removing the homestead exemption and lowering the trigger mechanisms, follow.

> . . . [W]hen this was first announced, and some of us first started looking at what it was that was being proposed in terms of tax credits, I don't think it really dawned on everyone that we were talking about multiple tax credits for someone that may in fact own multiple properties in the city, someone who has considerable wealth. . . . I think that is the basic flaw, at least in this section of this particular amendment, because it does not, in fact, make any sense from an equity standpoint. . . . I think this probably represents the most inequity of anything that we have done this session. . . .

> . . . [W]hen we started this debate we talked about trying to lessen the shock of revaluation. And moving some of the commercial taxes that businesses pay going onto the residential taxpayer, and we want to lessen that burden. So the proposal was if we have a shift of 20 percent or more to the residential property taxpayers, we are going to give you a tax credit on your property tax because you are struggling. . . . Now, when the bill comes out we are talking about 1.5 percent effective tax rate. . . . But let's see who might be eligible. Suffield: yes, that's a poor town. [But] Simsbury, Watertown, West Hartford; we are talking about people that can afford to pay some property taxes. . . . [I]t bothers me, the product that we have, the way it got here and I guess especially that we threw in the sweetener of the elderly to get this bill out of the senate.

> . . . [O]ne hears comments that suggest that the Finance Committee process was other than what it was. That it was not fair. That promises were made, or even on some cases, threats were made. . . .
>
> In the last few days and even in the last few weeks, many people have been represented by very capable and very effective advocates. . . . But . . . one group of people in Connecticut have not had advocates in the hallways, have not had the powerful and well-connected and very effective people to present their point of view, and they are Connecticut's homeowners. They are Connecticut's families. They are the elderly who are helped in this bill by the circuit-breaker amendment. They are the middle class and middle income who are trying to get by by trying to get their kids through school, a decent school, to try and own a home in a good and safe neighborhood, but who must contend with rising property values and skyrocketing property taxes.

> . . . I think there are good intentions in this legislation that we have before us. I think there was an effort to deal with property tax relief. I think we

mixed things up along the way. I have difficulty swallowing the pill that was placed in this particular legislation where the very wealthy get a $200 tax credit when there are other people throughout the state who are getting no relief whatsoever. . . . [T]he call we are making today is that $16 million out of $18 million of a program for tax relief is being directed into twelve communities without regard to income, ability to pay, or personal circumstances. I am going to make a difficult vote today. I am going to vote no on this bill. I am going to vote no because it is the worst solution to a complex problem that I have seen, and I would urge my colleagues to do also.

. . . I don't think we should be drafting legislation just to deal with one city's problems. . . . [T]here are thirty-five other senators in this Circle and we have to look at the larger picture. There is roughly three million people that live outside the boundaries of the city of Hartford and we have to look at legislation that would have a positive impact on them and would develop the most flexibility in terms of what they want to do with property tax relief.[11]

Additional floor comments from the bill's second consideration (with the homestead exemption removed by the house) follow.

I think this is a dark day for the State of Connecticut. We are embracing a piece of legislation that lacks reason, lacks consistency, lacks major miti-gation of a problem that we know exists. But, unfortunately, we are made up of two houses and an executive. There are checks and balances. And it requires for progressive legislation to pass through both houses and be signed by the governor. . . . This bill before us is what I consider a last ditch effort to provide a very minimal amount of mitigation to an awful lot of people that are going to require that mitigation. . . . I will vote for the bill. Because for those communities that will experience revaluation, I think that some mitigation is better than none.

I don't think in any way that we have addressed the question. The anxiety that we all feel here is we are not really doing much. . . . I think if we believe the property tax is unfair, we've got to explore alternatives.

I am going to support this provision before us. But only because it is the only game that we have to play with at this point. . . . We started off trying to tell the people of the State of Connecticut, that one of the major programs for this session was to provide meaningful tax relief. And we proceeded by robbing $52 million of a $70 million program to prove our intent. And then we gave $16 million away to only ten communities.

I rise to support the measure. We have come a long way to reach this point tonight. . . . In December, I don't think anyone would have placed much of a bet on the possibility of our being here tonight in agreement with the house and in agreement with the governor. . . . [W]e've got to take something and go with it.

As with the education finance bill, the senators' discussion of the property tax relief bill during the interviews reflected many of the same concerns voiced on the floor. Although the senators telling each of the narratives differed in their conceptualization of the issues involved and in their own positions on these issues, they were much closer in their assessments of what drove the bill's course through the legislature and why its ultimate outcome was what it was. The senators generally agreed that much of the course of the bill in the senate resulted from a personal, ego- and power-oriented struggle between a few members of the senate leadership, in particular the senate cochair of the Finance, Revenue, and Bonding Committee, and the governor, a struggle which ultimately carried each side beyond a consideration of the specific issues involved in the bill.

Although there were genuine differences in views between the governor and the senate leadership, based on the relative amount of emphasis placed on supporting business versus residences and on the progressivity of the tax system (differences that indeed probably undergirded the power struggle), the consensus among the senators was that the ensuing struggle was in large part a symbolic one over control of the legislative process. According to one senator, immediately after the bill was passed in its final form, "The vote up here wasn't about property taxes, it was whether the governor controlled the senate" (Fink 1988b). The senate leaders wished to establish independence from the governor, in preparation for a possible attempt at his office, while the governor wished to maintain the appearance of control, in preparation for a reelection bid and to discourage possible challengers. In addition, senators pointed to the influence of business interests, lobbying mostly through the governor's office, in the emasculation of the bill. This too was in large part a symbolic struggle, in that the outcome was important to the business interests in terms of their reputation for influence and political standing, as well as in terms of the dollars at stake through temporarily shifted mil rates.

Between business and the governor; I think the business side didn't want to go along because we also had the homestead [exemption] tacked onto it. . . . They thought they would lose a lot of money. Actually, United Technology gained $3 million [because of another bill passed]; now the homestead act would have cost them $500,000. But they were yelling and screaming that they would be losing money. . . . The governor was really twisting arms, I mean, he was twisting arms. . . .

A lot of senators really didn't want to support [the bill]. But because [the committee chair] wanted that bill, they figured they had nothing to lose—"I'll vote for it, and let it go to the house!"—they'll come out, no bruises.

The governor's personal opposition to the homestead [was important]; I think you had a personal clash of wills between [one of the bill's principal sponsors] and his supporters . . . , and the governor, the business community, and the Republicans. The result was perceived as a victory for the governor, although I don't think we would have gotten nearly as far as we did without [the clash].

The reason why the bill came out the way it did was because [Governor] O'Neill was against any real change in the system, from his concern for his political support from business. There wasn't enough support [for the homestead exemption] in the house or senate to override him; the issue hasn't hit home enough for a lot of us, but over the next couple of years many towns will have to revalue.

The heavy attention given to the bill's progress by the media fueled these symbolic struggles. It was a good story for the media—the senate versus the governor and big business—and the media reacted accordingly, and perhaps even helped to create the story in the first place. And as the bill's progress became more visible, the principal combatants appeared to become even more interested than usual in registering positions versus engaging each other in real exchanges of views; they increasingly began to talk past each other. This process was evident in the public hearing and committee meetings concerning the bill. The process also served to heighten an already present regional element in the bill's consideration, pitting the cities—especially Hartford—against the suburbs and smaller towns. This conflict overlaid nicely with the interpersonal, power struggle story, since the senate leadership represented districts in the Hartford area.

The prevalence of the personal-ego element in the bill sometimes influenced the senators' positions (and in a few cases even their votes), pushing them away from the bill when they might otherwise have been more strongly supportive. At the same time, however, the intensity of the conflict made the pressure from leadership even more acute.

Hartford was the key city in the state, because Hartford property taxes are way out of sight. And it was brought to my attention that the senator who sponsored the classification bill served on the city council in Hartford maybe ten years ago, and during that time a lot of tax benefits were given to . . . businesses to come to downtown Hartford. And this bill was correcting the many errors that took place ten years ago. . . . But I think you can't be that esoteric, you just can't pass a bill . . . or model a bill that's going to help one town.

I think it's [a senator's] personal political problems in the neighborhoods of Hartford that brought the issue to us, and had the entire senate standing on its head because of that problem. I don't think that's right; I don't think that's a good way to set basic policy. . . . I think [the proposals] would have discouraged and hurt a lot of businesses in some poor areas, like all of our companies that were trying to hang on and keep people working— we're going to keep penalizing them because Hartford's got a property tax problem. They've got a property tax problem because they've given all these major companies tax abatements to get them into Hartford . . . and because they haven't dealt with revaluation. . . . That issue is a great issue in terms of . . . [the leadership] pulling everybody together. Several senators who wanted to vote the other way really either didn't want to deal with the heat they might take from liberal groups at home, or they just didn't want to touch [a senator] and [another senator]. . . . The other part that comes into that is a challenge—I think those two people want to have some say in the next gubernatorial election—I think [one of them] is interested. This was an opportunity to take on the governor and show that they're not afraid to speak, so that next time when things happen they are looked upon as leaders and potential candidates. And that's why they took on the governor.

This highlights the interpersonal aspect of the legislative process, and the importance of influences other than beliefs and ideology. It is also interesting to note here, however, that most of the senators, although they recognized the personal power struggle underlying the bill, nonetheless conceptualized the issues in the bill and explained their own actions regarding it in other, more content-based, belief-oriented terms, which once again evoked their narratives of justice.

The critics' discussion of the bill clustered around three themes: a concern to help the cities, a desire for more progressivity in the entire tax structure, and a desire to cushion the effects of revaluation on homeowners more generally. They viewed the property tax system as a principal component of an antiquated revenue system that overburdens cities in its attempt to provide needed services. They also viewed the property tax system as regressive, both in the relation between residential and commercial owners and in the relation between less and more wealthy homeowners. Critics thus generally supported both the classification and homestead exemption proposals. As in the case of the education bill, the critics' views also generally matched the interests of their districts, which stood to gain from the implementation of the general contours of the property tax proposals, if not their manifestation in the final version of the bill.

The issues, overall, were: (1) providing a tax system that doesn't throw big increases in an unexpected way—predictability; and (2) the progressivity of the state's taxes—Connecticut has a regressive system comparatively, and the reliance on the property tax makes this more so. The homestead and classification measures weren't ideal, but at least they were comprehensive and helpful.

How in the world can you vote for this thing? You know you're getting the screws put to you, especially if you're coming from an urban area, especially if you're going to have reassessment this year. . . . What the governor is offering in this package is like a drop in the bucket; you're going to get $200 and your taxes are probably going to go up $1,000. What's $200? . . . They took $70 million out of the property tax relief fund to balance the budget, so they left $20 million for towns and cities to use. . . . It's not enough money to support those towns that are going to be affected. . . . The more I think about it, the more I think maybe we need an income tax. . . . We're going to have to find a better mechanism. . . .

This is the battle that we always have between the urban areas and the suburban areas and rural areas. They see the amount of dollars going to the [cities]. . . . They say, "what are you guys doing with all this money?" . . . We have all the problems; we're taking in regional problems. . . . All your poor come to the cities; all your sick come to the cities; local workers come to the city. You're using all our services; this is why we have such great problems. . . . It's hard to get this across to the other legislators.

The issue was whether or not we wanted to make the existing property tax system more progressive. Obviously, the solution that was opted for and given by the governor was to leave the current system intact, and to Band-Aid the problem caused by inequities in the system, by shooting some extra dollars in to fill some holes, and temporarily bridge some inequities that were created. But that's not a permanent solution. The business interests obviously opposed the plan for classification and homestead, which would put more of an onus on them to pay a greater share of property taxes, after a revaluation, which in essence would only have kept them at the same level they were before—they usually benefit after the revaluation, pay a lower percentage.

Supporters identified issues similar to those discussed by the critics, but were generally unsupportive of the entire package of tax relief proposals. They too saw the proposals in terms of aid to cities, and were therefore against them. The real problem was that the cities had not correctly managed their affairs; they had wasted their money on useless programs and did not deserve any additional money from other areas of the state. The proposals were in fact nothing other than a scam through which the cities, particularly Hartford, would rob the suburbs and towns of their money. In addition, the homestead and classification proposals were harmful to business. The supporters' concerns about squandering money on the cities fit well with the personal and regional struggles that attended the bill's progress through the legislature. Like the critics, the supporters' views generally well matched the interests of their districts.

> I think the issue was the city of Hartford not doing its revaluation and putting it off, and waiting for the state to come in and supplement it. . . . Geared toward the cities, certainly. . . . I felt it was very unfair. . . . For my towns it's a no-win, because my towns are the ones who are sending the money [to the state], to be redistributed. . . . I just felt the whole thing was inequitable. I feel, if you take a look at what the state sends back to communities right now, there's plenty of property tax relief built into it already. And to come out and specifically say, "we're going to give property tax relief" when you know darn well the money goes into the [town's] general fund, and the town can do with it as they please, they may not necessarily be giving people a tax break; they may just be adding to their budget. There's no guarantee that it's going to be property tax relief. To me, I guess the more money you keep in the town initially, or the budget that you control within the framework of the town, is property tax relief for individual homeowners and businesses.

> [One senator's] first and almost only concern is the city of Hartford. And the city of Hartford, 17 percent of their Grand List [of property value] is residential housing. So classification could very well work in the city of Hartford; give a little bang to the 17 percent, and it wouldn't amount to that much on the nonresidential tax roll. In other communities, . . . to help [residences], they would have to tax business to the extent that they would look elsewhere. . . . I think the so-called property tax relief is just another scam on the part of urban chief executives to get more money into their cities. [One large city] raises locally about 40 percent of its city budget.

And there really hasn't been a dent in the mil rate. Except at face value— that these urban chief executives say that they need more money— without finding out how the hell they're going to manage their city. And you can see what's happening in [that large city]. The city is obviously very poorly managed. And why the hell should people from [a neighboring area] and other communities just send money to [that city] willy-nilly so they can mismanage it and waste it? So in general I don't support those programs. They seldom benefit my communities.

Ambivalents displayed more heterogeneity in their discussion of the bill. As individuals they weighted the following items differently, but as a group they mixed explicit concerns for how their districts would fare with concerns about hurting the climate for business in the state and helping homeowners struggling with tax bills. Though many ambivalents supported the homestead exemption, they were uneasy about its impact on the business climate in the state. In contrast to both the critics and the supporters, the ambivalents also seemed less alienated by the fact that the legislation had taken on a personal-ego orientation and the possibility that it had a one city-specific origin. Their calculation of the power implications involved in the bill in fact contributed to their own decision making. Many ambivalents also shared the critics' desires for greater progressivity in the tax system, and a more general concern for the cities within the overall system of revenue in the state, but these concerns were for the most part less central to their discussion.

I had voted for classification back in 1987, and it had very little support. And I was bombarded by businesses in my district; that's one issue where CBIA sent the alarm out, to get to legislators. . . . The governor had said he would veto the [classification] bill, and was not flexible at all on it. The Speaker of the House said he didn't have the votes in the house for it. It was an issue where the governor's office started applying a lot of pressure to individual legislators. Being that he was going to veto it, being that I knew some background on the bill itself, I voted against classification . . . given the realities of the situation. . . .

I felt that trying to give property tax relief to the homeowner was very valid, and would benefit most of the people in my district. When they receive the bill for revaluation, I know how important that is. . . . Of course, business was very much against it, so that disturbed me. . . . So I was willing to go along with the senate and the leadership on this other issue [of homestead and classification] because of the experience I've had with revaluation and how people felt about it. . . . When it came back to the senate, it didn't seem worth continuing the fight, since we didn't have that kind of support and we knew the governor would veto. . . . Most of the lobbying was done by business.

The question was, to me: Are we going to change the rules to benefit the average taxpayer a little at the greater expense of businesses? I felt that in the ten-year cycle of taxation, there is fairness, there is equality. And to take the years that business benefits and the homeowner pays extra, without helping the homeowner too much and costing the businesses a lot, was terribly unfair. I have no problem with helping the property taxpayer, but I felt it should have been out of the General Fund as opposed to changing the system and going through the classification.

The real issue was that [one senator] represents a city where they have offered major tax incentives for there to be the building of commercial property. . . . In doing so, there has been a disproportionate amount of taxes coming from that [residential] segment. And they still continue to offer those incentives today. . . . As a political move, it's an effort for [that senator] to get the commercial property owners to be paying a higher percentage of the taxes in Hartford. . . . It's not that he's trying to correct the system; it's a purely political thing within his district. . . . You can't be critical of him; he certainly fought for it. . . . If he was doing it to benefit his constituents; hey, he's doing a good job. That's what he's elected for, to fight for the people he represents. . . .

Again, it's an election year. Understand the sex of going back to the people and saying, "I cut your property taxes," knowing there's two or three businesses that are now going to move to South Carolina because of it. . . . You may have the initial premise that you have saved someone something, but in the long run, you may have done more damage than not. So I don't believe in the classification, nor do I believe in the [homestead] exemption. . . . I don't look at business as the big, bad people, until it's proven to me that they're abusing their strength. They are the provider of jobs for everyone.

Plant Closings

The story of the plant closings bill is shorter than the stories of the education and the property tax relief bills, in large part because this bill died in committee.[12] But like both the education and property tax bills, the plant closings bill had a long prior history in the legislature. Similar measures had been attempted in recent sessions, but none had made it all the way through the process. In 1986, for example, two bills, one originating in the senate and the other in the house, called for expanding the state Labor Department's funding for retraining programs for employees affected by large-scale layoffs, plant relocations, or plant closings. Both bills were favorably reported out of the Labor Committee, but died in the Appropriations Committee. In 1987, three bills of note died in the Labor Committee: The first established a state fund to protect the health and life insurance benefits of employees who retired from companies that later became insolvent; the second funded the continued insurance coverage for employees under total disability when the employer stopped paying after closing a plant; and the third established a state program to assist workers in a business scheduled to close in order to purchase that business for themselves. Another bill, which allowed employees of a bankrupt company to continue receiving group insurance, died in the Insurance and Real Estate Committee. Most significant during the 1987 session, however, was a bill that would have required employers to give their employees three months' notice before a plant relocation, closing, or large-scale layoff. Companies violating this requirement would have been fined $3,000 per employee affected, and the money would have gone into a fund to retrain the workers. This bill successfully made its way through three committees, but was defeated on the house floor by a vote of 84–55. The group that defeated the bill was comprised of an interesting combination of Republicans upholding business interests and liberal Democrats, who apparently thought the measure was not strong enough in its protection of the workers. The governor had also opposed the bill, for reasons more similar to those of the Republicans.

The plant closings bill from the 1988 session that I am looking at here would have increased the maximum unemployment benefits available to employees from 51 percent to 75 percent of the state's average production wage if they received less than six months' notice of a layoff, closing, or relocation.[13] The bill would have applied only to enterprises employing twenty-five or more persons, and only if either 25 percent or more of the employees earning less than $1,000 per week or 25 percent of the collective bargaining unit had lost their jobs. It would have also required that in order to receive the increased benefits, the unemployed worker must have enrolled in a job-training program. The program would have been funded by the state's unemployment compensation fund, which in turn was funded by the unemployment compensation tax. The bill was favorably reported out of the Labor Committee, and then by the Appropriations Committee, but died in the Finance, Revenue, and Bonding Committee.

There were four other notable pieces of legislation pertaining to plant closings that were also considered during the 1988 session: The first required employers meeting the same conditions as those just described to extend payment for group insurance coverage for 120 days beyond a closing, relocation, or layoff (the current law required extended payment only in cases of closings and relocations, and only for companies with 100 or more employees); the second established a program in the state Department of Economic Development to assist troubled businesses in order to prevent layoffs and closings. These two bills died in the Insurance and Real Estate, and Planning and Development Committees, respectively. The other two bills were signed into law. The first bill, similar to a failed measure from the 1987 session, provided state funds to continue the health, accident, and life insurance for employees whose employers defaulted on these payments after closing or relocating the business; the second required that businesses receiving assistance from the Department of Economic Development repay that assistance if they move out of the state within three years of receiving it. An additional bill was passed by the legislature in the following year (1989), and was also signed into law. It made retroactive to 1985 the state funding to continue health, accident, and life insurance for employees affected by closings or relocations.

I have chosen to concentrate on the unemployment benefits bill because, of the various bills considered in the 1988 session, it offered the greatest (though still somewhat meager) challenge to the status quo; because it received the most attention in the legislature and the media; and because it appeared to be the most substantial, in monetary terms. Although, like most of the other closings bills before it, it did not succeed in reaching the full chamber, the senators could nonetheless discuss the bill intelligently during the interviews—or at least the kinds of measures it contained—because of the media coverage and their previous experience with similar pieces of legislation.

In large part, the plant closings bill reflected a symbolic struggle between labor and business for power and influence in the state, which extended beyond the specific concerns over what was in the bill. Listed under "nature and sources of support" on the Labor Committee's favorable report of the bill were the International Association of Machinists and Aerospace Workers, the Connecticut State Council of Machinists, and the Connecticut State AFL-CIO; listed as "opposition" were various chambers of commerce, CBIA, General Dynamics, and IBM, among others. During the public hearings on the bill, the testimony given came almost exclusively from CEOs of businesses, representatives of corporations, chambers of commerce, business lobbying organizations, and representatives of labor unions. Although it was always defeated, plant closing legislation was placed on the agenda every year, largely because it was pushed there by organized labor, which used the deliberations in part as a barometer of the state's political climate and as a test to determine friends and enemies in the legislature. Based on the outcomes, business was winning the contest. Perhaps even more decisive in terms of the bill's ultimate outcome, however, was the influence of the governor, who, again, was widely known as friendly toward the business interests in the state and opposed to plant closing legislation, as well as that of the commissioner of the state's Department of Economic Development, who was also actively opposed to any significant plant closing legislation. Finally, one legislator claimed that on this particular plant closing bill a deal was struck between the Labor Committee cochair and a key lobbying group opposed to it, in which the plant closing bill would not be strongly pushed in exchange for the absence of a strong lobbying effort against another piece of legislation that the cochair was more interested in.[14]

The argument most often advanced by critics of the plant closing legislation was that it inserted yet another cost of doing business in the state, and therefore made the state's business climate less competitive.[15] If other states did not have similar legislation, then businesses would simply choose to locate there instead. This argument is an instantiation of the problem of interstate competition, and the challenge it poses for progressive legislation (see chap. 7). Critics of the bill also argued that it robbed much-needed flexibility from plant and company managers trying to stave off bankruptcy, particularly those in smaller businesses that stayed afloat on a month-to-month basis and those in contract bid-based industries. Once it gave such notice, a company would have an extremely difficult time finding creditors and suppliers of necessary materials, and retaining customers. Furthermore, if it were forced to give advance notice every time it faced a possible bankruptcy, a company could not retain workers and maintain product quality; even worse, an army of informed and therefore embittered employees might vandalize or sabotage the workings of the plant during the remaining time period. Thus, companies facing severe difficulties would in fact be more likely to close, and to close faster than they would have without notification; therefore, the legislation would ultimately contribute to a net loss of jobs in the state. More generally, critics of the bill also argued that the legislation inappropriately inserted government into the collective bargaining process, a realm best left to management and labor. In addition, the legislation punished businesses for failing, which was a normal and necessary part of free economic enterprise. Finally, and in perhaps a more dangerous move vis-à-vis their general stance on plant closings, critics of the bill also argued that since the funding came from the unemployment compensation fund, companies that left the state entirely would not have to pay for their transgressions; the bill would instead be picked up by the remaining companies, in the form of higher insurance premiums. It is interesting to note that criticism from the Left also focused on this feature, claiming that the bill did not hold transgressing companies sufficiently responsible for their actions.

Proponents of the bill concentrated on the plight of those without jobs due to layoffs and closings, and the callous behavior of some companies toward their employees. They countered that the bill helped those employees who were in need of assistance and who were in no way responsible for their predicaments. Furthermore, through its retraining provision the bill actually improved the business climate by creating a more highly trained and flexible work force. Finally, proponents pointed out that the bill was, appropriately, nonpunitive, and did not levy penalties against individual businesses; the costs were instead spread out through payments into the unemployment compensation fund.

The two opposing camps thus agreed on many of the facts of the bill, but they interpreted these facts differently. These arguments may also have been at least in part symbolic, intertwining with a struggle for power and influence in the political process. Part of the problem may have been that the intent of the bill was left somewhat unclear. The bill did indeed fail to provide any real additional incentive for an individual company to supply advance notice of a layoff or a closing, or to avoid closing or layoffs in the first place. And in that regard, the arguments of the business community concerning the diminished ability of an individual company to stay afloat after making an announcement of an impending layoff or possible closing were largely irrelevant, though they were perhaps relevant to a larger debate about plant closing legislation in general. These arguments can be partially explained by recalling that the plant closing bill considered in 1987 did contain an individually based punitive element. Thus, the business community may have been refighting a previous battle, reestablishing a previous victory. And again, these arguments also become more intelligible if the bill is viewed as part of larger symbolic struggle for influence. The arguments offered by business about the state's business climate, in terms of higher unemployment insurance premiums, were more on target for this specific bill. On the other side, the bill's supporters' arguments about the plight of suddenly unemployed workers also appeared to be relevant; on its merits, the bill seemed to be more concerned with providing assistance to workers in need than it was with changing the behavior of irresponsible companies. But at the same time, their arguments that were directed to the irresponsible behavior of corporate managers were similarly irrelevant to this specific bill.

Several additional factors affected the policy environment within which the bill was considered, and worked against the passage of the legislation. First was the fact that national legislation concerning plant closings was also pending at this time. Many legislators viewed the possibility of national legislation as preemptive regarding any consideration of state legislation, especially since national legislation would have solved the problem of interstate competition vis-à-vis the business climate. The debate at the national level, however, also prompted the taking of public opinion polls, which indicated that approximately 80 percent of the nation's adult population favored plant closing legislation (Farnsworth 1988). This obviously made plant closing legislation seem more attractive to many legislators. Indeed, many legislators opposed to the state bill assumed what may have been a fallback position by claiming that they were indeed in favor of plant closing legislation in general, but only on a national basis. Second, the very fact that plant closing legislation had already come before the assembly several times and had always been defeated worked against the bill's passage. Labor and business had played out this hand before, and the trick had already been spotted. The legislators thus *expected* the bill to fail. Finally, the state's economic environment most likely affected the bill's policy environment, but it is unclear exactly how. The state as a whole had enjoyed dramatic economic success in the years prior to the 1988 session. While the good economic times may have reduced any sense of urgency about plant closing legislation, it may also have made it seem like a less costly or threatening measure. Few plants in the state had recently closed or endured large layoffs in 1988 (although these would come), and with the state's low unemployment rate displaced workers would have comparatively less trouble finding other jobs; however, to take just two examples, United Technologies Corporation and its subsidiary Pratt & Whitney, the largest employer in the state, had laid off 676 workers in the fourteen months prior to the bill's hearing (according to a company spokesperson), and while the bill was dying in committee, a pillow and mattress plant in Manchester suddenly closed, putting approximately 100 persons out of work (Robinson 1988).

On its face, the plant closings bill clearly engages the narratives of justice at a profound level. The bill implicates general questions about the fairness of distribution, in addition to more specific attitudes concerning management and labor and the degree to which they should be held accountable for conditions within and related to the workplace. The bill also gets at the heart of the debate over the proper role of government in the economy. In addition, it is a particularly interesting bill to examine at the state level, as it evokes the challenge levied by interstate competition to any kind of progressive legislation (again, see chap. 7). The senators telling each type of narrative engaged these questions in their discussions of the bill during the interviews, and many made explicit links back to earlier discussions on more general matters. Their discussions of this bill in fact provide a nice microcosm of many of their views, particularly those concerning the placement of blame for economic problems, as these problems are understood and rendered by each narrative type. Not surprisingly, critics placed much of the blame on management and supporters placed blame on labor, while ambivalents were reluctant to place any blame at all. Senators telling the different narratives also had somewhat different explanations for the bill's very existence and its ultimate fate, with critics and supporters both taking a more realpolitik view of the process.

Critics tended to conceptualize the bill and its purpose in terms of plant closings rather than assistance to unemployed workers; that is, they discussed the bill from the standpoint of punishing companies that act irresponsibly toward their employees (though some were aware that this bill did not level penalties to individual businesses). As I have already demonstrated, such discussions are largely off the mark regarding the specifics of this particular bill. Part of this tendency, however, may have been due to the way the bill was discussed by lobbyists, individual members of the legislature, and the media. It may also be due to the nature of the higher profile bill that was defeated in 1987, as well as to the more ideological viewpoint from which critics approached the issue. Perhaps needless to say at this point, they were supportive of this particular bill and of plant closing legislation in general, though one critic was against the bill for reasons of interstate competition. Their personal experiences appeared to be an important source of their support. They explained the final outcome of this bill in terms of a symbolic struggle between business and labor, with business having more (and too much) power in the political system. They also emphasized the influence of the governor working on behalf of business' interests.

> I think that we should have prior notification. I'm glad that it happened on the federal level, as any politician would be. . . . I would have supported it and would have taken the heat for it. Some plants have been closed down in my area, without any notification, and I think that's a bad way to treat your people. There will be some times where things get so bad they must be done and they must be done quickly. But I do believe that if there's any way you can alleviate the shock of not having a job, I think it's very important. . . . If you work for a company for ten or fifteen years, you're owed it.

> Had the bill come to the senate, I probably would have supported it. I support notification of plant closings—in general, I support it. . . . It's totally unfair for a plant just to pick up and go home with his marbles, and leave . . . employees just stranded with no hopes of achieving employment.

> I think [the issue] is either for or against; there's no in-between. You can't be neutral on that one. . . . I tend to believe in notification. . . . I've seen too many people whose lives have been totally destroyed. [One company]; whole families just went down the tubes on that. And [another company] is closing, and they just destroyed our neighborhood; tore down houses to build a parking lot that's not even being used. . . . I hate them for what they did to this community. Industry has the ability to swallow up a neighborhood.

> These [bills] were supposed to be incentives for them to give notice. . . . I supported that. . . . I think it was a bill that was intended to institute responsible social policy for businesses. And I think the concern about it

being a disincentive to do businesses and expand businesses is artificial. But it's another example, here in Connecticut, of how business interests control the outcome of the legislative process on a very critical issue. And they've controlled it for years. This is not the first time this bill has come before the legislature. . . . This [bill] was a weaker version. . . . Some argue, however, that if you're going to have [a plant closing bill] it's better to be done in Washington; . . . this way states do not become competitive with each other. Here's a state that has it, the next state doesn't. That may be true. I say it's just as well it was done nationally, though I don't believe it would have had the impact even if it were done strictly in some particular state, that some people thought it would have.

Supporters were against the bill, mostly because it hurt business. Like the critics, they conceptualized the bill as a punitive measure against companies that did not give advance notice. To the supporters, the bill provided yet another example of how labor organizations hurt the economy and even the interests of their own membership. Supporters also tended to explain both the initial introduction and the final outcome of the bill in terms similar to those of the critics.

The liberal faction of our General Assembly is representing labor. . . . When [the bills] get in committee after their public hearings, CBIA— they're able to point out to other senators—the meat of the information they're providing is convincing.

[There is] a very strong labor group in the state promoting their causes. . . . I don't think the labor unions are really serving the purposes they have, and maybe should take another look at themselves as to what their goals and achievements are now. . . .

[These bills] are killed for a reason. They're killed because the governor has made a deal with CBIA. . . . He's promised them no plant closing, and they turn around and they're very very generous to him in his campaigns. . . . That's the only reason we have not passed a plant closing bill, because the governor has opposed it.

Like the critics, the supporter group also contained one dissenter, who argued in favor of the bill on the grounds of individualism and the logic of economic freedom. Again, individual experience also appeared to have a significant influence in the formation of this particular opinion.

I think a conservative would be on the side of plant closing. . . . The individuals who work for these corporations—the economic freedom—

there's an abuse there, when somebody can be given forty-five minutes' notice after twenty-five years' work that they're never coming to work again. The employer—the partner—management . . . knew something about their business way in advance and deceived them. To me, that's an injustice. I know I made loans to people that I called for a first payment, and they said, "well, my shop closed up, we had a major layoff." And I said, "well, why . . . did you buy the money?" And he said, "we didn't know until we got our pink slip."

Ambivalents displayed a mix of positions on the bill, which varied with the relative emphasis placed on their shared concerns about the state's business climate, the desire to help unemployed workers and their families, and the recognition that these workers may need governmental protection from the vagaries of the private sector. The impact of interstate competition figured prominently in their efforts to balance these concerns, and personal experience also appeared to have a significant influence on whether or not they supported the bill.

The plant closing struggle here over the years has been a symbolic one between business and labor. And generally the image being labor pushing for the question of fairness and proper treatment of people about to lose their jobs, as opposed to business—and the governor supporting them— that . . . it would send a bad message to the business community . . . put a strike on the record of Connecticut. . . . I still think the best way to do it is at the federal level. That eliminates this issue of the symbolic message to the business community and employers that Connecticut is not a good environment. . . . I think in general the issue's been overplayed both by the business community and the labor unions. The vast majority of the labor unions' membership is never laid off; . . . most businesses, when they lay people off, give them notice. . . . In fact, I just had a layoff in my district. . . . They gave notice. . . .

I think the unions have happened to have used this issue very well for the last five or six years. They always get up on this issue, and when it comes down to nut crunching time, in exchange they get other things. It's a great bargaining chip.

I think it's almost symbolic now. If one were to ask at the beginning of each session what is labor's priority and CBIA's priority, [it would be] the plant closing bill. I think in reality, nobody wants to be beat on that one. . . . And while that isn't really their main priority, they continue to say that. . . . I happen to come from a city where they had a major close-down on Friday afternoon, and they gave everybody pink slips, and they brought in security so that the people would not get angry and start stealing . . . on their way out. It was very debilitating for people to be laid off, and then see that security was brought in from out of town. . . . It left a very bad taste, and rightfully so. . . . There's equal arguments on both sides, but I happen to come down on the side of the worker. I think it is inhumane to treat people that way.

The issue is civic responsibility and humanitarian concern. We had a plant [in my town] that employed 400 people. . . . After the second shift one night, they put the padlock on the door. . . . That was something that [the company] could have done, easily, with a sixty-day notice. It was in a difficult economic time for [the town]. People had just made commitments on mortgages, on cars, on long-term purchases. They could have used sixty days to back out of those, to retrain, to start looking for work. . . . The company was not at all bankrupt; it was a very rude and disgusting act on their part. On the other hand, we've had [another company] giving their workers a year-and-a-half notice that there was going to be layoffs. . . . Ironically, I was for it in 1981, but it really hit home [later] when [that company] locked people out of their plant. . . .

Of course I had [reservations]. If the economy stops, and orders stop, and a company has to take drastic action to remain afloat, then I understand it. If there has to be emergency action, so be it. But when a company has long-term plans that are known to the management . . . they should not act so harshly upon their work force as to just lock them out one day.

Plant closing in general: If it's the state of Connecticut doing it, it's negative, because if other states are not doing it . . . the climate for Connecticut is negative. You've got to balance benefits versus jobs. I don't want to give people a reason to be driven from the state beyond what we've already done. . . . But a company is the people that work there. And if I'm an employee and I've worked in a company for twenty, thirty years, and I've given a good day's work for a decent day's pay, and I've been loyal to that company, I shouldn't show up at the door Monday and find that the company closed. That's despicable to me. But to make it a formal piece of legislation which is very antibusiness, I couldn't support it.

In their explanations of the bill's outcome, ambivalents placed more emphasis on the debate on the merits of the issue, rather than on the power struggle; however, they too noted the symbolic overtones of the bill's disposition.

We've seen large layoffs, some with notice, some unfortunately without, and it was a protection that workers, especially the unions, felt was needed. . . . [It was killed] because the governor and the business forces in the Democratic Party . . . were concerned that it would be a disadvantage, a disincentive, to Connecticut businesses, and attracting new businesses, to compete with other states.

It's an annual fight in Hartford, between business and labor. If it wasn't passed during the time the Democrats controlled the legislature, its chances of ever passing are remote. . . . I think an argument has been made, successfully, by the business community. One must also look at the fact that the governor, again, is opposed to plant closing legislation. It's a fair observation . . . that when the governor does take a strong stand on an issue—he does it rarely—it's usually on the side of big business. . . . The point is, the governor's opposed to it, the business community's opposed to it. There are others of us who don't know whether the issue is notice so much as job retraining, job skills, those kinds of things. If the company's leaving, the company's leaving. The question is what happens to [the people] who worked there. . . . It died in Finance [Committee] because an effective case was made against it that it's a hindrance, that it makes the cost of doing business in Connecticut greater; the end result is that less companies will come in or those that are here are less likely to expand. The end result of that is lower employment. I think that case has been made effectively. . . . The winners were big business and the losers were displaced workers.

It's become a flagship issue, of a cause. It's a symbol [of] workers' rights versus shareholders/management's rights, I suppose. . . . Do we really need this? I don't think the need's been established. . . . There's just some absolute polarity that exists on some of these issues, where you've got two camps coming at it from two different points of view, and the twain will never meet. And I think this is one of them. . . . This one represents the cause for one group and the antichrist for another, and I don't see a chipping away effect happening.

CHAPTER 7

Beliefs and the Influences on Legislative Behavior

People are motivated to go [to the senate] for a variety of reasons. There are crusaders, there are people who want to have their influence on public policy in terms of that. And there are those who are caught by the whole political bug. . . . And then there are others who want personal gain. And everybody's in it because they've got an ego, and they like the system and the politics of it. There are those who utilize it to improve their own lot. There's a lot of all of that in the senate. I don't want to name names but there are those who really want the public office, there are those who want to make some money, and utilize contacts they make, get themselves on committees to get some work that they happen to be in, to help their firms. There are those who want to be perceived as very influential, and a leader, and therefore they try to pull everybody together to do certain things, right or wrong. There's a lot of pack mentality in there, which is unfortunate. . . . You're perceived as the leader: "boy, this guy can pull it together; therefore, he deserves three more credits towards being governor," or whatever. And to disagree, you don't do that. . . .

I'm not one who hesitates to vote against the party if I think they're going in the wrong direction, or what's in the best interests of my constituency. But you can't always do that, because then you have no influence at all yourself. You're no longer part of it; you're just an outsider. . . . If you're not part of the club, then you don't have any influence. . . .

It's not like people think, that you just go up there and vote on all these issues, and you vote what you think on the issues, because in order to get one piece through that you want, you've got to give over here. . . .

There's no doubt at all about [a time problem], and that's why you really depend on [others], especially in the senate, because things really move quickly there. . . . In the senate, unless somebody has been alerted to a problem, or unless they've really done their homework fairly well, and want to pick this kind of issue to deal with, you just sort of go along. I guess my discussions of philosophy and policy are really on more of the major bills. But the time frame is a real problem, real problem. Most senators don't know what's in most of the bills. They know their own committee work.[1]

In this chapter, I will consider the connections between beliefs and behavior in the senate from a more general perspective. I will examine the relations between the senators' beliefs and three elements of the policy process: the setting of legislative agendas, the specification of legislative alternatives within those agendas, and the ultimate decisions on those alternatives (Kingdon 1984). I will pay the closest attention to the second and third elements of this process. I will not, however, examine the fourth and final element in the policy process, the implementation of selected alternatives.

In the course of these examinations, I will also attempt to answer a question that I originally posed in chapter 3: Why does the critic's narrative not show up more prominently in the senate's legislative product? This question is my own, narrower version of Werner Sombart's question: Why is there no socialism in the United States? Although the critics are clearly a minority within the entire senate, they do constitute a quarter of the senate and more than a third of the majority party. We might thus expect to see some items emerge from the policy process bearing their distinctive mark. Although Connecticut's policies do appear to be fairly liberal, relative to the rest of the nation, the state is not known for policies that approach what the critics apparently endorse, even given the contradictions between their diagnosis and treatment of justice problems.[2] One might also pose the same question regarding the supporter's narrative, but since the supporters are located within the minority party, it is not as surprising that we do not find more supporter-oriented policies emerging from the policy process.

For the most part, the capitol provides the locus for the behavior I will study. The rationale for my choice is simple: Any activity that results in policy outcomes must ultimately come through the capitol. Granted, many important aspects of legislative behavior do take place away from the capitol, and thus I will also make use of the material I gathered from observation of the senators in their districts (Fenno, Jr. 1978). But I have nonetheless decided, for simplicity's sake, to concentrate primarily on capitol behavior.

Although my focus is capitol activity, and even more specifically, capitol legislative activity, I will not restrict my study to voting on the chamber floor. My examination will also include committee meetings and caucuses, party caucuses, and informal meetings with other legislators, constituents, and executive branch members. These are all important elements in the setting of legislative agendas and the specification of legislative alternatives, as well as in the voting decisions on those alternatives. By themselves, floor votes can tell us much about legislative behavior, and consequently they have been the subject of an enormous amount of empirical and theoretical research. But they are not the whole story, and we should be aware of the limitations of looking exclusively at voting, particularly in the attempt to understand the relations between beliefs and behavior.[3] Indeed, one of the senate leaders specifically counseled me to look for personal initiatives rather than floor behavior in order to understand the effects of philosophies and deep beliefs, while another senator commented:

> As an individual senator, I attempt to get more involved in some of the issues we've been discussing [during the interviews] by meeting with constituent units at home; by having my phone available, by having myself available, to try to help people wend their way through the bureaucracy; . . . by attempting to help people receive funding that they need to survive, by attempting to get funds, either through legislation or the governmental process, to keep the homeless shelter open for twenty-four hours, for example. So I think that as an individual senator, I can have more influence on addressing some of the problems and situations that I see that society has more so than I can by pushing a red or green button on the floor of the senate. That's not to say that there aren't issues that we vote on in the senate that have great or serious significance to the issues we've been discussing. But I think that is such a small portion of our time as public officials, that it's really not as significant as the other work we do. But I might parenthetically add that when we're looked at as elected officials come election time, we're generally looked at in scorecards as to how we voted on two or three key issues, by individual constituent groups. So, it's almost ironic. . . .

The limitations of the information presented in table 4 further illustrate the problems in looking only at roll-call voting. Table 4 presents a "Liberalism Index" of the senators' voting scores from 1987–88, broken down by narrative type and party. This index is based on the senate voting scores provided by three lobbying groups, the Connecticut Citizen Action Group (CCAG), the AFL-CIO, and the Connecticut Business and Industry Association (CBIA).[4] The indices for the respective narrative types indicate that the narratives are indeed correlated with different ideological voting patterns in ways we would expect; that is, critics have the highest liberalism index of voting, supporters have the lowest index, and ambivalents are in between (also note, however, that the distinctions by narrative type appear to be only slightly more finely grained than those by party alone). But as the senator's comment above indicates, and indicates correctly, these indices are based on a small subset of all roll-call votes. Most floor votes are in fact not controversial; once they reach the floor any serious controversy has usually been settled through the committee or caucus process, and the most controversial bills rarely make it to the floor at all. Only a very few floor votes, the most emotional and publicized, force voting to rub against beliefs in a public fashion. Indeed, CCAG had such a difficult time finding sufficiently important and relevant floor votes to determine its 1988

TABLE 4.   Average Liberalism Index of Voting, by Narrative and Party, 1987–88

	Critic	Ambivalent	Supporter	Democrat	Republican
Index score	71	62	45	68	46

Note: The Liberalism Index was determined by taking the average for each senator of the averaged sums of the 1987 and 1988 voting scores assigned by the Connecticut Citizen Action Group and the AFL-CIO, and the inverse (in terms of 100) of the average score derived from the Connecticut Business and Industry Association's 1987–88 published voting record. I derive the Liberalism Index from voting scores from both the 1987 and 1988 sessions, in the belief that the inclusion of scores from both the regular and fiscal sessions of the assembly yields a more complete and reliable picture of overall voting patterns during the period in which the interviews were conducted. There is no CCAG score from 1988, since CCAG reported only two senate floor votes that year. I have withheld the number of cases in order to further protect anonymity; one of the senators was elected in a special election, and did not register enough votes to be given a voting score.

scores that it gave up and opted to simply list the floor votes on just two bills. Its 1988 report explains that "only two senate floor votes have been indexed because the other bills of interest to CCAG were either never taken up in the senate, voted on unanimously, or decided on behind closed doors in Senate Democratic Caucus meetings" (Connecticut Citizen Action Group 1988). And even those votes that are controversial will not reveal the full range of views in the chamber; certain positions and proposals are likely to be systematically censored or filtered out in the process leading up to floor voting (Hall and Heflin 1995; see also the discussion that follows). This is likely to result in compression in the scores among the three groups; in terms of a continuum of views, much of the variation that would differentiate them will be chopped off.

Thus, although my Liberalism Index indicates that there is some behavioral connection involving the narrative types, by itself it does not tell us very much. Let us therefore look at the senate workings more broadly and deeply, with the assistance of a variety of sources.

Influences on Legislative Behavior

Although the senators may share the ultimate goals of reelection, influence within the chamber, and making good public policy, there are a variety of disparate influences on any individual legislator's behavior. Among these are the norms of the legislature, time limitations, fellow legislators, constituents, friends outside the legislature, employment outside the legislature, local political culture, level of state economic development and wealth, forms of state revenue, legislative leadership, committees, parties and the strategies that they adopt, interest groups and lobbyists, staff members, officials in the executive branch, the governor, other bureaucrats, and the media. And the list could of course go on. The relative strength and the specific behavioral effects of these sources will also vary with time and with the specific legislative contexts facing each senator. And for any given senator, these sources may affect behavior in conflicting ways. There may even be a number of other factors involved that are impossible to study systematically. One Connecticut state senator writing in 1980, for example, added this observation to an essay on the legislative process:

> In spite of all the theories of legislative behavior I have expressed above, a legislator's vote on a given bill may finally be determined by none of those but instead by whether he likes or dislikes the individual legislator who is proposing the bill, or whether his personality leads him to want to go along with his party or governor, or whether he had an argument with his wife that morning, or was up too late the night before, or has a cold that makes him experience the rest of the world more unhappily than is his normal instinct (Lieberman 1980, 50).

But though the senators may disagree over the relative influence of the various sources, there is nevertheless substantial agreement among them on what the specific sources are. I will discuss these sources in turn, using two broad categories as a means of organization: sources external to the legislature itself, such as constituency, state economics, or the executive; and sources internal to the body, such as norms and mores, the committee system, or party leadership. Within each category these sources can take different forms, such as actors versus procedures. These sources can also overlap and blend together, as for example when the party leadership adopts the governor's agenda as its own. They can also have mutually reinforcing relationships. We will see, for example, that time constraints add to the strength of the committee and chair system, which together contribute to deal making and vote trading, which in turn enhance the power of party leadership.

At least two lessons emerge from this treatment. First, as I have already indicated, the complete puzzle of legislative behavior is made up of many disparate pieces. Second, beliefs fit into this puzzle in different ways; sometimes their effects are reinforced by these other sources of influence, sometimes these sources act to constrain their effects, and sometimes beliefs and these sources each have unrelated effects.

Internal Influences on Legislative Behavior

The Limits of Time. For any one senator, there is simply too much to do in the Connecticut legislature. In addition to the myriad of bills that must be considered, which involve hearings, committee meetings, and individual research, there are also the demands of constituency service (both in the district and at the capital), service on investigative task forces, meetings with various policy and interest groups, and media relations. The legislator in Connecticut is placed under particularly severe time demands, as the state is usually among the national leaders in the number of bills introduced per year. And the fact that the legislature is officially a part-time institution means that most legislators must also respond to the time demands of a second job outside the legislature. It would seem that there are only two ways to accommodate all these demands: either adopt a constant, frantic level of activity directed only at the surface of each area, with no place for deeper deliberation, or simply choose to ignore one or more areas of service. Indeed, most of the senators complained about the problem of insufficient time to do their jobs properly.

Many of the senators complained that the time problem kept them from considering each proposal carefully, in terms of their own beliefs. The lack of time limited the information they could gather, master, and integrate into a decision, forcing much work to be done "by the gut," as one put it. Using the example of welfare reform, a senator telling the critic's narrative explained that the time problem was particularly damaging to his legislative agenda, because the successful advancement of his concerns required a more subtle understanding of the evidence, for which the time available simply did not allow. More generally, many of the senators pointed out that the time problem limited their careful attention to only those bills with the highest profiles. Somewhat ironically, it also deflected attention away from bills that required comparatively more work to develop and implement; legislators tended to introduce and pass the "easy bills" instead. Almost all the legislative product is thus incremental; as one senator phrased it, "[m]uch of the process is hitting at the margins." Another said, "[y]ou're in a political process, which is essentially a process of adjustment, and doing what's possible."

But the most significant consequence of the time problem is the reliance on others and the use of cues in decision making.[5] The problem of limited time forces specialization into respective areas of expertise, and deference to others with more information. In most cases, the senators know little about the bills that are outside of their own areas of specialization; that is, the areas of their committees.

> [Time] is definitely a limit. . . . The fact is you cannot, in any legislature these days, . . . you really can't read and understand all the legislation that comes to the floor. Even if you could, on the face of the legislation, you wouldn't have the opportunity to get any of the background information to really understand what's going on or how flawed the approach is. It's a matter of just the survivability of the legislative process; you have to, you use other—It's not just a lock-step thing, . . . you have a varying degree of reliance [on others] based on the profile of the issue—if it's a high profile issue, a highly politicized issue, obviously you're going to pay a little more attention to make sure you're not screwing something up for

yourself, your constituency. . . . Or if a particular committee chairman gains a reputation for not doing their homework, then you can't trust them. And then you find someone else in that committee to rely on; you may find another senator in caucus who emerges—if Senator X suddenly asks questions from Chairman Y who is talking about a bill in caucus, . . . then there may be a problem. . . . Here there are specific instances . . . I won't name names. Probably most members of the caucus could give you a rundown of which committee chairmen they have questions about, and others they have complete trust in, and others they may be intimidated to challenge.

Particularly because of the service aspect of [the job], which is a tremendous amount, most people don't have the opportunity to find out what the whole background is before a lot of the legislation comes forward. . . . Unless you're directly involved with it at a committee level, you pretty much have to rely upon what happens in your caucus, when it's explained during the bill review. . . . You're pretty much independent within the framework of the committee, and what you do on committee.

In particular, the problem of limited time forces a reliance on and deference to the chair or ranking member of each committee.[6] This senator is usually considered to be the specialist in that area. In caucus meetings, in informal exchanges, and on the chamber floor, the chair is often looked to to supply the information necessary to make a decision. Within the committee, this combination of time limitation and deference to the chair was most obvious when a meeting dragged on into the evening or ran up against another meeting. As the members began to shift in their seats and mumble about getting home or getting to the next meeting, more and more measures would inevitably be moved onto the Consent Calendar and acted on in bulk, at the suggestion of the chair. The kind of debate that had taken place just one or two hours earlier would then virtually cease, and the committee members would accede to the chair's wishes with little comment. The specialist system thus reinforces the committee system and its internal norms, and in turn enhances the power of the chair.

The Committee and Chair System, and Trading. Several other features contribute to the salience of the committee and chair system in the Connecticut senate. First, the legislature uses a "skeleton bill" system, meaning that all bills must be formulated by a committee. A legislator wishing to propose legislation must submit a proposed summary in nonstatutory language to the appropriate committee, which may then decide to formally write up the proposal as a proposed bill. This rule, combined with the fact that in comparison with other states, relatively few bills in the Connecticut legislature survive the committee reporting process (a result in part of the skeleton system itself), makes good relations with the relevant committee chair essential for any legislator wishing to push through a particular piece of legislation (Rosenthal 1981, 198–99; Swanson 1984, 75–76). Second, given the number of senators and the number of committees, almost every Democratic senator is a committee chair. Those who are not chairs are party leaders. By the same token, each Republican senator is a ranking member on two or more committees, or a member of the party leadership.

These aspects of the legislature's committee system have a great influence on what other senators outside of any given committee say and do when legislation from that committee is considered. They enforce among the membership a respect for and loyalty to the chair. In terms of voting on the floor, there is among the majority party, as one senator put it, a "prima facie deference" given to the chair of each committee. Another senator complained of "the pattern of the last two years of almost total support for anything that a committee chairman came out with." Senators support the chairs because of their greater expertise, but also because each senator needs the other chairs' assistance to get what he wants, and as a chair himself, he needs the assistance of the others to get his committee's bills passed once they reach the floor. Thus, each must depend on the others.

> What it comes down to is the time [available]. For example, a [certain] issue; I know this issue, I need your vote. You don't know as much about it; you're chair of [a different committee], you know the bill that you have and I don't know as much. You are convinced yours is good policy; I'm convinced mine is good policy. That's the horse trade: one good policy for another. That may be an idealistic view of it, but frankly I found that to be the case more than "hey, I need this for my district and my reelection." That sort of happens in the bonding package, but not in too many substantive issues. . . .
>
> There's a lot of [party votes and strategy]. . . . The reason being that each Democratic senator is a chair of a committee . . . or a leader.

> Most legislation here is worked out in committee or at some intermediate and not so formal step between committee action and floor action. . . . So that people might vote for things that if they had to work with from the ground up, they might never do. Not on a quickly graspable, understandable, electric issue like the death penalty, or something like that. But on other issues which may have far more impact on questions of social mobility and economic fairness. . . . These tend to get brokered out at a stage where fewer people call the shots. . . . I won't even read [a bill of this type from another committee], let alone read it and say, "well, I've got

all these questions I'm not too sure about, but out of respect. . . ." It's out of respect, confidence, and trust, and also the time imperatives, that you just back away and let it go.

Since all majority party senators are leaders in some capacity, and each senator thus has something to offer the others, this deference is mutual, and therefore takes the more specific form of trading and exchange. Trading is particularly facilitated by the wide dispersion of committee chairmanships, and the norm of deference to the chair within the committee further adds to the ability of the chair to engage in trading. Votes and support are bartered and exchanged in order to shepherd desired items through the process. Note, however, that most of this bargaining takes place within the majority party. Though a few senators were not at all uneasy with this system of trading, most expressed at least some concerns over how well it served the public interest, and also lamented the limits it placed on their ability to follow their own beliefs when they conflicted with the norm of trading support. At the same time, several senators also asserted that their "basic philosophies" set the boundaries on the deals that were struck.

Sometimes . . . someone votes for something, more than because they have any conviction or belief in it, they do it because . . . is it good for your district, do they owe a colleague a vote on something. . . . In the senate as opposed to the house, there's a tendency on nonbudgetary issues for chairmen of committees to be able to strike the deals . . . with their partisan colleagues. . . . In the house . . . different viewpoints are more easily expressed without as much clear concern that you should vote a certain way because the chair wants you to. In the senate it tends to operate more on the basis of an old boy network, a club atmosphere.

On certain issues, yes [there are deals]. You may feel that there's a proposal from the chairman of the Finance Committee that you're not exactly thrilled about, but he's also the one who's got control over whether or not you can get the bonding for the addition to the state college in your district. So you're not going to jump off the cliff for him . . . but you may just go along with some tax provision proposal that you're not too sure about, or have questions about, just to make sure you don't rock your project out of the boat.

[Making deals] definitely goes on; let's face it. It goes on in the senate more than it does in the house, because of the smaller numbers. It's easier to ask for favors knowing that you're going to be asked for them in return. But it's the numbers. . . . You have to be careful; you get a reputation for not being approachable, you'll get left out of the power game. . . . But then again, people also respect you for saying, "hey, I just can't do it this time." . . . It's a balance.

Sometimes this horse trading is a lot more subtle than an outside observer might really think it is. I mean, it's not "I'll go with this bill if you go with that bill." It's more where you had a bill before a certain committee where an individual chairperson made sure he or she got it out of committee for you, and then a month later they're coming to you saying, "can you give me a hand on this bill?" So you're not all that thrilled with the bill, but you remember that they got a bill out of committee for you. . . . I've bumped into very few senators or representatives that will remind you of what they may have done for you in the past.

If you're like me, and you don't play the game, you really get screwed. When it really comes right down to it, and you haven't been a trader, you haven't played the game of chits, I don't get anything coming my way. . . . I didn't promise anything to anybody so I didn't exact something in a trade; so it hurts people like me. . . . I just find a lot of that stuff to be happy horse-shit, wasteful of my time. I just don't want to engage in that game, because I'd be a full-time legislator if I did that.

Thus, although some senators did not perceive it to present a serious problem, Connecticut's version of the committee system appears to have dramatically different ramifications for policy outcomes than California's "author" system, for example, where each legislator controls her own bills from beginning to end.[7] The Connecticut senate's committee system appears to produce more trading than public interest, more political expediency than the "love of justice" found by William Muir in California (1982, 57).

According to the senators' comments, two committees seem to be particularly marked by this bargaining: the Finance, Revenue, and Bonding Committee and the Appropriations Committee. Here, senators trade support in order to get desired bond projects and funds for their districts for which they can claim credit, and which in turn help their reelection prospects. An anecdote from my observations of the senators illustrates a part of this process. I was following a senator on a morning the Finance Committee was to have an important meeting. The senator visited the committee office a few minutes before the meeting, in order to check on a couple of projects in his district. As with the Appropriations Committee office on the mornings before the budget was considered, lobbyists and legislators spilled out through the office door and into the hall. Just as we entered this crowd, the Finance Committee chair closed the office to everyone not on the committee, but not before the senator I was with could catch the chair's eye. The senator then patiently waited outside the door, and after a few minutes the chair emerged, walked over to us and touched the senator on the arm, and before the senator could inquire about his bond projects said to him, "Don't worry, we took care of you."

Although the relations and norms within each committee of course vary, certain shared themes nonetheless emerged from my observations and interviews. The first concerns the influence of the chair within the committee. The legislature operates under a joint committee system; that is, members from both the house and senate serve on the same committees. Connecticut is one of only two bicameral state legislatures to combine membership on committees, the other being Maine. Each committee has two chairs, one each from the house and senate, and in theory the two chairs share the duties and powers of chairmanship equally. From my own observations, it appears that the relative influence of house versus senate chairs varies with the personalities of the chairs themselves; I found instances of genuine partnerships, house chair dominance, and senate chair dominance. But relative to the rank-and-file committee members, both chairs are extremely influential within the committee. The chairs run the day-to-day operations of the committee, and although some committees attempt to maintain a more open, democratic process, there is an established norm of following the chair in one's party. Many bills are moved through by the chairs without much discussion, and in some instances discussion is actively discouraged. The power of the chair can even take the form of strong-arm tactics, as for example when a committee chair announced at the very end of one meeting that there would be no subsequent meetings to consider any new items for the agenda for that session. The motion to adjourn was subsequently passed over the shouts of protest of several minority party legislators.

The influence of the committee chairs is further enhanced by their role in the formal majority party committee caucuses, which are often held prior to full committee meetings. The stated purpose of these meetings is to count votes and attempt to marshal support for legislation—a bottom-up process. But in fact the chairs run these meetings as well; they introduce and describe each piece of legislation that the committee will consider, and then recommend a course of action. Thus the first committeewide views of legislation are those of the chairs, and they therefore have a unique opportunity to set the agenda and frame the subsequent discussion of legislation, both within and without the boundaries of the formal committee meeting.

There are also smaller, informal, ad hoc meetings that take place before and after committee meetings, and these seem to be more important for individual members' decisions than the formal committee meetings.[8] While it is not the case that the debates occurring in formal committee meetings are as irrelevant to individual decision making as the debates on the floor of the chamber, members nevertheless usually arrive at the full committee meetings either with their minds made up, or waiting to hear the appropriate decision from the committee chair. There were several occasions in my own observations, however, when I witnessed genuine, belief-driven debates in committee meetings, where minds actually changed. But such debates were exceptions rather than the rule. The point I wish to make here, however, is that committee chairs often figure prominently in the informal meetings as well; in fact, when they are present, the meetings usually take the form of information flows from the chair to the committee members.

In addition to providing opportunities for committee chairs to influence individual members' decisions, the committee system also provides an avenue for the influence of party leadership, especially majority party leadership. Party leadership works through the committee chairs to insure that the rank and file holds together on important pieces of legislation. On several occasions in committee party caucus meetings, I witnessed the leadership's "marching orders" being handed down by committee chairs to rank-and-file committee members. Thus, at the committee level, both majority party leadership and the committee chairs are the principal determinants of the final legislative product. I will now turn to the influence of party leadership and partisanship more directly.

Party Leadership, Partisanship, and the Party Caucus. Although the strength of Connecticut's political parties has declined somewhat in recent years, the state maintains its heritage of strong party organizations and party rule within its government. And though the strength of the parties in the legislature has apparently declined somewhat over the past twenty years, the parties nonetheless remain as key organizers of legislative behavior, or at least were so at the time of the interviews (three years later, party discipline broke down dramatically during the battle over a state income tax with the Independent Governor Lowell Weicker).[9] Indeed, in our conversations, the senators were extremely party-oriented in the way they described both their legislative activities and their interactions with one another.

The effect of party and partisanship on individual behavior within the Connecticut senate occurs mostly through the party leadership, which can draw on several sources of influence over the other senators. The influence of party leadership is apparent in the early development of legislation, committee work, and bargaining, as well as in voting on the chamber floor. This influence is also distinctly apparent within the party caucus, a particularly important forum in the senate. Party leaders supply important cues for voting decisions, and can guide an individual senator's decisions in the earlier stages of legislation development and coalition building. One senator, for example, spoke of the strength of the cue supplied when the leadership voted in a bloc on motions or amendments brought before the chamber; only when the leadership was split did he feel completely free to vote his own choice. This influence, however, appears to be much stronger and more pervasive in the majority party than the minority party, since in the minority party less is at stake concerning policy outcomes.

There are several more specific components of party leadership power. First, party leaders exert influence through their role as trade facilitators. They are able to influence other senate party members in part because they often serve as the focal point for the trades and exchanges among them. They also play a prominent role in the operation of certain key committees, the Finance, Revenue and Bonding and Appropriations Committees, which are themselves loci of trading. This further enhances their own power as well as the power of the chairs of these committees (since the leadership works through these chairs); in fact, the chairs of these committees are considered among the inner circle of the top party leadership. Attention to the wishes of leadership thus helps one to get precious bonding projects for one's district.

> Deals happen, yes. . . . That's the general legislative process to make deals—I don't mean deals in the negative sense, but in terms of [compromise]. . . .
>
> Yes, certainly certain types of issues [where I've wanted to vote differently]: taxes, finances, budgets, appropriations. Less of a sales tax, for example, because I thought that tax hurts poor people more. . . . In appropriations, more money for social programs. . . .
>
> A number of times a legislator or a speaker—I may have a couple of bills . . . that need some leadership or party support to get them through, so one hand washes the other. . . .
>
> In the senate, Democrats vote with the party line. . . . It's promise of bonding packages for your district, and some of the different committee heads get control, especially over freshmen, promising, "I'm going to do this for you, but you're going to do this for us." . . . You get something for the district, but the trade-off is that you vote with the majority.

They have to [stick with the party] because their appointments to committees come from that same party; their contributions to campaigns, many of them come from the leadership of that party. Their staffing levels come from within the leadership of that party. Whether they're going to have a clerk, whether they're going to be able to oversee a study committee which gives them staffing money during the interim, comes from the leadership. . . . You also have the governor. Your little projects that you're going to bring home; if the governor or your leadership don't put it on the bonding package, it doesn't exist. That's why you find the bonding package is one of the last bills that passes every session. They will keep the bonding package around long enough so that all the major bills that they need support for have gone first. . . . Leadership has tremendous impact. . . . But if you're a member of the Democratic Party, you'll see that happen more often.

Party leaders also control committee assignments. There is no strict seniority system that determines assignment; party leaders canvass the members for their preferences and then make the assignments. In addition to exerting influence on legislative behavior directly through their power over assignment, through this process leaders can also influence which committees are asked for or agreed to.[10]

Leaders screen bills before they come before the full chamber, and have the power to kill them.[11] They assign the status of bills: whether they are to be immediately considered or passed over for later consideration; whether they are to be sent to the other chamber after passage or retained by the senate; whether they are to be referred back to committee (though many of these decisions are predetermined by the committee chairs, due to the information they provide the leaders about remaining problems in the bills or the level of support they have). Indeed, members usually consult the party leadership early in the process, before submitting bills for consideration. Party leaders can also appoint their deputies; in most states these are elective positions. Leaders also control some of the resources for campaigns and much of the available staff support. And just like committee chairs, party leaders occupy unique positions from which to focus the discussion in party caucuses, introduce new items, and set agendas within meetings.

Outside of the leadership's influence, how does partisanship affect the connections between policy making and beliefs? In the most general sense, parties within legislatures marked by high levels of partisanship are more likely to use the policy issues involved in legislative decisions in order to protect and advance their own power bases. Of course, to the degree that parties and their use of these issues are based on competing ideologies, such behavior is directly linked to beliefs. But the simple fact that parties themselves are associated with different ideologies or some roughly coherent sets of beliefs does not mean that all partisan activity will necessarily reflect those differences. There may be other sources of partisan activity and other purposes served by that activity that may not be rooted in conflicts over beliefs, such as electoral competition, simple control over the policy product of the legislature, and the concentration of state spending among one party's legislative districts. In fact, party maneuverings on policy issues are often based on narrow electoral considerations, having little to do with ideological concerns.

Partisanship may affect the behavior of individuals in a legislature in at least three ways. First, there are the demands of party strategy, such as partisan gamesmanship. We may think of this type of influence as interparty influence. Second, there is the pressure to toe the "party line" in bargaining, speaking, and voting. This line is usually presented—or represented—to the members by the party leadership. We may think of this type of influence as intraparty influence. Finally, party may function directly as a behavioral cue or as a cue selector, without the mediation of leadership's direction or strategic considerations. These three types of influence are by no means meant to be exhaustive of the parties' influence, and they obviously overlap in their actual manifestations. Some additional conceptual clarity is retained, however, by treating them separately here.

The way the parties are distributed within a government will influence the extent of partisan behavior in the legislative body, and the strategy and tactics employed. During the 1987–88 legislature, the presence of a Democratic governor and a large Democratic majority in both legislative houses allowed the senate Democrats to legislate without the assistance of the Republicans. As a party, the Democrats could thus effectively shut the Republicans out of the legislative process without fear of losing their support at some later, critical point. The Republicans, on the other hand, were essentially forced into an obstructionist or "antilegislative" role in order to have any influence.[12] It was only when there was a conflict between the Democrats in the legislature and the governor (such as on the issue of property tax relief, or more recently, the institution of an income tax) that the minority party senators could play a more central and positive role in policy making.

This context of decisive Democratic control results in particular forms of partisan gamesmanship. And the more publicized an issue becomes, the more frequently such gamesmanship occurs. On the floor, Republican senators ask hypothetical questions concerning the implementation and application of the Democratic bills, primarily in an effort to embarrass the majority party by making it appear unprepared or incompetent. They also attempt to uncover technical and definitional problems that are severe enough to cause the bill to be referred back to the committee from which it came. Through amendments introduced on the senate floor, Republicans also attempt to "flag up" Democratic bills. These amendments are never intended to become law; their purpose is to be voted down by the majority on a recorded vote and thereby establish a record on which Democratic incumbents might be attacked in the next election, or immediately through press releases from the leadership office. The amendments often attempt to "improve" the proposed legislation by clarifying its language, increasing the benefits being distributed, tying the benefits to some standard of productivity or efficiency, or extending the inclusiveness of their coverage. The amendments are sometimes fiscally irresponsible (by the minority legislators' own admission in interviews), and are often directed to the short-term interests of certain identifiable groups within the state, particularly politically "sexy" groups, such as disabled elderly persons or emotionally disturbed children. Perhaps the most politically effective of these amendments, however, are the ones that increase the funds going into the Democratic senators' districts.[13]

On the majority side, the Democrats oblige the Republican strategy by automatically voting down all their proposals offered on the floor. This dynamic can produce strange ideological alignments in the floor voting, as Democrats sometimes end up rejecting more liberal or financially expansive proposals offered by Republicans. One result of this system is that many minority amendments that are in fact sincere and have legislative merit are never genuinely considered. According to a veteran Democratic house member, "many Republican amendments get shelved that shouldn't." Thus, on certain proposals the fog of partisanship in which the legislature operates clouds the majority legislators' perceptions of the situation and muffles the arguments they might otherwise hear clearly. This gamesmanship can be circumvented, however, if electoral considerations are temporarily set aside, or more specifically, if the majority party is allowed to claim credit for the minority's legislation. For example, prior to a legislative session, one of the senate Democratic leaders told me:

> The Republicans won't be a factor, if they wait until it comes to the floor to make amendments. That's just symbolic activity. But if [a Republican leader] came to me before and told me he had a problem with something, then we might need to sit down and talk. But if it's on the floor, it's not a factor.

On a separate occasion, the Republican leader referred to by the Democrat leader corroborated his statement:

> In terms of what you can extract from the majority leadership, I think that's done on a personal basis, for a district. I think it very much depends on the rapport that you have with the opposition leaders. Anything that I've been able to get out of here for my district—if it could be couched in terms that some Democrat could share some of the benefit, then of course you directly increase the probability that it will get out of committee, and onto the floor and get a positive vote. That's all part of the process here; you've got to strategically plan your way through this thing. I'll give you a very specific incident. I came up with a proposal last session to help regional schools. The chairman of the committee asked that I withdraw my proposal, my amendment, so that he could be one of the coauthors of it, which I was more than happy to do, because he also had a regional school in his district. The net result of that was that the amendment passed

unanimously out of the senate. Otherwise, it would have been a difficult problem for us in the minority.

Such arrangements, however, appear to be more the exception than the rule.

Similar gamesmanship is also found in committee meetings. Parties—especially the Democratic Party—vote in blocs based on signals from the party leaders within the committee; Republican proposals are usually ignored by Democrats; and Republican amendments are often offered with little intention of or even apparent desire for their passage. In some committee meetings, committee chairs publicly "release" their party members to vote for certain minority amendments that are deemed to be unimportant. But even on these amendments, the votes usually conform to party lines. Here again, one of the resulting problems is that genuine minority party proposals and amendments are not taken seriously.[14]

But beliefs are evident even in these games that the parties play with each other. During the session I observed, beliefs appeared to underlie the general themes of the partisan exchanges between the two parties. Republicans tended to emphasize fiscal responsibility, concerns about deficits, and future tax increases; Democrats stressed the provision of needed services and their concern for people rather than numbers.[15] Beliefs may also influence which strategies are chosen in a given situation, and when gamesmanship is employed in the first place.[16]

Within each party, there is an emphasis placed on hanging together as a group in voting on the floor and in committee. Again, this emphasis is stronger among Democrats, and results from their desire to maintain exclusive control over the legislative process and to appear unified before the media and the public. In contrast, individual Republicans did not find party unity to be a significant constraint on their behavior. The emphasis on party unity occurs primarily through the leadership, but it is also a generally held norm. At the same time, many Democratic senators seemed to resent the norm, even while recognizing its place in party strategy. They complained that the pressure to stick together as a party forces them to vote in ways they otherwise would not vote, and to make unpalatable compromises. This pressure is apparently reinforced by the implicit threat of sanctions from the leadership. The distribution of party membership in the senate once again affected the nature of this constraint; since the Democrats held a two-thirds majority, the leadership thought it could afford to "let go" or "release" a few senators on any given vote (but no more than four or five, I was told) and still easily maintain its dominance over the Republicans. Thus, although there is a strong norm for party unity, it is somewhat mitigated by the party's strength in the chamber. Nonetheless, the senators often felt constrained in their behavior by the emphasis on unity. Senators in both parties, however, were also quick to point out that much legislation is nonpartisan, and that most bills that are passed are unanimously supported and are usually placed on the Consent Calendar. There are only selected key battlegrounds, like the budget.

> If you got the votes, you got the votes, you got the votes. And [the Republicans] are going to get no credit for the good things, and hopefully, they'll share for the bad things! . . . I've always felt you live or die, basically, on straight party line stuff. Of course sometimes you do [feel constrained], but that's the process. I think the process is very important. I believe in the process, because that's the way you get things done. You have to judge all the time. . . . If you really feel strongly about something, then you do [follow your view]; there still may be other times when you feel strongly about something, but you'll do the opposite. It's hard to say, "well, where is the line strictly drawn?" . . . That's where the power comes in too. . . . You've got the votes, and you've got to responsibly put the votes together; that's why you're there. You have more influence as a member of the majority caucus than as a member of the minority caucus, because it sucks being in the minority. That means you've got to swallow hard on many things too. . . . But it sucks being in the minority.

> The Democrats want to say, "this is our bill." They don't want to say, "this is that Republican's bill." In a lot of cases what they would do is they would take that Republican's bill, and change it around and put their name on it, so now it's a Democratic bill instead of a Republican bill. . . . We're supposed to be here to serve the people of Connecticut, but you have this game that just serves Democrats only. . . . A Republican that everybody likes might get a bill through, but it's very tough.

> I think that leadership is more open-minded about a senator going to the president [pro tempore] or majority leader and saying, "look, I can't support you on the budget," and having the leader not force you to, or chastise you for the rest of the session if you don't support the budget. . . . My years in the house when I used to observe Joe Lieberman and Dick Schneller as leaders in the senate, I at times thought what it would be like to be a senator and have to toe the line on some of that stuff. . . . [But] don't get me wrong, there is that concept. We'll go into a caucus and our leaders will say, "unequivocally, absolutely"; the leadership will tell us . . . that we have to support certain party-line issues. . . . There are certain issues that it makes more sense to go in there with twenty-five solid votes and show the unity within the party . . . the budget is an obvious one.

The party caucus is perhaps the most significant forum in which leadership attempts to hold the party members together on votes. Caucuses are party meetings held during the legislative session, before or sometimes during full-chamber sessions. The Democratic caucuses are formally open, though at times they are closed to the public and the press. In practice, however, this means that the more important party meetings are often held informally, among a subset of the Democratic senators. The Republican caucuses are not formally open, but receive far less attention anyway from the press or public, owing to the Republicans' minority status. In general, it seemed that the Republican caucuses supplied more genuine forums of exchange than the Democratic caucuses; they were less formally structured meetings, and the leadership spent less time handing down "marching orders" and more time discussing the issues involved in the bills being considered. The typical instruction from the Republican leadership took the form of "this is what I think we should do, and this is what Senators X, Y, and Z are doing." In the Democratic caucuses, the leadership would give the status of each bill being considered, and then each committee chair would explain the bills originating from her committee that were to be taken up on the floor. The leadership would then usually suggest a vote, if the preferred vote was not already clear. Though more open discussions often ensued, the early comments of the leadership and the committee chairs largely set the tone.

Again, much of the difference between the two parties in this regard results from the structural differences in party strength; since the Republicans could never block any measures by themselves, there was less at stake in holding them together as a voting bloc. But the difference also probably results from a stronger "culture of leadership" among the Democratic senators. Having been in the majority in the senate for twenty-six of the previous thirty years, the Democrats had probably developed a tradition of governing within the chamber that reinforced the norm of leadership influence. On the other hand, being out of power for so long, Republican senators may have developed a norm of individual independence, which prevented them from being as disciplined as the Democrats. Indeed, in discussing the Republicans' two years of being in the majority from 1984 to 1986, one Republican senator lamented that "we used to hold our caucuses on the floor." Another Republican senator criticized the present minority caucus process for allowing too much independence, and pointed to the period from 1984 to 1986 as an example of the costs of such independence:

> You've seen our caucuses. I don't believe they're run as tightly as they should be. They're very loose, and everybody's allowed to go their own way. And I don't always agree with that. There are times when I think it's important that you be independent, and have a good reason for being independent. But there are other times when I really feel that the party structure is much too loose. . . . I think there should be an agenda on the

table, and . . . long before the [legislative] calendar comes up we should be discussing some of the things that are coming up, preparing everybody. . . . And when we get into caucus nobody listens anyway, so I think you need a little more discipline. I'm not saying that everybody has to march in lock-step, but I do think you have to have a parameter of some sort of control. . . .

I don't know how the other caucus works, but I just assume that they're marching to marching orders, which we definitely were not. . . . But I was watching the Democrats this time around and I really felt very badly for some of them; they really had to bite the bullet. Sometimes that has to be done. . . . But there are other times when I think, if this is better for this person's district, let them go. . . . Of course, [Republicans in the senate] are so small in numbers, that whatever we do, the impact is not there right now. . . .

I think it's very negative not to prepare to be the majority. It may never happen, but you still should be ready for it, so that when it does come, you can move right in. . . . I've been asked many questions about the '84–'86, and if I had to judge, it's the fact that they were so used to being the minority and doing whatever they wanted to do, that when the time came to pull together they didn't know how to pull together.

But the Democratic caucus cuts both ways. Although the Democratic caucuses are more highly structured affairs and provide leadership with a vehicle through which to constrain specific attitudes, voting behavior, and speech making, they nonetheless also provide a forum for the genuine exchange of views among all the Democratic senators. In fact, many of the Democratic senators cited the caucus as the place where the beliefs we had been discussing were most visible. It is at least a much more meaningful forum for the presentation and discussion of beliefs than the chamber floor. Indeed, I witnessed such discussions myself on several occasions, in debates over bills concerning Medicare and property tax, for example. The caucus is also the place where much of the cue taking occurs, not just from leadership but also from fellow party senators. These cues extend beyond the bills being considered on the floor that day to those that are still in committee, and even to more general policy opinions and opinions about intrachamber relations.

In the caucus, . . . generally there is—sometimes it's spoken and sometimes it's not—of our mission and our purpose, and the differences between us and the [other party]. . . . In the caucus you generally speak more . . . you make a more emphatic statement.

[In caucus] we try to get everything out front in terms of people's feelings before we went out on the floor. And it was good leadership to try to know where the votes were; not to bring something to a vote unless you had the votes.

The real debate in the senate goes on in the caucus; the real substantive debate, the real changes, the real horse-trading if you will, goes on in the Democratic caucus. The concerns of the various senators—"I think from a policy standpoint we ought to do it this way or that way"—that's where it's done. It's done there before it's brought to the floor. . . . Differences are worked out there. . . . What happens is . . . we'll take a hand-count—who can support this bill. And generally a Democratic senator will not bring a bill out until concerns have been worked out where he or she has the votes for a bill to become law. . . . We sit around the caucus table and it goes back and forth, and the concerns in the senate—and I'm really proud of this fact—generally the disagreements and the negotiations stem from policy disagreements. . . . I think it can be said that good policy makes good politics, in this state senate.

Professionalization and Staff. Like many other state legislatures, the Connecticut General Assembly has undergone a striking process of professionalization during the past twenty-five years. From the standpoint of the belief-behavior connection, professionalization helps in several respects. Professionalization enhances the legislative capacity of the body as a whole vis-à-vis the governor and various lobbying organizations, which better enables it to realize its own beliefs. In addition, professionalization tends to produce more individualism within the legislature; the strength of leadership, party solidarity, and other constraining norms decline as individual legislators pursue their own reelections and their own programs with professional independence. This individualism in turn allows legislators greater opportunities to follow their own beliefs.

The increase in staff has been a critical component in the professionalization process in the Connecticut legislature.[17] In addition to secretarial and other support staff, there is partisan staff under the direction of the senate party leadership (including policy, media, and campaign experts), committee staff, and in a more recent addition, one nonpartisan staff member for each senator. This last type of staff member handles much of the constituent service case work, but can also serve as a legislative assistant, depending on the senator. There is also a set of professional staff offices serving the legislature as a whole. These include the Legislative Commissioners' Office (for legal research and bill drafting), the Office of Legislative Research, and the Office of Fiscal Analysis. Finally, there is a large army of college interns. By assuming much of the constituent service, performing technical legislative work, and providing information, the increased staff better enables individual legislators to perceive the connections between specific alternatives and their beliefs, and therefore to institute their beliefs. It also provides each legislator with an independent source of information, which in turn makes them less reliant on leadership and party.

At the same time, however, legislators may become so dependent on staff that their decisions become insulated from their own beliefs. In my observations of committee meetings, for example, committee members would often rely on staff members from the professional offices. It also appeared that strong working relations had developed between many senators and the members of both personal and professional staffs, such that staff members would perform significant legislative work without much supervision from the senators. But these relations also seemed to be based in part on shared points of view (Kingdon 1989). Overall, staff members did not therefore appear to provide strong, independent, immediate cues for capitol behavior, particularly voting. Their immediate importance and influence in legislative decision making was more as information sources and sounding boards.

The individual independence brought by staff is part of a broader fragmentation process, however, which also affects the belief-behavior connection. As part of the professionalization process, legislatures are becoming more politicized; that is, legislative positions are perceived to be more desirable, and winning them has become more individually competitive. Though it has not reached congressional proportions, the attention paid at the state level to re-election, job security, and political advancement has increased dramatically. These concerns may decrease the tendency of any given legislator to advance his deep commitments, especially if those commitments are perceived to run counter to the mainstream of public opinion.

Furthermore, professionalization may bring to the legislature a new ethos of legislative service. Legislating itself may become a profession; that is, the generic production of a product or the yielding of a service (similar perhaps to law or medicine), which is separate from the more specific belief-driven "callings" that might have motivated a legislator to seek office in the first place.[18] Professionalization may thus suppress some sets of beliefs. In the extreme case, professionalization may cause only such service-oriented, ideologically removed candidates to be attracted to run for elective office. Overall, then, professionalization may ultimately result in a process that filters out, or at least tends to filter out, the most challenging or deviant activities and beliefs.

Friendship. Legislative research has consistently demonstrated that interpersonal relations and friendship are important factors in decision making (Caldeira and Patterson 1987; Jewell and Patterson 1977; Wahlke et al. 1962). My own observations of the Connecticut senate corroborated this wisdom. The capitol environment is intensely interpersonal; in fact, it is perhaps more inter-personally oriented than issue-oriented.[19] This is an obvious point to anyone familiar with politics, but it needs to be made. Senators spend much of their time at the capitol socializing and gossiping with other legislators, staff members, lobbyists, and the media. Their discussions of legislation and policy are often in terms of personal turf or territory, or the personalities of those involved—who the persons are rather than what they stand for. Several senators' considerations of the property tax relief measures during the 1988 session, for example, were heavily influenced by their personal dislike of one of the senate leaders most associated with the issue (see chap. 6 herein). This heavily interpersonal nature of the legislative environment will most likely inhibit to some degree the influence of deeper, normative beliefs on decision making, although the selection of friends, and the attitudes toward others more generally, are at the same time influenced by these beliefs (Kingdon 1989).

The social status of legislators, and concomitantly their desirability as friends, depends highly on their position in the legislative hierarchy, with leaders being more desirable than rank-and-file members. But status and desirability also depend on other factors; for example, the degree to which the legislators possess other desirable characteristics, such as a high sense of efficacy and a high level of tolerance toward other members; and the degree to which they share certain characteristics with the other legislators, such as party membership, age and tenure, attitudes about legislative service, and even physical location—both in the capitol and the chamber, and in the state itself (Caldeira and Patterson 1987). The expression of radical or deviant views has a negative impact on one's social standing within the legislature, and consequently, a negative impact on one's influence, including the ability to pass desired legislation and to obtain needed bonding packages for one's district through trading or going along (Caldeira and Patterson 1987, 961). The senators who are critics are particularly aware of this, and when combined with a sense of their own individual deviance (to be discussed in more detail below), the result is a feeling among them that they must adjust their statements and behavior accordingly. This effect is intensified by the structure of the distribution of committee chairmanships and leadership positions within the Democratic Party, which place a premium on being part of the group.

Technicalities. Many of the policy discussions and legislative debates that do take place at the capitol and in the district are technical in nature. This may result from the control of the legislature by one party, as discussed above, so that broader considerations are largely precluded by the Democratic lock on the process. It may also result from the fact that most policy changes are incremental, and from the increase in legislative professionalism. The limits of time might also contribute to the technical focus, in addition to the fact that the logistics of legislative deliberation can become so complicated that it is hard enough just to keep track of the most basic items.[20] But regardless of the ultimate sources of this behavior, senators devote much of their legislative work effort to understanding the language of proposed bills, determining just what they call for, and how they will be implemented. The discussions and debates that the senators engage in informally, in committees and public hearings, in party caucuses, and on the chamber floor, are often organized around these relatively technical tasks.

Just as the minority Republicans use the "flagging up" technique in their attempt to derail the Democratic legislation (or to make a record for the next election), they also attempt to uncover problems of language ambiguity, technical difficulties, and potential problems and ambiguities in implementation, either in the committee stage or on the chamber floor. In fact, this is their most effective strategy. In my own observations of the chamber, they succeeded in sending several bills back to the committee for refinement, and they were sometimes able to delay significantly the movement of bills through the committee process.

Like the interpersonal nature of legislative work, this technical focus would appear to inhibit the presence of deeper beliefs in the legislative process. But again, beliefs can serve as important cue-sorting mechanisms; that is, they can influence which technically oriented arguments one chooses to make, or which arguments one finds persuasive. They can also influence the choice of which bills and proposals to attack through technical or hypothetical-scenario means. But nonetheless, the kinds of beliefs tapped by the narratives—at least by the critic's and supporter's narratives—are sometimes only dimly visible through the cloud of incrementalism and technical concerns found within the senate.

Beliefs and External Influences on Legislative Behavior

The Governor, Lobbyists, and Media. Professionalization has considerably strengthened the legislature vis-à-vis other political actors in the state, but the governor still exerts a great amount of influence over the final legislative product.[21] Some senators in fact commented that most major initiatives come from the governor's office, and this observation is echoed by other observers of the state's politics (Swanson 1984, 104–5; Caruso 1980). Consider, for example, this lament from a Republican senator during the interviews:

Democrats seem to take what the governor gives them, and just carry it. They'll make some minor modifications, there might be a squabble or two. But generally, if the governor says jump they all respond. So it's not very creative. . . . If you really look at what the governor proposes as a budget, and what ultimately passes, they'll play with maybe $20 million, $30 million, but the budget's $6 billion. He's throwing them a bone.

As just one example of the executive's influence, representatives from the various state agencies and departments would often appear at committee meetings in order to provide information and advocacy for governor-sponsored legislation, and they appeared to be quite effective in this role. The governor's influence is also particularly strong when the governor and the majority in the legislature share a party identification, as was the case when the interviews took place. In addition, as the previous interview excerpt indicates, the governor plays the most salient role in what is certainly the most important legislative item, the budget. Of course, whether or not this level of gubernatorial influence advantages or disadvantages any of the narrative types depends largely on the person holding the office. From 1981 until 1990, this person was William A. O'Neill, a man generally known as a moderate-to-conservative Democrat who was friendly to business interests, and who had remained opposed to an income tax. He thus appeared to be a governor best suited for the ambivalents.

Regarding the influence of interest groups and their lobbyists at the capitol, the senators expressed conflicting views. Some saw the campaign money that they control as a powerful source of influence, while others primarily looked upon them as valuable additional sources of information. Several senators from both parties expressed concern that some of their colleagues were too beholden to the banking and insurance industries. In the extreme case, one senator spoke of a conspiracy between some lobbyists and legislators to introduce ripper bills, which had no other purpose than to be killed, but which also threatened certain wealthy interests. The lobbyist would then approach these interests and offer to get the bill killed for a certain sum, which would subsequently be divided between the lobbyist and legislator after the bill was summarily killed. But perhaps the most typical of the senators' comments about the influence of interest groups and lobbyists on their own behavior was the following observation from an ambivalent:

> I have found myself voting against issues, but not speaking against issues, so as not to alienate groups that I oppose on one issue. Again, dealing with opposition gingerly, and possibly trying to convince other legislators without being outspoken publicly. . . . Dealing with a special interest that I differ with with a very gentlemanly way, so that they understand that when I oppose them it's with reason and it's with consideration.

From my own observations at the capitol, the most striking thing about the lobbyists was their ubiquitous presence; they were everywhere, all the time.[22]

They lined the corridors where committee meetings and public hearings were held (the legislators called these corridors "shark alley," and the lobbyists "sharks"). They would show up even for meetings that were pro forma and lasted only ten minutes. More specifically, the lobbyists appeared to enjoy a natural advantage in the period leading up to the committee meetings where final action was taken on legislation. Legislators would spend much of this time, especially during the "out of session" period, meeting with different organizations, or the individuals representing them. There was a distinct group bias to these meetings, and in them these lobbyists were usually both listened to and heard. Their access to the legislative process at the critical early stages was real.

Though business interests still dominate the lobbying activity in the state, other interests have increasingly made their presence felt.[23] Perhaps foremost among these are public interest groups and political leaders at other levels of government, such as urban leaders. Two notable examples of their influence in recent years are the urban leaders' influence in blocking passage of a governor's budget, and the Connecticut Citizen Action Group's influence in the passage of a "bottle bill."

Another potentially important external source of influence is the media. The need to present an image or get a political message through the media, particularly through television, pushes the legislators toward the gamesmanship tactics discussed above. More generally, based on my observations at the capitol, the influence of the media on the behavior of the senators appears to come from the fact that the legislators follow themselves closely in the press. They are their own most attentive public. I noticed that each senator collected the articles that included coverage of himself, and as a group the senators gossiped and joked about how they appeared in these articles.[24] The influence that this coverage had on subsequent behavior is difficult to measure, but to me it appeared to have only a marginal direct impact.

The Electoral Connection and Constituency Influence. The potential influence of constituents on legislative behavior can take many forms. In terms of the electoral process, constituents can act as filters on legislative behavior through a Darwinian process of natural selection. This includes the selection of who decides (or is encouraged) to seek office in the first place, as well as who ultimately wins the election. It is no surprise, for example, that supporters tend to come from rural and suburban districts, while critics tend to come from urban districts. Once a candidate gains office the influence becomes more direct—letters, phone calls, meetings, public hearings, and so on. Much of this influence is electively driven; the legislator pays attention to the desires of her constituents, or her *perception* of the desires of her constituents, because of the electoral incentives to do so. As John Kingdon points out, part of the advantage held by incumbents results from the fact that "they avoid taking positions contrary to constituent preferences most of the time" (1989, xii). And although the direct links between constituency opinion and legislative voting records may be weak, legislators may nonetheless anticipate how their votes could be used against them and vote accordingly, even on issues that are less visible at the time. Thus, even citizens' "potential preferences" can become important sources of influence on legislative behavior (Arnold 1990, 9–13, 11; Kingdon 1989, 60–68). In a more indirect form of constituent influence, the legislator may be driven to mold herself into the general shape, or her *perception* of the general shape of the entire legislative body, in order to better accomplish the kinds of things—such as bonding projects and discrete local projects and programs—for which she can claim the most credit at election time. She may also be driven to produce these things quickly, indeed produce almost anything, to demonstrate effective activity on behalf of her constituency.

Note again that all of this appears to work against the critics in terms of realizing their deeper legislative concerns. While most of the other senators shared the notion that their views were pretty close to those of their constituents, the critics tended to see themselves as different, more liberal. Some saw a fair amount of connection in the "blue collar" qualities of parts of their districts, but overall, there was a significant degree of perceived difference. The effect of this perception is compounded by the critics' individually held senses of their own distinctiveness within the senate chamber, combined with the need to produce tangible results for their districts.[25] Indeed, the laments of three senators illustrate this problem well:

Every year there's at least 4,000 bills. . . . There's just all these crazy bills. As long as we keep running on a two-year legislature, this is what we're going to get. Because those legislators are running scared, because they want to go back to their constituents and say, "look, this is what I passed, these are the bills I have." And they want to show what they've done for two years. And it's crazy; it's too much pressure.

Too many of us look as far as the next election. If you're going to be that short-sighted, you can't really do any thinking. Because anything that requires any substantial thought process really is going beyond the next election. . . . Everybody wants to do something so they can take credit, so they can go back to their voters within the next year, so they can take credit for it, and get reelected. Steeple for a church! . . . It bugs me that we are so politically motivated towards the election, to do what's right.

My tendency would probably be to be a liberal. . . . I'm regulated by the district I represent in the legislature—if I was a liberal, I'd probably be run out of office. . . . To some degree, my legislative district has made it kind of hard for me to come out on issues. For instance, to vote for a state income tax. . . . A state income tax probably would be a fairer way to resolve the issues, but I certainly have to be governed by the constituency that I represent. When it comes to fiscal issues, I have a responsibility to vote their pocketbook, and if I don't do that, then I don't think I'm acting responsibly in that area. . . . As long as you're not voting for stuff like a state income tax, you can take fairly liberal positions on social questions. . . .

I ended up getting beat by about 5,000 votes the first time I ran, with George McGovern. So I decided I wasn't going to be a liberal anymore. . . . I had very progressive thoughts at the time. My district . . . to some degree has governed my thoughts or has restricted my innate liberalism. For instance, if I was in another type of district, I'd probably be far more progressive.

Additional comments by other senators further illustrate this tension.

In a general sense I vote on certain issues by conscience and what I feel, and on certain issues what my constituency—what I perceive they're telling me how to vote. So I don't think there's a specific answer to the question of how I determine the votes in a broader sense. . . . I tend to have fairly strong liberal/progressive beliefs . . . but I do think at times when I vote I vote with an ear to the constituency, and I think the overall constituency in this district, for example, is not as liberal as I am, so I will politicize—if that's the right word—politicize my vote to some extent. . . . But I won't do that on an issue that I consider social conscience.

I don't think that there's any doubt that my ideas on the tax structure in this state are not acceptable. People do not want to see massive changes in the tax structure, and I happen to believe that there's an opportunity here for straightening some things out that are wrong with the state. But that's not an acceptable stance in terms of—if you put it to referendum in the district it would lose 80–20, I can guarantee that. . . . And if I ran on that platform I'd probably get my head handed to me. But the people have accepted the fact that that's something that I think about and I talk about, but as long as I don't actively do—or succeed!

There are reasons to think that the Connecticut senate would be particularly fertile ground for the effect of such electoral incentives. First, elections are held every two years. Second, Connecticut senate elections are relatively competitive; between 1968 and 1986, the margin of victory for senate incumbents was extremely low in comparison to other states, and the proportion of incumbents who were reelected was also comparatively low (although the actual proportion was still quite high, at 80 percent) (Garand 1991, 12, 16).[26] Third, since Connecticut is a small state, senators continue to live among their constituents even while they are legislating; they usually commute to and from the capitol during the session. This allows the district constituency to remain a highly salient reference group even when the senators are working at the capitol (Swanson 1984, 64).

But as the last two interview excerpts presented above indicate, there are other reasons to think that the effects of these electoral incentives are heavily muted. First, a recent survey-based study of legislative behavior found that constituency had little independent effect on decision making in the Connecticut lower house (Entman 1983). Second, some studies have suggested that district sentiments are perceived by legislators in terms of those citizens who are most active, and who are in turn most like the legislators themselves (West 1988; Fenno, Jr. 1977, 1978). There was some evidence of this type of thinking among the senators. Third, through their own behavior, legislators are often able to socialize their constituents into expectations of representational styles that allow the legislators more freedom concerning policy decisions (Entman 1983, 164).

[A]nyone that's any good should be able to mold [constituent] opinion on many subjects by the information that you let out on that subject.

I'm a trustee and not a delegate. . . . I'm not going to go poll my district to find out what the majority believes, and then cast my vote accordingly. . . . The way that the public reacts [to my activity], by phone, letter, public demonstrations, petitions, letters to the editor, you name it—I'm going to respond to that. . . . It has an effect, and I will listen to that. . . . In that sense the public can have some input. . . . As a legislature, in general, we do things reacting to popular sentiment more than we should. Things in public policy are less logical than they could be. . . .

Two or 3 percent of the people know what I'm doing, and care, and the other group doesn't. The other group is more aware of me because I took care of a social security check for their neighbor down the street, sent Johnny a letter when he graduated from. . . . So that's all biased by the name-identification tactics that you can employ. I do that, because I feel like it's my job to serve my district, to be a problem solver. So I don't think it's as issue-directed as it is of another nature.

I had said that a legislator might be able to concentrate on three out of sixteen committees or committee areas; well people might be aware of five issues completely. State government doesn't affect them directly, and obviously. It's very subtle, it's something that affects different people in different ways. . . . Most people are concerned with their family, their job, and with their leisure time, and really don't see how government affects them unless there's a pothole in the road, or there's a road construction down the street and they're delaying traffic five minutes or an hour because of that—that's when they realize that state government is or isn't working. . . . They're more concerned about their own job and keeping it and getting a raise than about diversification of the economy.

There are still other factors that argue against the strong control of constituency over legislative behavior at the expense of beliefs. First, as both the research concerning representational roles and legislative decision making more generally has determined, constituencies rarely provide legislators with clear policy preferences. And constituencies can also vary within districts. Thus, as John Kingdon concludes, "[t]he mass public sets rather vague boundaries that leave politicians quite a bit of discretion" (1989, xiii; see also Jewell 1982).

With the district that I represent, no view that I take matches up completely with that constituency, because it changes dramatically depending on whether I'm talking about [a modest town] or [a wealthy town]. That's one of the interesting things about a district that's as diverse as the one that I have. My thoughts on economic justice are not perhaps even considered by a large portion of that district; it's not a concern of theirs in [the wealthier towns]. . . . The really good thing about the district that I have is that as a result of that diversity, they give me a lot of flexibility, knowing full well that I have to represent a bigger arena. As long as I don't get really crazy on something, it's not a problem.

Second, although the prevailing scholarly wisdom is that highly visible issue positions often bring more harm than good, and therefore legislators wish to avoid such positions and instead promote themselves as individuals through "soft press," a study based on one congressional district indicates that information on legislators available to constituents is more likely to be used to increase the strength of previously held evaluations (Larson 1990). If constituents already have a favorable opinion of the legislator, they will more easily learn the "good" information about him rather than the dissonant positions he may take. More generally, constituents appear to base their evaluations of individual incumbent legislators more on their impressions of constituency service, accessibility, personal characteristics such as trustworthiness, and personal reputation (Jewell 1982, 175–77; Entman 1983; Parker and Davidson 1979). And state legislators are usually even less visible to the constituents on policy issues than are members of Congress (Jewell 1982, 171; Entman 1983). Furthermore, in Connecticut an incumbent's loss is usually the result of party competition across the state, enhanced by the coattail effects of those running at the top of the ticket (1984 and 1986 are particularly good examples), so in many respects negative electoral outcomes in the state are beyond the control of any one individual senator.[27] Also note, however, that these arguments do not address the degree to which legislators are aware of these mitigating factors.

Overall, the Connecticut senators seemed to feel relatively secure in their jobs. One senator, for example, described a "rule of thumb" for reelection, where once a senator had served two terms, he should have little problem in serving as long as he wished. Many other senators cited their name recognition as giving them a distinct advantage once they were in office. This sense of security should engender the connections between beliefs and behavior. The beliefs of the legislators may also have a profound effect on the way they experience the wishes and influence of their constituencies, particularly if their districts are diverse. This effect is part of the notion of beliefs as filters, which I have introduced at several earlier points in this work. Legislators' beliefs can help to define who they think they are representing at the capitol. The natural selection process of the electoral system also involves beliefs; a legislator's base, or reelection constituency, has indeed chosen that legislator, so there is presumably some fit between the constituency and the legislator that reflects shared beliefs, at least at some level.

Constituency concerns probably have their greatest effect, however, not on how specific policy-oriented legislative decisions are made, but rather on where legislators focus their time and attention. Constituency concerns increase the service orientation of legislative behavior; legislators spend more time in the district, more time on case work, and so on.[28] To demonstrate the extreme forms that this service can take, one of the legislators I followed spent part of his day editing a constituent's résumé, as part of the job-hunting assistance he was giving him. And as described above, district work and constituency relations have an overwhelmingly interpersonal orientation. Even when it does involve legislation, this realm of activities is not heavily issue-oriented. Thus, a heavier concentration on constituency concerns means more time allocated to interpersonal activities, at the expense of issue content.

> Unfortunately, constituent work takes up more time than it should, and I don't say that because I don't believe in constituent work. Often legislators are the best hope for people. But getting bureaucracy to move on a certain minor problem often takes a lot of time away from what should be a senator's role, which is concern about policy questions.

External Agenda Constraints: Economics, Public Opinion, and Interstate Competition. Three aspects of Connecticut's political climate in 1988 had a particular impact on the ability of policy alternatives to make it onto the decision-making agenda and to become viable: budget constraints, public mood, and interstate competition.[29]

The state budget, and more generally the structure of the revenue system and the economic health of the state, are important constraining elements in the policy-making process. Of course, on the one hand the budget and the revenue system are themselves the products of legislative behavior, and in the long term they are subject to change, a dependent variable. But in the short term, say, of one legislature, they are more of a given, an independent variable. Richard Winters, for example, has shown how the method of revenue generation can itself greatly influence the policy climate (1980). Winters studied the dramatic differences between Vermont's and New Hampshire's public policies, including the level of state expenditures, the progressivity of revenue generation, and the degree of policy activism. The differences were particularly intriguing because the two states shared so many social, cultural, and economic characteristics, and the beliefs of their lawmakers were also similar. Winters determined that these differences in policy largely dated back to Vermont's institution of an income tax system in 1931. This tax system subsequently yielded a more elastic source of revenue, which in turn engendered an entrepreneurial and acquisitive style of political administration, and a more progressive and activist policy orientation among Vermont's political actors.

Connecticut had no individual income tax in 1988; it relied instead on sales, corporate, and use taxes. We can thus expect that state lawmakers operated under the constraints of the state's particular system of revenue generation, and that the entire budgetary climate, indeed the entire policy-making climate, was in turn influenced by the revenue system. But the years leading up to 1988 had nonetheless been good ones for state government. The economic boom in the state during the 1980s allowed the government to increase its spending significantly, while leaving tax rates the same, even lowering them in some years. This growth had run its course by 1988, however, and during the legislative session just prior to the interviews, the legislators faced lower revenue estimates, lower rates of state economic growth, and real concerns about a budget deficit. Indeed, the senators in all three narrative types shared an awareness of what the state could reasonably afford and what was politically possible, within the given system of revenue generation. There simply were limits on what the state government could do.

The public mood would seem to be a slippery concept. Nonetheless, it has been widely studied, particularly at the national level, and has in fact received an increasing amount of scholarly attention of late. Public mood as I am using the term here is a broader concept than constituency opinion. It concerns general aspects of public feeling and interest, such as, to use the terminology of two of its observers, the relative emphasis placed on "public purpose" versus "private interest," or the periodic expression of a "creedal passion" (Schlesinger, Jr. 1986; Huntington 1981). Public moods are particularly relevant here as influences on legislative agendas because, as David Mayhew points out, "[m]oods seem to overrepresent elite views and to give great weight to opinion intensity and citizen action. They have a profile, in short, that is more likely to engage politicians than designers of surveys" (1991, 172). Mayhew goes on to consider moods as primary causes of legislative surges at the national and subnational levels. John Kingdon states that "[p]eople in and around government sense a national mood. They are comfortable discussing its content, and believe they know when the mood shifts." Furthermore, "these changes . . . have important impacts on policy agendas and policy outcomes" (1984, 153, 156).

Most observers of the public mood agree that it has been relatively conservative since the mid to late 1970s (at least up until the late 1980s). This has lowered the likelihood of any state embarking on new, ambitious policy initiatives. The senators were indeed aware of this mood; they often referred to the tenor of the times in the course of commenting on the limits of the budget and on their constituencies. It is another component in the senators' sense of what is possible. Given its recent nature, the public mood is particularly constraining on the critics' agendas. And once again, the effects of the public mood on the critic's narrative are intensified by the critics' own sense that they are swimming against its current. Since they perceive themselves to be in opposition to the dominant public mood, they are even quicker, as one phrased it, to "pull in their wings" than they might have been otherwise.

Finally, interstate competition for business constrains the ability of certain items to survive in the policy process. The concern here among state policy makers is that policies that are too expensive, redistributive, or progressive will cause businesses and the wealthier strata to leave the state, thus deteriorating the revenue base. In addition, the state's economic performance may influence election outcomes, which further constrains legislative behavior.[30] Interstate competition has become more of a concern for state lawmakers as the economy has deindustrialized, and as businesses have consequently become less tied physically to a particular location. In spite of the fact that the state had one of the highest taxes on business, or perhaps because of it, the Connecticut senators were extremely cognizant of the problem of interstate competition.[31] In fact, their own conceptions of the problem's dimensions appeared to exceed reality. Interstate competition was a commonly made and powerful argument in legislative discussions of anything that involved spending a significant amount of money, especially items that were thought to affect the "business climate" in the state, such as plant-closing legislation (see chap. 6 herein). During the

interviews, supporters and ambivalents more heavily emphasized considerations of interstate competition than did the critics, though almost all senators
mentioned it at least once.

The Narratives and the Perception of Influence and Constraint

As a whole, the senators' perceptions of the degree to which beliefs affect
legislative behavior have in large part already emerged from my descriptions of
the various sources of influences on their behavior. I now wish, however, to
consider their perceptions more specifically in terms of the narratives.

Despite the influences I have just described, all three narrative groups
shared the sense that the beliefs of the kind that we had been discussing in the
interviews mattered in the legislative process; only a few senators thought that
the beliefs did not matter much. Beliefs were generally thought to be rooted in
the senators' personalities, their backgrounds, and their experiences. They
provided a frame of reference for the daily senate activities, an "internalized
sense of good," a "background theme," or the "computer in the mind," as three
of them phrased it. In the same vein, another senator concluded:

> Sometimes [the beliefs] do get lost. I think there is a sense of doing right
> for people, within a pragmatic—there's only so much you can do. . . .
> Your philosophy is something that you internalize; you experience, you
> believe in. I don't think you say, "well, let me see now. I have this
> philosophy, then I should therefore be doing this."

A senate staffer was also close to the mark when he observed that I would not
find much "political philosophy" in the discussion over and making of legislation, but rather a kind of "intuitive philosophy." At the same time, the senators
also perceived limits to the influence of these kinds of beliefs. These limits
took the general form of "practical" or "pragmatic" considerations, as two
senators phrased it, and the more specific forms of the political and electoral
constraints that I have described throughout this chapter.

The group that perceived the least connection between beliefs and behavior was the Republican segment of those senators telling the ambivalent's
narrative. This may have resulted from their greater affinity for the proposals of
the majority Democratic Party, relative to their own party colleagues, combined with the fact that they were nonetheless largely excluded from the
legislative process due to their party affiliation. But according to them, neither
their own beliefs nor those of the Democrats counted for much in the actual
process. Senators positing the greatest connection tended to reside in the
Democratic segment of the ambivalent's narrative. This finding is not surpris-

ing, as this group constitutes a plurality within the senate. The senators in this group grumbled a bit about certain aspects of the process, but did not level any harsh critiques.

We might think that because their views are less legislated, the critics would perceive less connection between beliefs and behavior within the senate than the other senators. This is not the case, however. The explanation for this turns on the critics' individually held perceptions of their own distinctiveness. First, the perception by each critic that he is different from the rest of the senate has a profound impact, not only on his perceptions of the legislative process, but also on his behavior itself. Critical senators do not share a sense of solidarity; they do not even seem to be aware that they constitute a significant group within the senate. As individuals, they believe that the rest of the senators largely fail to recognize their concerns as legitimate political issues.

> [My beliefs] guide me, and they provide me with a conceptual framework where the day-to-day or month-to-month kinds of tasks fit. I'd like to think I know what I'm doing, in the sense of that I have a vision of where I want us to get. . . . I think what I do is rather consistent. If someone else were to look at it, they may have some difficulty finding that consistency, but that's perhaps because they wouldn't necessarily know . . . much about me. . . . My sense about the senate is, first of all, probably most people don't share my views. I find myself somewhat in a minority situation.

> The governor exerts pressure on us, and our leaders in turn put pressure on the rank and file. . . . There are times when I find myself, even now— particularly in an election year—there are things I'd like to say I can't say, because if I say what I think I'm going to turn off a whole group of people.

> Clearly, most [other senators] don't share the forms of the types of solutions that I've talked about. They probably think of them as too extreme. They're much more gradualist in what they would propose. . . . The level of concern and the level of immediacy they would feel—I don't get the sense, in dealing with my colleagues on these issues that it's something any of them ever go home in the evening and lose a night's sleep over.

It is thus reasonable to expect that as the critics look out at the rest of the membership, they would conclude that in general, beliefs matter; it is just that these beliefs are different from their own. If the critic's narrative receives little legislative attention, that is to be expected; after all, collectively they think they are just one senator out of the entire body. Furthermore, since they perceive themselves individually to be so different, they must be especially careful in tending to the things necessary for success within the chamber, and for reelection itself, such as trading support and generally fitting in with their perceptions of the rest of the Democrats in the senate. In addition they must be careful to minimize the differences between themselves and their constituencies, differences that they perceive to be significant. In short, the critics' perceptions of their own distinctiveness exacerbate the constraining effect of all the factors I have previously described. Their self-perceptions cause the anticipated reactions from fellow senators and constituents to what they might otherwise do to assume ominous forms.

The self-perceptions of the critics may also add to the explanation of their narrative's apparent paradox between diagnosis and treatment. Recall from the initial presentation of the critic's narrative in chapter 3 that the critics described distributive problems that ran quite deeply in the economic system; in some tellings these problems were even structurally embedded. At the same time, the specific proposals they put forward to remedy these wrongs were somewhat soft and individually oriented, relative to the problems. This paradox may therefore be explained in part by the critics' sense of their own distinctiveness, and the subjectively held limits that this distinctiveness imposes on the realization of any more direct or structural remedies. Thus, the critics' proposed remedies may reflect a cognitively driven adjustment on their part, in response to reality as they perceive it.

The Overall Effect of Beliefs: Sorting Devices and Filters

If we consider the entire account in this and the previous chapter, beliefs appear to have their greatest influence on legislative behavior as cue sorters and cognitive filters. We could in fact view many of the various sources of influences on legislative behavior considered in this chapter, in particular the collection of legislative actors both within and without the legislative body, as suppliers of cues in a senator's decision-making process; the more salient the cues supplied by a given source, the more powerful it is as a source of influence. But just as deep beliefs can influence the very perception and even conception of one's own self-interest, they can also influence the perceptions and conceptions of these decision-making cues. Beliefs can influence, for example, a legislator's perceptions of his constituency, the public mood, and party competition. Beliefs can also influence the request of committee assignments. In addition, beliefs can directly influence behavior and decision making *within* any of the parameters set by the features discussed in this chapter.

If we follow the dominant trend in cognitive theory and consider the senators as cognitive misers, who seek efficiency rather than complete mastery in their processing of incoming information, it in turn follows that they will also seek out cognitive shortcuts in their decision making. The problem of the modern legislature, namely too many decisions to make and too little time in which to make them, only increases the limits on any one legislator's ability to process, retain, and organize relevant information, and thus intensifies her search for these shortcuts. Under such conditions of what John Kingdon calls "bounded rationality," that is, "imperfect information, limited time, incomplete canvass of alternatives, and a dramatic deficit of ability to consider floor votes thoroughly in the light of the tremendous volume of decisions to be made," legislators will look for cues from other sources in order to make their decisions (1989, xiii). The limits on their own cognitive powers force them to be selective in processing information, and cues supply a handy device in making these selections. Potential cue sources include fellow legislators, legislative leaders, lobbyists, constituents, staff members, and other political actors, such as the governor and agency officials. Even the apparently interpersonally oriented gossip about who is for and against a certain bill may be a form of cue taking. In a study on decision making in state legislatures, Malcolm Jewell specifically considers whether Kingdon's model for members of Congress is applicable to state legislators. Jewell concludes that the model is extremely applicable; in fact, "[i]t may be even more important for state legislators to minimize the cost of getting information and simplifying choices, because they have less time and staff" (1982, 130). Other students of state legislative politics have similarly observed that cues may be even more important to state legislators than they are to members of Congress (Jewell and Patterson 1977; Uslaner and Weber 1977).

In this system, beliefs emerge as important filters of the cues themselves. Accordingly, Kingdon (1989) remarks on the central importance of legislative policy attitudes, both directly, in legislators' attempts to enact good policy, and indirectly, in the selection of cues. This filtering effect is intensified by the fact that it is easier to retain information that is consistent with previously held beliefs (Larson 1990).[32] Thus, beliefs affect not only which cues will be most sought out, but also which cues will be best remembered and most easily accessed. When do beliefs matter most? According to both Kingdon and related cognitive theories, as the intensity of conflict in the legislative environment increases, the legislator's own attitudes and beliefs become more important; the filtering process becomes more pronounced.[33] The senators' responses in the interviews appeared to substantiate this finding about the relative influence of beliefs. Beliefs thus seem to matter most when there are salient, conflicting points of view.

CHAPTER 8

Endings

In this final chapter I wish to return to a consideration of the narratives themselves, but from a different, more speculative perspective. Do the narratives of justice have any implications for our understanding of contemporary American politics, and American political ideology and political beliefs? I believe that the narratives help to illuminate several related and contentious subjects of ongoing debate: the relative salience of ideology in our political system and the degree of monism in American political ideology and beliefs; the prospects for constructively addressing the problem of normative incommensurability; and the viability of the Left in American politics. Though these three subjects are indeed closely related, I shall discuss the implications of the narratives regarding each of them in turn.

The Narratives and American Exceptionalism Reconsidered

It seems clear that the collection of the three narratives supplies yet another powerful counterfactual to the notion that the United States is not heavily marked by ideology in its politics; that is, that competing commitments to normative frameworks are not as important as pragmatic approaches to problem solving, and that political differences in the United States are more about means than about ends. Such statements have usually been made with particular reference to the United States' peer nations in Western Europe. These observations, while popular in the 1950s and 1960s, have already been decisively discredited by the Reagan and post-Reagan years. My evidence further supports this rejection. The diversity of views found in the narratives, their level of normative commitment, and the real challenges they level at the status quo from both the Left and the Right drive another nail into the coffin of the "end of ideology" thesis.

In fact, as I set forth in chapters 1 and 3, much of the received scholarly wisdom now agrees that the United States is indeed a strongly ideological nation, but that there is also a monistic quality to that ideology. The most distinctive feature of American political beliefs is widespread consensus, which is centered around the traditional liberal tenets of individualism, and concomitantly, economic opportunity. The classic statement of this view is found in Louis Hartz's *The Liberal Tradition in America* (1955).[1] There is thus, according to Samuel Huntington, one "American Creed," and political protest in the United States therefore assumes the form of a periodic radicalization of the center, mobilized against institutions that are perceived to violate that creed (1981).[2] The narratives offer a commentary upon this notion as well.

Although each narrative, including the critic's narrative, bears distinctively American markings, and although the narrative told by the largest number of senators is indeed a centrist one, as a group the narratives nonetheless contradict this characterization of American political beliefs. There is much that is different among the three narratives. They appear to differ significantly in their views of how persons at different levels of socioeconomic achievement should be treated; their notions of which resources are social and which are individual, and how they in turn should be distributed; their approaches toward solving differently conceived social problems; their conceptions of the appropriate role of the state; and their ways of defining key political and economic terms. They appear to differ significantly in their visions of the good society, the extent of our mutual obligations to one another, and the place of compassion versus competition in that society. They appear to choose different—even opposing—sets of heroes and villains.

I am certainly not the first person to make such a counterclaim; see, for just one example, the large block of literature during the last twenty years that rediscovers the classical republican underpinnings of the founding period, as well as a newer set of literature rediscovering persistent ascriptive hierarchical strains in American political thought (Wildavsky 1990; Smith 1993). Furthermore, I do not claim, as others have, that Hartz is entirely wrong about political ideology in the United States. It is the ambivalents who are the dominant narrative type, after all, and they tell a story that is consistent with the Hartzian view. The American exceptionalism thesis, however, is not just a claim about the center of gravity in American political beliefs; it is also a claim about the range of discussion and the range of viable alternatives. Bearing that in mind, I argue that there are significant variations within the existing liberal theme that threaten to break it apart; therefore, as J. David Greenstone (1986) also argues, these variations are of primary rather than secondary importance. The very nature and the genuine range of American political beliefs have been distorted and underestimated by most political observers because of their reliance on the labels of certain long-standing institutions of these liberal tenets—labels like opportunity, upward mobility, self-reliance, and individualism—and their assumptions of a consensus on and about them. Such distortions are particularly likely with the use of surveys that begin with these assumptions, since they must precategorize the answers, and almost always use a standard set of items that are themselves based on the assumptions. If nothing else, the evidence from the narratives demonstrates that the meanings of these labels need to be examined more closely. In particular, the nature and the salience of the critic's narrative makes the case for such reexaminations all the more compelling.

It may also be the case that the continuing presence of these assumptions among most political scientists and political observers and their analogous forms among members of the media has contributed to the fact that we do not see around us more noticeable pieces of evidence of the critic's narrative, the narrative that most directly challenges this supposed consensus. We have just seen in chapter 7 how the critics' individually held senses of their own exceptionalism exacerbate the limiting effects of a preexisting set of legislative conditions, which in turn further disadvantage the appearance of their narrative in policy output. More generally, these assumptions about the character of American political beliefs, and the intuitive awareness of such assumptions, may contribute to what Elisabeth Noelle-Neumann (1986) calls a "spiral of silence" among the critics themselves, and among other potential critics in the general public. This is a spiral in which, due to the fear of social isolation, it is increasingly unlikely that apparently deviant opinions will be heard, even though a substantial number of persons might hold those opinions. And in a state legislature, such isolation carries with it dangers that extend well beyond one's psychological and social comfort. Once a spiral of silence is in place, threats to the apparently prevailing opinions are largely precluded.

But the critical senators nonetheless emerged, at least during the interviews. One question, then, is why. While the environment I attempted to provide during the interviews certainly fell short of any situation of Habermasian free speech or the conditions that obtain in a psychotherapy session, I tried nonetheless to be as supportive and nonjudgmental as possible. The environment was also more academic and anonymous, and therefore less politically threatening, than that produced, say, in an interview with a member of the press. In addition, the respondents could easily assume the role of teacher, which is arguably an empowering experience that would instill additional confidence in one's opinions. All these factors may have helped to break the spiral of silence. The fact that the critics did emerge may strike a hopeful chord for those who would like to see a greater variety in American political discourse.[3]

An offshoot of the debate over the nature and range of American beliefs that also deserves mention here is the division between materialist and postmaterialist concerns. Some political observers have argued that the postmodern world, or at least the industrialized portion of it, has largely shifted its political battleground from materialist to postmaterialist issues (Inglehart 1977, 1990). Although there are some similarities between the critic's narrative and postmaterialism, particularly in the narrative's approach toward solving social problems, the three narratives taken together, along with the lines of cleavage that separate them, suggest the continued relevance of material issues as the basis for ideological divisions. The debate between the three narratives does not ignore scarcity. Furthermore, the set of postmaterial concerns does not fully capture the critic's narrative taken by itself; there are many material concerns in the narrative in addition to those regarding empathy and mutual understanding, and even the concern for empathy and mutual understanding is in part a way for the critics to bring more material prosperity to those in need. What I may have found instead is the same thing that another study discovered in its examination of Dutch elite beliefs: that materialist and postmaterialist debates overlap one another, and result in overlapping ideological divisions (Eldersveld, Kooiman, and van der Tak 1981, 131–33). That study also found that an emphasis on postmaterialist concerns usually accompanies traditional, materialist-oriented support of state economic intervention, a finding consistent with the fact that it is my critics who have many of the post-materialist concerns.

How the Narratives Relate to One Another: The Problem of Normative Incommensurability

But if American normative beliefs are more varied than we might have thought, is there a way to bring them together? More specifically, what are the relations between the narratives of justice? Do they offer the potential for finding common ground, or do they exist as three separate visions, destined to argue endlessly with each other?

The possibility of endless debate, also known as the problem of incommensurable or essentially contestable normative positions, is a problem that political and ethical theorists have been wrestling with, in one way or another, for at least two centuries.[4] The basic notion is that all normative statements are inherently rooted in a particular perspective, interest, or context that renders them invalid as unbiased ethical principles. Granted, different persons will of course disagree with each other on important matters. The problem here, however, is that these disagreements may not have a common base to which they can refer for adjudication; that is, what one thinks, says, and does may ultimately be based on who one is and where one sits, in such a way as to render the prospect of real normative communication remote, perhaps even impossible. Combatants cannot engage each other on meaningfully shared terms, and normative disagreements become analogous to statements of taste or preference. Disagreements based on different normative perspectives, which in turn are based on different worldviews and basic conceptions of reality, thus end in what Robert Grafstein calls "a mutual shrugging of shoulders" (1988, 9).

As a group, the three narratives appear to fit the incommensurability thesis disturbingly well; they arrive at the discussion of fairness and justice from dramatically different perspectives, in such a way that establishing common ground and a mutually acceptable basis for adjudication appears extremely unlikely, if at all possible. In the face of these differences, how can the narratives be brought together? In what follows, I consider three potential answers to this question, along with considerations of the arguments that might be leveled against each proposal. These potential answers concern the narrative structure itself, the empirical assumptions made by the senators, and the narratives' views about education and opportunity. The previous descriptions of the three narratives of justice have demonstrated how they are different. I will now attempt a more difficult task: to show how they are similar, or at least that they share some significant—perhaps decisively significant—points of contact. But before I launch into a consideration of the three narratives, I should further sketch, in broad strokes, the philosophical problem that leads me to this inquiry.

The Theoretical Problem. The related philosophical problems of incommensurability, essential contestability, lack of closure in moral reasoning, and subjectivism in moral judgments have all been subjected to an exhaustive treatment, one that I will render here in only the briefest and most general fashion. Under the general rubric of these problems, one could also include the deconstruction and contextual dependency of moral positions, particularism, and ethical relativism. These problems, and the theorists who work with them, find their recent heritage in the work of Marx, Nietzsche, and Foucault (each with his own distinctive contributions), and beyond that in Hume, and perhaps, under some interpretations, even Plato.[5] Some theorists have argued that these problems are built into the very logic of Enlightenment liberalism, with its emphasis on neutrality, empiricism, and skepticism (we could spin even deeper into the problem by stating that the concept of neutrality itself presupposes a particular, contestable view of rationality and justice) (Fishkin 1984, 153–57; MacIntyre 1988).

Basically, the claim is that all normative statements are inherently rooted in a particular perspective, interest, or context that renders them invalid as objective, universalizable principles of action.[6] Parties divided by deep moral disagreements will argue against each other from these different perspectives. They will never be able to reach closure or agreement; in fact, they will never be able to agree even on the standards by which to adjudicate their competing claims. As Alasdair MacIntyre observes:

> [D]ebate between fundamentally opposed standpoints does occur; but it is inevitably inconclusive. Each warring position characteristically appears irrefutable to its own adherents; indeed in its own terms and by its own standards of argument it *is* in practice irrefutable. But each warring posi-

tion equally seems to its opponents to be insufficiently warranted by rational argument. (1990, 7)

[W]hen disagreements between contending views are sufficiently fundamental . . . those disagreements will extend even to the answers to the question of how to proceed in order to resolve those same disagreements. (1990, 4)

Much of the work in this vein examines the contested and incommensurable nature of the fundamental concepts used in formulating normative claims.[7] In many readings of normative debate, the contextually based disagreements I have just described reach down into these fundamental concepts, so that "[e]ach party's insights . . . can only be appreciated by those sharing the value-laden conception on which those insights depend" (Grafstein 1988, 9). The problem of incommensurability thus envelops the very language used to communicate normatively. Such conceptual disagreements are not surprising; indeed it would seem to follow naturally that persons disagreeing over fundamental moral positions will also disagree over the terms and concepts used to express these positions (Connolly 1983, 10–41; Gutmann 1982, 39–43). Before we are able to reach agreement on the content of our views about justice, we must first be able to specify what concepts such as "political party" or "liberty" mean. And if these concepts themselves are contextually based and therefore essentially contestable, such agreement is not possible.

The upshot of this deconstructive analysis is that justice claims are always contextually dependent. As James Fishkin observes, in discussing the problem of moral subjectivism:

If I say "X is right," and you say, "X is wrong," we think we are disagreeing about something. But . . . these statements are logically compatible once they are interpreted as "From my perspective X is right" and "From your perspective X is wrong." They become reports on the attributes of perspectives or points of view rather than statements about the attributes of the action X. (1984, 145)

This contextual dependency in turn casts suspicion on any kind of claim to justice. The prospects for its impartiality and objective validity are slim, if they exist at all, because, in the words of Amy Gutmann, a critic can always reply to the proponent of a moral principle:

Is it not possible that your intuitions are wrong? Since the ultimate support for your moral intuitions is not rational argument but the social life into which you have been educated and socialized, and since you do not have sure standards by which to choose among forms of social life, how can particular intuitions or your entire system of beliefs be *correct* standards for moral argument? (1982, 40)

We are thus left uneasy, since as William Connolly argues, "[a]ny authoritative set of norms and standards is, at its best, an ambiguous achievement; it excludes and denigrates that which does not fit into its confines" (1987, 138). In even more critical views, justice claims are ultimately expressions of such morally unacceptable motivations as preference, will, and self-interest. According to this view, "beliefs, allegiances to conceptions of justice, and the use of particular modes of reasoning about action . . . appear . . . as disguises assumed by arbitrary will to further its projects, to empower itself" (MacIntyre 1988, 396). This view is a contemporary reformulation of Marx's argument concerning ideology and Nietzsche's argument concerning morality.

This lack of closure, essential contestability, or incommensurability certainly exists regarding differences and disagreements *between* different social systems and different cultures, but it is also an inherent problem for the deep conflicts that occur between individuals and points of view *within* social systems and cultures. And it is the second version of this problem that I am concerned with here. Indeed, the three narratives of justice are found within a relatively specific and narrowly defined social system, a particular state's legislature.

Though some theorists would of course disagree with the following assessment (contestably?), it nonetheless appears that in their relentless pounding at objective, universal principles the antifoundationalists have carried the day.[8] There is at least a growing agreement among theorists on the assertion that there can be no agreement. But now that the theorists have opened the Pandora's box of incommensurability and subjectivism, they have not helped much to contain the effects. In fact, they seem to make their best contributions by showcasing the disagreements and the gaps, and by exposing the sources of the gaps, without making much effort to close them or to show how we might go about closing them.[9] Deconstruction is not construction, and little deconstruction is undertaken in order to lay a new foundation. Just as a house divided against itself cannot stand, neither can a house built on air. Given that we may never be able to realize the Enlightenment dream of moral closure among rational persons, the proper task of philosophy now seems to be the reconstruction, in the midst of the ruins, of some kind of valid ethical theory.[10] If we can never say never again, we must find out what we *can* in fact say. Do the narratives teach us anything about this?

An Empirical Solution? Although the problem of incommensurability appears real enough regarding the debates among political theorists given the ways in which they themselves have framed their normative discourse, it still remains largely an open question as to whether or not these same conditions of incommensurability exist among real political actors (though the theory of essential contestability would at least imply that this is indeed the case). While closure or agreement among these real political actors certainly has not occurred in fact, it is not as certain that closure or agreement is not possible, that there are no grounds available upon which to achieve closure. As Norman Care has observed, "it does not follow that the concepts which are, according to the thesis in question, essentially contestable for the social scientist are also essentially contestable for participants in such particulars as political parties or educational institutions" (1974, 13).[11]

This empirical question is more important to political life than the question with which the theorists have been wrestling.[12] The argument can and should be joined at a more concrete level. I would also argue that this empirical question is that which the theorists' debate is ultimately directed toward answering (though it has done little to answer it); otherwise, their efforts are of limited use. Again, as Care argues:

If it should turn out that social concepts may be essentially contestable for social scientists but somehow not be essentially contestable for participants in institutions and parties to practices, it may be that the importance of the thesis is limited somewhat. . . . But if it should turn out that the social concepts which are essentially contestable for social scientists are also essentially contestable for participants, then . . . the general importance of the thesis is great; it then bears on how we understand, say, our prospects for social reform and social progress. (1974, 14)

Such a discovery would drive yet another—perhaps the final—nail into the coffin of valid normative positions. Just as the theorists have concluded from their debates among themselves, we would now have empirical evidence to support the view that all such normative positions are "subject to the shifting sands of interests and expectations, ideology and custom" (Care 1974, 15).

One way to get at this question is to attempt to discover the nature of normative arguments from the participants themselves, in their own words, as they relate them in a relatively nonconfrontational setting such as an in-depth, semistructured interview. In this way we might make progress toward our primary concern of discovering whether or not closure is possible, and through this discovery toward our ultimate goal of finding a way in which to achieve that closure. I am attempting here a preliminary reconnaissance for such a discovery, through in-depth, textured, empirical evidence from a set of political actors.

One notable extant study of this kind is James Fishkin's *Beyond Subjective Morality*. Fishkin uses interviews with undergraduate and graduate students at Yale and Cambridge Universities to investigate whether or not people in fact endorse a subjectivist view of morality. He finds that they do have such a view, which can only be resolved by "a basic revision in moral culture, through an adjustment in our expectations about what a nonsubjective morality might be like" (1984, 26). He argues for a "middle ground" of "minimal objectivism" between extreme subjectivism and absolutism, an objectivism whose "principles do not lay claim to being rationally unquestionable," but nonetheless avoids "the route to subjectivism" (1984, 129).

But this solution begs a difficult question, one that I too must face in discussing the relations between the narratives of justice: How can a profoundly theoretical reworking solve what was found to be an empirical problem? Fishkin claims that "once the measure of truth in subjectivist arguments is granted, there is still room for positions that provide morality with a basis that is not entirely 'arbitrary,' not entirely 'subjective'" (1984, 140). But will his interview subjects think any differently in response to his reworking of what should count as objective morality? By the same token, what good is my ability to bring together the senators' narratives if they themselves still have a sense that they are too far apart? These questions get at the age-old challenge of the tangled relations among social inquiry, theory, and political praxis. Such a task may be beyond the scope of Fishkin's project, but it still must ultimately be addressed. One possible response to the challenge is that if these persons knew the researcher's argument, they would change their views. In this way theory becomes praxis. Indeed, that may be the last best hope of the social scientist. I shall now turn to the three potential answers to the incommensurability problem that are suggested by the narratives.

Narrative as the Level of Normative Belief. As I set forth in chapter 2, the concept of narrative indicates a story with a plot and a cast of characters possessing certain qualities, in which the interactions between these characters and the circumstances that they encounter are used by the teller of the narrative to both explain and judge perceived outcomes. The fact that the beliefs themselves are organized into such narratives might offer a way out of the incommensurability problem, in that the basic formats of these normative beliefs are similarly structured in a contextually independent fashion. Furthermore, this narrative structure does not appear to be generated by the competing patterns of reasoning that the contemporary political theorists have culled from conflicting conceptions of justice. The narratives of justice do not have their origins in incommensurable philosophical methods. Narrative may thus offer a meta-structure of normative thinking that provides a common ground for disagreement, a basis of adjudication.

But just how useful is the common ground of narrative structure in grappling with the challenge of incommensurability? Will not narratives themselves conflict? The fact that we may think normatively in terms of a narrative does not preclude the adoption of incommensurable positions within the constraints of a shared narrative framework. In terms of the *content* of the stories that we tell ourselves and others, many different, fundamentally opposed narratives are obviously still possible. Again, just as with the liberal tradition itself, the substantive variations within the narrative structure may be of primary rather than secondary importance. The actual content of a narrative can be just as contextually bound and unadjudicable as any other kind of normative claim. Indeed, the supporter's and critic's narratives appear to be prime examples of such contestable positions. Given these considerations, is there any way to bring the actual narratives together?

The distinctive value of narrative in this regard may lie not so much in the shared structure of beliefs, but rather in the way that we can understand and evaluate competing narratives as opposed to competing principles of justice. We all can weigh the truth of a narrative. While we may not be able to decide between competing abstract principles of justice, we are better able to judge between penetrating and convincing stories, and shallow and specious ones (Beiner 1983, 126). In this way, narrative may provide a more accessible—and shared—means of evaluating competing claims, albeit a fairly intuitive one, through which we can escape contestability and incommensurability.

But this aspect of narrative still does not solve the problem. First, it is unclear whether judgments that distinguish more compelling from less compelling stories are any less controversial or contestable than moral judgments based on abstract principles of justice. The fact that we may find narratives more normatively accessible and easier to evaluate than abstract principles does not preclude the possibility, again, of the adoption of incommensurable positions within the constraints of a shared narrative framework. In addition, different persons may weigh narratives differently. Furthermore, such an approach to solving the problem threatens to conflate literary analysis with moral reasoning (Hadari 1988, 671–72). We may thus wish to consider other options.

The Empirical Assumptions of the Narratives. To bring the competing narratives together, we still must attempt to accommodate their differing specific contents. It is not enough to rely on their similar structures. But before we can bring the narratives together we must know why they differ. On what bases do the narratives' contents differ? What drives their competing story lines? If we can discover the answers to these questions we can then begin the attempt to construct a common ground for the narratives.

Upon a close examination of the three narratives, it appears that many of the differences between the three narratives are driven by the empirical assumptions that they make. The narratives' views of justice are heavily informed by their views of the history of social and economic relations, the past and present patterns of economic distribution, and more generally the respective historical paths through which persons have arrived at their present situations. These views appear to be in turn largely shaped by the senators' personal experiences, particularly the experiences they had as they were growing up, including the influence of their parents. These early experiences heavily influence the meanings assigned to the empirical information that the senators later receive. Recall, for example, how the supporters' views about the appropriateness and efficacy of government activism began to approach those of the other senators in two areas where the supporters either experienced or observed real problems among those with whom they were familiar—affordable housing and small business viability.

The fact that the narratives of justice differ around their empirical assumptions is not surprising, given the nature of the incommensurability thesis itself. If moral reasoning is inherently contextually bound, and closure depends on a common context, then the assessments of and notions about that context should be key materials—perhaps even determining materials—in the construction of any normative position.

Consider for example the narratives' views about equal opportunity. Each narrative endorses a notion of equal opportunity and looks for conditions of equal opportunity as a barometer of the condition of economic fairness. The actual content of equal opportunity is obviously constructed differently in each of the three narratives: there is a movement from a voluntaristic conception in the supporter's narrative toward a stronger, more positive or interventionist conception in the critic's narrative. But the narratives' competing conceptions of the normative concept of equal opportunity are heavily influenced by their respective views of what has happened to individuals and groups in the past. Their views of the past, largely based on assumption and personal experience, structure their perceptions of the present, and their proffered solutions to the perceived problems.

Perhaps the most influential empirical assumptions are the views that each narrative has about human nature. Each narrative has its own vision of human nature, which collectively are reminiscent of Thomas Sowell's (1987) two-part division of unconstrained versus constrained world visions and the respective conceptions of human personality that undergird them. The critic's narrative assumes the dynamic, perfectible notion of human nature of the unconstrained vision, while the supporter's narrative assumes the harsher, more static, self-interested based notion of the constrained vision. The ambivalent's narrative assumes a somewhat vague hybrid of these two notions (perhaps balanced is more accurate), though it is more static than dynamic. These assumed notions of human nature are also reminiscent of the two views about human personality that, according to J. David Greenstone (1986), undergird the respective strains of American liberalism that have competed with each other throughout the nation's history (and that I alluded to earlier). The Protestant non-Lockean strain of liberalism, more supportive of progressive movements, is based on a relatively dynamic notion of personality, while the secular Lockean strain, more supportive of traditional liberal—and therefore typically conservative—positions, is based on a relatively static notion.

The competing notions of human nature underlie and in some cases explain the most important differences between the narratives. The views about human nature inform the views about the "other," which in turn explain the basic orientation each narrative has toward the capacity and means for social reform. In the critic's narrative, for example, the comparatively distinctive theme of compassion and empathy appears to be in large part driven by the narrative's approach toward the problem of the other, and in turn its sense of human nature. The respective views of human nature also underlie the three narratives' respective notions of liberty. The dynamic conception of the critic's narrative informs its more positive, "freedom to" notion of liberty, while the static conception of the supporter's narrative informs its more negative, "freedom from" notion. By the same token, the more vague sense of human nature of the ambivalent's narrative also appears to inform its more vaguely defined notion of liberty (again, perhaps balanced is a more accurate word). The fact that the ambivalent narrative's conception of human nature is more static than dynamic also supports the fact that its notion of liberty is more negative than positive. Finally, the respective conceptions of human nature support the respective views each narrative has about equal opportunity; the dynamic view of the critic's narrative, for example, supports its stronger notion of empowering and enabling persons to better themselves.

The argument concerning the importance of empirical assumptions is further supported by other scholars' works. For example, Gerald MacCallum advances a related argument in his notable contribution to the apparently incommensurable debate among political theorists concerning the concepts of liberty and freedom (1972). The theorists appear to be mired in arguments between the competing, apparently contestable conceptions of negative and positive liberty. This theoretical problem is particularly relevant here because the respective narratives of justice seem to take similarly contestable positions concerning liberty and freedom. MacCallum first unmasks much of the debate by stating that

> disputes about the nature of freedom are certainly historically best understood as a series of attempts by parties opposing each other on very many issues to capture for their own side the favourable attitudes attaching to the notion of freedom. It has commonly been advantageous for partisans to link the presence or absence of freedom as closely as possible to the presence or absence of those other social benefits believed to be secured or denied by the forms of social organization advocated or condemned. (1972, 175)

But MacCallum stops short of claiming that such strategic positioning explains all of the debate; there is also "a genuine confusion concerning the concept of freedom" (1972, 175). He then posits that in each of its conceptions freedom is always a "triadic relation" between three variables, and that the camps advancing each conception are in fact reaching for the same goal, but that they differ on the "ranges of the term variables" that constitute that relation; that is, they differ about

> the ("true") identities of the agents whose freedom is in question, on what counts as an obstacle to or interference with the freedom of such agents, or on the range of what such agents might or might not be free to do or become. (1972, 176, 180)[13]

Debates over freedom, then, "rather than being about what *freedom* is," are really debates "about what persons are, and about what can count as an obstacle to or interference with the freedom of persons so conceived" (1972, 181; emphasis in original). It thus follows from MacCallum's analysis that a key factor in the construction of these variables will be the set of empirical assumptions that individuals bring with them into the freedom debate. These will include assumptions about the items I have discussed above; that is, assumptions about human nature ("what persons are") and the nature of the obstacles to freedom.

When we reconsider the narratives' respective views concerning liberty and freedom, it does indeed seem possible to place the three narratives' views at distinct locations in the triadic relation (or to have distinct versions of the relation). Furthermore, their placement in this relation appears to result from the empirical assumptions that each narrative makes about human nature, the nature of the obstacles to freedom—especially past obstacles, and the beliefs of others opposing it. MacCallum's typology thus seems particularly appropriate to a comparative analysis of the narratives, and therefore appears to provide a potential solution to their seeming incommensurability.

But, as I will argue below, the argument from empirical assumption also contains flaws. In MacCallum's case, for example, what are we to do about the very real possibility that persons will have incommensurable notions of the ranges of the term variables concerning freedom, which are in turn based on radically different empirical assumptions?

Problems with the Argument for Empirical Assumption. It is tempting to conclude that the differences between the narratives are mainly empirically based; that if, for example, the supporters could only see the same extent and depth of social problems that the critics see, their commitments to a stronger form of equal opportunity and an enhanced empathy would match those of the critics. But several problems remain. Following up on the objection raised against MacCallum's argument concerning liberty, one could argue that the empirical assumptions about such core elements as human nature are fundamental and prior to other assumptions, and therefore differing empirical assumptions about these elements may themselves be incommensurable. I wish to set aside this objection, however, in order to consider two deeper problems.

First, the implication of the argument from empirical assumption is that the way out of the incommensurability problem lies in having persons undergo similar experiences. In this regard, it is interesting to note that the critics in particular emphasize the need to integrate the lives of different citizens, in order to provide a means through which they can achieve mutual understanding. For the critics, education is particularly important precisely because of its role in the development of this mutual understanding; it is the best means through which persons at an impressionable age can learn about others and absorb the values of empathy and compassion. Although the critics are probably largely unaware of incommensurability as a philosophical problem, they may nonetheless provide a valuable insight into its solution in their emphasis on the noncoercive creation of integrative experiences. It is through the creation of such experiences that the problem of incommensurable empirical assumptions may be solved.

But how is this to be accomplished? Our collective experience with regimes that attempt to establish unitary experiences through fiat or force should be sufficient to deter us from advocating this option. Beyond education, how do we then confront the problem of different experiences? Indeed, some of the senators have radically different experiences. Are these experiences so far apart that we cannot possibly harmonize them? How do we bring together the senator who "grew up a little rich kid, went to private schools . . . a preppy punk" with the senator who grew up witnessing "discrimination on a firsthand basis"? We are thus left with the problem of how to address the likelihood that persons have "incommensurable experiences" leading to incommensurable empirical assumptions, as well as incommensurable normative commitments and normative conceptions. Perhaps Rousseau and other ancient and republican thinkers are right in assuming that democracy can only function properly in a relatively small, homogeneous community, where interests and experiences are widely shared.

Second, we are still left with the question of why persons draw the lessons that they do from their experiences. The normative commitments that I have been treating here as largely derivative of empirical assumptions and lived experiences are in fact important sources of influence themselves on the meanings that individuals assign to experiences, as well as on their formulation of empirical assumptions. Deriving a meaning from an experience is not something that occurs only at the time of the experience. It is an ongoing process, involving much retrospection. Normative commitments exert an important, relatively independent influence in this retrospection. One of the themes of my earlier discussions of beliefs in chapters 2 and 7 is that these beliefs organize and give meaning to one's perceptions of empirical conditions, one's own self-interest, and one's processing of incoming information. These beliefs also act as important filters on perceptions. In short, they influence the construction of the empirical world. They certainly influence the construction of human nature, which I have argued is one of the key empirical assumptions of the narratives. Incommensurable beliefs may thus be the product of a complicated, dynamic interplay between the normative and empirical realms, an interplay that can be distinctive to each individual. The argument from empirical assumption thus becomes circular; we need somehow to get beyond competing normative frameworks in order to achieve a shared sense of the empirical, which is in turn required to achieve a shared normative framework.

This critique is supported by evidence from the narratives themselves. Though experience certainly plays a large role in the formation of beliefs, it does not always play a determinative role. For example, the notion of experience informing normative commitments appears to work well in explaining the differences between critics and supporters, but runs into problems in explaining the differences between critics and ambivalents; ambivalents and critics have similar experiences, but different sets of beliefs.

Postscript: Social Science and the Argument for Empirical Assumption and a Note on the Critics' Assumptions. The observation that much of the contested material in the three narratives appears to be based on differing empirical assumptions also suggests an intriguing argument about the relations among social science, political ideology, and legitimate normative claims. What are the most reliable procedures and sources of information upon which to base a set of empirical judgments? One might argue that social science, while normatively contentious, is certainly a more reliable informant of empirical judgments than individual personal experience. It is thus at this juncture in an individual's moral reasoning that social science may be of most use to us normatively. Heretofore, we have tended to focus our concerns about theory and normative praxis on political philosophy; however, it may be social science—normatively oriented in terms of the questions it is trying to answer—that is more useful in this regard.

A final observation regarding empirical assumptions: it is interesting to note that regarding the empirical assumptions that can be easily verified, such as perceptions of incomes, levels of achievement among different groups, and present amounts of social assistance, the critics tend to be more accurate than the other two narrative groups.[14]

The Narratives' Views about Education. The final escape route out of the trap of incommensurability I wish to consider concerns education, and its place in the narratives. Recall that all the narrative types emphasize the importance of education, and of providing access to it. Indeed, many observers of American politics and American political thinking have noted the unique position occupied by public education in public policy and in general attitudes about government spending. Although the United States is distinct in comparison to Western European nations in terms of the comparatively smaller size and more limited scope of its state, especially in areas of social welfare (a fact that undergirds the exceptionalism thesis regarding beliefs), the U.S. state's educational expenditures generally exceed those of these same nations (King 1973; U.S. Bureau of the Census 1990). This apparent anomaly in the relative size of the U.S. public sector is not surprising when we consider the place of education in the concept of equal opportunity. We have seen already the power of the concept of equal opportunity in all three narratives, and it has been widely recognized by students of American political thinking to be a central concept of both the American Left and Right. If the concept of equal opportunity offers, in the words of Jennifer Hochschild, a bridge spanning "the gap between the promise of political and social equality and the fact of economic inequality," then education occupies a privileged place in the American style of crossing that bridge (1988, 168). Education offers an individually oriented approach to a collective problem, an approach that is not blatantly redistributive. Anthony King thus explains the anomaly of the American commitment to public education:

> [E]ducation is an issue that lies athwart the predominantly anti-Statist tendency of American thinking. American cultural values contain a latent dilemma [between social equality and upward mobility, and individualism]. . . . Education seems to reconcile equality with individualism. Largely for this reason, in America it became . . . a substitute for other forms of social action. (1973, 420)

To a large extent, all three narratives share this notion of education. There are of course differences in their views. Critics expand this notion, and use education as a primary device through which to develop empathy and mutual understanding. Ambivalents also consider the sphere of public education rather broadly; it goes well beyond what takes place in the classroom, and includes efforts to foster social and emotional development. Ambivalents thus place particular importance on early education and programs of early development. For them, education is the principal means through which the state can provide individuals with the equipment to enter into and succeed within the market. In addition to these programs' correspondence to the ambivalents' predisposition against interfering with the market, they are also thought to have the highest probability of success. At the same time, however, the ambivalents' conception of education is not as broad as that of the critics; it does not extend to a personality-transforming experience. Supporters concentrate their notion of education primarily in terms of an enabling device, but recall that education was one area in which they were more favorably disposed toward greater government activity and largess. In addition, education was an area in which supporters were more responsive to relative need.

What emerges from the narratives' views about education, then, is the suggestion that although this subject is itself highly contentious, education may nonetheless offer the potential of a significant normative point of contact. That being said, we must not overlook the fact, regarding the narratives themselves, that dramatically different notions of the rights and purposes of education remain, as well as dramatically different notions of the range and scope of the right of opportunity, and the implications of that right for more specific social policy.

The Viability of the American Left and the Critic's Narrative

My final conclusion here is the most speculative, and may push the findings up against the limit where they can reasonably be taken, but when certain items are considered together—the presence of the critic's narrative, its incidence of nine out of the thirty-five respondents, the degree and intensity of its leftism relative to standard accounts of American political beliefs, along with the possibility that on some important issues the gulf between the narratives may not be as great as it first appears—all these may indicate that some form of American leftism is more viable than we tend to assume. At the very least, the critic's narrative suggests that a significant portion of American liberal politicians may be more left than we think, once we get them past button-pushing, campaign-stock, consensus-hegemonic answers. This assertion of viability runs counter to the trend of striking successes by conservatives during the past sixteen years, a period in which many political pundits have pronounced welfare liberalism to be dead (or, in 1994, dead again). Nonetheless, the rendition of the narratives offers, I think, some insights into both the potential and nature of that Left.

Where would this Left be located? As Michael Harrington and others have argued, it does seem that an American Left will have to manifest itself through the Democratic Party. And if the critic's narrative is any evidence of its presence, it *is* in the Democratic Party. In the Connecticut senate, it is my impression that there are also some Democratic ambivalents who would be quite sympathetic to the critics' views, if they had the opportunity to give them a fair and thorough hearing. At the same time, any such potential Left will have many hurdles to overcome in the legislative sphere. As I described in the previous two chapters, there is a plethora of internalized boundaries and constraints, as well as institutional and external political constraints. Its leaders will also have to recognize and understand its distinctively American context, and their own Americanism, an awareness that Louis Hartz points out was lacking in earlier progressive movements (1955, 12–13).

It is also interesting to note here that the narratives themselves may offer an important piece of advice for those trying to advance a left agenda. They may meet with more success if they are careful to present their case in the form of a narrative, or a story. And though they must tell a left-based story, they must also tell a distinctively American story. It is in this way that their views have the best chance of being heard in terms that are relevant to the way in which citizens and political actors themselves appear to understand, remember, and relate political and economic matters.[15]

Ultimately, an American Left's greatest success may occur at the symbolic level; it may have more success in redefining conceptions of self-interest, human nature, and the attitudes toward those previously considered to be deviant, than it has in directly changing patterns of distribution. This fits well indeed with the critic's narrative, for it suggests the manifestation at the level of actual political life of what I have called at earlier points the narrative's "soft side," which is, after all, a symbolically oriented argument. In fact, this is where my presentation of the narratives may be most effective as a piece of political praxis, in that the publication of these findings may cause others who think similarly to recognize that they are not as alone as they might have thought.

Appendixes

Contexts: State Demographics, Political Climate, Recent Political History, and the State Senators

In order to provide a more complete context for the interviews upon which this work is based, what follows are brief descriptions of the state's demographics, political climate, and political history leading up to the time of the interviews, as well as a brief description of the state senators themselves.

State Demographics

In contrast to many other states, in the years immediately prior to the interviews Connecticut's economy had been consistently growing at a rapid rate.[1] In 1986, Connecticut supplanted Alaska as the state with the nation's highest per capita income ($19,600; $14,629 across the nation) (U.S. Bureau of the Census 1988, 417). From 1978 to 1987, personal income in the state grew at an average rate of 3.7 percent, adjusted for inflation. The comparable rate of growth for the nation as a whole was 2.9 percent (Office of Fiscal Analysis 1988b, 181). In 1988, median family income in the state was $42,000, while across the nation it was $32,400.[2] State unemployment in 1987 was a mere 3.3 percent, while across the nation it ran at 6.2 percent (U.S. Bureau of the Census 1989, 378). During the same year, only 3.4 percent of the state's population received food stamps, while across the nation this figure was 7.5 percent (U.S. Bureau of the Census 1989, xx). In 1988, the state's General Assistance caseload hit a modern all-time low (Office of Legislative Research 1991, 1).[3] Finally, a study of the state's "Index of Social Health," an overall indicator of the state's social well-being, found that for most of the 1980s, the state's index was substantially higher than that of the entire nation (Judson 1994). The index included data on child abuse, health costs, and crime, among other factors.

There were notable exceptions to the state's prosperity and well-being, however, such as Hartford, New Haven, and Bridgeport, three of the poorest cities in the nation for their population sizes. The plight of these three cities in part reflected a change occurring not only in the state, but also in the rest of the nation as a whole: the conversion to a service and information-processing economy. Between 1965 and 1988, the state's finance, service, and trade sectors grew in their relative proportions while the manufacturing sector declined. Construction, utilities, and government remained about the same in proportion (Office of Fiscal Analysis 1988b, 180; 1988a, 167).[4] The defense industry is— or at least was, at the time of the interviews in 1988—a mainstay of the state's economy; in 1986 the state accounted for more defense contract funds, per capita, than any other state in the nation (Connecticut Department of Economic Development 1986, iii).

Regarding religious preference, Connecticut is a substantially Catholic state; 45 percent of its adult residents assert a Catholic religious preference (the state senate is even more heavily Catholic; see below). Protestants account for 35 percent and Jews account for 4 percent, while adherents to other religions, agnostics, and atheists account for 13 percent of the adult population (Institute for Social Inquiry 1988, Poll #88 [November-December]).[5]

Regarding population distribution, the state has become progressively more suburban, at the expense of cities and larger rural towns. In 1980, 74 percent of the state's population lived within urbanized areas (over 50,000): 32 percent within the central cities and 42 percent in their fringes. Towns outside urban areas and between 2,500 and 50,000 in population accounted for 4 percent of the state's residents, with the remaining 21 percent in rural areas (U.S. Bureau of the Census 1982) (the percentages do not total 100 due to rounding). Across the nation, the state ranks fifteenth in urbanization (Office of Legislative Research 1992, 5).

In 1988, 12 percent of Connecticut's adult population was nonwhite (most of which was black and Hispanic). Across the nation this proportion was 21 percent (U.S. Bureau of the Census 1989, 23).[6] Although the state has proportionately more whites than the rest of the nation, it has become increasingly diverse in recent years. Between 1980 and 1990, the number of blacks in the state grew by 26 percent, the number of Hispanics grew by 71 percent, and the number of Asians grew by 167 percent, while the number of whites grew by only 2 percent (Fiske 1991). Minority populations in the state are for the most part concentrated in the large cities, in particular Bridgeport, Hartford, and New Haven. Like their counterparts across the nation, black and Hispanic minorities in the state lag far behind whites in economic attainment, though in general blacks tend to do better in the state than they do across the nation as a whole, and during the 1980s they made up ground faster than they did across the nation. In 1980, 25 percent of the state's black residents lived below the poverty level, in contrast to 8 percent for the state's entire population (31 percent for blacks across the nation). Among Hispanics, this figure was 33 percent (22 percent across the nation) (Connecticut Department of Labor 1988, 6; U.S. Bureau of the Census 1988, 433). In 1979, the median family income among blacks was 61 percent of the state's median family income, while among Hispanics the median was 55 percent of the state's median (Connecticut

Department of Labor 1988, 6). By 1989, these figures had changed to 67 percent and 60 percent, respectively (in 1989 across the nation the figures were 66 percent and 80 percent, respectively) (Barringer 1992). It is interesting to note here that regarding poverty rates and incomes, Hispanics are worse off in Connecticut than they are across the nation. The 1980 unemployment rates of blacks and Hispanics were 10 percent and 9 percent, respectively, compared to 5 percent for the state as a whole. In 1985, the unemployment rate for blacks and Hispanics in the state was still more than double the rate for whites (Connecticut Department of Labor 1988, 6).

A similar picture emerges regarding educational attainment. In 1980, 70 percent of the state's adult population had completed high school while 21 percent had completed four or more years of college (Connecticut Department of Labor 1988, 6). Across the entire nation, these figures were 67 percent and 16 percent, respectively (U.S. Bureau of the Census 1988, 125). Among the state's adult black residents, 57 percent had completed high school and only 9 percent had completed college (across the nation, 32 percent and 4 percent). Among Hispanics, these figures were 42 percent and 9 percent (across the nation, 32 percent and 5 percent) (Connecticut Department of Labor 1988, 6; U.S. Bureau of the Census 1988, 125).

Political Culture

A 1987 study of state political cultures, making use of CBS and *New York Times* surveys, concluded that Connecticut, perhaps paradoxically, is somewhat more liberal and considerably more Republican than its own demographics would indicate (Erikson, McIver, and Wright, Jr. 1987).[7] Relative to the rest of the nation, it found, again perhaps paradoxically, that the state was slightly more Republican and substantially more liberal. Another presentation of the same overall study placed the state in the top seven states in terms of liberalism of public opinion (Wright, Jr., Erikson, and McIver 1987, 989). It also placed the state in the top eight states in terms of "composite policy liberalism" (1987, 989).[8] A 1974 study of the public policies among the states ranked Connecticut tenth in terms of liberalism regarding welfare and education policy (Hofferbert 1974, 217). When asked about their ideological orientations, 22 percent of the state's citizens considered themselves to be liberal, 31 percent considered themselves to be conservative, and 43 percent considered themselves to be moderate (Institute for Social Inquiry 1988, Poll #80 [March]).[9] These percentages were from a poll conducted just prior to the beginning of the interviews in May 1988; prior to the November 1986 election (in which the senators interviewed were either elected or reelected) the percentages were 18 percent liberal, 34 percent conservative, and 38 percent moderate (Institute for Social Inquiry 1986, Poll #66 [October]).[10] A less scientific view of the state's political culture was presented to me by a careful observer and lay historian of the state's politics, who was also a senior Republican senate staff member. He maintained that by all rights the state should be Republican, with its growing affluence, increasingly suburban character, and heritage of ethnic Italian conservatism. He likened the state to New Jersey, and predicted: "One day it will get a decent Republican governor, and that will be the end of the Democrats."

Perhaps that day has arrived; in November 1994, the state's voters selected Republican John Rowland to be their governor, and gave Republicans a one-seat edge in the state senate (however, Democrats retained a majority in the House, and in fact gained more seats than in any other chamber in the nation). During the previous forty years, control of the governorship had mostly remained in Democratic hands, with the exceptions of 1971–75 (Thomas Meskill, Republican) and 1991–95 (Lowell Weicker, Independent). Since reapportionment in 1965, Republicans controlled the entire General Assembly for only two legislative sessions, 1973–75 and 1985–87; otherwise, both chambers of the assembly remained in Democratic control.[11]

Among the public, in October 1986, Democrats in the state accounted for 40 percent of registered voters and Republicans accounted for 27 percent, while 33 percent went unaffiliated and less than 0.1 percent were registered with another party (Connecticut Secretary of State 1987, 777).[12] Over the ten years prior to that time, Democrats had gained slowly in membership, from 37 percent in 1976, while Republicans had remained constant (Swanson 1984, 25). It is interesting to note that unaffiliated voters *dropped* from 36 percent. Regarding the vitality of the party system itself, over the years Connecticut has enjoyed a comparatively healthy and competitive party system.[13] Finally, voter turnout in Connecticut has been consistently among the highest in the nation.

Government Activity, Revenues, and Taxes

During the 1960s and early 1970s, the growth in the state budget rapidly outpaced growth in personal income. Budget growth then slowed between 1976 and 1979. Between 1979 and 1988, budget growth significantly outpaced income growth, though not by the margins over income growth posted in the latter half of the 1960s (U.S. Bureau of Economic Analysis 1984, 39–41; Office of Fiscal Analysis 1988b, 122, 182; Office of Fiscal Analysis 1988a, 160). Across the nation, state government expenditures increased 9 percent between 1985 and 1986. In Connecticut this figure was 11 percent (Council of State Governments 1988, 230–31). In 1985, the amount of combined state and local government spending per capita in Connecticut was just slightly above the national average (ranking 22 out of 50), but in relation to income, combined spending was the second lowest in the nation (exceeding only New Hampshire)

(Price Waterhouse 1988, 14). By function, the largest proportion of the appropriated state expenditures for 1988–89 went to education, at 30 percent, followed by welfare, at 21 percent, health and hospitals, at 11 percent, and transportation, at 5 percent (Office of Fiscal Analysis 1988c, v). Among all the states, these percentages in 1986 were 32 percent for education, 17 percent for welfare, 7 percent for health and hospitals, and 8 percent for transportation (Council of State Governments 1988, 232–33). Connecticut's General Assembly is required to pass a balanced budget, as is the case in thirty-six other states with similar laws or constitutional provisions (Council of State Governments 1988, 229).

Like ten other states, Connecticut had no individual income tax in 1988, though it did impose a graduated tax on capital gains, dividends, and interest, once a personal income of $50,000 was surpassed (Council of State Governments 1988, 257). At 7.5 percent, it had the highest state sales tax in the nation.[14] It also had one of the highest business taxes. In 1988, the state collected 40 percent of its General Fund revenues through sales and use taxes, 13 percent through corporate taxes, 8 percent through capital gains, dividends, and interest taxes, and 5 percent through public service taxes (Office of Fiscal Analysis 1988b, 4). The relative burden that the state's taxes placed on its citizens appears differently depending on how it is considered; in particular, depending on whether the figures are considered per capita or per income dollar. In 1987, its per capita tax revenue ranked fifth nationally, at $1,358 (Council of State Governments 1988, 268).[15] But according to the Connecticut Public Expenditure Council, a nonprofit research concern, in 1987 Connecticut state tax as a percentage of per capita income was only twenty-third highest in the nation, and 1 percent below the national average (Johnson 1989b). According to the U.S. Census Bureau (1989, xix), in 1987 the state ranked forty-first in state tax collections as a percentage of individual income. When the state's citizens themselves were asked in 1988 about their state taxes, 51 percent of them responded that they were too high, 42 percent responded that they were "just about right," and another 2 percent responded that they were too low. Similarly, 45 percent responded that state spending was too high, 32 percent responded that it was about right, and 4 percent responded that it was too low (Institute for Social Inquiry 1988, Poll #88 [November-December]).[16]

Because sales and use taxes are almost always assessed at flat rates, and because they cover many basic goods, states that rely on them tend to have less progressive tax structures than states relying on income taxes. Prior to the 1991 switch to an income tax, Connecticut citizens with annual incomes below $10,000 lost 3.1 percent of their incomes to the state's sales tax, whereas those with incomes above $75,000 lost only 2.2 percent of their income to the tax (Johnson 1989b). But in comparison to other states, Connecticut may not be that regressive. A study of the progressivity of forty-six state tax systems, based on data from 1975–76, found that only thirteen states had more progressive state tax systems than Connecticut's, while another nine had equally progressive systems. When both state and local tax systems were taken into account, thirteen states still had more progressive systems, while only one additional state had an equally progressive system (Lowery 1987). The paradoxical results for Connecticut are probably due to the rapidly growing economy of the state during this period, as well as the state's relatively high level of party competition (Lowery 1987, 155).

Another fact associated with the lack of an income tax is that localities must pay much more of their own way for services. In 1987, Connecticut's towns were the second most self-sufficient in the country. Towns in New Hampshire, a state without an income or a sales tax, were the most self-sufficient (Johnson 1989a). This arrangement sets up a system in which the poorer towns and cities are much more heavily burdened than the wealthier ones. This burden is compounded in Connecticut by the fact that the funding scheme the state uses to distribute many of its funds to localities is not sensitive to relative need.[17] The tax arrangement also adds to the lack of tax progressivity regarding individual citizens, since most local revenues in the state derive from property taxes—58 percent in 1987—which are almost always less progressive than income taxes (Johnson 1989a).[18]

The Connecticut General Assembly, 1987–88

Politics in the two yearly sessions of the legislative cycle prior to the interview meetings was not particularly unusual. The full two-year legislative cycle contains two different types of sessions. In odd-numbered years, "regular" sessions, the General Assembly meets from January to June. In even-numbered years, "fiscal" sessions, it meets from February to May. In principle, the fiscal session is limited in scope to "only budgetary, revenue and financial matters," committee bills, and matters "of an emergency nature," but in practice this limitation is not always strictly adhered to.[19] In the regular 1987 session, the General Assembly went along with most of the Democratic governor's requests, including the passage in relatively unaltered form of his proposed budget (the central focus of almost any state legislative session), which increased state spending by 15 percent. A significant surplus, estimated at the end of the session to be $324 million, punctuated the 1987 budget year.

Some of the more significant legislative initiatives that marked 1987 included a raising of the state minimum wage; additional state funds to cities and towns to alleviate property taxes; increases in medical assistance for low income and elderly patients, including a requirement that doctors accept Medicare reimbursement as full payment from low income patients; a comparable worth pay provision for state employees; a mail-in voter registration procedure; the removal of parkway tolls; a plan to phase in mandatory trash recycling; and an adjustment of the capital gains tax to prevent the state from gaining a windfall from the federal tax revisions of 1986. Some notable proposals that were rejected included a provision to make English the official state language, a gay rights measure, and an income tax on nonresident workers. Two major issues left unresolved at the end of the session were a proposed exemption on the service tax on business where the service is provided to a wholly owned subsidiary, and further measures regarding local town and city property tax relief. In a special session of the General Assembly, a one-year exemption from the business service tax was approved.

The 1988 session was to some degree overshadowed by lower revenue estimates, apparently due in large part to changes in the federal tax laws and some slowing in the rate of growth of the state's economy.[20] As the session progressed, concerns about a budget deficit grew based on revenue projections for 1988 and 1989 (an estimated shortfall of approximately $250 million ultimately resulted, and a projected deficit of over $880 million was forecast for the following year).[21] Nevertheless, the assembly passed a budget largely unaltered from that proposed by the governor, which increased spending by 14 percent over the previous year and drew some funds from the property tax relief and the emergency or "rainy day" funds in order to balance. A rush at the conclusion of the session resulted in a frenzied, chaotic set of maneuvers, with many issues dying as the constitutionally mandated adjournment time arrived. Some legislators claimed that the rushed conclusion of the 1988 session was the worst finish they had ever seen.

Significant legislation from this session included a new formula to distribute state aid for education to towns and cities, based more heavily on the financial and educational needs of the residents in each location. This measure, examined in detail in chapter 6, replaced a prior set of formulas emanating from a 1977 state supreme court ruling in the case of *Horton v. Meskill,* which found that the heavy reliance on local property taxes to finance education resulted in unconstitutional inequities in educational opportunity. Other initiatives included a relatively modest local property tax relief package (a source of some conflict between the senate and the governor, also examined in chap. 6); a permanent extension of the business service tax exemption passed the previous year; a record high bonding package; an emergency financial assistance package for the city of Bridgeport; and an increase in the required percentage regarding minority-owned business set-aside contracts awarded by the state. Some of the proposals that were rejected included the prohibition of lobbyist contributions to legislators during legislative sessions and, on a tie vote in the senate, the extension of the deadline concerning physician compliance with the Medicare fee legislation passed during the previous session (a decision thus going against physicians).

The State Senators

Though we now have some sense of the larger political context within which the interviews occurred, we still need to know something about the respondents. Who are these senators? As a group the people I interviewed have more in common than in distinction; they share political backgrounds, experiences, and institutional settings. The following facts give some indication in the very broadest terms of the nature of that background and experience. To be sure there are great individual differences contained within the averaged and aggregated characteristics that follow, but the summaries nonetheless provide a basic sense of some of the more salient features of the membership.[22]

The respondents included thirty-five of the thirty-six total members of the senate. Due largely to the fact that the Democrats had recaptured control of the senate from the Republicans in the 1986 election, thirteen of the thirty-five interviewed members were serving in their first terms. The thirty-five members were comprised of twenty-four Democrats and eleven Republicans, of whom six were female (two Republicans, four Democrats) and twenty-nine male, three black (all Democrats), and the remainder white. More than half considered themselves to be of some ethnic extraction (four Republicans, sixteen Democrats), the most common of these being Irish and Italian, but also including, for example, a Polish senator and a senator who claimed to be "ethnic Yankee." Their average age was forty-eight; fifty-three for Republicans and forty-five for Democrats. Out of the thirty-five senators, nine were either single or divorced, while the remaining twenty-six were married.[23] The average number of children per capita was identical for members of both parties, at 1.7. All except one of the senators were raised in a particular religion, and of those so raised, twenty-one claimed to be still actively practicing. Raised Catholics constituted by far the largest proportion (three Republicans, eighteen Democrats), followed by a smattering of Jews (two Republicans, one Democrat), Episcopalians (3 Republicans), and Methodists (2 Republicans, 1 Democrat). There was one each (all Democrat) of Quaker, Baptist, and Greek Orthodox.

All the senators were, or had been, upwardly mobile. Many were the first great socioeconomic successes in their families. Their average years of university-level education was 5.0; 4.3 for Republicans, 5.3 for Democrats.[24] Average family income was $73,000; $81,000 for Republicans, $70,000 for Democrats.[25] The average number of real properties owned by each family was 1.9; 1.3 for Republicans, 2.3 for Democrats.[26] The average number of securities each in excess of $5,000 held by each family was 3.2; 3.5 for Republicans, 3.1 for Democrats.[27]

The Connecticut General Assembly is formally a part-time institution. From what I can tell, however, in practice this usually means it is a full-time institution that (due to its salary) requires its members to work at some other job either half- or three-quarter-time.[28] Thus, many senators have other career occupations in addition to the senate. Attorneys headed up this list of occupations, with ten (one Republican, nine Democrats), followed by three bankers (two Republicans, one Democrat), three realtors (two Republicans, one Democrat), and two in private business (one in each party). There were also an appraiser (Democrat), a funeral director (Democrat), a jet mechanic (Democrat), an insurer (Democrat), a physician (Republican), a salesperson (Democrat), and a teacher (Democrat).[29] This left ten others who either had no other occupation or were retired (four Republicans, six Democrats).

Many of the senators apparently inherited their political activity from their families; eleven came from families with direct political involvement (two Republicans, nine Democrats), while several others were from families that were politically active.[30] Only three senators came from families where the parents were split regarding party identification, and only three others had party identifications that were different from those of their parents when they were growing up. A single senator came from a family where the parents had no party identification whatsoever. The remaining senators had party identifications that were identical to those of both parents. All except six had held elective office sometime prior to being elected senator, and all except nine were native to the state.[31] They are also a politically ambitious lot; fifteen were actively interested in other political offices (three Republicans, twelve Democrats), even if they were not making specific plans to run for any one in particular. Since the interviews, at least seven senators have actively sought other offices: one for the mayoralty of a large city (successfully); one for state attorney general (successfully); three for governor (all unsuccessfully); and three for the U.S. Congress (all unsuccessfully) (one senator has run for two offices). Several others have been discussed as likely candidates for higher offices, including governor.[32]

In sum, then, the senators are a financially comfortable, well-educated, highly motivated, yet socially diverse group. They were certainly interesting people to talk to.

Additional Notes on Methods

Chapter 1 offers a brief discussion of my methods. What follows here is a more detailed description of the interviews, the interview process, the additional sources I make use of, and my methods of analysis.

The Interview

The interview is divided into four main sections. The first section is directed toward discovering what the senators think about distributive justice. It contains mostly open-ended questions, and in the main moves from the general to the specific. It includes subsections on the following items: the definitions of terms; political economy; work; classes, social mobility, and race; equality and equal opportunity; wages and wealth; taxes; power and democracy; welfare; and views of the future.

The second section concerns the workings of the senate body (with an eye toward the manifestation of beliefs) and the senators' perceptions of themselves as actors within it. The third section concerns some specific bills and policy initiatives that were considered during the 1988 legislative session. John Kingdon argues that in studying voting behavior it is much more useful to ask legislators about specific votes, preferably as soon after the vote as possible, than to ask them about how they go about voting in general (1989, 13).[1] Through the inclusion of the second and third sections, I have tried to combine both techniques. Granted, the questions on specific bills did not immediately follow their consideration in the senate, but nonetheless the senators' memories of the bills and their actions on them were in most cases still fresh. The bills concerned education financing, property tax, and plant closings. Each was selected for its high salience, controversial character, and its relation to an issue of distributive justice.[2] But the bills were clearly not average or typical of the usual stream that ran through the halls of the capitol, and thus any conclusions we might draw from their treatment are obviously limited. One might further object that since the discussion of the bills followed on the heels of lengthy discussions of beliefs about distributive justice, it would come as no surprise if we were to discover the presence of these beliefs in their discussions of the bills—that I have in effect primed the senators for such a discussion. There may be some truth to this critique, but in response I should point out that the interviews rarely were completed in one meeting, and more often than not the section on specific bills occasioned the start to the second or third session in the interview. Thus, there was some kind of break in the minds of most of the senators before discussing specific bills.

The interview concludes with a section containing questions about the senators' political and personal lives, including questions about their earliest memories of their political thoughts, the evolution of their views, and their interest in and recruitment into politics. This section was placed at the end because it was easier to stretch the patience of the senators, if it needed to be stretched, by asking questions about more personal matters. They were more inclined to give a little more of their time if the end was less difficult, and indeed most senators welcomed the chance to reminisce about their political careers. This topic therefore provided a nice ending point.

Format and Method of Interview Meetings

In the end I managed to meet with thirty-five of the thirty-six members of the senate. Of the thirty-five interviews, two went uncompleted, though enough material was covered to get an adequate sense of each senator's beliefs. The bulk of the interviews took place between May and October 1988, the period between the end of the 1988 legislative session and the November general election. A few meetings spilled over into November 1988 through January 1989. The summer provided a good period in which to conduct the interviews; the capitol had a more relaxed atmosphere, and I sensed a greater distance from the heated rhetoric of the session. As the election approached, appointments became more difficult to arrange and responses sometimes tended to become a little more canned.

In most cases the interview consisted of three meetings, but was some-times spread over as many as five. The time for a completed interview ranged anywhere from a short of fifty minutes to a long of six hours, and typically ran about three-and-a-half to four hours. Our discussions took place in many different locations, including homes, restaurants, work offices, capitol offices, district offices, local town halls, and in one case an automobile. The most common locations were state capitol offices in Hartford, followed by work offices.

The method I used to arrange the interview consisted of sending a letter at the end of the 1988 session requesting an interview sometime thereafter and then following up the letter with phone calls if necessary. In some cases I already knew the senator from my earlier observation period during the session or from having been introduced at some point earlier, and in that instance I called to make an appointment and then sent a letter. I had purposely waited until after the finish of the legislative session to conduct the interviews, not only for the purposes of the interview itself (as some questions were about the session) and the accommodation of the senators' busy schedules, but also to allow myself the time to become somewhat known around the capitol through my observation. In this regard, I was following the strategy of John Wahlke and his colleagues (1962) in their classic interview-based study of state legislators from three decades ago. In retrospect, I think this strategy helped me greatly to gain access.

In the letter I described myself and my project, though in accord with the cumulative wisdom on the subject I did not go into detail as to what kind of material I was after. I described my project as a work "on the ways legislators approach issues." I also listed the senators from the respective party with whom I had spent time earlier in the session. I was able to arrange most of the meetings without problem. Only two senators flatly refused to meet. One claimed that I would not need to talk to him since his district was so far away from my own. Although my initial attempts to persuade him to meet with me failed, I was finally able to set up an interview with the help of a staff member from his party's leadership office. Regarding the one senator whom I ultimately failed to interview, I never made it past his secretary.

When the meetings actually began, I would again introduce the project and the interview, and assure the senators that I would try as much as possible to keep their answers anonymous.[3] I told them I would not use their names and that I would change or omit identifying details. I asked that I be allowed to tape-record the interviews. I then briefly told them that I had a collection of questions regarding certain issues, mostly economic. I did not use the word *justice.* I told them that some of the questions might seem difficult or impossible to answer while others might seem overly simple, but that I was interested in their reactions to all of them. I also informed them that there were questions on actual bills and their political lives. I then told them to feel free to elaborate on any question or topic that they liked; I was interested in hearing their complete opinions.

During the interview, I tried to be as flexible as possible. Although I had a clear interview schedule in front of me, I would depart from it in the interests of building rapport, pursuing an interesting subject brought up by a response, or avoiding redundancy. Following Robert Lane, I tried to make the interviews *dialectical,* by often probing responses or asking follow-up questions (1962, 9). I also tried as much as possible to let them remain *discursive;* letting the senators' responses to any particular question go on as they liked, even rambling perhaps, in order to see their trains of thought rather than mine. I often made use of silence during the interview, in order to draw out a response or ask for a further explanation. Silence is often the most effective probe; it supplies the least offensive and perhaps the most effective means of indicating that the interviewer suspects that some additional item is being hidden or held back. It also functions as a rapport builder; it encourages the respondent to control and structure the interview and demonstrates interest on the part of the interviewer (Reik 1972, 124–25; Gordon 1969, chap. 5).

Although I tape-recorded the interviews, I took notes as well. I sometimes found in the course of the interviews that my note taking made the senators feel more at ease, perhaps because they didn't always have someone staring at them while they tried to grapple with often difficult questions. Many senators seemed to talk more, and more freely, when I was taking notes versus when I was not.

As soon as possible after the conclusion of each meeting, I would write up an account from notes and memory. My analysis of the material is based on these written accounts, and when necessary on references back to the original tape recordings. All excerpted quotes are taken verbatim from the tapes. Names have been replaced by numbers, used consistently throughout the book, and identifying details have been changed.

Honesty and Cooperation

Obviously, the success of this project depended on the cooperation and sincerity of the respondents. And in general, the senators were very coopera-tive. Only one was overly suspicious of our meetings; he refused the tape recorder and insisted on a power of review over any quotes used in the book. During the interviews themselves, I was continually impressed by the senators' sincerity and their efforts to take the questions seriously. I was also impressed by what they knew, and daunted by what they were expected to know.

Reflecting back on the interview experiences, I think there were a number of factors contributing to this cooperation. Foremost perhaps was the sense that in giving some of their time to me, and taking our meetings seriously, they were performing a public service. Some of this was no doubt ego-based; they saw themselves as important enough to make the study of their own opinions something of consequence. In addition, on several possible counts they re-ceived something of benefit themselves. First, they had the opportunity to talk with an understanding stranger about difficult issues, and related to this, to explain themselves and their views, to clear up misconceptions, and to defend themselves against past and potential attacks by others. Second, our meetings gave them the opportunity to teach an academic about politics. Third, in talking about their beliefs, they had the opportunity to organize their own thoughts, to teach themselves, so to speak. Fourth, our conversations provided them with an opportunity to register their positions on various matters (albeit anonymously), something politicians often seek to do.[4] Finally, and perhaps related to the previous point, I also sensed the presence of something I will call "the book phenomenon": Many senators for whatever reason wanted to be in the book they knew I would ultimately write.

I tried to keep the interview from becoming too taxing, and toward this end I would suggest a break or a later meeting when I sensed a senator was tiring. Even so, some senators tended to fatigue as the interview wore on. The questions were, after all, of a kind rarely if ever put to them before, and required much thought and introspection on their part. One senator even exclaimed somewhat tongue-in-cheek as I turned off the tape recorder, "That was torture!"

Due to the generally held stereotypes of party culture, I had expected to find the Democratic senators as a group to be more accessible, open, and gregarious than the Republican senators, but this was not the case.[5] If anything, it was the opposite. I asked a few senators and staffers about this difference, and the consensus that emerged was that as individuals the Democrats in the senate may indeed have had different personality types from the Republicans in the opposite direction from what I had expected, but they were also affected collectively by the fact that they were the party in power; they were the ones responsible for policy. The Republicans' position was in many ways an easier and freer-wheeling one, with less at stake regarding what they had to say and with fewer demands on their time.

Bias and Interviewer Effect

HAMLET: Do you see yonder cloud that's almost in shape of a camel?
POLONIUS: By th'mass and 'tis, like a camel indeed.
HAMLET: Methinks it is like a weasel.
POLONIUS: It is backed like a weasel.
HAMLET: Or like a whale.
POLONIUS: Very like a whale.[6]

The problems of bias and suggestion are particularly difficult when one is trying to elicit deep beliefs. The interviewer cannot be completely objective; if she is, she may not obtain what she is after. The method I adopted was to be as supportive as possible toward the respondents themselves, but as objective as possible toward their points of view.[7] It is likely, however, that the senators made some assumptions about my own views. It is also likely that their assumptions about my views affected their answers to some extent, but as the following two anecdotes suggest, I did not make a consistently one-sided impression. At the end of the interview, two senators, one from each party, spontaneously commented on their impressions of me. The Democrat asked me about my own political views, and then told me that he had assumed throughout our interview that I was a conservative. The Republican, on the other hand, thought that I was a liberal.

I was somewhat concerned that the questions themselves may have seemed to have a liberal agenda; one might argue that their basic presumption is, to borrow from *Hamlet* again, that something is rotten in the state of the United States. If this is indeed the case, then so be it. The questions reflect my decisions as to what are the most important and best things to know about what the senators think. More troubling to me was the discovery that the questions may have had a slight male bias in that they were more conducive to abstract, objective, rules-based types of answers (Furby 1986; Gilligan 1982). Those were the kinds of answers that I most likely had in mind when designing the questions. In the course of the interviews I found that the female senators, as a group, more strongly resisted answering the questions in these terms than did the male senators (for more on this gender-based difference, see chap. 2).

Extrainterview Sources

In addition to the interview materials themselves, I make use of a number of other sources and techniques. These include observation of the legislators at the capitol and in their districts; observation of public hearings, committee meetings, and caucuses; transcripts from public hearings and floor discussions; materials used by committees; interviews with selected house members regarding the specific bills discussed earlier; individual senator voting scores generated by several lobbying organizations; and senate voting records on selected bills. My observation merits further elaboration.

In the months prior to and during the legislative session that preceded the interview meetings, I spent some time with several senate and house members, accompanying them as they went about their jobs at the capitol and in the district. I also spent some time unaccompanied observing events at the capitol. Richard Fenno refers to this as "participant observation" or "soaking and poking—or just hanging around" (1978, 249).[8] The purpose of this activity was to get a better sense of the context within which the senators operate, and to add to my understanding of their points of view, a necessary element in the understanding of something as idiosyncratic as the beliefs about justice. In following them around I cannot claim to have seen the world as they see it, but I can claim, at least in a limited sense, to have seen their world. In general I was successful in my efforts; most legislators made efforts to include me in everything they did during the day and to explain to me what they were doing while they were doing it. In several instances I was able to see things normally not open to the public; my ticket of "he's with me" gave me admission to a few "back room" scenes I had not planned on seeing.

What always struck me above anything else on these jaunts (as it had also struck Fenno) was the incredible stamina of the legislators and the mass of policy and personal information that the people with whom they came into contact expected them to know. At the end of the day I was exhausted just by following them. Observing them could also become tedious at times; I once spent an hour watching a house member open and read her mail. It struck me at the time that I would appear to another observer as a caricature of the social scientist, sitting there in a chair, cradling pad and pen—the scientist studying behavior—while she read through her mail.

But in spite of the fatigue and occasional tedium, one element of the legislative context I began to experience particularly well as my travels wore on was the political "bug" that often motivates these people to seek office in the first place. I began to understand why someone would want the job badly enough to sacrifice so much for it. Once, prior to a lunch with lobbyists, two senators bantered back and forth, each claiming that they could on that day walk away from politics. Neither believed the other. They then lamented the fate of another former senator who after his defeat could not let go. He was still often seen at the capitol, and would play the election he lost over and over to any senator who would be willing to listen.

At some points in my observation experience, the problem of "going native" threatened to distort the process. For example, by the end of the day, one senator was introducing me to the various local officials he met simply as "my friend Grant." Our day ended at 9 P.M. in a local bar, where over a couple beers he virtually whispered what he considered to be secrets about the state's politics. At another point a different senator suggested a preinterview meeting, offering "[t]here are things about some of the senators I could tell you." This problem also had its amusing side, usually owing to situations where local citizens would remain stubbornly unconvinced of my status as an outside observer and would attempt to lobby or persuade me just as heavily as they would the legislator. I tried to remain as objective as possible in these situations, but on one occasion I was gently but firmly pressed into telling the nuns that their students' science projects were indeed quite impressive.

I was also able to accomplish a sizable amount of soaking and poking while waiting to conduct or arrange an interview, hanging around an office after an interview had been completed, or during the slower moments in a day of following someone around.[9] This usually took the form of watching or talking to the senate staff as they went about their jobs. They were usually quite open about what they were doing, and often eager to tell me about some facet of the politics of the day. What I have referred to earlier as "the book phenomenon" seemed to play a large part in this, but regardless of its source, it resulted in good information.

The Interview Schedule

[For a description of how the interview was approached and handled, see chapter 1 and appendix B. Obviously, the entire set of questions presented here could not be covered with any individual senator; rather, it supplied a schedule, which I would readily depart from and edit, depending on the circumstances.]

A. Introduction

I have here a collection of questions regarding certain issues, mostly economic. They start with the very general, and move to the more specific, ending with questions on a few actual bills considered by the senate this session. Some of the questions will seem very difficult, even impossible to answer completely, and others will seem too simple, but I am interested in your reactions and opinions on all of them, so if you could bear with me . . . If there's a question that piques your interest in particular, feel free to elaborate; I'm interested in hearing your complete opinions. After we discuss the actual bills, there are a few questions about your political life and some basic questions about yourself.

Lastly, please feel free to pass over any question that makes you uncomfortable, or any question that you don't want to answer.

B. Preliminary Locaters

1. We hear a lot about "liberals" and "liberalism" and "conservatives" and "conservatism." What do these terms mean to you?
   How would you describe yourself in terms of these labels?
2. We also hear the phrases "capitalism" and "socialism." What do these mean to you?
3. What about the term "radical," what would you say this means?
   Have you ever considered yourself to be a radical?
4. About the economy: What kinds of things would you look for in judging whether an economic system was successful?
5. What does the term "justice" mean to you, in terms of the economic world?

Would you say that overall, our society is just?
What things promote justice?
   In what ways?
What things promote injustice?
   In what ways?

Now, I'd like to ask you some questions that go into more detail about these kinds of things.

C. The Political Economy

6. Which of the following two economic conditions are you most concerned about: inflation or unemployment?
   Why?
7. Regarding employment, it is sometimes said that people have a right to a job. What do you think is meant by this phrase?
   Using this sense, do you agree?
   Is there another sense in which you think someone has a right to a job?
   (Should the government act to ensure this right, and how?)
8. Out of every sales dollar about how much of that sales dollar do you think a manufacturer is able to keep, on average, as profit, after all costs and taxes are paid?
9. What should this rate be? (What do you think is a fair rate of profit?)
10. Where do most of these profits go?
11. How do you think the interests of businesses and corporations to make a profit and the public interest fit together? (Are they in harmony or opposition?)
12. When the economy in Connecticut is generally considered to be performing well, are there any groups in particular that get most of the benefit?
13. How would you say that the interests of employer and employee fit together; are they basically opposed, or harmonious, or in some other relation?
14. When corporations get into serious economic trouble, they sometimes seek government aid. Do you favor this?
   Why/what course would you recommend?

D. Work

15. The following question is about work. It's terribly oversimplified, so if you'd like to add anything, please feel free. The question is:

Which of the three following statements is closest to your notion or view of work:

    (1) an activity that provides an individual's identification, meaning, dignity, and fulfillment;

    (2) something that actually threatens those things;

    (3) something that one puts up with for the sake of private things, which are more important to life?

(Does it depend on the job? what kinds of jobs are more rewarding than others? what keeps work from being more meaningful?)

E. Classes, Social Mobility, and Race

16. Do you think there are social or economic classes in this country?
    How would you describe them?
    What are their relative sizes, approximately?
17. How important do you think classes are in America today?
18. Do you think that the interests of these classes tend to conflict?
    Over what? (Why not?)
19. How easy or difficult do you think it is for a person born and raised in one class to move up into another? (If the notion of classes has been rejected, from one income group to another)
    What does this move depend on?
20. In general, do people end up where they deserve to be?
    Why?
21. People sometimes speak of the "working people," or "working class," or simply "workers."
    When you hear these terms, whom do you think of?
22. Do you think our economic system pays them fairly?
    Do they work as hard as others do? Harder?
23. When you hear the term "the poor," whom do you think of?
24. Consider the poor. How did they get where they are?
25. Consider the rich. How did they get there?
26. Do they have special responsibilities or functions in society that are different from those of the others?
    Do they meet them?
27. It is a fact in this country that in particular nonwhites, as a group, earn lower incomes than whites.
    Why do you think this occurs?
28. What if I told you that it is also a fact that in the last twenty years, the relative difference or gap between the incomes of blacks and whites has become even greater, and the difference or gap in the unemploy-

ment rates has also become even greater.
Why has this happened?

29. Is there an underclass in our society?
What is it? How would you define it?
Why does it always seem to exist?

30. It is also apparently a fact that women earn less than men, even when they are in similar positions and life situations.
Again, why?

31. Many thinkers reflecting on American society are somewhat puzzled by the apparent fact that people in the lower social strata, or in the lower half of society, do not emphasize and form political and social movements for a more equal distribution of wealth and income and a somewhat different organization of the economy. Another way to put this is that since the median level of income and wealth, that which half are above and half are below, is lower than the average, meaning that the lower half has less than half of the total, some thinkers find it puzzling that the lower half has not made any significant attempts to vote itself more money, so to speak.
Do you see this absence of movement?
Do you find it puzzling?
How would you explain it?

F. Equality

32. The Declaration of Independence contains this famous phrase: "All men are created equal."
How do you think this was meant?
In what sense or senses do you think people *are* equal?
Unequal?

33. What would it take to make people more equal in terms of (ways they are seen as unequal)?

34. What would you think of attempting this?
Is there anything government can do about this?

G. Equal Opportunity

35. The phrase "equal opportunity" is often used in discussing education, jobs, and overall life achievement.
What do you think it means?
Do you favor this equal opportunity?
Is there another form of it that you prefer?

36. Do we have equal opportunity in that sense in America?

37. Sometimes the metaphor of a fair race is used to talk about equal opportunity. In this metaphor, there are two runners, with one runner artificially bound or hindered in some way. This metaphor has at least two interpretations. It is said by some that equal opportunity should remove those impediments to running, so that one can run as fast as one can and therefore the best runner wins; and the race is fair. Others say that removing the impediments does not compensate for the unfair beginning or first part of the race; the person presently behind never has a chance to catch up. The hindered runner must not only be unbound but brought up to an equal place with the unbound runner, and then the race can continue fairly.

    What do you think of this metaphor in general; is it a good way to represent what happens in society?

    What about replacing individual runners with whole groups of people?

    What are your thoughts about the two interpretations?

38. What do you think is required to make opportunities genuinely equal? What can government do about this?

39. What do you think about the use of quotas in job hiring?

    What goals are they designed to achieve? Are they a good way to achieve these goals?

    How about using them in school admissions?

40. If you were a school teacher, and you had a class with ten smart children and ten slower children, how would you decide to give out your time and attention?

H.1. Wages and Wealth

41. I am going to read to you some occupations. For each one, tell me what you think they make for a yearly income, on average:
    —a police patrol officer
    —the top executive at a top financial services corporation
    —a doctor
    —a middle-level engineer (no supervisory responsibility)
    —a janitor
    —a high school teacher
    —a bank teller
    —an industrial production worker in private industry
    —a printing press operator in a large city

42. Now, for each one, tell me what you think they *should* be paid.

43. Why do you think they are paid these amounts?

44. Are there other occupations in particular that I haven't mentioned that stick out in your mind as over- or underpaid?
    Why are they paid this way?

45. What are the main things that *should* determine what people are paid? (probes: seniority, need, character, merit, productivity, effort)
    Should people with boring jobs get paid more than people with interesting jobs?
    Should people with dangerous jobs get paid more than people with safe jobs?
    Should people with hard physical jobs . . . than less physically demanding jobs?
    Should someone who produces the same as another, but exerts more effort, tries harder to do it, . . . than a very skilled or efficient person who doesn't work as hard?
    How about someone with a handicap or poor health who can't work a full day; should they be paid for a full day?

46. In the last forty years, how do you think the distribution of wealth in this country, overall, has changed?

47. In the next forty years, how do you think the distribution will change?

48. What do you think would happen if incomes and wealth were made more equal?

49. What would happen if everyone made between $20,000 and $60,000 a year?
    What would society look like?

50. Should the government attempt to reduce the income gaps between the rich and the poor?
    Why/not?
    What methods might you favor; upper limits, minimum levels?

H.2. Wages and Wealth: Taxes

51. If you were devising an overall federal tax plan, what are the general principles that would guide you in setting it up?

52. About taxes more specifically: What do you think about tax rates that tax at an increasing percentage as incomes and wealth go up, that is, progressive taxes?

53. Do you have any thoughts or reactions to large inheritances?
    How should they be taxed?

54. Do you have any thoughts or particular reactions regarding taxing businesses?

I.1. Power and Democracy: Government

55. Should all persons have approximately the same political influence?
56. Are there certain groups or persons who exert more influence on political decisions than they should?
57. Are there groups or persons who do not have as much influence as they should?
58. Some thinkers have argued that the public is not competent to guide important matters of policy, and therefore democracy needs to be limited. What do you think of this?

I.2. Power and Democracy: Workplace

59. Regarding the workplace: Do you think it would be a good idea to send managers down to the assembly line, or to the customer line of a service operation so to speak, in order to give them a better sense of what it's like to be there?
60. Do you think it would be a good idea to send the nonmanagement employees up to the management levels for a while to see what it's like being the manager?
61. What do you think about employees having a say in the choice of bosses and managers?
    How much and in what way?
    What would you think about elections?
62. What do you think about employees making some of the decisions commonly made by management, such as setting production goals, making decisions about working conditions or the workplace, and such?
    Why/How much?

J. Welfare

63. Is there a basic minimum level of certain things, such as food, medical care, housing, or education that everyone is entitled to?
    How would you characterize these levels?
    Can government effectively do anything about this; achieve these levels?
64. What proportion of the federal budget do you think goes to assistance that is targeted to income, or means-tested, such as welfare, food stamps, AFDC, Medicaid, and so on?
65. What proportion of the state government budget goes to this kind of spending?

66. What do you think about the amount of money government spends on means-tested welfare?
67. What is the main reason that people go on welfare, in your opinion?
68. Do many people on welfare try to take advantage of the system? How?

    About what proportion do this?

    What can be done about this; is government capable of doing anything about it?
69. Are there certain kinds of welfare or programs that you favor over others?
70. Some have been advocating a concept known as workfare.

    What do you think of this idea?

K. Government

71. Overall, how does the federal government affect the quality of life in the nation?

    What things in particular does it do that make it better?

    That make it worse?

    Does too much emphasis go to certain groups or people?
72. How about the state government, how does it affect the quality of life in the state?

    What things in particular does it do that make it better?

    That make it worse?

    Does too much emphasis go to certain groups or people?

L. End Questions for General Section

73. Over the next twenty years, how do you think the country is going to do economically?

    Will it become much richer, in real terms?

    Will there be certain groups or sectors in particular that will benefit most from these patterns over the next twenty years?
74. Now, for the state: Over the next twenty years, how do you think it is going to do economically?

    Will it become much richer, in real terms?

    Will there be certain groups or sectors in particular that will benefit most from these patterns?
75. The fields have narrowed in the past few months, but of the original candidates, which Democratic or Republican presidential candidate did you like the best?

    What are the most important reasons for this pick?

M. Political Connections

I'd like to now ask you some questions that are more directed to the senate itself.

76. How much would you say that the kinds of issues, concerns, and views that we've been talking about here enter into the senate work that goes on at the capitol?
    In what ways does this occur?

77. What are the limits on the influence of what legislators think about these things on the actual work and product of the senate?
    (probes: limits of time, issue complexity, deals for legislation, interest groups, legislative processes, party unity and machinations)
    How do they operate; why are they there?

78. Since I've been up here, I've seen a lot of votes on the floor and in committees go along strict party lines. Tell me about these votes; do they ever significantly constrain you from what you would otherwise do (for leaders: Do you think they significantly constrain your party members from doing what they would otherwise do?)
    In what ways? Is it troublesome? Why do you do it?

79. I know this is a very difficult question, but on the whole, how would you say your constituents' views on the kinds of things we've been discussing match with yours?
    Are there any particular areas of major disagreement?

80. People usually see themselves as occupying certain roles as they perform certain activities. A senator might see himself or herself as a representative, a lawyer, and a social reformer. Another might see herself or himself as a businessperson, a member of the black community, and a representative. Yet another might think of herself as a woman, an environmentalist, and a representative.
    What roles do you see yourself in here at the capitol?
    Is there one that is primary? Would you describe how you see this role in more detail?

81. Are some of these roles more prominent in your mind when certain issues come up?
    Which issues and roles?
    What directions do they move you in?

N. Specific Bills

Now I would like to ask you about a few specific items of legislation that the senate considered during the session.

N.1. Property Tax Relief

82. First, the property tax relief bill. Tell me about this bill: As you see it, what do you think were the issues involved in this bill?

83. I've both heard and read this issue described as a big-city, mainly Hartford, versus the rest of the state fight, the progressives against moderates and conservatives, the governor versus the senate, and businesses versus homeowners.
   Are any of these descriptions particularly apt?
   Did any group or interest, or person, win or lose in this bill?
   Why was the outcome what it was?

84. Did you get involved with this bill? What did you do?
   What things counted most heavily in your involvement?

85. Are any of your district towns affected by this bill?

86. What do you think about the classification proposal that was considered originally?

87. What about the homestead exemption?

88. Why were these proposals dropped?

89. I've heard and read that this relief doesn't work well, because the aid goes to everyone in a qualifying town, regardless of wealth, and because the poorest people don't own houses to begin with. What do you think about this view?

N.2. Education

90. About the school finance bill: What were the issues involved here? How did you come down on them?

   (similar follow-up questions from above bill)

91. I got the sense that there might have been a city versus suburban and small town contest going on.
   How much of the bill formation was due to this, do you think?

92. Is this something the state can afford? (Should afford?)

93. I've heard and read objections that the bill rewards failure, not merit, and provides a disincentive to achievement. Do you have any reactions to this?

94. There was a Republican-sponsored amendment to the education bill that I wanted to ask you about. It was offered on the day that the bill itself passed the senate (and earlier in committee, where it was also rejected), and would have, as I understood it, required school districts to raise their education budgets by the amount of increased state aid

they were receiving for that purpose; in other words, it was to make sure that the money the town receives for education goes to education. This was rejected by a strict party vote.
Why?

95. There was another education bill I wanted to ask you about. Early in the session, a bill was introduced to decrease differences in amounts of money spent on education through limiting a town's eligibility to receive state money when its own education expenditures reach certain levels—a cap of sorts. This bill died in the Education Committee.
What do you think about this bill?

N.3. Plant Closings

The next two bills never made it to the floor of the senate, so you may not know that much about them.

96. I'd like to know what you have to say about the plant closing bills. I'm referring to 5077, the bill that would increase the unemployment benefits paid to workers where their factories closed or moved, or had a substantial layoff, without providing them six months' notice; and 5071, the bill that would have made employers extend employees' health insurance coverage if they lose their jobs due to closings, relocations, or layoffs (adds layoffs to closings and relocations of original law).
What were the issues involved? What do you think about them?

(similar follow-up questions)

97. Do workers have an interest in being notified?
98. How does the employee's interest compare with a business's interest in being able to move, relocate quickly?
99. Why do these kinds of bills seem to come up in recent sessions and continually get killed?

O. Personal/Political

Now, I have a few questions about your political career and about your political life.

100. Do you remember your political views when you were young?
101. Did your views ever subsequently change suddenly?
Why?

102. What were your parents' views?
103. How did you become seriously interested in politics?
104. What was the political office you first ran for?
105. How did you come to run for that political office?
106. How did you come to run for state senator?
107. Do you see yourself ever running for a different office?

P. Demographics

I have some final questions regarding certain facts about you. The purpose of these is to allow me to make some basic comparisons of the responses. I would appreciate you answering all of them, but if you'd rather pass on some, that's fine.

108. In what year were you born?
109. Do you have any brothers and sisters?
     What birth order were you in your family?
110. How long have you lived in the state?
     In the town where you live now?
111. What is your marital status?
112. What is your highest level of education?
     Where did you earn this degree?
     Where did you do your undergraduate work?
113. We were talking about social classes earlier. Which one would you say you fit into best?
114. What class would you say your parents fit or would have fit into?
115. Do you consider yourself a full-time senator?
     Do you have any other occupations that provide you with income?
     When you're not being a senator, what is your occupation?
116. Were you raised in a particular religion?
117. Do you consider yourself to be practicing now?
118. Do you consider yourself to be an ethnic American?
119. To the nearest $10,000 or $20,000, what is your family income (before taxes)?
     Whom are you including in your family?

Notes

Chapter 1

Epigraph from a press conference, 1983; quoted in Hochschild 1988, 168.

Epigraph from a speech delivered at Howard University, June 4, 1965, in Johnson 1971, 166.

1. There are varying interpretations of the trends in these conditions since the 1970s, depending on which sets of statistics are employed, how these statistics are gathered, and which years are used as bases. This is particularly true regarding the issue of economic progress among minorities. For persuasive accounts of inequality, see among others Levy 1988; Phillips 1990; and Congressional Budget Office 1991.

2. These and subsequent figures are from the U.S. House of Representatives Ways and Means Committee, the Congressional Budget Office, and the Internal Revenue Service, as reported in *The New York Times*. See Uchitelle 1990a; Nasar 1992a, 1992c, 1992d; and Passell 1992.

3. For these figures, see, respectively, Pear 1991; Johnson 1989; and DeParle 1992a. For more general treatments of racial inequality, see among many others Schiller 1989; Harris and Wilkins 1988; Ezorsky 1991; and Hacker 1992.

4. On the other hand, it should also be noted that the number of black families with annual incomes of $50,000 or more quadrupled from 1967 to 1989, while the number of white families with similar incomes only doubled. And in terms of household income, between 1979 and 1989, black income increased from 62 to 63 percent of white income. See "Study Finds Gains for Black Middle Class" 1991; and Barringer 1992.

5. Among many others, see Hochschild 1981; Lamb 1982; McClosky and Zaller 1984; and Verba and Orren 1985.

6. As an example of such American exceptionalism, consider the fact that the most egalitarian of the various "challenging" U.S. groups surveyed by Sidney Verba et al. was still found to favor more income inequality than the least egalitarian group in Sweden (1987, 263).

7. To what degree such goods are actually social (or which ones are social) rather than purely private is itself a contentious issue within distributive justice.

8. See McClosky and Zaller 1984, 12–13, 97–100, 246–63. See also McClosky and Brill 1983 and Eulau 1976. Note that the McClosky/Zaller model assumes Conversian notions of constraint concerning belief systems, a subject I will take up in chapter 2, herein.

9. Regarding the two authors' views on the rich cited here, see F. Scott Fitzgerald,

"The Rich Boy," and Ernest Hemingway, "The Snows of Kilimanjaro." Irving Kristol invokes the same phrases to describe politicians, though he leaves out the reference to Fitzgerald and seems to endorse the Hemingway response (1978, 103).

10. Almost all students of state government have made this observation, but for brief summaries of the trend, see Rosenthal 1988, 1989. Concerning the Connecticut legislature more specifically, see Ogle 1990.

11. Malcolm Jewell argues, for example, that as state legislatures become more professional and modern, findings on Congress should become more applicable to state legislatures (1982, 183). Conversely, we might argue that as state legislatures become more professional, research findings regarding them become more relevant to understanding Congress, though this is a weaker claim.

12. In 1971 the General Assembly, reacting to a budget crisis, passed an income tax, only to repeal it six weeks later amidst a hail of protest. For more on the problems leading up to the 1990 budget crisis, see appendix A.

13. But in the 1992 elections, the state's voters appeared not to punish legislators for supporting an income tax; while a few prominent tax supporters were defeated or retired, overall the legislature was left intact.

14. I am greatly tempted to add an in-depth study of the income tax debate to my consideration of the relations between beliefs and behavior in chapters 6 and 7, herein, but I have decided against it in order to better protect the anonymity of the individual respondents.

15. Note that John Kingdon makes a similar access-based choice of subjects in choosing to focus on the U.S. House of Representatives instead of the Senate (1989, 15).

16. Rosenthal makes this point well in reviewing John Straayer's book on the Colorado state legislature: "Some students of state legislatures aspire to build theory or explain structure, behavior, process, and even outputs. They tend to extract specific variables from the rich variety of legislative life, subjecting them to comparative and statistical scrutiny. Other students of state legislatures propose to add to our understanding of one political institution within the context of a single state. They tend to be more descriptive, less quantitative, and intent upon giving the reader a feel for the broader subject under examination. . . . The question is not so much the particular approach as how successful the author is in achieving his or her objectives" (1991, 656).

17. Robert Putnam offers this comment on the importance of having a period of normal politics in which to conduct interviews on beliefs: "Politicians, like most of us, live in a world of foreshortened time perspective, and when talking about politics, talk about today's, or yesterday's, or (more rarely) tomorrow's. It is doubtful that the style of their thought or the pattern of their ideals changes markedly from day to day, but the events to which they apply their thought and ideals do. It is, therefore, important and reassuring that the events of these periods were not radically abnormal in any important respect. It was by and large a period of 'politics as usual'" (1973, 12).

18. Examples of the kind of interview situations I attempted are provided by Hochschild 1981 and Lane 1962. Their interviews generally were much longer than mine, however. A more recent study based on in-depth interviews of approximately the same length as mine is Reinarman 1987. His study is similar to mine in some other relevant respects, including his selection of respondents based on their occupations and his prior observation of their work lives. Reinarman is concerned with uncovering his

respondents' thinking about the "social charter," which concerns the relation between the market and the state.

19. See Lane 1962, 9–10 and Fenno, Jr. 1986. Richard Ashcraft argues that such an approach is largely missing in political science, yet is required for the deeper understanding of beliefs and ideology. "What contemporary political scientists need are not formal abstract concepts of ideology or psychologistic assertions about subjectively constructed meanings but rather a methodological approach that is sensitive to the contextualist and situational features of political thought and action" (1990, 288). It is my claim that the individualized in-depth approach, as I have described it here, does this best.

20. This danger, however, is inherent in any effort to categorize responses, including my own effort here. It is a matter of degree. See chapter 2, herein.

21. My strategy here was similar to Robert Putnam's: to create an interview that would "suggest certain topics for discussion, striving for a formulation as constant as possible across interviews, but striving also to maintain the tone of a genuine conversation" (1973, 19).

22. I use the phrase "deep beliefs" to connote the beliefs about such things as distributive justice. Obviously, beliefs about some things, at some level, greatly influence behavior, even when it is subject to a variety of other disparate forces. The use of deep beliefs is meant to connote those fundamental beliefs (about justice in this case) that one might think would fade in importance in the face of such other forces.

23. I recognize, however, that given the basic design of my study I can offer only indicative findings on the relations between beliefs and behavior.

Chapter 2

1. See Rosenberg 1988, 31, 41, 47.

2. Note that although I make use of some studies that concern beliefs and behavior on a collective level, the focus of my study is on the individual. I am interested in understanding beliefs and their influence regarding individual legislators rather than, for example, dominant collective belief patterns and entire institutions or societies. These two levels of analysis are of course ultimately linked, for it is only through individuals that institutions possess their characters, and any changes in institutions must also manifest themselves in the individuals that populate them. Nonetheless, their different foci result in different starting points for research. But even with an individually oriented approach it is still possible, with great caution, to infer certain features about individuals from information gathered on collectives, and thus at several points I will adduce some of the evidence from other researchers' collectively oriented studies.

3. For a summary of subsequent studies reaching similar conclusions, see Kinder 1983.

4. See Converse 1964, 218, 223–25, 228–29 and Campbell et al. 1960, chap. 10, "The Formation of Issue Concepts and Partisan Change."

5. See Converse 1964, 206, 213, 225, 228–29, 232, 239. For a more recent finding of elite attitude constraint, see Kritzer 1978.

6. It should be noted, however, that open-ended questions were part of the survey instrument used in *The American Voter* (Campbell et al. 1960). In chapter 10, for

instance, Converse relied on open-ended questions about what respondents liked and disliked about the two parties and their presidential candidates (Eisenhower and Stevenson) in order to determine the four "levels of conceptualization" among the public. In "The Nature of Belief Systems," Converse added to these questions a set of both open- and close-ended questions designed to identify the degree of ideological constraint. See Converse 1964, 219–20.

7. See Reik 1972, 144–53 and Bruner 1979, 1986, 3–54. Bruner thus describes this approach in the inquiry into the nature of knowing: "It is an approach whose medium of exchange seems to be the metaphor paid out by the left hand. It is a way that grows happy hunches and 'lucky' guesses, that is stirred into connective activity by the poet and necromancer looking sidewise rather than directly. Their hunches and intuitions generate a grammar of their own—searching out connections, suggesting similarities, weaving ideas loosely in a trial web" (Bruner 1979, 4).

8. Several similar examples of responses whose meanings would have been misinterpreted had they been considered simply as bits of survey data emerge in Reinarman 1987, especially 79–82.

9. See also Lasswell 1948. In addition to a source of beliefs, the Lasswell model might also be considered alternately as a limit on the consequences of beliefs or as an influence on the motivations of actors, in that, on the one hand, beliefs serve personally oriented functions and are not genuinely directed toward external objects, and, on the other hand, that compensatory motivations inform the reasons for getting into politics in the first place. In either case, however, these limits relate back to the sources of beliefs, and thus I have chosen to include the Lasswell model here.

10. For Barber, legislative behavior was considered to represent "a collection of adjustive techniques or strategies by which [a legislator] attempts to maximize the satisfaction of his needs" (1965, 213). The strategies adopted depended on the needs and the environment. The lone noncompensatory type, the "lawmaker," accounted for 34 percent of his sample. The lawmaker was goal-oriented and motivated by a need for rational mastery, and derived satisfaction from the workings of the representative body itself and its legislative products, rather than the satisfactions external to the legislative process emphasized by the other legislative types.

11. See also Rothberg 1981; Sniderman 1975; and Milbrath and Goel 1977.

12. In this view, ideology functions as a distortion, serving to conceal the contradictions inherent in presocialist economic and social relations. The materialist view of ideas is a theme that runs throughout most of the Marxist corpus, but it is found in particular in *The Communist Manifesto* and *The German Ideology.*

13. In addition to the works I am about to cite, see, on an individual level, Hochschild 1981 and Kluegel and Smith 1986. On a societal level, see Geertz 1964 and Wildavsky 1987.

14. In their article, Kinder and Kiewiet are careful to distinguish their claims about sociotropic politics from claims about self-interested versus altruistic-based voting decisions, but nonetheless their findings regarding the *scope* of the voting decision shed light on this issue (Kinder and Kiewiet 1981). Their findings were challenged by Kramer 1983. Kramer argues that Kinder and Kiewiet's findings are artifacts of their statistical methodology.

15. See Edinger and Searing 1967; Putnam 1973, 238–39; 1976, 93–102; and Aber-

bach, Putnam, and Rockman 1981, 158–62. For more anecdotally based evidence (particularly persuasive for the case of Democrats), see Broder 1980, especially 30–130, 478–79. See also the classic study by Wahlke et al. 1962, especially chapter 4.

16. This relation is not unidirectional, however. Different members come to Congress with different goals, and seek out committees that will help them to achieve those goals, thus shaping and reinforcing the characters of the committees themselves.

17. Michael X. Delli Carpini (1986) has written directly about the long-term political impact of the 1960s. Although he locates a fairly specific 1960s political generation among the general public, he argues that this generation has not demonstrated a lasting distinctiveness in terms of its views and values. He concedes, however, that there is not much evidence available regarding elites at the state and local level. See in particular chapter 15.

Craig Reinarman's study comes to similar conclusions regarding the lasting impact of the 1960s: "The ways in which my specific cases failed to fit neatly under any 1960s generation umbrella suggests that it is a mistake to assume that 'the 1960s' existed as such in the 1960s" (1987, 180).

18. See also Entman 1983, 164 and Fiorina 1974. Keith Poole argues, however, that Clausen's policy dimension theory of voting is not inconsistent with the models of voting that focus on beliefs (Poole 1988, 120).

19. I should also note, however, that a recent study following in the footsteps of Mayhew retains a significant amount of influence for personal policy beliefs in the decision-making process. See Arnold 1990.

20. The gamesmanship takes other, more humorous forms as well. I spent the opening day of the 1988 session with one of the Republican senate leaders. On that day, the governor also presented his budget to the assembly. The senator told me that his "mission" that day was to find two or three quick things for the party to use against the budget that would come across well on television and in the papers. With his staff, he settled on a theme of a "credit card budget," and created a money game he played with dollars he took from one pocket and put in another. He had also planned during a television interview in the office to hold up a credit card and use the "credit card budget" line, when during his rehearsal for the interview, someone on his staff (in addition to this observer) noticed that he had been holding up an American Express Gold Card. Thinking that this would not look good to the citizens of Connecticut, he quickly switched to a more plebeian card before the television crew arrived, but during the interview he mistakenly pulled out the Gold Card again, and was forced to quickly shove it back into his pocket. After the crew left he glanced my way, sheepishly smiled, and offered, "It's all such a game."

21. Similarly, Robert Entman surveys recent studies of ideology and concludes that "[r]ecent studies of ideology indicate that it should not be viewed solely as a source of moral crusades or rigid extremism. Rather, it can be a tool for temperate, sober decision makers who, facing complexity, seek to reduce information costs, simplify information processing, and diminish psychic stress" (1983, 165). Such a model of ideology is also found in Anthony Downs's classic work, *An Economic Theory of Democracy* (1957).

22. Among many others, see Collie 1985; Poole 1985, 393–96; 1988; 1991; Schneider 1979; and Entman 1983.

23. More anecdotally, Alan Ehrenhalt has recently traced the effects on policy out-

comes of changes in the beliefs of legislators in several state legislatures (1991, 125–42, 164–207).

24. In this vein, see also Reich 1988.

25. They determined that "a decision maker's basic ideological stance predicts and helps explain his views on specific issues of policy, as well as his vision of the future of the society" (Aberbach et al. 1981, 118).

26. For much of what follows in this paragraph, see Seliger 1976; and also Robert Entman's review of the book (1978).

27. A congressional legislative assistant once explained to me how, coming from New York, he ended up on the staff of a Virginia congressman. He said that he based his job search solely on the Americans for Democratic Action (ADA) ratings, and sent a letter of inquiry to every member above a certain score.

28. Robert Putnam makes a similar point regarding precision in *The Beliefs of Politicians*. Invoking Aristotle's *Nicomachean Ethics*, he quotes: "We must be content, then, in speaking of such subjects and with such premisses to indicate the truth roughly and in outline, and in speaking about things which are only for the most part true and with premisses of the same kind to reach conclusions that are no better. In that same spirit, therefore, should each type of statement be *received;* for it is the mark of an educated man to look for precision in each class of things just so far as the nature of the subject admits" (Putnam 1973, 27, emphasis in original).

29. Here she is quoting Robert Redfield.

30. For an elaboration of storytelling as the common form of moral argument, and its implications, see also Walzer 1987, particularly 65–66.

31. Bruner also suggests that narrative is at the base of the way we think and make decisions: "The economist Robert Heilbroner once remarked that when forecasts based on economic theory fail, he and his colleagues take to telling stories—about Japanese managers, about the Zurich 'snake,' about the Bank of England's 'determination' to keep sterling from falling. There is a curious anomaly here: businessmen and bankers today (like men of affairs of all ages) guide their decisions by just such stories—even when a workable theory is available. These narratives, once acted out, 'make' events and 'make' history. They contribute to the reality of the participants. . . . Narratives may be the last resort of economic theorists. But they are probably the life stuff of those whose behavior they study" (Bruner 1986, 42–43). In a similar vein, he continues later: "Journals of science do not give space to rambles through metaphor, to the processes by which we get ideas worth testing—that is, worth falsifying. Yet a great deal of the time of scientists is spent in just such rambling" (1986, 50–51). Similarly, Alasdair MacIntyre argues that "dramatic narrative is the crucial form for the understanding of human action." Dramatic narrative allows for the resolution of epistemological crises; that is, of the existence of "mutually incompatible accounts of what is going on around [one]" (1977, 464, 454).

32. However, the state did rank in the top seven in terms of the degree of liberalism of its public opinion, and in the top eight in terms of the liberalism of its policies (Wright, Jr., Erikson, and McIver 1987). See also the discussion of state political culture in appendix A.

33. The differences between the critics' and the supporters' conceptions of distributive justice are to some degree captured by the debate between Rawlsian and Nozickian

notions of justice, though this is an oversimplification. See Rawls 1971 and Nozick 1974. See also Arthur and Shaw 1978 and Hayek 1960.

34. This notion is similar in some ways to the classic division between ideas emphasizing being and ideas emphasizing becoming. See, for example, Baumer 1977.

35. Reich is not, of course, the first person to employ such a term, but his use of it is close to mine here.

36. Verba and Orren's discussion of the role of desert in the thinking of the American elite yields similar findings (1985, 82–83).

37. See Hochschild 1981, 238–60; Reinarman 1987, 94–97, 167; Verba and Orren 1985, 5–20; and Kluegel and Smith 1986, 6–8, 11–12, 298–302.

38. This probably reflects a slight male bias in the interview questions, as these were the kinds of answers that I most likely had in mind when designing the questions. But this finding regarding style of response is similar to that of Jennifer Hochschild's in her study of the beliefs of private citizens: "[T]he men tend to have stronger, more clearly etched views than the women . . . [who] tend to be both more ambivalent in their views and more diffident about them" (1981, 229).

39. For accounts of the feminine approach and its critics, see Gilligan 1982; Furby 1986; and Tavris 1992. For studies of legislators in this vein, see among others Kathlene 1989; Thomas and Welch 1991; Githens and Prestage 1978; and Saint-Germain 1989.

Chapter 3

1. A recent work, however, has traced an increasing distrust of business and, more generally, an increasing cynicism among American workers of all classes. See Kanter and Mirvis 1989.

2. See Schlozman and Verba 1979, 190–231, for a demonstration, through public opinion surveys, of the weak support for progressive income taxation, and the strong resistance to upper limits on income. They also argue, however, that deep divisions over the distribution of economic benefits remain prevalent.

3. Furthermore, neither public opinion on distributional and public policy issues nor vote choice appears to vary much with occupational stratum. See Schlozman and Verba 1979, 190–231; Alford 1963, 94–122, 219–49; and Bennett and Resnick 1990. Two recent works take issue with the view that Americans are not significantly class conscious. See Jackman and Jackman 1983 and Vanneman and Cannon 1987.

4. This difference between political leaders and members of the public appears to be true both in objective terms, based on respective issue positions taken by each group, and in subjective terms, based on the way in which each group describes its own political views. See McClosky, Hoffmann, and O'Hara 1960 and Jackson, Brown, and Bositis 1982. Note, however, that these studies are based solely on survey responses.

5. Jennifer Hochschild (1986) describes problems in McClosky and Brill's analysis and offers another view concerning tolerance: elites are not more tolerant per se, but rather are more directly tapped into the opinions of the U.S. Supreme Court. Regarding issues on which the Court has been "murky," for example, McClosky and Brill found no significant differences between elite and nonelite opinions.

6. For a recent argument in favor of considering the problem of the underclass as primarily a class versus a race issue, see Wilson 1987. This view contrasts with some

recent interpretations of contemporary American politics, which have argued that race has largely replaced economic class as the dominant political division. Edward Carmines and James Stimson (1990), for example, claim that the present national party alignment is based primarily upon race. See also Edsall and Edsall 1992; Huckfeldt and Kohfeld 1989; and in a more economic vein, Boston 1988.

7. But Rousseau was not this simplistic in his own allegory or narrative. He goes on to clarify: "For this idea of property, depending on many prior ideas which could only have arisen successively, was not conceived all at once in the human mind. . . . Therefore let us start further back in time . . ." (1964, 142).

8. The significance of this should not be overlooked; arguably, in one way or another such an attitude has dominated the mainstream approach to the problems of poverty and minority status for the past twenty years, via the notion of the "culture of poverty." See for example Daniel Patrick Moynihan's 1964 Labor Department report, "The Negro Family: The Case for National Action." The pervasive influence of this report on the media, and in turn on policy thinking, is traced in Ginsburg 1989.

9. These distinctions regarding liberty are part of a larger division between two arguably different kinds of morality, a division that implicates the problem of incommensurability (see chap. 8 herein). See, for example, W. B. Gallie 1956b. As will become clear in the presentation of the critic's narrative, in many respects the critics' responses indicate such a division. This division is not the whole story, however. For example, critics do not cast off the "commutative," merit-oriented conception of getting "what one deserves," found in liberal morality (Gallie 1956b, 123–24). Rather, they believe that certain groups of people are continually being cheated.

10. Thus, though it is not named as such, a "third face" of power is seen to be at work. The first face of power is the ability to influence the outcomes of decisions and behavior in a direct fashion. The second face is the ability to structure the agenda of decisions and to influence what will be nondecisions as well as decisions. The third face concerns influence over the more subjective orientations of the system's members, including self-esteem and perceptions of self-interest. See Lukes 1974 and Gaventa 1980. The faces-of-power debate, in large part pitting critical against behavioral theories of power and politics, remains one of the most contested in political science. For a brief and insightful rendition of the major positions see Rae 1988.

11. For more on this kind of inward looking among blacks see Blauner 1989. Blauner's findings are based on twenty-two years of intensive interviews of twenty-eight respondents. He is careful to distinguish the inward emphasis he identifies from political conservatism, characterizing it instead as "Black Power redefined."

12. One of the classic treatments in this vein is Piven and Cloward 1971. Many conservative criticisms reach the same conclusion about the welfare system being a perpetuator of poverty, but take a different path in reaching that conclusion and draw different lessons from it (see, e.g., Murray 1984).

13. Furthermore, the market, when it is invoked, is not defended in and of itself, but rather for the socially desirable outcomes (which theoretically precede the market) toward which it is seen to contribute, such as achievement, productivity, the reward for hard work, or having goods efficiently exchanged for their just value. Market relations do not obviate other relations.

14. Although none of the senators advanced a concept of justice that involved rea-

soning from an original position behind a veil of ignorance, in light of their notion of an equal moral worth with distributive implications, they nonetheless might be considered to be Rawlsians in some important respects (see Rawls 1971).

15. These kinds of concerns particularly resonate with the concerns found in some of the movements of the 1960s (Miller 1987).

16. To help preserve the anonymity of the individual respondents, I have omitted nonessential identifying details in this excerpt, and in the excerpts from the critics' personal stories, which appear below. In addition, I have suspended the use of the numbering system, so that any identification that might be made of these excerpts cannot be traced back to the other comments excerpted earlier. These excerpts will be indicated by (*).

17. The emphasis on empathy and compassion also evokes one of Reich's four basic morality tales, "the benevolent community." This tale is "the story of neighbors and friends rolling up their sleeves and pitching in to help one another, of self-sacrifice, community pride, and patriotism. It is about Americans' essential generosity and compassion toward those in need" (1987, 10).

18. The dividing line for the critics is similar to what Reich identifies in his tale of "The rot at the top." The critics' "other" may thus consist of "business tycoons, wealthy aristocrats, Washington insiders, or any others who seem to exercise unaccountable power or enjoy unearned privilege" (1987, 18).

19. And the paradox may only be apparent. I am reminded of a statement by George Orwell: "I had at that time no interest in Socialism or any other economic theory. It seemed to me then—it sometimes seems to me now, for that matter—that economic injustice will stop the moment we want it to stop, and no sooner, and if we genuinely want it to stop the method adopted hardly matters" (1958, 149).

20. I take the general term *government* to mean the entire array of national, state, and local governmental entities. When the senators spoke of government in general terms, it was usually clear that this entire conglomerate was what they meant. Sometimes the term government referred primarily to the national government.

21. The most recent research concerning effective ways to fight various forms of bias indicates that the critics are correct in this view (Goleman 1991).

22. But some recent surveys, particularly of the nation's youth, indicate that this optimism is fading.

23. Although it has received substantial criticism, equity theory has nonetheless emerged as a popular social-psychological model of the way in which people think about economic and distributive justice. Based on experiments drawing on interviews and mock social situations, its central thesis is the contributions rule: People judge the fairness of distributions based on interpersonal comparisons of input and output, and believe that justice is achieved when, for all the individuals involved in the distribution, the ratio of one's contribution or input to one's receipt or outcome is perceived to be equal. Contributions are generally considered in terms of production, thus placing an emphasis on productivity and performance. For more on equity theory and its problems, see among others Furby 1986; Folger 1984; and Deutsch 1975.

This equity-based justice might also be considered to be an attention to human needs, in terms of a basic need to be rewarded through the market for what one has produced.

24. Nathan Glazer argues that since the 1970s, the public conception of affirmative

action as a term has come to include quotas, in much the same way that desegregation has come to include busing (1988, 102–3). He also cites data indicating that three-quarters of the American public oppose quotas (1988, 108).

25. The groups included leaders from business, labor, farming, academia and arts, media, political parties, blacks, feminists, and college youth. Blacks and feminists were considered to constitute "challenging" groups.

26. Verba and Orren found a similar accuracy among their respondents, which in their case extended to the executive's income (though the executive was defined differently) (1985, 154–55).

27. The comments of the senators during the interviews, however, indicated that they were on unsure footing concerning this particular occupation.

28. In the Verba and Orren study, the estimated lowest paid occupation is an elevator operator. I did not include this occupation on the grounds that it was too obscure, perhaps even obsolete. Fortunately, Verba and Orren also included the bank teller. The comparisons of the ratios of the highest to lowest paid occupations, however, are based on Verba and Orren's figures for the elevator operator. The specific figure posited for the bank teller by each group was unavailable from Verba and Orren's published data. If the bank teller had been used, however, the differences between the critics' ratio and the various groups' ratios would be even greater.

29. Here, the income figure for the bank teller is available from the Verba and Orren data. See the note above.

30. See Miller 1987, 21–126, 185–87; Isserman 1987; and regarding family background in particular, Flacks 1967, 1970.

31. The average age of the critics at the time of the interviews was forty-seven, matching the state senate average of forty-eight.

32. Party agents and coopted candidates are two of the four categories of state legislative candidates identified by Kim, Green, and Patterson 1976. The other two categories are careerists and entrepreneurs. The critics do not appear to fit any of these categories well, but probably come closest to the careerists. Careerists are self-starters, with a serious commitment to politics, while entrepreneurs view political life more as an instrumental activity to promote their private careers. Entrepreneurs are similar in many ways to the "advertisers" of James David Barber's earlier study of Connecticut house members (1965). The advertiser is one of four patterns of legislative behavior styles, which are organized around the two variables of activity level and expressed willingness to return to the legislature for future terms of service. In terms of overall background, recruitment, and activity patterns, critics do not fit neatly into any of Barber's four categories, but probably come closest to "lawmakers."

33. For reasons of anonymity, some of the more interesting and illustrative examples of these personal stories cannot be included here, but the following excerpt begins to indicate their patterns of recruitment.

> GR: How did you come to run for state senate?
> A couple of reasons. One, the heir-apparent to the seat was no longer available. Number two, the gentleman that I ran against was a young man, never served in government before, came from a rather wealthy family. He had a different perspective in terms of the role of government; he was very conservative, he

believed that government had no role in people's lives. . . . His philosophy was so different from me, and my concern was the direction that government was going to take. I was ready to run for [another] term [in another office], probably would have been my last term [in that office]. . . . As I thought about it, I said to myself, you know if there's a chance for me to win, there may be a chance for me to do something for the people, to really bring an agenda for the people to the state level. (*)

34. The critics' average family income was $57,000, compared with $73,000 for the entire senate. The average number of securities in excess of $5,000 each held by each critic's family was 3.4, above the senate average of 3.2. The critics' average, however, is skewed upward by one critic's holdings; six critics held no such securities. The average number of real properties owned by each critic's family was 1.7, compared with 1.9 for the entire senate. The critics' average years of university-level education was 4.3, compared with 5.0 for the entire senate.

For further descriptions of these data categories and their sources, see appendix A.

35. Sidney Verba and Gary Orren, however, find age to have little effect on attitudes toward equality (1985, 174–75). Milton Rokeach, on the other hand, finds a "complex, undulating pattern of development" concerning values about equality, which does appear to include a conservatizing trend during this transition (1973, 80).

36. Much of the Populism scholarship on the Left or progressive side involves Harry Boyte (Boyte 1980; Boyte, Booth, and Max 1986; Boyte and Riessman 1986). For treatments of Populism on the Right, see, among many others, Crawford 1980 and Phillips 1982.

The amount of scholarship on the earlier forms of American Populism is legion. Two excellent works are Goodwyn 1978 and Hofstadter 1955.

37. I should also point out here, however, that my questions themselves may have caused the critics to talk more about economic distribution than about power.

38. See Young 1977, 24–51, 130–44; Diggins 1973, 3–27, 155–96; Gorman 1989, 48–52; and Flacks 1967.

39. On participatory democracy, see also Miller 1987; Hayden 1988, 73–102; and Young 1977, 44–50.

40. "[T]hey believed that just as the sinner can be cleansed and saved, so the nation could be redeemed if the citizens awoke to their responsibilities" (Hofstadter 1955, 11). More generally, see Hofstadter 1955, 204–14 and Hofstadter 1963.

41. To many of the Progressives, the economic realm was considered "as a field for the expression of character" (Hofstadter 1955, 315). This view is shared by the supporter's narrative, though it carries different ramifications.

42. See, among others, Harrington 1970, 248, 326; Wolfe 1978; and von Beyme 1985, 37. And Richard Hofstadter writes of a "social-democratic tinge" in the latter phase of the New Deal, owing to "[t]he demands of a large and powerful labor movement, coupled with the interests of the unemployed" (1955, 308).

43. In the 1950s, John Kenneth Galbraith observed a similar change in American liberalism, stemming from the Great Depression and the Keynesian system (1958, 186–92).

Chapter 4

1. The choice of Trump for the name of the first chapter was made prior to his fall.

2. In the interview, the underclass was defined as "a systematically deprived group that is not connected to the American ethos of advancement, and that is overwhelmingly made up of nonwhites." Critics tended to bring up the existence of an underclass on their own, for which they provided their own definitions, which were roughly similar to the one above.

3. See, for example, Friedrich Hayek's (1960) distinction between value and merit in his defense of the market.

4. This position is similar to that resulting from the reluctance to make interpersonal comparisons of utility, a reluctance that informs much of the normative elements in neoclassical economics, as well as the application of neoclassical economics to political questions. For a helpful review of this literature, see Mueller 1979.

There is arguably a relation between this kind of economic conservatism and more traditional forms of European conservatism, in that both share an epistemological skepticism.

5. Perhaps the most influential contemporary statement of this position is Murray 1984. For a view opposed to Murray's, see Schwarz 1983.

6. This is in contrast to many recent characterizations of the "New Right," where the new version of American conservatism is painted as radically antielitist and individualistic, and critical of institutions of the "establishment" (with the exception of the defense establishment). In many of these characterizations the new conservatism becomes an anticonservative populism of the Right, which is particularly popular among the white lower middle class. See, for example, Crawford 1980, especially chaps. 6 and 8; Phillips 1982, especially chaps. 1 and 3; and Peele 1984. Jerome Himmelstein takes issue with this view (1989, chap. 3). See also Schlesinger, Jr. 1986.

Students of the New Right have located within the movement reassertions of authority, but these have been for the most part limited to a religious orientation, concentrating on such issues as homosexuality, pornography, and abortion. See Peele 1984. The assertions of authority made by the supporters appear to extend well beyond these concerns.

The authoritarianism in the supporter's narrative may in fact be linked to a darker side of populism, which has been observed even by its sympathetic students. This side is an "authoritarian populism [which] affirms communities of exclusion for white middle Americans—combining the nostalgia for small town America and values of self-reliance with attacks on urban decadence, minority dependence, feminist immorality, union greed, worker indolence, government intrusion and foreign subversion." Ann Bastian, quoted (without reference) in Greer and Goldberg 1986, 174–88, 187.

7. John Gray makes a similar point in a work on Friedrich Hayek: "[U]nplanned social evolution may throw up results deeply subversive of the liberal order" (1986, 139). See also Rowland 1988.

This problem poses a challenge for the new conservative thinking, not only at the level of the unintended social consequences of individual activity, but also at the level of the individual's motivations. Unfettered individuals still need to constrain themselves within *some* moral strictures. Irving Kristol presents the problem most succinctly: "And what if the 'self' that is 'realized' under the conditions of liberal capitalism is a self that despises liberal capitalism, and uses its liberty to subvert and abolish a free society?" (1978, 68). One solution, dating back at least to Adam Smith, is to posit that there are natural, internalized checks on self-interested behavior. This positive view of ultimate human nature, however, seems more at home in the critic's narrative than in the supporter's narrative.

8. Calling attention to these prior factors forms the basis of much of the criticism of both neoclassical economics and the attempt to apply it to politics and political philosophy. See, for example, Shapiro 1986, 151–204.

9. This senator's invocation of these black politicians as examples of success stories is somewhat ironic, since they have advanced and achieved in large part by promulgating the view that there are deep problems concerning equal opportunity and upward mobility, and by attempting to address these problems.

10. I should note here that one supporter endorsed labor unions in an abstract sense, as an element of the market economy. Unions offer a product—labor—at a price. The senator also supported, on roughly the same grounds, legislation at the state level to protect workers from the effects of plant closings, which was an unusual position for a Republican to take, especially a supporter.

> If you really take a look at unions, they're nothing more than a capitalistic unit. They have a product, and they're going to their employer saying, "This is my product. This is what we think it's worth." And the employer says "No, it's not worth that." And they negotiate and come up with a value for that product, much as I do when I go buy a car. (12)

11. Concerning the most recent segment of U.S. history, this view appears to be incorrect. See chapter 1, herein.

12. The blaming of the poor for their situation has enjoyed a long history in this country. For its more recent forms, see Patterson 1981.

13. See, for example, Sumner 1982. It is interesting to compare Sumner's "forgotten man" to the common, "triumphant individual" found in the supporter's narrative. The forgotten man is the supplier of productive services who suffers when inefficient transfers are made from the rich to the poor. Like the hero of the supporter's narrative, the forgotten man is "worthy, industrious, independent, and self-supporting" (1982, 110). The only help he needs is "to be freed from the parasites who are living on him" (1982, 111).

14. I discussed three "additional items" in the critic's narrative. One of these items, internationally comparative assessments, did not surface in the supporters' responses. They simply did not pay much attention to other nations, though it was apparent from their descriptions of U.S. practices that they believed that the United States was a uniquely favored nation. One senator did make a point of criticizing Sweden (compare this with some of the comments of the critics about Sweden), but this topic was usually left alone.

15. The supporters' average age was 57; the senate average was 48. The supporters' average yearly family income was $78,000, compared with $73,000 for the entire senate. Two senators' income figures are missing from the supporters' data; one due to

an incomplete interview, and the other due to a refusal to state income. In the second case, the income was described as "in the six figures." The average number of securities in excess of $5,000 each held by each supporter's family was 5.3, higher than the senate average of 3.2. Two supporters, however, held no such securities. The average number of real properties owned by each supporter's family was 1.4, slightly less than the senate average of 1.9. The supporter's average years of university-level education was 3.9, below the senate average of 5.0.

For further descriptions of these data categories and their sources, see appendix A.

16. The fact that some supporters were recruited by others does not necessarily mean that they are any less enthusiastic about their jobs than the self-starters. See Sokolow 1989, 29.

17. For the economic theories of the New Right, see Thompson 1990, and Waligorski 1990.

18. In this endorsement, supporters differ from the general public, which has a deep distrust of corporate management. See, for example, Lipset and Schneider 1983.

19. See also Eatwell and O'Sullivan 1990.

20. This concern with moral decline could be the product of the supporters' own generational characteristics or, as mentioned earlier, the distant echo of a civic republicanism.

Chapter 5

Due to the large number of ambivalent senators, I will not quote every senator in presenting this narrative (as I have done in the previously presented narratives). I believe, however, that my presentation is representative of all the ambivalent senators' remarks.

1. Note that like the supporter's narrative, the ambivalent narrative's attitude toward the market is distinct from the subset of conservative defenses that attempts to separate value from merit. For an argument for such a separation, see Hayek 1960. In the supporter's and ambivalent's narratives, markets are supported as distributional mechanisms precisely because they join value and merit; the link between value and merit is a criterion of fairness that stands outside of and prior to the support of the market. It is thus interesting to note that no one in the Connecticut senate endorses the market for the same reasons that Hayek and others in his camp do.

2. One limitation of this method of handling social problems is that its benefits are usually based exclusively on membership in certain specified groups. It is also interesting to note that some leaders in the minority communities are critical of an overemphasis on civil rights for precisely the reason that civil rights-based policies are less explicitly redistributive; such an overemphasis misses the real problem of basic class-based distributional inequities.

3. I owe this observation to David Mayhew.

4. The account of the ambivalent's narrative concerning poverty is thus similar to the "culture of poverty" accounts that have circulated for the past thirty years. See the note on the culture of poverty in "The Big Fish Eat the Little Fish" section of chapter 3 herein.

5. I have withheld the number identification in this and in subsequent interview excerpts marked with an asterisk in order to further preserve anonymity.

6. Recall that equity emphasizes a consistency of return from a given amount of input or effort.

7. I do not think it necessary to provide a comparison of the income data here with that offered by Verba and Orren (1985), as I did in the presentation of the critic's and supporter's narratives. The reader wishing to do so may consult that work and chapters 3 and 4 herein.

8. I do not mean to imply that the ambivalent's narrative is either more rational or reasonable than the critic's and supporter's narratives. I also do not mean to imply that because of its coolness it is any less ideological.

9. The word caucus has two related meanings. In this excerpt, the senator is using caucus to refer to the entire collection of senators within a party. Caucus also refers to the formal meetings of the senators within each party.

10. The average age of the ambivalents is 44; that of the senate as a whole is 48, of the critics is 47, and of the supporters is 57. The average number of terms served by ambivalents is 2.4; that of the senate as a whole is 2.9, of the critics is 2.6, and of the supporters is 4.6.

11. The ambivalents' average family income was $80,000, compared with $73,000 for the entire senate ($57,000 for critics and $78,000 for supporters). Only three of the ambivalents had family incomes under $60,000. Three ambivalents refused to state their family incomes, and I have reason to believe that these incomes were substantially higher than the senate average, perhaps spectacularly so. The number of real properties owned by each ambivalent's family was 2.3, compared with 1.9 for the entire senate (1.7 for the critics and 1.4 for the supporters). On the other hand, it should also be noted that the average number of securities in excess of $5,000 each held by each ambivalent's family was 2.3, compared with 3.2 for the entire senate (3.4 for the critics and 5.3 for the supporters).

12. The ambivalents' average years of university-level education was 5.6, compared with 5.0 for the entire senate and 4.3 and 3.9 for the critics and supporters, respectively. In terms of the relative prevalence of lawyers among ambivalents, the difference between that group and the others is striking; 42 percent of the ambivalents were lawyers, compared with only 13 percent of the other two narrative groups (taken together).

13. Republican ambivalents, a much smaller group, were much more often self-recruited. This is not surprising, given their deviance in many respects from standard party beliefs.

14. For evidence of just such an adjustment process among ambitious California city councilmen, see Prewitt and Nowlin 1969.

In terms of their overall background, recruitment, and ambition patterns, the ambivalents appear to blend together the characteristics of both the "advertisers" and "lawmakers" of James David Barber's earlier study of Connecticut house members (1965, 69–76, 165–71).

15. In this regard, consider the following observation by Randall Rothenberg: "The neoliberals' most important contribution to current political discourse is their establishment of a rational middle ground between the automatic reliance on government spending with which the Democratic Party has been associated and the equally instinctive

rejection of government solutions now accepted as doctrine by the Republican Party"
(1984, 244).

Chapter 6

1. In 1974, for example, local levels of government provided 73 percent of the entire state expenditure for public education, while state funding accounted for only 24 percent of the total. The court held that the wealthier towns in the state, with higher property values, could more easily supply quality public education than could other towns, particularly the larger cities. This ruling was rendered despite a 1973 ruling by the U.S. Supreme Court that inequalities in educational funding based on a reliance on property taxes did not violate the U.S. Constitution.

2. The legislature operates under a joint committee system; thus each committee has two chairs, one each from the house and senate. See chapter 7 herein.

3. The test score system was actually based on average scores, but was designed to yield an enrollment adjustment equal to what I have described here.

4. I base these opinions on the remarks made on the senate floor and in the Republican senate caucus.

5. This comment and subsequent comments from the senate floor are taken from the transcripts kept by the Senate Clerk's Office. I have excerpted them verbatim, but at a few points I have added necessary punctuation and corrected obvious errors in transcription.

6. In this and all subsequent interview excerpts in chapters 6 and 7, I have omitted the numbered references that indicate which senator is speaking. I have done this in the interest of anonymity, since the senators' comments are now embedded in a much more concrete setting, from which they could be identified. I do not want these comments to link them to their earlier statements of belief.

7. Additional data on the distribution of Connecticut's tax burdens can be found in appendix A. The institution of a state income tax in 1991 might be thought to lessen the relative dependence on local property tax, but since the state has not yet assumed a significant additional burden for local funding, the relative dependence remains.

8. In a similar vein, it is also interesting to consider some of the other bills concerning property tax relief that were introduced into the session but did not make it very far. The fact that these bills did not move through the assembly may have had more to do with the fact that they did not originate with the cochairs of the Finance, Revenue, and Bonding Committee than with their policy content. In addition to the two bills to expand the circuit-breaker program to cover the state's residents regardless of age, there were two other bills of note. One bill would have provided more significant increases in direct tax relief aid to towns and cities on a need basis, while another would have made tax relief grants contingent on local efforts to promote affordable housing and desegregate schools. Both of these bills were tabled in committee and never even received a public hearing.

9. In addition, the senate's disposition of the bill was postponed for a day due to a technical problem uncovered by a Republican senator (an amendment to the bill had not been cleared by the Appropriations Committee; the committee then held a meeting to approve the amendment that evening).

10. As the day dragged on, two additional amendments planned by the Republicans were withdrawn on the floor by the minority leader.

11. The entity of the full senate in the chamber is often referred to as "the Circle," because the desks are arrayed in a large circle.

12. My retelling of the story of the plant closings legislation is based in part on lengthy interviews with a senior house member of the Labor and Public Employees Committee and another senior house member.

13. The benefits would have been increased to 75 percent of gross pay or 90 percent of net pay, whichever was less.

14. I was unable to verify this claim, but its source was very reliable. A member of the Labor Committee also once spoke of a general agreement by employers not to contest a raise in unemployment compensation, which he tied to the outcome of the plant closing bill.

15. One of the more curious arguments made against the bill during the public hearings came from a lobbyist from CBIA, who claimed on two separate occasions that if the bill were passed companies would deliberately, out of benevolence, not provide notice of layoffs or closings so that their employees could collect higher unemployment benefits. The Labor Committee member I interviewed dismissed this argument as "bullshit."

Chapter 7

1. Such statements by the senators introduce the question of the meaning of the word "political," which by all rights is an extremely inclusive term. When the senators use it in this context, however, they obviously mean something much more narrow. John Kingdon supplies a good definition of the term in its narrow, intracapitol sense: "'Political' factors in such parlance are electoral, partisan, or pressure group factors. As one talks to practitioners of the art, they use 'political' motivations, for example, to refer to politicians' attention to voter reactions, their skewering of members of the opposite political party, and their efforts to obtain the support of important interest group leaders" (1984, 152).

2. See my discussion of this apparent paradox between diagnosis and treatment in chapter 3, herein, and my brief discussion of several measures of Connecticut's liberalism in appendix A.

3. Consider the following anecdote. During a party caucus meeting immediately before a legislative session, a senator expressed concern over a bill that was to be placed on the Consent Calendar (bills that are approved in bulk, by unanimous consent). The concern was based on the fact that when the bill had first come through the senate earlier in the year, four of the caucus members had voted against it. Now it was to be placed on the Consent Calendar. Why? One of the four senators then explained that during the previous vote on the bill, he had rushed into the session and voted against it, "without any idea of what I was voting on." The other three senators then voted against the bill so as not to let the first senator "hang out in the wind."

4. See Connecticut Citizen Action Group 1987; Connecticut Business and Industry Association 1987, 1988; and Connecticut AFL-CIO 1987, 1988. I selected the scores of these three groups because they are widely recognized and are often cited by both the

media and the legislators themselves. For kindred examples and accompanying discussions of this method of measuring voting behavior in terms of ideology, see among others Entman 1983 and Kritzer 1978.

5. The use of cues in individual legislative decision making has been well studied at both the national and state level. For two excellent examples see Kingdon 1989 and Muir, Jr. 1982.

6. This norm of reliance and deference is less strongly held by members of the minority party. See the following discussion of partisanship.

7. In this regard, see also Frank Smallwood's experiences as a state senator in Vermont (1976).

8. For similar findings at the national level, see Hall 1987.

9. In addition to the legacy of the state's party system, the enduring strength of parties in the legislature is in part due to the fact that each party represents a relatively distinct set of regions and interests within the state. In fact, Connecticut fits well Malcolm Jewell's "obvious example" of a state where party discipline within the legislature is likely to be strong: "a state where the Democrats represent the major cities and the Republicans represent suburbs, small towns, and rural areas" (1982, 6). In Connecticut, Democrats add to their strength in the cities with support in the middle-class white-collar and blue-collar rural areas in the eastern part of the state.

10. I observed a humorous example of this influence in the house when two legislators elected in a special election arrived at the leadership office for their first day of service. The leader canvassed their preferences about committee assignments and then suggested some others, including for both of them an assignment that each balked at, for different sets of reasons. There were two open spots on this particular committee, which the leader was trying to fill. Later in the day, when the committee assignments were again discussed more specifically, the leader once again suggested this particular assignment for each new legislator. He cited reasons why they would be well suited for the assignment, reasons that, for the two members taken together, seemed to be self-contradictory. But after some further discussion, each member acceded to the committee assignment. After the second of the two legislators had left the office, a member of the leadership staff, who had witnessed the entire set of conversations, said to the leader, "you are in the wrong business, my friend. I've got some snake oil and used cars that I think we could sell. Not just one [committee] assignment, but two! Incredible! They come in, they're new, and they don't know. Do they know what issues are being considered by [that committee]?" The leader laughed and replied that he did in fact mention to them the issues presently on the committee's agenda (which he did, but without emphasizing the political ramifications).

11. There are provisions for individual members to override leadership in order to introduce legislation, by gathering sufficient support from the rank and file. But these provisions are invoked very rarely.

12. The Republicans did propose alternatives to the most important pieces of legislation considered, but these were offered mostly as a formality, accompanied by a sense of futility, and usually were not taken that seriously by either party.

13. Alan Rosenthal notes that Connecticut is one of several states in which such partisan positioning through recorded votes on floor amendments—"making a record"—has become routine (1989, 93). And such a technique is obviously not entirely

new, at least not in Connecticut; writing in the 1950s, then State Senator Duane Lockard described it as the "improve-it-to-death weapon" in the struggle between two chambers under divided party control (1959b, 296).

14. A particularly distressing example of this problem occurred during an Appropriations Committee meeting. Toward the end of the meeting, a Republican legislator offered an amendment concerning drunk driving. In a passionate argument in its favor, he referred to the practice of making a record against the Democrats, but swore that this was not part of that strategy. He emphasized that the amendment spent no more money than the provisions it was designed to replace, only that it spent the money earlier. Democratic leaders then argued against the amendment, out of fiscal considerations. This was somewhat ironic, as the committee had just spent most of the previous two hours approving, on party votes, provisions recognized by members of both parties as "pork-barrel" items for the Democratic legislators. The drunk driving amendment was defeated, again on a party vote. Some members of an organization called Remove Intoxicated Drivers (RID), who had been invited to the meeting by the Republican legislator, openly wept over the decision.

15. Similarly, Alan Rosenthal observes that, typically, "Democrats will try to get Republicans on record against teachers or environmental interests, while Republicans will try to get Democrats on record against economic development" (1989, 93).

16. A good example of this influence comes from my observations of a house leader. He discussed how he planned to use a possible obscure problem in the implementation of a bill concerning guaranteed breaks for employees. Though he was using a non-ideological technical problem to derail the bill, his actions were driven, according to his own self-observations, by a more general, ideological reaction against prolabor (or antibusiness) legislation.

17. As recently as 1970, there were only 12 permanent full-time employees working for the entire General Assembly. In 1982 there were 176 (Swanson 1984, 86).

18. But at the same time, the professionalization of the legislature along these lines may naturally produce a more politically liberal legislative atmosphere, given the likely attitudes and career backgrounds of those persons wishing to make a full-time career out of public service. See, for example, Alan Ehrenhalt's descriptions of the changes in the Wisconsin and Alabama state legislatures (1992, 125–42, 164–85).

19. One piece of behavioral evidence for this claim is the amount of physical touching that occurs in the capitol; the only occupation where I have seen more physical touching is professional sports.

The district environment is even more subject to an interpersonal or service orientation. As I followed the legislators into their districts, and we flitted from place to place and meeting to meeting, they would reiterate the need "to poke my head in" or "be seen" there, or "work the network," but they would spend little time discussing issues or policy, let alone setting forward their beliefs. Furthermore, constituents coming in contact with legislators want to talk about getting the road sign or the traffic light (or some larger project), or often just want to talk, rather than discuss larger issues such as justice. At the close of one meeting I attended between a senator and some local officials, a town mayor kept repeating—almost like a mantra—as the senator and I walked out of the building, "Just get the sign, just get the sign."

20. This latter point appeared to hold particularly true in committee meetings, when

various amendments would be tacked onto bills, and other bills would be split into two or more revised bills. Such occasions furthered the strength of the chair, who often led the rank-and-file members through the changes step by step.

21. In earlier periods, the governor, along with state party leaders, virtually dominated the legislature.

22. A 1991 General Assembly Office of Legislative Research study of lobbyists at the state level found that Connecticut had the tenth-highest ratio of lobbyists to legislators in the country, with 7.5 registered lobbyists per legislator.

23. Regarding the domination of business interests in lobbying activity, see Swanson 1984, 58–59. According to Swanson, legislators also perceive that, along with labor and education, business interests are the most effective at lobbying.

24. This kind of influence is similar to that described by Frank Smallwood (1976, 193).

25. One piece of evidence that contradicts my argument, however, is the fact that the margins of victory for critics are the highest of the three narrative groups. In the election prior to the interviews, the critics' average margin of victory was 37 percent, while the ambivalents' and supporters' average margins were 24 percent and 18 percent, respectively. This pattern may be explained in part by the party identifications of the three narratives and the fact that Democrats are more electively secure than Republicans; recall that all critics are Democrats, all supporters are Republicans, and ambivalents are mixed.

26. But note that Garand found that for the entire sample of state senates the relation between increasing victory margin and proportion of winning incumbents was not significant, and for the Connecticut Senate it was even negative (though still not significant). This finding is similar to Gary Jacobson's 1987 finding concerning congressional elections.

Alan Rosenthal, however, argues that the elections of 1984 and 1986 were aberrations in the state, with unusually strong coattail effects from Ronald Reagan and Governor William O'Neill, respectively. Under normal conditions, the reelection rate is about 90 percent (1989, 83–84).

27. This phenomenon was reinforced by the optional party lever, which was eliminated in 1988.

28. On the first day of the 1988 legislative session, for example, the president pro tempore of the senate delivered the keynote speech to the senate chamber. It was an eloquent, inspirational speech, evoking Disraeli, about "the two Connecticuts," one rich, one poor. He then followed this speech by introducing and bringing into the center of the chamber two state champion football teams from his district.

29. Here I am following Kingdon's "policy stream" analysis (1984).

30. Ironically, voters apparently do not hold state politicians responsible for the state's economic performance (though they of course still do not like taxes) (Chubb 1988). The fact that state legislators still *believe* that it matters, however, is more relevant here than the reality.

31. The concern over the business tax and interstate competition figured largely in the debate over a state income tax, and was an important contributor to its ultimate passage. On the state's business tax, see appendix A.

32. More generally, see the work in schema theory.

33. See, for example, Lau, Smith, and Fiske 1991. See also Hurwitz 1986 and Songer et al. 1986.

Chapter 8

1. Note that this emphasis on sameness appears to undercut any empirical concerns about normative incommensurability right from the start; if there is a profoundly held consensus on the core issue of distributional fairness, then incommensurability becomes a rather distant problem.

2. Huntington sees his work as a challenge to the consensus theorists, in that he identifies the presence of deep value-driven conflict in American politics. But the creed he describes, though internally inconsistent, is relatively monistic. Huntington also argues for the exclusion of economic and class-based cleavages in the creedal passion periods; the most important political cleavages are thus vertical rather than horizontal.

3. In addition, the emergence of the critic's narrative through the methods I employed supplies yet another reason for using these methods; the narrative probably would not have surfaced through voting studies or a content analysis of speeches delivered on the chamber floor, or through surveys.

4. On the issue of essential contestability, see among others Care 1974; Connolly 1983; Gallie 1956a; Grafstein 1988; and MacIntyre 1974. Much of the work on this problem examines the contested and incommensurable nature of the fundamental concepts and terms used in formulating and advancing normative claims.

5. For an interesting summary of the variants of the problem, along with an attempt to place them within an "isomorphic structure" (though I find the claims for the novelty of this structure to be overstated), see Hadari 1988.

6. In more critical treatments, these normative statements are also the products of the power relations within a given social system. The exposure of the power relations embedded in normative claims, as well as the particularistic perspectives of normative claims more generally, is the principal task of deconstructive analysis.

7. See among others Care 1974; Connolly 1983; Gallie 1956a (the phrase "essential contestability" is Gallie's); Grafstein 1988; and MacIntyre 1974.

8. A recent, powerful statement of disagreement with this view is Midgley 1991.

9. But to their credit not all the theorists working with these problems conclude that all hope is lost, or that certain kinds of political orders and normative frameworks can never be justified. Richard Rorty, for example, argues for a "democratic, progressive, pluralist community" of "postmodernist bourgeois liberalism" (1991, especially 21–34, 197–202). William Connolly (1987) argues for a kind of theoretical and political pluralism that recognizes, tolerates, even encourages the "other," rather than trying to overcome it. Jürgen Habermas argues for conditions of "rational consensus" expressing "generalizable interests" (1975, 111). Finally, Alasdair MacIntyre argues that closure through rational debate is possible, because "an admission of significant incommensurability and untranslatability in the relations between two opposed systems of thought and practice can be a prologue not only to rational debate, but to that kind of debate from which one party can emerge as undoubtedly rationally superior . . . if only because exposure to such debate may reveal that one of the contending standpoints fails in its own terms and by its own standards" (1990, 5). See also MacIntyre 1988, 326–403.

10. Perhaps the most notable and celebrated attempt at positive construction during the last fifty years is John Rawls's *A Theory of Justice* (1971). But even this work has been subjected to similar critiques that it is ultimately contextually bound. Perhaps the second most notable attempt is Michael Walzer's *Spheres of Justice* (1983), though this is a far more controversial claim. Walzer rejects universal principles, but argues that within a given context of time, place, and social good, we can establish valid principles of justice.

11. See also Hadari 1988.

12. I do not mean to imply here, however, that the theorists have ignored this question entirely. Much of Foucault's work, for example, has an empirical orientation. I am arguing instead that the empirical side of this question has been greatly understudied.

13. Freedom is a triadic relation, in that "it is thus always *of* something (an agent or agents), *from* something, *to* do, not do, become, or not become something" (MacCallum 1972, 176; emphasis in original).

14. For an interesting attempt to subject normative political theories commonly understood as "ideal" to empirical analysis, see Frohock and Sylvan 1983. The authors conclude that traditional liberal theory is based on dubious empirical assumptions, particularly those concerning the supposed trade-offs between liberty and levels of economic well-being. Their assessment also supports (at a deeper level) my claim that the critics are more empirically accurate than the other two narrative groups, as the critic's narrative implicitly challenges the assumption of these trade-offs.

15. For a similar argument in a more theoretical vein, see Walzer 1987 and Shapiro 1990, 55–88.

The research into jury decision making by Nancy Pennington and Reid Hastie (1988, 1991) is also instructive here. They find that jurors piece together and make sense of the presented evidence through the stories that they tell to themselves about what happened. In one of their studies, for example, different sets of college student mock juries were provided the same information in story order versus witness order (each witness telling everything she knew about the case). The probability of the jurors returning a verdict in favor of a given side went up dramatically when that side presented its case in story order. Pennington and Hastie also find that jurors are led to different verdicts depending on the kind of story that they tell, which includes assumptions about factors not presented in the trial, including certain facts, motives, and psychological states. These assumptions appear to be derived from the jurors' own backgrounds and experiences.

Appendix A

1. But in the middle of 1989, it began to show signs of slowing down. Subsequently, the state experienced a recession, along with the other states in the Northeast. Construction, defense, real estate, banking, and insurance industries all fell off. By late 1990, the unemployment rate had eclipsed 5 percent, and the annual rate of growth for personal income had fallen below 3 percent. See Uchitelle 1990b.

2. These figures are from the Connecticut Census Data Center in Hartford, Connecticut.

3. The caseload increased dramatically after 1988.

4. The number of production workers in the state declined 10 percent between 1982 and 1986 (U.S. Bureau of the Census 1989, xxiv).

5. A final 3 percent remained in the "Don't know, etc." category.

6. These figures are for people over eighteen years of age. I treat all Hispanics as nonwhite. In 1980, 14 percent of the entire state population was nonwhite. Across the nation, this proportion was 23 percent (U.S. Bureau of the Census 1981, 32).

7. Political culture is often treated as largely derivative of demographics. Erikson et al.'s study indicates, however, that there are distinct political cultures within the states, not reducible to demographics, which exert significant influence on the partisanship and ideology of a particular state.

Also note that Connecticut's combination of Republicanism and liberalism is less paradoxical in historical perspective, given its New England heritage.

8. The measure of policy liberalism is based on various indices of particular policies during the early 1980s.

9. Five percent went unclassified into one of the three groups. The sample consisted of 990 "likely voters," surveyed by telephone.

10. Ten percent went unclassified.

11. Prior to the 1965 reapportionment, the allocation of house districts was based on the state's 169 towns instead of population—at least one representative for each town, and no more than two for any one town. In 1959 the apportionment for the house was the worst in the nation; the ratio of the population of the largest district to that of the smallest district was 682, and a scant 9.6 percent of the state's voting population could elect a majority of the representatives. This method of districting furnished the Republican Party with a great electoral advantage, owing to its strength in the numerous small towns; indeed, it held unbroken control of the house from 1876 to 1958. See Lockard 1959a, 269–72. Regarding the senate districts, there was a slight bias toward the larger population centers, and therefore toward the Democratic Party.

12. The self-reported figures from the *Connecticut Poll #66* (October 1986) are 32 percent Democrat, 28 percent Republican, and 37 percent independent (Institute for Social Inquiry 1986). The inconsistency between these figures and those based on actual registration rolls is somewhat puzzling, perhaps indicating that the state Republican Party is stronger among all adults than among registered voters only, or that many registered Democrats have switched or dropped their party orientation without changing their registration.

13. See Mayhew 1986, 27–32. Mayhew's data are based on the late 1960s. For more recently focused studies, see Garand 1991 and Weber, Tucker, and Brace 1991. Garand's data, for example, shows that out of a sixteen-state sample, from 1968 to 1986 Connecticut's senate elections yielded the lowest average incumbent vote proportions and the lowest proportion of incumbent winners.

14. The sales tax was increased from 7.5 percent to 8 percent during the 1989 legislative session. The comparison with the other states is based on 1988 data in Council of State Governments 1988, 254.

15. According to the Connecticut Public Expenditure Council, however, in 1987 Connecticut ranked fourth in tax payments per person, with an average of $2,216. It based this finding on recent census figures (Johnson 1989b).

16. Other categories account for 5 percent and 19 percent of the responses, respectively.

17. See, for example, "State Spending Slights Basic Needs" 1989.

18. For the regressivity of Connecticut's property tax system (prior to the income tax), see Price Waterhouse 1988, 31–45.

But also note here that the present state income tax system does not provide a complete remedy for these problems. The original income tax system proposed by Governor Weicker was only marginally more progressive than the old system. The income tax itself became somewhat more progressive in the course of subsequent budget iterations between the governor and the legislature, but at the same time the corresponding decrease in the sales tax was trimmed back. In the final version, families earning between $60,000 and $90,000 (a large group in Connecticut) paid comparatively more in taxes than families earning higher incomes. For some of its incarnations along the way, see Johnson, 1991a, 1991b, 1991c, 1992.

19. *Amendments to the Constitution of Connecticut, 1970,* Article III.

20. One Republican senate staffer claimed that the changes in federal tax law were more excuses than reasons for the state's fiscal troubles (Berthoud 1989). He posited instead that Democrats intentionally inflated original revenue estimates in order to have a scapegoat, in the form of tax reform, for spending levels that were simply too high given economic growth rates.

21. In 1989, the legislature did indeed face a budget crisis. In the end, it instituted nearly $1 billion in new taxes and approved a budget of $6.82 billion, which increased state spending by 8 percent over the previous year. Later, the state was able to announce that it was once again running a surplus, due to the new taxes. The same problems returned with a vengeance in 1990, however, as the state's economy fell into recession, along with the rest of New England, and as the federal government continued to supply fewer funds to the state. As a percentage of state spending, the projected 1991 deficit was higher than that of any other state (Uchitelle 1990b). On June 30, 1991, the state ended the fiscal year 1990 with a deficit of $937 million.

22. For a few of the items listed below, the figures do not include every interview respondent. Thus not all numbers may total. With the exception of reported income, only one or two cases are missing from the totals.

23. At least one of those married had been previously divorced.

24. More than anything else, the difference between these numbers indicates the Democrats' greater percentage of lawyers; Republicans had only one attorney.

25. These figures are self-reported and include senate salaries. There are seven missing cases here; two Republicans, five Democrats. I have reason to suspect that several of these missing incomes would have been substantially higher than the top reported incomes. The reported incomes range from $23,000 to $130,000. One of those who refused to name a specific income described it as "in the six figures."

26. The figures for properties and securities in excess of $5,000 are from the Connecticut State Ethics Commission Annual Statements of Financial Interests for the year 1988, and thus no cases are missing. Family-owned property includes "all real property . . . whether property was owned by (or held in the name of a corporation, partnership, or trust for the benefit of) the individual, or the individual's spouse or dependent children residing in the individual's household . . . at any time during the calendar

year." Securities include "securities . . . that involve an interest in a corporation or other business entity and that were at some time during the past calendar year, while having a fair market value in excess of $5,000, owned by (or held in the name of a corporation, partnership, or trust for the benefit of) the individual or the individual's spouse or dependent children residing in the individual's household."

The number of properties held ranges from zero to eight.

27. These figures range from zero to twenty-seven.

28. In 1988, Connecticut senators earned about $23,000 per year, including personal expenses and small bonuses for committee chairs, ranking memberships, and such. This placed the state near the national mean.

Frank Smallwood, a Dartmouth College government professor who served a term as a state senator in Vermont, has this to say about the myth of the part-time legislator: "So forget the theories about the part-time citizen legislator. As far as I could see, there is no such animal: when the political life is pursued with any reasonable degree of diligence, it becomes an all-consuming business. . . . [A]ny one who is interested in making a major commitment to politics had best be prepared literally to give up all else if this commitment is to be fulfilled" (1976, 221–23). More recently, Alan Ehrenhalt concludes an in-depth examination of legislative politics in Wisconsin, Connecticut, Alabama, and Colorado with this observation: "To say that the notion of time has become crucial to the process is to address a question broader than whether sessions take four months or six months. . . . What matters more is the time consumed by an open political system as practiced in Colorado and states like it across the country. Colorado legislators need to commit the time it takes to provide the constituent service that has come to be expected, to meet with the local pressure groups that did not exist twenty years ago, and to solicit the campaign funds that frighten away serious opposition at election season. Those are the ingredients of full-time work . . ." (1991, 207). In a similar vein, see also Jewell 1982, 182–88 and Kolbert 1989.

29. There are several former teachers who now hold different occupations.

30. "Direct political involvement" means that at some point, either a parent or a sibling held or ran for some office, including party office. "Politically active" can mean anything from actively working for a party or candidate to regular political discussions at the dinner table.

31. "Native" means spending most of one's childhood in the state, rather than moving into it after college or high school. Most senators were native to the district they presently represented.

32. Such ambitions among state legislators are becoming increasingly common. See for example Rosenthal 1981, 1989 and Muir, Jr. 1982.

Appendix B

1. Though I agree with Kingdon's point about proximity and validity, many of the senators I spoke with had no trouble defining in general terms how they vote on bills.

2. The education finance bill itself was not that controversial, but the issues from which it sprang, and which surrounded it, were more so.

3. This assurance was important to some, while many others had no concerns at all about anonymity.

4. "The ways in which positions can be registered are numerous and often imaginative. There are floor addresses ranging from weighty orations to mass-produced 'nationality day statements.' There are speeches before home groups, television appearances, letters, newsletters, press releases, ghostwritten books, *Playboy* articles, even interviews with political scientists" (Mayhew 1974, 61–77, 63).

5. In the Vermont legislature, Frank Smallwood found the Democrats and Republicans to fit these stereotypes (1976, 139–42). See also Rossiter 1960.

6. William Shakespeare, *Hamlet,* III, ii, 360–68. This excerpt also appears in a chapter concerning suggestion in Schuman and Presser 1981, 203.

7. This was easy for me to do, since access was so critical to the success of the project. I was happy to be there, regardless of my opinions on their views.

8. Fenno's thoughts about participant observation are collected in the appendix to *Home Style* (1978), and in *Watching Politicians* (1990).

9. I did a lot of waiting in the course of the research for this project.

References

Aberbach, Joel D., Robert D. Putnam, and Bert A. Rockman. 1981. *Bureaucrats and Politicians in Western Democracies.* Cambridge, Mass.: Harvard University Press.

Alford, Robert R. 1963. *Party and Society: The Anglo-American Democracies.* Chicago, Ill.: Rand McNally.

Alperovitz, Gar. 1986. "Toward a Tough-Minded Populism." In *The New Populism: The Politics of Empowerment,* ed. Harry C. Boyte and Frank Riessman. Philadelphia, Penn.: Temple University Press.

Arnold, R. Douglas. 1990. *The Logic of Congressional Action.* New Haven, Conn.: Yale University Press.

Arthur, John, and William H. Shaw, eds. 1978. *Justice and Economic Distribution.* Englewood Cliffs, N.J.: Prentice-Hall.

Ashcraft, Richard. 1990. Review of *Reason, Ideology and Politics,* by Shawn W. Rosenberg and *Political Reasoning and Cognition: A Piagetian View,* by Shawn Rosenberg, Dana Ward, and Stephen Chilton. *American Political Science Review* 84:286–88.

Barber, James David. 1965. *The Lawmakers: Recruitment and Adaptation to Legislative Life.* New Haven, Conn.: Yale University Press.

Barrett, Edith J., and Fay Lomax Cook. 1991. "Congressional Attitudes and Voting Behavior: An Examination of Support for Social Welfare." *Legislative Studies Quarterly* 16:375–92.

Barringer, Felicity. 1992. "White-Black Disparity in Income Narrowed in 80's, Census Shows." *New York Times,* July 24.

Baumer, Franklin L. 1977. *Modern European Thought.* New York, N.Y.: Macmillan.

Beer, Samuel. 1978. "In Search of a New Public Philosophy." In *The New American Political System,* ed. Anthony King. Washington, D.C.: American Enterprise Institute.

Beiner, Ronald. 1983. *Political Judgment.* Chicago, Ill.: University of Chicago Press.

Bell, Daniel. 1960. *The End of Ideology: On the Exhaustion of Political Ideas in the Fifties.* New York, N.Y.: Free Press.

Bennett, Stephen Earl, and David Resnick. 1990. "The Implications of Nonvoting for Democracy in America." *American Journal of Political Science* 34:771–802.

Berlin, Isaiah. 1969. "Two Concepts of Liberty." In *Four Essays on Liberty.* Oxford, England: Oxford University Press.

Berthoud, John E. 1989. "Passing the Buck on Revenue Shortages." *Wall Street Journal,* February 21 (letter to the editor).

"Beware of This Tax Reform." 1988. *Hartford Courant,* May 1 (op-ed.).

Birchall, Ian. 1986. *Bailing Out the System; Reformist Socialism in Western Europe: 1944–1985.* London, England: Bookmarks.

Blauner, Bob. 1989. *Black Lives, White Lives: Three Decades of Race Relations in America.* Berkeley, Calif.: University of California Press.

Boston, Thomas D. 1988. *Race, Class, and Conservatism.* Boston, Mass.: Unwin Hyman.

Boyte, Harry C. 1980. *The Backyard Revolution: Understanding the New Citizen Movement.* Philadelphia, Penn.: Temple University Press.

Boyte, Harry C., Heather Booth, and Steve Max. 1986. *Citizen Action and the New American Populism.* Philadelphia, Penn.: Temple University Press.

Boyte, Harry C., and Frank Riessman, eds. 1986. *The New Populism: The Politics of Empowerment.* Philadelphia, Penn.: Temple University Press.

Bradsher, Keith. 1995. "Gap in Wealth in U.S. Called Widest in West." *New York Times,* April 17.

Broder, David S. 1980. *Changing of the Guard: Power and Leadership in America.* New York, N.Y.: Simon and Schuster.

Bruner, Jerome. 1979. *On Knowing: Essays for the Left Hand.* Cambridge, Mass.: Harvard University Press.

Bruner, Jerome. 1986. *Actual Minds, Possible Worlds.* Cambridge, Mass.: Harvard University Press.

Caldeira, Gregory A., and Samuel C. Patterson. 1987. "Political Friendship in the Legislature." *Journal of Politics* 49:953–75.

Campbell, Angus, Philip E. Converse, Warren E. Miller, and Donald E. Stokes. 1960. *The American Voter.* New York, N.Y.: John Wiley and Sons.

Care, Norman S. 1974. "On Fixing Social Concepts." *Ethics* 84:10–21.

Carmines, Edward G., and James A. Stimson. 1990. *Issue Evolution: Race and the Transformation of American Politics.* Princeton, N.J.: Princeton University Press.

Caruso, Ralph. 1980. "The Legislature's Most Important Bill." In *Perspectives of a State Legislature.* 2d ed., ed. Clyde D. McKee, Jr. Hartford, Conn.: Trinity College.

Chubb, John E. 1988. "Institutions, the Economy, and the Dynamics of State Elections." *American Political Science Review* 82:133–54.

Clausen, Aage R. 1973. *How Congressmen Decide.* New York, N.Y.: St. Martin's Press.

Collie, Melissa P. 1985. "Voting Behavior in Legislatures." In *Handbook of Legislative Research,* ed. Gerhard Loewenburg, Samuel C. Patterson, and Malcolm E. Jewell. Cambridge, Mass.: Harvard University Press.

Congressional Budget Office. 1991. *Green Book.* Washington, D.C.

Connecticut AFL-CIO. 1987, 1988. "Cope Scorecard." Hartford, Conn.

Connecticut Business and Industry Association. 1987, 1988. "General Assembly Report." Hartford, Conn.

Connecticut Citizen Action Group. 1987, 1988. "CCAG Legislative Index." Hartford, Conn.

Connecticut Department of Economic Development. 1986. *Connecticut Market Data: 1986.* Hartford, Conn.

Connecticut Department of Labor. 1988. *The Connecticut Workplace to the Year 2000.* Hartford, Conn.

Connecticut Secretary of State. 1987. *Connecticut State Register and Manual: 1987.* Hartford, Conn.

Connolly, William E. 1983. *The Terms of Political Discourse.* 2d ed. Princeton, N.J.: Princeton University Press.

Connolly, William E. 1987. *Politics and Ambiguity.* Madison, Wis.: University of Wisconsin Press.

Converse, Philip E. 1964. "The Nature of Belief Systems in Mass Publics." In *Ideology and Discontent,* ed. David E. Apter. New York, N.Y.: Free Press.

Converse, Philip E. 1975. "Public Opinion and Voting Behavior." In *Handbook of Political Science: Nongovernmental Politics,* vol. 4, ed. Fred Greenstein and Nelson Polsby. Reading, Mass.: Addison-Wesley.

Council of State Governments. 1988. *The Book of the States, 1988–1989.* Lexington, Ky.

Crawford, Alan. 1980. *Thunder on the Right: The "New Right" and the Politics of Resentment.* New York, N.Y.: Pantheon Books.

Crosland, C. A. R. 1956. *The Future of Socialism.* London, England: Cape.

Delli Carpini, Michael X. 1986. *Stability and Change in American Politics: The Coming of Age of the Generation of the 1960s.* New York, N.Y.: New York University Press.

DeParle, Jason. 1992a. "Young Families Poorer, Study Finds." *New York Times,* April 15.

DeParle, Jason. 1992b. "Report, Delayed Months, Says Lowest Income Group Grew Sharply." *New York Times,* May 12.

DeParle, Jason. 1994. "Census Sees Falling Income and More Poor." *New York Times,* October 7.

Deutsch, Morton. 1975. "Equity, Equality, and Need: What Determines Which Value Will Be Used as the Basis of Distributive Justice." *Journal of Social Issues* 31:137–49.

Diggins, John P. 1973. *The American Left in the Twentieth Century.* New York, N.Y.: Harcourt Brace Jovanovich.

Downs, Anthony. 1957. *An Economic Theory of Democracy.* New York, N.Y.: Harper and Row.

Eatwell, Roger, and Noel O'Sullivan, eds. 1990. *The Nature of the Right: American and European Politics and Political Thought since 1789.* Boston, Mass.: Twayne.

Edinger, Lewis J., and Donald D. Searing. 1967. "Social Background in Elite Analysis: A Methodological Inquiry." *American Political Science Review* 61:428–45.

Edsall, Thomas Byrne, and Mary Edsall. 1992. *Chain Reaction: The Impact of Race, Rights, and Taxes on American Politics.* New York, N.Y.: W. W. Norton.

Ehrenhalt, Alan. 1991. *The United States of Ambition: Politicians, Power, and the Pursuit of Office.* New York, N.Y.: Times Books.

Eldersveld, Samuel J., Jan Kooiman, and Theo van der Tak. 1981. *Elite Images of Dutch Politics: Accommodation and Conflict.* Ann Arbor, Mich.: University of Michigan Press.

Entman, Robert M. 1978. Review of *Ideology and Politics,* by Martin Seliger. *Policy Sciences* 9:364–67.

Entman, Robert M. 1983. "The Impact of Ideology on Legislative Behavior and Public Policy in the States." *Journal of Politics* 45:163–82.

Erikson, Robert S., John P. McIver, and Gerald C. Wright, Jr. 1987. "State Political Culture and Public Opinion." *American Political Science Review* 81:797–813.

Esping-Andersen, Gøsta. 1985. *Politics against Markets: The Social Democratic Road to Power.* Princeton, N.J.: Princeton University Press.

Eulau, Heinz. 1976. "Elite Analysis and Democratic Theory: The Contribution of Harold D. Lasswell." In *Elite Recruitment in Democratic Politics,* ed. Heinz Eulau and Moshe Czudnowski. New York, N.Y.: John Wiley and Sons.

Ezorsky, Gertrude. 1991. *Racism and Justice: The Case for Affirmative Action.* Ithaca, N.Y.: Cornell University Press.

Farnsworth, Clyde H. 1988. "Republicans in Senate Fail to Block Plant-Closing Bill." *New York Times,* June 28.

Feldman, Stanley. 1988. "Structure and Consistency in Public Opinion: The Role of Core Beliefs and Values." *American Journal of Political Science* 32:416–40.

Fenno, Richard F., Jr. 1973. *Congressmen in Committees.* Boston, Mass.: Little, Brown.

Fenno, Richard F., Jr. 1977. "U.S. House Members in Their Constituencies: An Explanation." *American Political Science Review* 71:883–917.

Fenno, Richard F., Jr. 1978. *Home Style: House Members in Their Districts.* Boston, Mass.: Little, Brown.

Fenno, Richard F., Jr. 1986. "Observation, Context, and Sequence in the Study of Politics." *American Political Science Review* 80:3–16.

Fenno, Richard F., Jr. 1990. *Watching Politicians: Essays on Participant Observation.* Berkeley, Calif.: Institute of Governmental Studies Press.

Fink, David. 1988a. "O'Neill to Unveil Tax Plan." *Hartford Courant,* March 19.

Fink, David. 1988b. "Who Won Fight over Tax Relief?" *Hartford Courant,* May 8.

Fiorina, Morris P. 1974. *Representatives, Roll Calls, and Constituencies.* Lexington, Mass.: D.C. Heath.

Fishbein, Martin. 1967. "Attitude and the Prediction of Behavior." In *Readings in Attitude Theory and Measurement,* ed. Martin Fishbein. New York, N.Y.: John Wiley and Sons.

Fishkin, James S. 1984. *Beyond Subjective Morality: Ethical Reasoning and Political Philosophy.* New Haven, Conn.: Yale University Press.

Fiske, Edward B. 1991. "Racial Mix in Connecticut Rose in 80's." *New York Times,* February 15.

Flacks, Richard. 1967. "The Liberated Generation: An Exploration of the Roots of Student Protest." *Journal of Social Issues* 23:52–75.

Flacks, Richard. 1970. "Who Protests: The Social Bases of the Student Movement." In *Protest! Student Activism in America,* ed. Julian Foster and Durward Long. New York, N.Y.: William Morrow.

Folger, Robert. 1984. "Emerging Issues in the Social Psychology of Justice." In *The Sense of Injustice: Social Psychological Perspectives,* ed. Robert Folger. New York, N.Y.: Plenum Press.

Foner, Eric. 1984. "Why Is There No Socialism in the United States?" *History Workshop* 17:57–80.

Frahm, Robert A. 1988. "Reform Results Visible in State." *Hartford Courant,* April 26.

Frohock, Fred M., and David J. Sylvan. 1983. "Liberty, Economics, and Evidence." *Political Studies* 31:541–55.

Furby, Lita. 1986. "Psychology and Justice." In *Justice: Views from the Social Sciences,* ed. Ronald L. Cohen. New York, N.Y.: Plenum Press.

Galbraith, John Kenneth. 1958. *The Affluent Society.* Boston, Mass.: Houghton Mifflin.

Gallie, W. B. 1956a. "Essentially Contested Concepts." *Proceedings of the Aristotelian Society* 56:167–98.

Gallie, W. B. 1956b. "Liberal Morality and Socialist Morality." In *Philosophy, Politics and Society,* ed. Peter Laslett. Oxford, England: Basil Blackwell.

Garand, James C. 1991. "Electoral Marginality in State Legislative Elections, 1968–86." *Legislative Studies Quarterly* 16:7–28.

Gaventa, John. 1980. *Power and Powerlessness: Quiescence and Rebellion in an Appalachian Valley.* Urbana, Ill.: University of Illinois Press.

Geertz, Clifford. 1964. "Ideology as a Cultural System." In *Ideology and Discontent,* ed. David Apter. New York, N.Y.: Free Press.

Gilligan, Carol. 1982. *In a Different Voice.* Cambridge, Mass.: Harvard University Press.

Ginsburg, Carl. 1989. *Race and Media.* New York, N.Y.: Institute for Media Analysis.

Githens, Marianne, and Jewel Prestage. 1978. "Women State Legislators: Styles and Priorities." *Policy Studies Journal* 7:264–70.

Glazer, Nathan. 1988. "The Affirmative Action Stalemate." *The Public Interest* 90:99–115.

Goleman, Daniel. 1991. "New Way to Battle Bias: Fight Acts, Not Feelings." *New York Times,* July 16.

Goodwyn, Lawrence. 1978. *The Populist Moment: A Short History of the Agrarian Revolt in America.* London, England: Oxford University Press.

Gordon, Raymond L. 1969. *Interviewing: Strategy, Techniques, and Tactics.* Homewood, Ill.: The Dorsey Press.

Gorman, Robert A. 1989. *Yankee Red: Nonorthodox Marxism in Liberal America.* New York, N.Y.: Praeger.

Grafstein, Robert. 1988. "A Realist Foundation for Essentially Contested Political Concepts." *Western Political Quarterly* 41:9–28.

Gray, John. 1986. *Hayek on Liberty.* 2d ed. New York, N.Y.: Basil Blackwell.

Greenstein, Fred I. 1969. *Personality and Politics.* Chicago, Ill.: Markham.

Greenstein, Fred I. 1971. "The Study of Personality and Politics: Overall Considerations." In *A Source Book for the Study of Personality and Politics,* ed. Fred I. Greenstein and Michael Lerner. Chicago, Ill.: Markham.

Greenstone, J. David. 1986. "Political Culture and American Political Development: Liberty, Union, and the Liberal Bipolarity." *Studies in American Political Development* 1:1–49.

Greer, Colin, and Barry Goldberg. 1986. "Populism, Ethnicity, and Public Policy." In *The New Populism: The Politics of Empowerment,* ed. Harry C. Boyte and Frank Riessman. Philadelphia, Penn.: Temple University Press.

Gutmann, Amy. 1982. "Moral Philosophy and Political Problems." *Political Theory* 10:33–47.

Habermas, Jürgen. 1975. *Legitimation Crisis*. Trans. Thomas McCarthy. Boston, Mass.: Beacon Press.

Hacker, Andrew. 1992. *Two Nations: Black and White, Separate, Hostile, Unequal*. New York, N.Y.: Charles Scribner's Sons.

Hadari, Saguiv A. 1988. "Value Trade-off." *Journal of Politics* 50:655–76.

Hall, Richard L. 1987. "Participation and Purpose in Committee Decision Making." *American Political Science Review* 81:105–27.

Hall, Richard L., and Colleen M. Heflin. 1995. "The Importance of Color in Congress." Ann Arbor, Mich.: Unpublished manuscript.

Harrington, Michael. 1970. *Socialism*. New York, N.Y.: Bantam.

Harris, Fred R., and Roger W. Wilkins, eds. 1988. *Quiet Riots: Race and Poverty in the United States*. New York, N.Y.: Pantheon Books.

Hartz, Louis. 1955. *The Liberal Tradition in America*. New York, N.Y.: Harcourt Brace Jovanovich.

Hayden, Tom. 1988. *Reunion: A Memoir*. New York, N.Y.: Random House.

Hayek, Friedrich A. 1960. *The Constitution of Liberty*. Chicago, Ill.: University of Chicago Press.

Himmelstein, Jerome L. 1989. *To the Right: The Transformation of American Conservatism*. Berkeley, Calif.: University of California Press.

Hochschild, Jennifer L. 1981. *What's Fair? American Beliefs about Distributive Justice*. Cambridge, Mass.: Harvard University Press.

Hochschild, Jennifer L. 1986. "Dimensions of Liberal Self-Satisfaction: Civil Liberties, Liberal Theory, and Elite-Mass Differences." *Ethics* 96:386–99.

Hochschild, Jennifer L. 1988. "The Double-Edged Sword of Equal Opportunity." In *Power, Inequality, and Democratic Politics: Essays in Honor of Robert A. Dahl*, ed. Ian Shapiro and Grant Reeher. Boulder, Colo.: Westview Press.

Hodgkinson, Harold L. 1988. "Connecticut: The State and Its Educational System." Washington, D.C.: Institute for Educational Leadership.

Hofferbert, Richard I. 1974. *The Study of Public Policy*. New York, N.Y.: Bobbs-Merrill.

Hofstadter, Richard. 1948. *The American Political Tradition*. New York, N.Y.: Vintage Books.

Hofstadter, Richard. 1955. *The Age of Reform: From Bryan to F. D. R.* New York, N.Y.: Vintage Books.

Hofstadter, Richard. 1963. "Introduction: The Meaning of the Progressive Movement." In *The Progressive Movement 1900–1915*, ed. Richard Hofstadter. Englewood Cliffs, N.J.: Prentice-Hall.

Holmes, Steven A. 1995. "Income Gap Persists for Blacks and Whites." *New York Times*, February 23.

Huckfeldt, Robert, and Carol Weitzel Kohfeld. 1989. *Race and the Decline of Class in American Politics*. Champaign, Ill.: University of Illinois Press.

Huntington, Samuel P. 1957. "Conservatism as an Ideology." *American Political Science Review* 51:454–73.

Huntington, Samuel P. 1981. *American Politics: The Promise of Disharmony*. Cambridge, Mass.: Harvard University Press.

Hurwitz, Jon. 1986. "Issue Perception and Legislative Decision Making: An Application of Social Judgment Theory." *American Politics Quarterly* 14:150–85.

Inglehart, Ronald. 1977. *The Silent Revolution: Changing Values and Political Styles among Western Publics.* Princeton, N.J.: Princeton University Press.

Inglehart, Ronald. 1990. *Culture Shift in Advanced Industrial Society.* Princeton, N.J.: Princeton University Press.

Institute for Social Inquiry. 1986–88. *Connecticut Poll* (various polls). Storrs, Conn.: University of Connecticut.

Irving, R. E. M. 1979. *The Christian Democratic Parties of Western Europe.* London, England: George Allen and Unwin.

Isserman, Maurice. 1987. *If I Had a Hammer . . . The Death of the Old Left and the Birth of the New Left.* New York, N.Y.: Basic Books.

Jackman, Mary R., and Robert W. Jackman. 1983. *Class Awareness in the United States.* Berkeley, Calif.: University of California Press.

Jackson, John E. 1974. *Constituencies and Leaders in Congress.* Cambridge, Mass.: Harvard University Press.

Jackson, John S. III, Barbara Leavitt Brown, and David Bositis. 1982. "Herbert McClosky and Friends Revisited: Party Elites Compared to the Mass Public." *American Politics Quarterly* 10:158–80.

Jacobson, Gary C. 1987. *The Politics of Congressional Elections.* 2d ed. Glenview, Ill.: Scott, Foresman and Co.

Jewell, Malcolm E. 1982. *Representation in State Legislatures.* Lexington, Ky.: University of Kentucky Press.

Jewell, Malcolm E., and Samuel C. Patterson. 1977. *The Legislative Process in the United States.* 3d ed. New York, N.Y.: Random House.

Johnson, Julie. 1989. "Childhood Is Not Safe, Congress Study Warns." *New York Times,* October 2.

Johnson, Kirk. 1989a. "Region's Budgets: The 3 States Pursue Different Routes to Overcome Their Financial Woes." *New York Times,* February 10.

Johnson, Kirk. 1989b. "Unseen Levies Confound the Issue of Tax Burden." *New York Times,* March 12 (Connecticut Weekly section).

Johnson, Kirk. 1991a. "Weicker Proposes an Income Tax in Fiscal Overhaul for Connecticut." *New York Times,* February 14.

Johnson, Kirk. 1991b. "Weicker Says New Budget Is Compromise." *New York Times,* June 12.

Johnson, Kirk. 1991c. "Budget Is Passed for Connecticut with Income Tax." *New York Times,* August 23.

Johnson, Kirk. 1992. "Tax Revision a Priority, Says New Speaker." *New York Times,* November 7.

Johnson, Lyndon Baines. 1971. *The Vantage Point: Perspectives of the Presidency 1963–1969.* New York, N.Y.: Holt, Rinehart and Winston.

Judson, George. 1994. "State's Quality of Life Has Dropped Sharply in Last 10 Years, a Study Finds." *New York Times,* December 5.

Kanter, Donald L., and Philip H. Mirvis. 1989. *The Cynical Americans: Living and Working in an Age of Discontent and Disillusion.* San Francisco, Calif.: Jossey-Bass.

Kaplan, Abraham. 1964. *The Conduct of Inquiry: Methodology for Behavioral Science.* San Francisco, Calif.: Chandler.

Kathlene, Lyn. 1989. "Uncovering the Political Impacts of Gender: An Exploratory Study." *Western Political Quarterly* 42:397–421.

Kelman, Steven. 1987. *Making Public Policy: A Hopeful View of American Government.* New York, N.Y.: Basic Books.

Key, V. O. 1961. *Public Opinion and American Democracy.* New York, N.Y.: Knopf.

Kilborn, Peter T. 1995. "Up from Welfare: It's Harder and Harder." *New York Times,* April 10.

Kim, Chong Lim, Justin Green, and Samuel Patterson. 1976. "Partisanship in the Recruitment and Performance of American State Legislators." In *Elite Recruitment in Democratic Polities,* ed. Heinz Eulau and Moshe Czudnowski. New York, N.Y.: John Wiley and Sons.

Kinder, Donald R. 1983. "Diversity and Complexity in American Public Opinion." In *Political Science: The State of the Discipline,* ed. Ada Finifter. Washington, D.C.: American Political Science Association.

Kinder, Donald R., and D. Roderick Kiewiet. 1981. "Sociotropic Politics: The American Case." *British Journal of Political Science* 11:129–61.

King, Anthony. 1973. "Ideas, Institutions and the Policies of Governments: A Comparative Analysis, Parts I–III." *British Journal of Political Science* 3:291–313, 409–23.

Kingdon, John W. 1984. *Agendas, Alternatives, and Public Policies.* Boston, Mass.: Little, Brown.

Kingdon, John W. 1989. *Congressmen's Voting Decisions.* 3d ed. Ann Arbor, Mich.: University of Michigan Press.

Kluegel, James, and Eliot Smith. 1986. *Beliefs about Inequality: Americans' Views of What Is and What Ought To Be.* New York, N.Y.: Aldine de Gruyter.

Kolbert, Elizabeth. 1989. "Lawmaking in States Evolves Into Full-Time Job." *New York Times,* June 4.

Kramer, Gerald H. 1983. "The Ecological Fallacy Revisited: Aggregate versus Individual-Level Findings on Economics and Elections, and Sociotropic Voting." *American Political Science Review* 77:92–107.

Kristol, Irving. 1978. *Two Cheers for Capitalism.* New York, N.Y.: Basic Books.

Kristol, Irving. 1983. *Reflections of a Neoconservative.* New York, N.Y.: Basic Books.

Kritzer, Herbert M. 1978. "Ideology and American Political Elites." *Public Opinion Quarterly* 42:484–502.

Lamb, Karl A. 1982. *The Guardians: Leadership Values and the American Tradition.* New York, N.Y.: W. W. Norton.

Lane, Robert E. 1959. *Political Life: Why People Get Involved in Politics.* New York, N.Y.: Free Press.

Lane, Robert E. 1962. *Political Ideology: Why the Common Man Believes What He Does.* New York, N.Y.: Free Press.

Lane, Robert E. 1969. *Political Thinking and Consciousness: The Private Life of the Political Mind.* Chicago, Ill.: Markham.

Lane, Robert E. 1972. *Political Man.* New York, N.Y.: Free Press.

Lane, Robert E. 1973. "Patterns of Political Belief." In *Handbook of Political Psychology,* ed. Jeanne N. Knutson. San Francisco, Calif.: Jossey-Bass.

Larson, Stephanie Greco. 1990. "Information and Learning in a Congressional District: A Social Experiment." *American Journal of Political Science* 34:1102–18.

Lasswell, Harold D. 1936. *Politics: Who Gets What, When, How.* New York, N.Y.: Whittlesey House.

Lasswell, Harold D. 1948. *Power and Personality.* New York, N.Y.: Norton.

Lasswell, Harold D. [1930, 1948] 1960. *Psychopathology and Politics.* New York, N.Y.: Viking.

Lau, Richard R., and David O. Sears. 1986. "Social Cognition and Political Cognition: The Past, the Present, and the Future." In *Political Cognition,* ed. Richard Lau and David Sears. Hillsdale, N.J.: Lawrence Erlbaum Associates.

Lau, Richard R., Richard A. Smith, and Susan T. Fiske. 1991. "Political Beliefs, Policy Interpretations, and Political Persuasion." *Journal of Politics* 53:644–75.

Levy, Frank. 1988. *Dollars and Dreams: The Changing American Income Distribution.* New York, N.Y.: W. W. Norton.

Libov, Charlotte. 1988. "Resistance Grows on Teacher Pay." *New York Times,* July 3.

Lieberman, Joseph I. 1980. "Guidelines for Initiating Legislation and Understanding Its Scope." In *Perspectives of a State Legislature.* 2d ed., ed. Clyde D. McKee, Jr. Hartford, Conn.: Trinity College.

Lipset, Seymour Martin. 1988. "American Exceptionalism." Unpublished manuscript.

Lipset, Seymour Martin, and William Schneider. 1983. *The Confidence Gap: Business, Labor, and Government in the Public Mind.* New York, N.Y.: Free Press.

Lockard, Duane. 1959a. *New England State Politics.* Princeton, N.J.: Princeton University Press.

Lockard, Duane. 1959b. "The Tribulations of a State Senator." In *Legislative Behavior: A Reader in Theory and Research,* ed. John C. Wahlke and Heinz Eulau. Glencoe, Ill.: Free Press.

Lowery, David. 1987. "The Distribution of Tax Burdens in the American States: The Determinants of Fiscal Incidence." *Western Political Quarterly* 40:137–58.

Lukes, Steven. 1974. *Power: A Radical View.* London, England: Macmillan.

MacCallum, Gerald C., Jr. 1972. "Negative and Positive Freedom." In *Philosophy, Politics and Society, Fourth Series,* ed. Peter Laslett, W. G. Runciman, and Quentin Skinner. Oxford, England: Blackwell.

McClosky, Herbert. 1964. "Consensus and Ideology in American Politics." *American Political Science Review* 58:361–82.

McClosky, Herbert, and Alida Brill. 1983. *Dimensions of Tolerance: What Americans Believe about Civil Liberties.* New York, N.Y.: Russell Sage Foundation.

McClosky, Herbert, Paul J. Hoffmann, and Rosemary O'Hara. 1960. "Issue Conflict and Consensus among Party Leaders and Followers." *American Political Science Review* 54:406–27.

McClosky, Herbert, and John Zaller. 1984. *The American Ethos: Public Attitudes toward Capitalism and Democracy.* Cambridge, Mass.: Harvard University Press.

MacIntyre, Alasdair. 1974. "The Essential Contestability of Some Social Concepts." *Ethics* 84:1–9.

MacIntyre, Alasdair. 1977. "Epistemological Crises, Dramatic Narrative and the Philosophy of Science." *The Monist* 60:453–72.

MacIntyre, Alasdair. 1984. *After Virtue.* 2d ed. Notre Dame, Ind.: University of Notre Dame Press.

MacIntyre, Alasdair. 1988. *Whose Justice? Which Rationality?* Notre Dame, Ind.: University of Notre Dame Press.

MacIntyre, Alasdair. 1990. *Three Rival Versions of Moral Enquiry: Encyclopaedia, Genealogy, and Tradition.* Notre Dame, Ind.: University of Notre Dame Press.

Macpherson, C. B. 1973. "Berlin's Division of Liberty." In *Democratic Theory: Essays in Retrieval.* Oxford, England: Oxford University Press.

Mandler, Jean Matter. 1984. *Stories, Scripts, and Scenes: Aspects of Schema Theory.* Hillsdale, N.J.: Lawrence Erlbaum Associates.

Matthews, Donald R. 1985. "Legislative Recruitment and Legislative Careers." In *Handbook of Legislative Research,* ed. Gerhard Loewenburg, Samuel C. Patterson, and Malcolm E. Jewell. Cambridge, Mass.: Harvard University Press.

Mayhew, David R. 1974. *Congress: The Electoral Connection.* New Haven, Conn.: Yale University Press.

Mayhew, David R. 1986. *Placing Parties in American Politics.* Princeton, N.J.: Princeton University Press.

Mayhew, David R. 1991. *Divided We Govern: Party Control, Lawmaking, and Investigations, 1946–1990.* New Haven, Conn.: Yale University Press.

Merton, Robert K., Marjorie Fiske, and Patricia L. Kendall. 1956. *The Focused Interview.* Glencoe, Ill.: Free Press.

Midgley, Mary. 1991. *Can't We Make Moral Judgements?* New York, N.Y.: St. Martin's Press.

Milbrath, Lester, and M. L. Goel. 1977. *Political Participation.* 2d ed. Chicago, Ill.: Rand McNally.

Miller, David. 1976. *Social Justice.* Oxford, England: Oxford University Press.

Miller, James. 1987. *Democracy Is in the Streets.* New York, N.Y.: Simon and Schuster.

Miller, Mike. 1986. "Populist Promises and Problems." In *The New Populism: The Politics of Empowerment,* ed. Harry C. Boyte and Frank Riessman. Philadelphia, Penn.: Temple University Press.

Mueller, Dennis C. 1979. *Public Choice.* Cambridge, England: Cambridge University Press.

Muir, William K., Jr. 1982. *Legislature: California's School for Politics.* Chicago, Ill.: University of Chicago Press.

Murray, Charles. 1984. *Losing Ground: American Social Policy 1950–1980.* New York, N.Y.: Basic Books.

Nasar, Sylvia. 1992a. "Even Among the Well-Off, the Richest Get Richer." *New York Times,* March 5.

Nasar, Sylvia. 1992b. "Fed Gives New Evidence of 80s Gains by Richest." *New York Times,* April 21.

Nasar, Sylvia. 1992c. "However You Slice the Data the Richest Did Get Richer." *New York Times,* May 11.

Nasar, Sylvia. 1992d. "Who Paid the Most Taxes in the 80s? The Superrich." *New York Times,* May 31.

Nice, David C. 1987. "State-Financed Property Tax Relief to Individuals: A Research Note." *Western Political Quarterly* 40:179–85.

Noelle-Neumann, Elisabeth. 1986. *The Spiral of Silence: Public Opinion—Our Social Skin.* Chicago, Ill.: University of Chicago Press.

Nozick, Robert. 1974. *Anarchy, State, and Utopia.* New York, N.Y.: Basic Books.

Office of Fiscal Analysis, Connecticut General Assembly. 1988a. *A History of Connecticut Taxes, Budget and Economic Data, Fiscal Years 1960–1987.* Hartford, Conn.

Office of Fiscal Analysis, Connecticut General Assembly. 1988b. *Connecticut Revenue, Budget and Economic Data, Fiscal Years 1969–1988.* Hartford, Conn.

Office of Fiscal Analysis, Connecticut General Assembly. 1988c. *The State Budget for the 1988–1989 Fiscal Year.* Hartford, Conn.

Office of Legislative Research, Connecticut General Assembly. 1991. "States Slash General Assistance." *OLReporter* 49 (November). Hartford, Conn.

Office of Legislative Research, Connecticut General Assembly. 1992. "Northeast Becoming More Rural." *OLReporter* 52 (February). Hartford, Conn.

Ogle, David. 1990. "The General Assembly, 1969–1989: Two Decades of Transformation." *OLReporter* 29 (January). Hartford, Conn.: Office of Legislative Research, Connecticut General Assembly.

Okun, Arthur. 1975. *Equality and Efficiency: The Big Tradeoff.* Washington, D.C.: The Brookings Institution.

Orwell, George. [1937] 1958. *The Road to Wigan Pier.* New York, N.Y.: Harcourt Brace Jovanovich.

Parker, Glenn R., and Roger H. Davidson. 1979. "Why Do Americans Love Their Congressmen So Much More Than Their Congress?" *Legislative Studies Quarterly* 4:53–62.

Passell, Peter. 1992. "The Wage Gap: Sins of Omission." *New York Times,* May 27.

Paterson, William E., and Alastair H. Thomas, eds. 1986. *The Future of Social Democracy: Problems and Prospects of Social Democratic Parties in Western Europe.* Oxford, England: Oxford University Press.

Patterson, James. 1981. *America's Struggle against Poverty 1900–1980.* Cambridge, Mass.: Harvard University Press.

Pear, Robert. 1991. "Rich Got Richer in 80's; Others Held Even." *New York Times,* January 11.

Peele, Gillian. 1984. *Revival and Reaction: The Right in Contemporary America.* Oxford, England: Oxford University Press.

Pennington, Nancy, and Reid Hastie. 1988. "Explanation-Based Decision Making: Effects of Memory Structure on Judgment." *Journal of Experimental Psychology* 14:521–33.

Pennington, Nancy, and Reid Hastie. 1991. "A Cognitive Theory of Juror Decision Making: The Story Model." *Cardozo Law Review* 13:519–57.

Phillips, Kevin P. 1982. *Post-Conservative America: People, Politics, and Ideology in a Time of Crisis.* New York, N.Y.: Random House.

Phillips, Kevin P. 1990. *The Politics of Rich and Poor: Wealth and the American Electorate in the Reagan Aftermath.* New York, N.Y.: Random House.

Piven, Frances Fox, and Richard A. Cloward. 1971. *Regulating the Poor: The Functions of Public Welfare.* New York, N.Y.: Random House.

Poole, Keith T. 1985. "Ideology, Party, and Voting in the U.S. Congress, 1959–1980." *American Political Science Review* 79:373–99.

Poole, Keith T. 1988. "Recent Developments in Analytical Models of Voting in the U.S. Congress." *Legislative Studies Quarterly* 13:117–33.

Poole, Keith T. 1991. "Congressional Attitudes and Voting Behavior: An Examination of Support for Social Welfare." *Legislative Studies Quarterly* 16:375–92.

Prewitt, Kenneth, and William Nowlin. 1969. "Political Ambitions and the Behavior of Incumbent Politicians." *Western Political Quarterly* 22:298–308.

Price Waterhouse. 1988. "Property Assessment and Property Tax Relief in Connecticut." Report submitted to the Property Tax Assessment Task Force, Connecticut General Assembly. Washington, D.C.

Putnam, Robert D. 1973. *The Beliefs of Politicians: Ideology, Conflict, and Democracy in Britain and Italy.* New Haven, Conn.: Yale University Press.

Putnam, Robert D. 1976. *The Comparative Study of Political Elites.* Englewood Cliffs, N.J.: Prentice-Hall.

Rae, Douglas W. 1988. "Knowing Power: A Working Paper." In *Power, Inequality, and Democratic Politics: Essays in Honor of Robert A. Dahl,* ed. Ian Shapiro and Grant Reeher. Boulder, Colo.: Westview Press.

Rawls, John. 1971. *A Theory of Justice.* Cambridge, Mass.: Harvard University Press.

Reich, Robert B. 1987. *Tales of a New America.* New York, N.Y.: Times Books.

Reich, Robert B., ed. 1988. *The Power of Public Ideas.* Cambridge, Mass.: Ballinger Press.

Reik, Theodor. [1948] 1972. *Listening with the Third Ear: The Inner Experience of a Psychoanalyst.* New York, N.Y.: Arena Books.

Reinarman, Craig. 1987. *American States of Mind: Political Beliefs and Behavior among Private and Public Workers.* New Haven, Conn.: Yale University Press.

Robinson, James. 1988. "100 to Lose Jobs in Plant Closing in Manchester." *Hartford Courant,* April 27.

Rokeach, Milton. 1973. *The Nature of Human Values.* New York, N.Y.: Free Press.

Rorty, Richard. 1991. *Objectivity, Relativism, and Truth.* New York, N.Y.: Cambridge University Press.

Rosenberg, Shawn W. 1988. *Reason, Ideology and Politics.* Cambridge, England: Polity Press.

Rosenthal, Alan. 1981. *Legislative Life: People, Politics, and Performance in the States.* New York, N.Y.: Harper and Row.

Rosenthal, Alan. 1988. "State Legislatures—Where It's At." *The Political Science Teacher* 1:1–5.

Rosenthal, Alan. 1989. "The Legislative Institution: Transformed and at Risk." In *The State of the States,* ed. Carl E. Van Horn. Washington, D.C.: Congressional Quarterly Press.

Rosenthal, Alan. 1991. Review of *The Colorado General Assembly,* by John Straaver. *American Political Science Review* 85:656.

Rossiter, Clinton. 1960. *Parties and Politics in America.* New York, N.Y.: Signet.

Rothberg, David L. 1981. *Insecurity and Success in Organizational Life.* New York, N.Y.: Praeger.

Rothenberg, Randall. 1984. *The Neoliberals: Creating the New American Politics.* New York, N.Y.: Simon and Schuster.

Rousseau, Jean-Jacques. [1754] 1964. *Discourse on the Origin and Foundations of*

Inequality among Men. In *The First and Second Discourses,* ed. Roger D. Masters, trans. Roger D. and Judith R. Masters. New York, N.Y.: St. Martin's Press.

Rowland, Barbara M. 1988. "The Impact of Contemporary Conservatism on Modern Political Thought." *Western Political Quarterly* 41:401–12.

Rutherford, Brent M. 1971. "Psychopathology, Decision-Making, and Political Involvement." In *A Source Book for the Study of Personality and Politics,* ed. Fred I. Greenstein and Michael Lerner. Chicago, Ill.: Markham.

Saint-Germain, Michelle. 1989. "Does Their Difference Make a Difference? The Impact of Women on Public Policy in the Arizona Legislature." *Social Science Quarterly* 70:956–68.

Schattschneider, E. E. 1942. *Party Government.* New York, N.Y.: Farrar and Rinehart.

Schier, Steven E. 1992. *A Decade of Deficits: Congressional Thought and Fiscal Action.* Albany, N.Y.: State University of New York Press.

Schiller, Bradley R. 1989. *The Economics of Poverty and Discrimination.* 5th ed. Englewood Cliffs, N.J.: Prentice Hall.

Schlesinger, Arthur M., Jr. 1986. "The Cycles of American Politics." In *The Cycles of American History.* Boston, Mass.: Houghton Mifflin Co.

Schlozman, Kay Lehman, and Sidney Verba. 1979. *Injury to Insult: Unemployment, Class, and Political Response.* Cambridge, Mass.: Harvard University Press.

Schneider, Jerrold. 1979. *Ideological Coalitions in Congress.* Westport, Conn.: Greenwood Press.

Schuman, Howard, and Stanley Presser. 1981. *Questions and Answers in Attitude Surveys: Experiments on Question Form, Wording, and Context.* New York, N.Y.: Academic Press.

Schwarz, John E. 1983. *America's Hidden Success: A Reassessment of Twenty Years of Public Policy.* New York, N.Y.: Norton.

Seliger, Martin. 1976. *Ideology and Politics.* New York, N.Y.: Free Press.

Seligman, Adam. 1987. "The American System of Stratification: Some Notes towards Understanding Its Symbolic and Institutional Concomitants." In S. N. Eisenstadt, L. Roniger, and A. Seligman, *Centre Formation, Protest Movements and Class Structure in Europe and the United States.* London, England: Frances Pinter.

Shapiro, Ian. 1986. *The Evolution of Rights in Liberal Theory.* Cambridge, England: Cambridge University Press.

Shapiro, Ian. 1990. *Political Criticism.* Berkeley, Calif.: University of California Press.

Smallwood, Frank. 1976. *Free and Independent.* Brattleboro, Vt.: Stephen Greene Press.

Smith, Rogers M. 1993. "Beyond Tocqueville, Myrdal, and Hartz: The Multiple Traditions in America." *American Political Science Review* 87:549–66.

Sniderman, Paul M. 1975. *Personality and Democratic Politics.* Berkeley, Calif.: University of California Press.

Sokolow, Alvin D. 1989. "Legislators without Ambition: Why Small-Town Citizens Seek Public Office." *State and Local Government Review* 21:23–29.

Sombart, Werner. 1976. *Why Is There No Socialism in the United States?* Trans. Patricia M. Hocking and C. T. Husbands. White Plains, N.Y.: M. E. Sharpe.

Songer, Donald R., Sonja G. Dillon, Darla W. Kite, Patricia E. Jameson, James M. Underwood, and William D. Underwood. 1986. "The Influence of Issues on

Choice of Voting Cues Utilized by State Legislators." *Western Political Quarterly* 39:118–25.

Sowell, Thomas. 1987. *A Conflict of Visions*. New York, N.Y.: William Morrow.

Squire, Peverill. 1992. "Legislative Professionalization and Membership Diversity in State Legislatures." *Legislative Studies Quarterly* 17:69–79.

"State Spending Slights Basic Needs." 1989. *New Haven Register,* February 6 (op-ed.).

"Study Finds Gains for Black Middle Class." 1991. *New York Times,* August 10.

Sumner, William Graham. [1883] 1982. *What the Social Classes Owe to Each Other.* Caldwell, Idaho: Caxton Printers.

Swanson, Wayne R. 1984. *Lawmaking in Connecticut: The General Assembly.* New London, Conn.: Connecticut College.

Tavris, Carol. 1992. *The Mismeasure of Woman.* New York, N.Y.: Simon and Schuster.

Thomas, Sue, and Susan Welch. 1991. "The Impact of Gender on Activities and Priorities of State Legislators." *Western Political Quarterly* 44:445–56.

Thompson, Grahame. 1990. *The Political Economy of the New Right.* Boston, Mass.: Twayne.

Tindall, George Brown, ed. 1976. *A Populist Reader: Selections from the Works of American Populist Leaders.* Gloucester, Mass.: Peter Smith.

Uchitelle, Louis. 1990a. "Threshold of Pain: Will All this Tax Talk Lead to New Taxes?" *New York Times,* March 25.

Uchitelle, Louis. 1990b. "Tough Choices for Connecticut as Boom Ends." *New York Times,* December 13.

U.S. Bureau of the Census. 1981, 1988, 1989, 1990. *Statistical Abstract of the United States.* Washington, D.C.

U.S. Bureau of the Census. 1982. *1980 Census of Population: Characteristics of the Population: Connecticut.* Washington, D.C.

U.S. Bureau of Economic Analysis. 1984. *State Personal Income, 1929–1982.* Washington, D.C.

Uslaner, Eric M., and Ronald E. Weber. 1975. "The 'Politics' of Redistribution: Towards a Model of the Policy-Making Process in the American States." *American Politics Quarterly* 3:130–70.

Uslaner, Eric M., and Ronald E. Weber. 1977. *Patterns of Decision Making in State Legislatures.* New York, N.Y.: Praeger.

Vanneman, Reeve, and Lynn Weber Cannon. 1987. *The American Perception of Class.* Philadelphia, Penn.: Temple University Press.

Verba, Sidney, Steven Kelman, Gary R. Orren, Ichiro Miyake, Joji Watanaki, Ikuo Kabashima, and G. Donald Ferree, Jr. 1987. *Elites and the Idea of Equality: A Comparison of Japan, Sweden, and the United States.* Cambridge, Mass.: Harvard University Press.

Verba, Sidney, and Gary R. Orren. 1985. *Equality in America: The View from the Top.* Cambridge, Mass.: Harvard University Press.

von Beyme, Klaus. 1985. *Political Parties in Western Democracies.* Trans. Eileen Martin. Aldershot, England: Gower.

Wahlke, John C., Heinz Eulau, William Buchanan, and LeRoy C. Ferguson. 1962. *The Legislative System.* New York, N.Y.: John Wiley and Sons.

Waligorski, Conrad P. 1990. *The Political Theory of Conservative Economists.* Lawrence, Kans.: University Press of Kansas.

Walzer, Michael. 1983. *Spheres of Justice: A Defense of Pluralism and Equality.* New York, N.Y.: Basic Books.

Walzer, Michael. 1987. *Interpretation and Social Criticism.* Cambridge, Mass.: Harvard University Press.

Weber, Ronald E., Harvey J. Tucker, and Paul Brace. 1991. "Vanishing Marginals in State Legislative Elections." *Legislative Studies Quarterly* 16:29–48.

West, Darrell M. 1988. "Activists and Economic Policymaking in Congress." *American Journal of Political Science* 32:662–80.

Wildavsky, Aaron. 1987. "Choosing Preferences by Constructing Institutions: A Cultural Theory of Preference Formation." *American Political Science Review* 81:3–21.

Wildavsky, Aaron. 1990. "A World of Difference—The Public Philosophies and Political Behaviors of Rival American Cultures." In *The New American Political System, Second Version,* ed. Anthony King. Washington, D.C.: American Enterprise Institute.

Williams, Robin M., Jr. 1979. "Change and Stability in Values and Value Systems: A Sociological Perspective." In *Understanding Human Values,* ed. Milton Rokeach. New York, N.Y.: Free Press.

Wilson, William Julius. 1987. *The Truly Disadvantaged: The Inner City, the Underclass, and Public Policy.* Chicago, Ill.: University of Chicago Press.

Wines, Michael. 1994. "Taxpayers Are Angry. They're Expensive, Too." *New York Times,* November 20.

Winters, Richard. 1980. "Political Choice and Expenditure Change in New Hampshire and Vermont." *Polity* 12:598–621.

Wolfe, Alan. 1978. "Review Article: Has Social Democracy a Future?" *Comparative Politics* 11:100–125.

Wright, Gerald, C., Jr., Robert S. Erikson, and John P. McIver. 1987. "Public Opinion and Policy Liberalism in the American States." *American Journal of Political Science* 31:980–1001.

Young, Nigel. 1977. *An Infantile Disorder? The Crisis and Decline of the New Left.* London, England: Routledge and Kegan Paul.

Index

Aberbach, Joel, 28
AFL-CIO, 205
Aid to Families with Dependent Children (AFDC), 165
Ambition, 185, 223, 269. *See also* Narrative
American "exceptionalism." *See* Beliefs
American Voter, The, 16, 293n.6
Appropriations Committee, 212, 215
Aristotle, 5, 296n.28

Barber, James David, 20, 294n.10, 300n.32, 305n.14
Bargaining. *See* State legislators
Beer, Samuel, 86
Beliefs
  aging effect on, 301n.35 (*see also* Narrative)
  ambivalence in, 35 (*see also* Narrative)
  American "exceptionalism" in, 4, 12, 38, 43, 76, 241–43, 256–58, 291n.6, 297n.2
  and behavior, 8, 11, 23–30, 40, 163–64, 170, 182, 187, 196, 203–39, 243 (*see also* Narrative, critic's; State legislators)
  cognitive strategies in, 43, 107, 238–39
  constraint in, 16–17
  deep, 15, 292n.22
  early socialization and, 22–23, 35, 251, 254–55 (*see also* Narrative)
  empirical assumptions in, 32, 34, 35, 250–55

  filtering effect of, 23–24, 29–31, 163, 238–39, 255
  and gender, 35, 43, 116–17, 129, 140, 142, 149, 297n.38
  about human nature, 34, 87, 251–53, 258, 302n.7 (*see also* Narrative)
  later socialization and, 22 (*see also* Narrative)
  learning model of, 5
  leftism in, 12, 84–89, 257–58
  and legislative voting behavior, 27–28, 205–6 (*see also* Narrative)
  and party attachment, 41, 81, 95, 119, 129 (*see also* Narrative)
  psychopathology model of, 20
  self-interest and, 20–21, 29, 247, 258
  and social science, 255
  sources of, 19–23
  "spiral of silence" in, 243
  systems of, 16–17
  See also Narrative
Bills
  introduced, 208
  screening process, 216
  skeleton bill system, 209
  survival, 209
  See also under specific bills
Bond, Julian, 98
Boyte, Harry, 84
Bruner, Jerome, 31–32, 123, 294n.7, 296n.31

Calvin, John, 125
Care, Norman, 248
Christian democracy, 89
Civic republicanism, 94, 242

333

Habermas, Jürgen, 243
Hadari, Saguiv, 311n.5
Hamlet, 275
Harrington, Michael, 257
Hart, Gary, 160
Hartz, Louis, 242, 258
Hastie, Reid, 312n.15
Hayden, Tom, 86
Hayek, Friedrich, 302n.3, 304n.1
Heilbroner, Robert, 296n.31
Hochschild, Jennifer, 8, 39, 40, 77, 256,
  297nn. 5, 38
Horton v. Meskill, 164
Human nature. *See* Beliefs; Narrative
Hume, David, 245
Huntington, Samuel, 120–21, 242
Hurwitz, Jon, 30

Ideology, 11–12, 33, 197, 241–44
  and dogmatism, 26–27, 295n.21
  end of ideology thesis, 241
  in a legislature, 26–28
  See also Beliefs; Narrative
Income distribution
  and race, 3, 291n.4,
  trends in, 2–3
  See also Narrative
Income tax, 6–7, 234, 292nn. 12, 14,
  314n.18
Incrementalism, 208
Individualism, 3–4, 38–39, 43, 241–42,
  302n.7. *See also* Narrative
Interest groups. *See* Lobbying
Interstate competition, 194, 197–99,
  235–36
Interviews. *See* Methods

Jackson, Jesse, 98, 99, 136
Jackson, John, 24
Jewell, Malcolm, 239, 292n.11, 308n.9
Johnson, Lyndon, 1

Kant, Immanuel, 68
Kelman, Steven, 28
Kennedy, John, 158, 160
Kennedy, Ted, 160

Key, V. O., 12
Kiewiet, D. Roderick, 21
Kinder, Donald, 21
King, Anthony, 256
King, Martin Luther, Jr., 82, 98, 137
Kingdon, John, 24, 27, 29, 31, 228, 232,
  235, 239, 292n.15, 307n.1,
  310n.29
Kristol, Irving, 39

Labor Committee, 192
Lane, Robert, 9, 17, 39, 273
Lasswell, Harold, 20
Legislative behavior. *See* Ambition; Be-
  liefs; Elections; Lobbying; Me-
  dia, the; Narrative; State
  legislators
Legislative Commissioners' Office,
  223
Legislative staff, 25. *See also* State
  legislators
Liberalism, 87–88, 242, 245, 251
Liberalism Index, 205
Liberty, 87, 252–54. *See also* Narrative
Lieberman, Joseph, 220
Lincoln, Abraham, 99
Lobbying, 205–6, 227–28. *See also* Ed-
  ucation, finance bill; Plant clos-
  ings bill; Property tax, relief bill
Lockard, Duane, 308n.13

MacCallum, Gerald, 252–54
MacIntyre, Alasdair, 31, 32, 245,
  296n.31, 311n.9
Malcolm X, 82
Market, the. *See* Narrative
Marx, Karl, 21, 48, 61, 245, 247
Marxism, 86
Matthews, Donald, 22
Mayhew, David, 25, 235, 304n.3
McCarthy, Eugene, 118
McClosky, Herbert, 5, 38
McGovern, George, 230
Media, the, 186, 228
Merton, Robert, 9
Meskill, Thomas, 264